PRINCIPLES OF COST ACCOUNTING

SEVENTH EDITION

ROBERT E. SCHMIEDICKE, MA, CPA
Vice President for Administration and Finance
Davenport College of Business
Grand Rapids, Michigan

CHARLES F. NAGY, PhD, CPA
Professor of Accounting
Cleveland State University
Cleveland, Ohio

Published by

A67 **SOUTH-WESTERN PUBLISHING CO.**

CINCINNATI   WEST CHICAGO, ILL.   DALLAS   PELHAM MANOR, N.Y.   PALO ALTO, CALIF.

ISBN: 0-538-01670-1
Library of Congress Catalog Card Number: 81-84299

3 4 5 6 7 8 D 8 7 6 5
Printed in the United States of America

PREFACE

The concepts of accounting for costs permeate all organizations. However, the use and understanding of such concepts are vital to business organizations which are primarily concerned with the manufacture of products. The increasing importance of costing can be judged by the number of new textbooks arriving at colleges and universities from various publishers. The new titles are not typically "Cost Accounting," but rather "Costing" with some emphasis on managerial or management accounting.

Although cost accounting, managerial accounting, and management accounting share many common ideas and concepts, it is difficult to isolate any one facet as exclusive to any particular area. However, it does seem apparent that the solid foundation of study in any of these areas should rest on the cost systems, with the premise that a more complete understanding of the systems will result in a more in depth analysis of management problems. In this edition, the seventh, we present a thorough and contemporary view of all commonly used cost accounting systems, along with the special problem-solving techniques which are used with routine and nonroutine cost problems requiring solution by management.

The first chapter is an overview of subjects which are more thoroughly examined in subsequent chapters. The subject matter includes discussions of the elements of cost, job order costing, process costing, and standard costing. The first chapter outlines the schematic for the more complete and thorough discussions which follow. The overall view is presented to overcome any criticism that the subsequent study of the "pieces" cannot be fitted to the overall system.

The second, third, and fourth chapters are detailed discussions of the cost elements: materials, labor, and factory overhead. Practice and theory are blended throughout the discussions in all chapters; however, in these chapters the theoretical aspects of the elemental studies may be more apparent because of the emphasis on internal control requirements.

The fifth chapter reviews the material covered in the previous four chapters by illustrating one month of manufacturing operations for a corporation. An optional practice set is available which continues the corporation's activities in the subsequent month.

The sixth and seventh chapters cover process costing. The sixth chapter introduces the general procedures involved with process costing that include departmental and nondepartmental factories, equivalent production with the average cost method, and the department-to-department flow of costs. The seventh chapter covers the more specialized techniques of process costing. They include equivalent production determinations when the cost elements are not uniformly added to a process, accounting for lost units and an increase in units, the first-in, first-out method, joint products, by-products, and whether to sell a product or process it further.

The eighth and ninth chapters cover standard costs. The eighth chapter stresses the general procedures of standard cost systems and the procedures that pertain to materials and labor. These procedures include determining materials and labor variances and their analyses. Yield and mix variance analyses have been added to the subjects covered in this edition. The ninth chapter emphasizes the standard variances for factory overhead. The two- and three-variance overhead analysis methods are presented. The chapter also discusses the budgeting of factory overhead and budgets in general.

Chapter 10 focuses on managerial uses of cost data. The chapter covers direct costing, segment reporting, cost-volume-profit analysis, distribution costing, special problems involving decisions to make or buy, operate or shut down, and differential costing.

Discussion questions, short exercises, and comprehensive problems are presented at the end of each chapter. The seventh addition includes a greater number of exercises and problems than the previous edition, and at least one exercise or problem is provided for each major topic covered in the text.

Although this revision has been updated and changed to meet the contemporary standard for a principles of cost accounting textbook, we have stood steadfastly by the goals established in the previous editions that clarity in the subject matter presentation and the text's teachability would not be sacrificed with the additions and changes.

The authors wish to thank the American Institute of Certified Public Accountants for permission to use their materials in this publication.

Robert E. Schmiedicke
Charles F. Nagy

CONTENTS

1

Introduction to Cost Accounting

Over the past several years, there has been a steady, significant increase in the costs of materials, labor, and other manufacturing needs, and it appears that this trend will continue. The inclination is to pass on the higher costs of manufactured products to the consumer by increasing selling prices. Quite often, however, a company is precluded from doing this by intense domestic and foreign competition. As a result, many companies today are faced with the dilemma of increasing costs and relatively restricted selling prices. In addition, changing consumer demands and new technologies require the development of new and attractive products as well as more effective methods of marketing and servicing these goods. In order to remain competitive today, manufacturers must have control of costs and be ready to exploit new opportunities. Otherwise, they can be forced into declining economic growth and a vicious downward spiral of reduced capital expansion, decreasing profits, a declining work force, loss of markets, and eventual oblivion.

The importance of sound financial information including specific cost data, has always been recognized, but in the current economic environment, such information is crucial to the survival of business and industry. The function of **cost accounting** is to provide the detailed cost data which are essential to management in controlling current operations and planning for the future. It provides the infor-

1

mation that management needs in order to allocate resources to the most efficient and profitable areas of operation.

All types of business entities — manufacturing, merchandising, and service businesses — require **information systems** which provide the necessary financial data. Because of the nature of the manufacturing process, the information systems of manufacturing entities must be designed to accumulate detailed cost data relating to the production process. Thus, it is common today for small, medium, and large manufacturing companies to have structured **cost accounting systems**. Stated simply, these systems show what costs were incurred and where and how these costs were utilized. While cost accounting principles and procedures discussed in this text are used primarily by the manufacturing industry, many of the basic principles of control are also used by merchandising and service businesses. Cost accounting today is recognized as being essential to efficient operations of business and industry.

THE MANUFACTURING PROCESS

In order to appreciate the importance of an efficient cost system, it is necessary to understand the nature of the manufacturing process. In many ways, the activities of the manufacturing organization are similar to those of the merchandising business. Both are concerned with purchasing, storing, and selling of goods; both must have efficient management and adequate sources of capital; both may employ hundreds or thousands of workers. In the manufacturing process itself, we see the distinction between the two, for while merchandisers buy items in marketable form to be resold to their customers, manufacturers must make the goods they sell. Once the merchandising organization has acquired and stored goods, it is ready to carry out the marketing function. The purchase of materials by a manufacturer, however, is only the beginning of a long, and sometimes complex, chain of events that will eventually produce a finished article ready for sale.

The **manufacturing process** involves the conversion of raw materials into finished goods through the application of labor and the incurrence of various factory expenses. The manufacturer must make a major investment in physical facilities, such as factory buildings and warehouses, and acquire many specialized types of machinery and equipment. In order to carry out the manufacturing process, the manufacturer must purchase appropriate quantities of raw materials, supplies, and parts and build up a work force to convert these raw materials, supplies, and parts into finished goods.

In addition to the cost of materials and labor, the manufacturer incurs other expenses in the production process. Many of these costs, such as depreciation, taxes, insurance, and utilities, are similar to those incurred by a merchandising concern. Other costs, such as machine maintenance and repair, materials handling, and inspection, are peculiar to the manufacturing industry.

Once the goods have been manufactured and are ready for sale, the manufacturer performs basically the same functions as the merchandiser in storing and marketing the goods. The methods of accounting for sales, cost of goods sold, and selling and administrative expenses are similar to those of the merchandising organization.

USES OF COST ACCOUNTING DATA

Principles of cost accounting have been developed which enable the manufacturer to process the many different costs associated with manufacturing and to provide built-in control features. The information produced by a cost accounting system provides a basis for determining product costs and aids management in planning and controlling operations.

Determining Product Costs

Cost accounting procedures provide the means to gather the data needed to determine product costs and thus to generate meaningful financial statements and other reports, schedules, and analyses that are relevant to management. In preparing financial statements, knowledge of product costs is necessary for determining the cost of goods sold and for valuing inventories.

Cost procedures must be designed to permit the determination of **unit costs** as well as total product costs. The fact that a factory spent $10,000 for labor in a certain month is not, in itself, significant information; but if this labor produced 5,000 finished units, the fact that the cost of labor was $2 per unit is important because this figure can be compared to the unit labor cost of other periods and the trends analyzed.

Unit cost information is also useful in making a variety of important marketing decisions:

(1) *Determining the selling price of a product.* A knowledge of the cost of manufacturing a unit of product aids in setting the selling price. This price should be high enough to absorb the cost of producing the item, pay a portion of marketing and administrative expenses, and provide a profit.

(2) *Meeting competition.* If a product is being undersold by a competitor, detailed information regarding unit costs can be effectively used to determine whether the problem can be resolved by a reduction in selling price, a reduction of manufacturing costs, or the elimination of the item.

(3) *Bidding.* Many manufacturing organizations must submit competitive bids in order to be awarded manufacturing contracts from government, business, and industry. An analysis of the costs relating to the manufacture of any particular item is of great importance in determining the bid price.

(4) *Analyzing profitability.* Management can determine the amount of profit that each product earns and possibly eliminate those that are least profitable, thereby concentrating all efforts on those items that are most profitable. It is not uncommon, however, for some companies to retain a certain line of goods yielding a very low profit, or even a loss, in order to provide the variety of items that will attract customers who also purchase the more profitable items.

Planning and Control

The ultimate value of cost accounting lies in the use of the data accumulated and reported. One of the most important functions of cost accounting is the development of information which can be used by management in planning and controlling operations.

Planning is the process of selecting goals and objectives for the firm and determining the means by which the firm will attain these objectives. Effective planning is facilitated by the following:

(1) *Clearly defined objectives of the manufacturing operation.* These objectives may be expressed in terms of the number of units to be produced, the desired quality at the lowest cost, and the timing necessary to meet the needs of consumer demand while avoiding the financial strain of being overstocked.

(2) *The development of a program that will assist and guide the company in reaching its objectives.* This detailed plan includes a description of necessary manufacturing operations to be performed, a projection of personnel needs for the period, and the coordination of the timely acquisition of materials and facilities.

Cost accounting aids in the development of plans by providing historical costs that serve as a basis for projecting data for planning. Management can analyze trends and relationships among such data as an aid in estimating future costs and operating results and in making decisions regarding the acquisition of additional facilities, changes in marketing strategies, and obtaining additional capital.

The word "control" is used in many different ways, but from the viewpoint of the manufacturing concern, **control** is the process of monitoring the company's operations and determining whether the objectives identified in the planning process are being accomplished. Effective control is achieved through:

(**1**) Assigning responsibility
(**2**) Periodically measuring results
(**3**) Taking necessary corrective action
(**4**) Searching for ways to reduce costs

Assigning Responsibility. Responsibility should be assigned for each detail of the master production plan. All managers and supervisors should know precisely what their responsibilities are in terms of efficiency, operations, production, and costs. The key to proper control involves the use of responsibility accounting and cost centers.

The essence of **responsibility accounting** is the assignment of accountability for costs or production results to those individuals who have the authority to influence costs or production. It involves an information system that traces these data to the managers who are responsible for them.

A **cost center** is a unit of activity within the factory to which costs may be practically and equitably assigned. A cost center may be a department or a group of workers; it could represent one job, one process, or one manufacturing operation. The criteria for a cost center are (**1**) a reasonable basis on which manufacturing costs can be allocated and (**2**) a person who has control over and is accountable for many of the costs charged to that center.

It is important to recognize that, with responsibility accounting, the manager of a department is accountable only for those costs that are controllable by that person. For instance, the costs of labor and materials will be charged to the cost center, but the department head may be responsible only for the quantity of materials used and the number of labor hours worked. This person would probably not be accountable for the unit cost of raw materials or the hourly rate paid the employees because these are normally beyond the control of the department head, being handled by the purchasing and personnel departments and affected by company policy. The manager may be responsible for the cost of machinery maintenance and repair due to misuse in the cost center, but would not be responsible for the costs of depreciation, taxes and insurance on the machinery. If production in a given period is lower than planned, this could be due to poor supervision which is the department head's responsibility, or, it may be that less-skilled workers are being hired — not a factor that can be controlled by the supervisor.

Periodic reports for a cost center may reflect all costs charged to that department and related production information. With the responsibility accounting system, the data for which the manager is specifically and individually responsible would be highlighted or segregated for the purpose of evaluating that manager's performance and initiating action to correct deficiencies. Quite often, however, both a departmental cost and production report and a separate performance report will be prepared for a cost center; the **performance report** will include only those costs and production data that are controllable by the center's manager.

It is imperative that these reports be furnished at regular intervals (monthly, weekly, or daily) on a timely basis. In order for them to provide the maximum benefit, they must be available as soon as possible after the end of the period being reported. Reports that are not produced in a timely fashion will lose their effectiveness as a control device.

Periodically Measuring Results. Actual operating results should be measured periodically and compared with the objectives established in the planning process. This analysis, which might be made monthly, weekly, or even on a daily basis, is a major part of cost control because it points out how current performance compares with the overall plan. The actual results in terms of dollars, units produced, hours worked, or materials used are compared with the master plan. This comparison is a primary feature of cost analysis. The number of dollars expended or the quantity of units produced have little significance until compared with the objective. Comparisons may also be made with actual results of prior periods, thus serving to point out meaningful trends.

Taking Necessary Corrective Action. The reports produced by the measurement and analysis of the results of operations may identify problem areas and deviations from the plan. Corrective action should be planned and implemented where necessary. A significant variation is a signal for attention. An investigation may reveal an area that needs adjustment or may show an area of strength where an especially efficient condition may be better utilized.

Management wants to know not only the results, but how the results — whether favorable or unfavorable — compare with a plan, why things happened, and who was responsible. Management must be prepared to improve or change existing conditions; otherwise, the periodic measurement of activity has little value.

Searching for Ways to Reduce Costs. Management has the responsibility not only to control costs, but also to reduce them in every possible way consistent with the type of operation and quality of product. There must be a continuing search for less expensive materials, for more efficient methods of operating, and for improved usage of materials and labor.

RELATIONSHIP OF COST ACCOUNTING TO FINANCIAL ACCOUNTING

The objective of accounting in general is the accumulation of financial information that is useful in making economic decisions. **Financial accounting** focuses upon the gathering of information to be used in the preparation of financial statements which meet the needs of investors, creditors, and regulatory and taxing authorities. Although these financial statements are useful to management, additional reports, schedules, and analyses are required for internal use in planning and control. **Cost accounting** provides the additional information required by management, and also provides data necessary for the preparation of financial statements. Cost accounting procedures are necessary for the determination of cost of goods sold on the income statement and the valuation of inventories on the balance sheet.

Cost of Goods Sold

For the merchandising concern, the cost of goods sold is computed as follows:

> Beginning merchandise inventory
> Add **purchases** (merchandise)
>
> Merchandise available for sale
> Less ending merchandise inventory
>
> Cost of goods sold

The amount of purchases represents the cost of the goods which were acquired during the period for resale.

Since the manufacturing concern *makes* rather than *buys* the products it has available for sale, the term "cost of goods manufactured" replaces "purchases" in determining the cost of goods sold:

> Beginning finished goods inventory
> Add **cost of goods manufactured**
>
> Finished goods available for sale
> Less ending finished goods inventory
>
> Cost of goods sold

The amount for the cost of goods manufactured is supported by a manufacturing schedule detailing the costs of materials, labor, and the expenses of maintaining and operating a factory.

The format of the income statement for a manufacturer is not significantly different from that for a merchandiser. However, the cost accounting procedures involved in gathering the data for the determination of the cost of goods manufactured are considerably more complex than the recording of merchandise purchases, and these procedures are discussed in detail in subsequent chapters.

Inventories

If the merchandiser has on hand unsold items of merchandise purchased for resale, the cost of these items is reflected in the current asset section of the balance sheet in the following manner:

> Current assets:
>   Cash
>   Accounts receivable
>   **Merchandise inventory**

On the balance sheet of the manufacturing concern, the current asset section is expanded as follows:

> Current assets:
>   Cash
>   Accounts receivable
>   Inventories:
>   **Finished goods**
>   **Work in process**
>   **Materials**

The balance in the **finished goods** account represents the total cost incurred in manufacturing goods that are complete but still on hand at the end of the period. The balance of the **work in process** account includes all of the manufacturing costs incurred to date for goods that are not yet completed. The balance of the **materials** account represents the cost of all materials purchased and on hand to be used in the manufacturing process, including raw materials, prefabricated parts, and other factory materials and supplies. Raw materials for one company are often the finished product of another company. For example, plastic to be used in the formation of office machine cases would be the finished product of a plastics manufacturer. Prefabricated parts would include units, such as electric motors, assembled by another manufacturer to be used in the manufacture of a product such as office machines. Other materials and supplies might include screws, nails, rivets, lubricants, and solvents.

Valuation of Inventories. The inventory accounts peculiar to manufacturing concerns simply represent costs gathered both by cost accounting procedures and by conventional inventory accounting procedures. Valuation of raw materials and supplies on hand is made through use of the inventory costing techniques that might be used by any business — first-in, first-out (fifo), last-in, first-out (lifo), or moving average. The company might maintain a **perpetual inventory** system, which involves keeping a continuous record of purchases, issues, and new balances of all goods in stock. Generally, these data are verified by periodic counts of selected items throughout the year. Under the perpetual system, inventory valuation data for financial statement purposes are available at any time, as distinguished from other methods that might require estimating inventory during the year for interim statements and shutting down operations to count all inventory items at the end of the year.

In addition to providing inventory valuation data for the financial statements, the detailed cost data and inventory records provide the information necessary for the control of inventory levels, the timely availability of materials for the factory, and the detection of pilferage, waste, and spoilage. Inventory valuation and control are discussed in detail in Chapter 2.

Inventory Ledgers. Both the merchandiser and the manufacturer may have the usual subsidiary ledgers, such as that for accounts receivable. In addition, the manufacturer generally maintains subsidiary ledgers for the general ledger inventory control accounts, Finished Goods, Work in Process, and Materials. The purpose of these subsidiary ledgers is to maintain a perpetual inventory and to furnish the detailed balances and information to support and prove the accuracy of the control accounts.

Some manufacturers, especially those that are decentralized, use a **factory ledger** which contains all of the accounts relating to manufacturing, including the inventory accounts. This self-balancing ledger, which is maintained at the factory, is tied in to the general ledger at the main office through the use of reciprocal control accounts.

ELEMENTS OF COST

Manufacturing or **production costs** are classified into three basic elements: **(1) direct materials**, **(2) direct labor**, and **(3) factory overhead**.

Direct Materials

The costs of materials which become part of the item being manufactured or which can be specifically identified with a certain product are classified as **direct materials**. Examples are: lumber used in making furniture, fabric used in the production of clothing, iron ore used in the manufacture of steel products, and rubber used in the production of tires.

There are many types of materials and supplies which are necessary for the manufacturing process but which cannot be specifically identified with any particular item manufactured or whose relative cost is too insignificant to measure. The costs of items such as sandpaper used in sanding furniture, lubricants used on machinery and other items for general factory use are classified as **indirect materials** and are included in factory overhead. Similarly classified are materials that actually become part of the finished product but whose costs are relatively insignificant, such as thread, screws, rivets, nails, and glue.

Direct Labor

The cost of labor for those employees who perform some work on the item manufactured, such as machine operators or assembly line workers, is considered **direct labor**. The wages of those employees who are required for the manufacturing process but who do not work directly on the units being manufactured are considered **indirect labor** and are included in factory overhead. Under this classification would be the wages of department heads, inspectors, materials handlers and maintenance personnel.

Payroll related costs, such as payroll taxes, group insurance, sick pay, vacation and holiday pay, retirement program contributions, and other fringe benefits can be considered as part of direct labor costs, but are usually included in factory overhead.

Factory Overhead

Factory overhead is known by various names — *factory burden, manufacturing expenses, indirect costs, overhead,* and *factory expenses* — and includes all costs related to the manufacturing of a product except direct materials and direct labor. This includes indirect materials and indirect labor as well as other manufacturing expenses, such as depreciation on the factory building and on machinery and equipment, supplies, heat, light, power, maintenance, insurance, and taxes.

The costs of direct materials and direct labor are sometimes combined and described as the **prime cost** of manufacturing a product.

Prime cost plus factory overhead equals total cost of manufacturing. Direct labor cost and factory overhead, which are necessary to convert the materials into finished goods, can be combined and described as **conversion cost**.

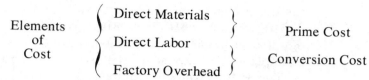

Elements of Cost
{ Direct Materials } Prime Cost
Direct Labor
Factory Overhead } Conversion Cost

Marketing or selling expenses, general administrative costs, and other nonfactory expenditures are not included in the costs of manufacturing. However, some costs incurred by a manufacturer may benefit both factory and nonfactory operations. An example is depreciation, insurance, and property taxes on a building that houses both the factory and the administrative offices. In this situation an allocation of cost must be made.

FLOW OF COSTS

All three elements of manufacturing cost flow through the work in process inventory account. The cost of direct materials used in production and direct labor costs incurred are charged (debited) directly to Work in Process. All other factory costs — indirect labor, indirect materials, and other factory expenses — are charged to the factory overhead account and later transferred to Work in Process. When goods are completed, the total costs incurred in producing the goods are transferred from Work in Process to the finished goods inventory account. The flow of manufacturing costs can be illustrated very simply as follows:

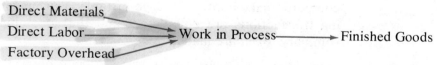

Direct Materials
Direct Labor ——————→ Work in Process ——————→ Finished Goods
Factory Overhead

When goods are sold, the costs incurred to manufacture the goods are transferred from the finished goods inventory account to the cost of goods sold account.

Finished Goods ——————→ Cost of Goods Sold

A more detailed illustration of cost flows is presented in "T-account" form on page 21.

ILLUSTRATION OF ACCOUNTING FOR MANUFACTURING COSTS

Cost accounting procedures are used as a means of accumulating and allocating all elements of manufacturing cost in a manner that will produce meaningful data for the internal use of management and for the preparation of financial statements. The following example illustrates basic cost accounting procedures, utilizing the terminology and principles that have been previously discussed. Later, this example will be expanded to illustrate more advanced procedures.

The Patio Products Company is a small, newly organized company that manufactures wood patio tables and benches. The firm's products are sold to jobbers, or wholesale distributors, who in turn sell them to retailers. The basic steps in the company's manufacturing process are as follows:

(1) Lumber is cut to size for table tops, seats, legs and braces.
(2) The individual pieces of cut lumber are painted a redwood tone.
(3) The pieces are assembled into tables and benches.

The beginning balance sheet for the company on January 1 of the current year is presented below.

PATIO PRODUCTS COMPANY
Balance Sheet
January 1, 19--

Assets		Liabilities and Owners' Equity	
Cash..............................	$ 50,000	Capital............................	$332,000
Building..........................	210,000		
Machinery and equipment	72,000	Total liabilities and	
Total assets....................	$332,000	owners' equity..............	$332,000

Assume, for the purpose of simplification, that in January the company makes only one style of table. During January the following transactions are completed, and the accompanying entries, in summary form, are made:

1. Materials (lumber, paint, screws, lubricants, and solvents) are purchased at a cost of $20,000.

Materials...	20,000	
Vouchers Payable		20,000

The cost of materials purchased is charged to the inventory control account, Materials. This treatment is based on the assumption that the company uses a perpetual inventory system.

2. During the month, direct materials (lumber and paint) costing $15,000 and indirect materials (screws, lubricants for machines, and solvents for cleaning) costing $900 are issued to the factory.

Work in Process 15,000
Factory Overhead (Indirect Materials) 900
    Materials... 15,900

Direct materials issued are charged directly to the work in process control account, but the indirect materials are charged to the factory overhead account. The latter account will be used to accumulate various factory expenses that will later be transferred to Work in Process.

3. Total gross wages and salaries earned for the month were: factory employees working on the product, $8,600; factory supervision, maintenance, and custodial employees, $2,990; sales and administrative employees, $3,400.

Work in Process 8,600
Factory Overhead (Indirect Labor)................. 2,990
Selling and Administrative Expense (Salaries) ... 3,400
    Payroll.. 14,990

The wages earned by those employees working directly on the product are charged to Work in Process, while the salaries and wages of the factory supervisor and the maintenance and custodial personnel, who do not work directly on the product, are charged to Factory Overhead as indirect labor. The salaries of nonfactory employees are debited to a separate expense account.

In order to focus on specific cost accounting procedures as distinguished from general accounting procedures, the general ledger account Selling and Administrative Expense will be used to accumulate all nonmanufacturing expenses. In the usual situation, there would be a general ledger account for each category of expense.

4. Depreciation expense for the building is 4% of cost per year. The office occupies one tenth of the total building, and the factory operation is contained in the other nine tenths. The expense for one month is recorded as follows:

Factory Overhead (Depreciation of Building) 630
Selling and Administrative Expense
    (Depreciation of Building)......................... 70
        Accumulated Depreciation — Building....... 700

The cost accounting principle illustrated is that only those costs directly related to production should be charged to Factory Overhead. Depreciation on the portion of the building used as office space is an administrative expense and should not be treated as an element of production cost.

5. Depreciation expense for machinery and equipment is 10% of cost per year.

Factory Overhead (Depreciation of Machinery and Equipment)	600	
Accumulated Depreciation — Machinery and Equipment		600

All of the machinery is used in the factory for production purposes, so the depreciation expense, which generally cannot be traced to a certain unit of product, is properly charged to Factory Overhead.

6. The cost of heat, light, and power for the month was $1,200.

Factory Overhead (Utilities)	1,080	
Selling and Administrative Expense (Utilities) ...	120	
Vouchers Payable		1,200

Because one tenth of the building is used for office purposes, 10% of the total utilities cost is allocated to Selling and Administrative Expense.

7. Miscellaneous expenses for the telephone, office supplies, and travel expenses totaled $520.

Selling and Administrative Expense.................	520	
Vouchers Payable		520

There are many other expenses that a manufacturing organization might have, but for purposes of simplicity, it is assumed that no other expenses are incurred during the month. After posting the journal entries, the debits in the factory overhead account will be as follows:

Transaction	Description	Amount
(2)	Indirect materials...	$ 900
(3)	Indirect labor..	2,990
(4)	Depreciation of building..	630
(5)	Depreciation of machinery and equipment..............	600
(6)	Utilities...	1,080
	Total...	$6,200

8. The balance in Factory Overhead is transferred to Work in Process.

Work in Process	6,200	
Factory Overhead		6,200

The three elements of manufacturing cost — direct materials, direct labor, and factory overhead — are now accumulated in Work in Process, and the debits in the account are as follows:

Transaction	Description	Amount
(2)	Direct materials	$15,000
(3)	Direct labor	8,600
(8)	Factory overhead	6,200
	Total	$29,800

The fact that indirect factory expenses are first accumulated in Factory Overhead and subsequently transferred by journal entry to Work in Process rather than being charged directly to Work in Process may be perplexing. However, justification of this procedure will be offered in subsequent chapters when a more complete discussion of the allocation of factory overhead to jobs, processes, and departments is presented.

9. Assuming that all goods started in process have been finished, the following entry is made:

Finished Goods	29,800	
Work in Process		29,800

Assuming that 4,000 tables were produced during the month, the unit cost is $7.45 ($29,800 ÷ 4,000). This unit cost serves as a basis for establishing the selling price of the tables. After considering the anticipated selling and administrative expenses, a selling price can be established that should provide a reasonable profit.

The unit cost for each element of manufacturing cost is calculated as follows:

	Total	Units Produced	Unit Cost
Direct materials	$15,000	4,000	$3.75
Direct labor	8,600	4,000	2.15
Factory overhead	6,200	4,000	1.55
	$29,800		$7.45

If the same type of table is produced in future periods, the unit costs of those periods can be compared with the unit costs determined above, and any differences could be analyzed so that management might take appropriate action. In later periods, it might be found that this particular item cannot be sold at a price high enough to provide a reasonable profit. Through analysis of the unit costs, management might effect a cost-cutting measure, or perhaps even discontinue production of the item.

From this example, it is apparent that an accurate picture of cost for inventory valuation purposes is available. At any given time, the cost of each article in inventory is known. It should be reemphasized that one function of cost accounting is the accurate determination of the cost of producing a unit of product. This knowledge of unit cost aids management in planning and controlling operations and in making marketing decisions.

To continue with the example, assume that the following transactions take place in January in addition to those already recorded:

10. Vouchers of $14,000 are paid.

| Vouchers Payable | 14,000 | |
| Cash | | 14,000 |

11. Gross salaries and wages totaling $14,990 were vouchered and paid.

(a) Payroll	14,990	
Vouchers Payable		14,990
(b) Vouchers Payable	14,990	
Cash		14,990

In these transactions, the usual items of purchases discount, payroll taxes, and payroll accrued at the end of the month have been ignored to allow concentration on those transactions affecting cost flow and cost accounting procedures. These items will be discussed in subsequent chapters.

12. 3,500 tables are sold to jobbers at a net price of $9.95 each.

Accounts Receivable	34,825	
Sales		34,825
Cost of Goods Sold (3,500 × $7.45)	26,075	
Finished Goods		26,075

Because the unit cost of each item is known, the cost of goods sold can be determined without a physical inventory or cost estimate.

13. Cash totaling $22,575 is collected on accounts receivable.

| Cash | 22,575 | |
| Accounts Receivable | | 22,575 |

The accounts in the general ledger will reflect the entries as follows:

	CASH				ACCOUNTS RECEIVABLE		
1/1	50,000	(10)	14,000	(12)	34,825	(13)	22,575
(13)	22,575	(11)	14,990				
	72,575		28,990				
	43,585				*12,250*		

	FINISHED GOODS		
(9)	29,800	(12)	26,075
	3,725		

WORK IN PROCESS

(2) Direct materials	15,000	(9)	29,800
(3) Direct labor	8,600		
(8) Factory overhead	6,200		
	29,800		

MATERIALS

(1)	20,000	(2)	15,900
	4,100		

BUILDING

1/1	210,000		

ACCUMULATED DEPRECIATION —
BUILDING

		(4)	700

MACHINERY AND EQUIPMENT

1/1	72,000		

ACCUMULATED DEPRECIATION —
MACHINERY AND EQUIPMENT

		(5)	600

VOUCHERS PAYABLE

(10)	14,000	(1)	20,000
(11)	14,990	(6)	1,200
	28,990	(7)	520
		(11)	14,990
			36,710
		7,720	

PAYROLL

(11)	14,990	(3)	14,990

CAPITAL

		1/1	332,000

SALES

		(12)	34,825

COST OF GOODS SOLD

(12)	26,075		

FACTORY OVERHEAD

(2) Indirect materials	900	(8)	6,200
(3) Indirect labor	2,990		
(4) Depreciation of building	630		
(5) Depreciation of machinery & equip.	600		
(6) Utilities	1,080		
	6,200		

SELLING AND ADMINISTRATIVE EXPENSE

(3) Salaries	3,400		
(4) Depreciation of building	70		
(6) Utilities	120		
(7) Other	520		
	4,110		

After determining the balance of each general ledger account, the equality of the debits and credits is proven by preparing a trial balance as follows:

PATIO PRODUCTS COMPANY
Trial Balance
January 31, 19--

Cash..	43,585	
Accounts Receivable...	12,250	
Finished Goods..	3,725	
Work in Process..	—0—	
Materials	4,100	
Building..	210,000	
Accumulated Depreciation — Building		700
Machinery and Equipment...................................	72,000	
Accumulated Depreciation — Machinery and Equipment		600
Vouchers Payable		7,720
Payroll...		—0—
Capital...		332,000
Sales...		34,825
Cost of Goods Sold...	26,075	
Factory Overhead...	—0—	
Selling and Administrative Expense	4,110	
	375,845	375,845

Note that the finished goods control account reflects the cost of the 500 units still on hand — 500 × $7.45 = $3,725.

From an analysis of the general ledger accounts and the trial balance, the financial statements for the period are prepared as illustrated below and on the following page.

PATIO PRODUCTS COMPANY
Statement of Cost of Goods Manufactured
For the Month Ended January 31, 19--

Materials:			
Inventory, January 1..	—0—		
Purchases..	$20,000		
Total cost of available materials............................	$20,000		
Less inventory, January 31.................................	4,100		
Cost of materials used.....................................	$15,900		
Less indirect materials used..............................	900		
Cost of direct materials used in production...............		$15,000	
Direct labor..		8,600	
Factory overhead:			
Indirect materials	$ 900		
Indirect labor	2,990		
Depreciation of building	630		
Depreciation of machinery and equipment................	600		
Utilities	1,080		
Total factory overhead.....................................		6,200	
Cost of goods manufactured		$29,800	

[handwritten annotations in margin: Direct material, Direct labor, Factory overhead, finished goods]

PATIO PRODUCTS COMPANY
Income Statement
For the Month Ended January 31, 19--

Net sales		$34,825
Cost of goods sold:		
Finished goods inventory, January 1.........................	—0—	
Add cost of goods manufactured	$29,800	
Goods available for sale	$29,800	
Less finished goods inventory, January 31	3,725	26,075
Gross profit on sales...		$ 8,750
Selling and administrative expenses:		
Selling and administrative salaries...........................	$ 3,400	
Depreciation of building	70	
Utilities	120	
Miscellaneous	520	4,110
Net income		$ 4,640

PATIO PRODUCTS COMPANY
Balance Sheet
January 31, 19--

Assets

Current assets:			
Cash...			$ 43,585
Accounts receivable.......................................			12,250
Inventories:			
Finished goods		$ 3,725	
Work in process..		—0—	
Materials		4,100	7,825
Total current assets			$ 63,660
Plant and equipment:			
Building..	$210,000		
Less accumulated depreciation	700	$209,300	
Machinery and equipment..................	$ 72,000		
Less accumulated depreciation	600	71,400	
Total plant and equipment............................			280,700
Total assets..			$344,360

Liabilities and Owners' Equity

Current liabilities:			
Vouchers payable..		$ 7,720	
Total current liabilities			$ 7,720
Owners' Equity:			
Capital, January 1...		$332,000	
Net income		4,640	
Capital, January 31			336,640
Total liabilities and owners' equity			$344,360

The figures in the manufacturing statement were obtained by analyzing the appropriate general ledger accounts. The materials inventory account had no beginning balance but has an ending balance of $4,100. The amount of purchases during the period is determined by analysis of the debits to the materials account. Usually this amount could be obtained from a purchases journal. The cost of direct materials used of $15,000 and direct labor cost of $8,600 can be readily found as charges to the work in process account. These figures would normally be determined from supplementary records which will be discussed in a subsequent chapter. All of the other items in the manufacturing statement represent indirect factory overhead and are available from inspection of the factory overhead account in the general ledger. These costs could also be gathered in separate accounts before they are transferred to the factory overhead account and then to the work in process account, thus making available the amount incurred for each expense and eliminating the necessity for analysis of the factory overhead account. However, as more advanced cost accounting procedures are presented in subsequent chapters, the common practice of maintaining a subsidiary ledger with an account for each type of expense will be discussed. Following this procedure, the factory overhead account acts as a control account, with its balance supported by the sum of the balances of the expenses recorded in separate accounts in the subsidiary ledger.

A complete cycle in cost accounting procedures has been presented. Before proceeding, a careful review of the basic elements of terminology and flow of costs is recommended. More complex procedures will be presented, and a firm grasp of the fundamentals already covered will be of considerable value in comprehending the ensuing material.

A graphic illustration of the flow of costs is on page 21. Study this carefully, following each line to trace the costs. Compare this diagram with the ledger accounts illustrated and the journal entries that were made for Transactions 1 through 13.

COST ACCOUNTING SYSTEMS

In the previous example, the basic foundation of a cost accounting system was presented. In that illustration, costs were accumulated for the month, and at the end of the month these costs were divided by the total units produced to give the average unit cost. This accomplished one function of cost accounting, the determination of product costs — both total costs for the period and cost per

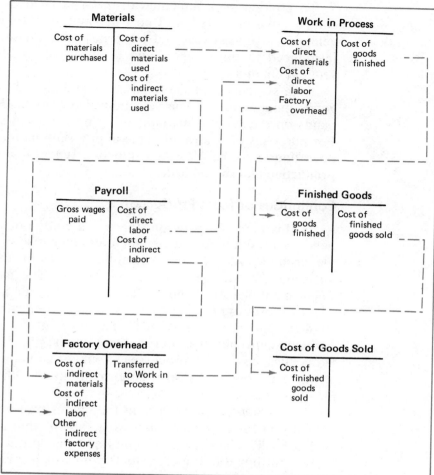

CHART 1-1
Flow of Costs

unit. However, another important objective of a cost accounting system — cost control — could not be satisfactorily achieved using the described procedure. The statement was made that the unit costs could be compared with similar costs in future periods to see if costs were increasing. Assuming that in a subsequent month the cost of direct labor had risen to $2.50 per unit, it is necessary to investigate and determine whether something can be done to correct the situation. The described accounting procedure restricts any investigation, because it is not known exactly where in the factory this increase has occurred. Labor costs went up; but did they go up because of a general rise in wages, or because of inefficiency? Did labor costs increase for a particular department or job? Answers to such questions are not readily available using the procedures described in the earlier example.

To provide management with the data needed for effective cost control, two basic types of cost accounting systems have been developed — **process cost** and **job order cost**. These two systems are introduced in this chapter and discussed in greater detail in subsequent chapters.

Both systems are used to gather cost data and to allocate costs to goods manufactured. The selection of one method or the other depends on the type of manufacturing operation of a given company. For purposes of determining the appropriate method, manufacturing operations may be classified into two types — **continuous or mass production** and **special order**.

Continuous or Mass Production

In this type of operation, there is a continuous output of homogeneous products for stock. Such an enterprise may produce a single product, such as an automobile, or many different products, such as cereal foods or patent medicines. The factory generally is departmentally organized. Industries of this type include those manufacturing automobiles, tires, cement, chemicals, canned goods, lumber, paper, candy, foodstuffs, flour, glass, soap, toothpaste, chewing gum, petroleum products, textiles, plastics, and paints, and firms engaged in such processes as rubber compounding and vulcanizing. A **process cost system** is normally used with this type of manufacturing enterprise.

The characteristic feature of the manufacturing conditions under which process cost accounting is suitable is that the final product is substantially identical in all units and that production basically involves turning out units for stock from which sales are made. There are no separate jobs presenting substantially different characteristics; rather, the company (or a department within the company) makes large numbers of virtually identical items from the aggregate of which sales (or transfers to other departments) are made as orders are received.

Special Order

In this type of operation, the output consists of special- or custom-made products; the product is made to order. Each order may be of external or internal origin; that is, it may represent a customer order, or it may represent an internal order for a predetermined quantity of products to be placed in stock for sale. Industries of this type include those manufacturing or producing locomotives, ships, aircraft, machine tools, engines, structural steel, books and magazines, directories and catalogs; and specialty shops producing custom-made products such as clothing, shoes and hats. The **job order cost system** is appropriate in these instances.

Illustration of Process Costing

With the process cost system, costs are allocated by departments (or processes). To illustrate how this is accomplished, the Patio Products Company model will be revised with certain transactions recorded as they would be when a departmentalized process cost system is used.

The main innovation from the previous example is that all factory costs will be charged to the various departments. These departments or cost centers are named in accordance with their processing function — Cutting, Painting, and Assembly. Only the transactions affecting the work in process accounts will be presented; the other entries would be recorded in the same way as previously described.

To record the issue of materials to the factory, the entry No. 2 was:

Work in Process	15,000	
Factory Overhead	900	
Materials		15,900

Assume that certain materials records showed that materials had been issued as follows:

Cutting Department — lumber	$13,800
Painting Department — paint	1,200
Miscellaneous materials and supplies	900

With a process cost system, the entry would be made as follows:

Work in Process — Cutting Department	13,800	
Work in Process — Painting Department	1,200	
Factory Overhead	900	
Materials		15,900

Instead of charging the direct materials to one work in process account, the materials have been charged to the departments that will use them. This is the first indication that costs will be accumulated by departments, a basic procedure in a process cost system. For indirect materials, nothing has changed; the items that cannot be specifically identified with the product are still charged to the factory overhead account.

The next applicable entry is No. 3, which illustrates the recording of the payroll for the month by the following entry:

Work in Process	8,600	
Factory Overhead	2,990	
Selling and Administrative Expense	3,400	
Payroll		14,990

Assume that an analysis of the cost of labor for the factory disclosed the following data:

Cutting Department..	$2,800
Painting Department	2,600
Assembly Department..	3,200
	$8,600

The labor costs would be recorded in general journal form as follows:

Work in Process — Cutting Department	2,800	
Work in Process — Painting Department	2,600	
Work in Process — Assembly Department........	3,200	
Factory Overhead	2,990	
Selling and Administrative Expense.................	3,400	
Payroll...		14,990

Entries Nos. 4, 5, and 6, recording factory overhead for depreciation of the building, depreciation of machinery and equipment, and utilities, and entry No. 7, for selling and administrative expense, would be made in the same way as in the first example.

Now that the costs for direct materials and direct labor have been recorded in the work in process accounts for each department, only the distribution of factory overhead to these departments remains to be completed, thus involving one of the more complex problems of cost accounting. As has been illustrated, it is relatively easy to allocate direct materials and direct labor to a specific department, but this is not true with the other manufacturing expenses. Some method must be devised to distribute factory overhead to the departments on an equitable basis. Two common approaches to distributing factory overhead are: **(1)** the **allocation or apportionment method** and **(2)** the **predetermined rate method**. Both methods will be discussed in a subsequent chapter.

Assume that the following distribution of factory overhead expenses has been prepared for the company.

SCHEDULE OF FACTORY OVERHEAD DISTRIBUTION

Costs	Total	Cutting	Painting	Assembly
Indirect materials	$ 900	$ 240	$ 540	$ 120
Indirect labor	2,990	1,150	860	980
Depreciation — building.............	630	210	320	100
Depreciation — machinery and equipment	600	360	180	60
Utilities	1,080	600	300	180
Total	$6,200	$2,560	$2,200	$1,440

The schedule provides the basis for making the following entry to distribute factory overhead to the departments.

Work in Process — Cutting Department	2,560
Work in Process — Painting Department	2,200
Work in Process — Assembly Department	1,440
Factory Overhead	6,200

The departmental work in process accounts appear as follows:

WORK IN PROCESS — CUTTING DEPT.

(2) Direct materials	13,800	
(3) Direct labor	2,800	
(8) Factory overhead	2,560	
	19,160	

WORK IN PROCESS — PAINTING DEPT.

(2) Direct materials	1,200	
(3) Direct labor	2,600	
(8) Factory Overhead	2,200	
	6,000	

WORK IN PROCESS — ASSEMBLY DEPT.

(3) Direct labor	3,200	
(8) Factory overhead	1,440	
	4,640	

From this information, the following summary of production costs is prepared.

PATIO PRODUCTS COMPANY
Summary of Production Costs
For the Month Ended January 31, 19--

	Cutting	Painting	Assembly	Total
Total costs:				
Direct materials....................	$13,800	$1,200	—0—	$15,000
Direct labor.........................	2,800	2,600	$3,200	8,600
Factory overhead.................	2,560	2,200	1,440	6,200
Total	$19,160	$6,000	$4,640	$29,800
Number of units produced........	4,000	4,000	4,000	4,000
Unit costs:				
Direct materials....................	$3.45	$ .30	—0—	$3.75
Direct labor.........................	.70	.65	$ .80	2.15
Factory overhead.................	.64	.55	.36	1.55
Total	$4.79	$1.50	$1.16	$7.45

This summary provides a detailed breakdown of each element of cost in each department. As unit costs are determined in subsequent months, a comparison of costs on a month-to-month basis by cost element within each department is available, and any unanticipated fluctuations in costs can be referred to the department supervisor for accountability. At the same time, accurate data are available for inventory valuation.

The final entries can now be made that will transfer the costs from each department to the next, following the flow of goods through the factory.

Work in Process — Painting Department 19,160
    Work in Process — Cutting Department   19,160

Work in Process — Assembly Department 25,160
    Work in Process — Painting Department   25,160

Finished Goods 29,800
    Work in Process — Assembly Department   29,800

After these entries have been made, the work in process accounts will appear as follows:

WORK IN PROCESS — CUTTING DEPT.

(2) Direct materials	13,800	To transfer costs	
(3) Direct labor	2,800	to Painting Dept.	19,160
(8) Factory overhead	2,560		

WORK IN PROCESS — PAINTING DEPT.

(2) Direct materials	1,200	To transfer costs	
(3) Direct labor	2,600	to Assembly Dept.	25,160
(8) Factory overhead	2,200		
From Cutting Dept.	19,160		

WORK IN PROCESS — ASSEMBLY DEPT.

(3) Direct labor	3,200	To transfer costs	
(8) Factory overhead	1,440	to Finished Goods	29,800
From Painting Dept.	25,160		

The cost of the goods manufactured has now been transferred through the various departments to the inventory control account, Finished Goods. Additional entries such as those for sales and cost of goods sold will be the same as in the first illustration.

Illustration of Job Order Costing

With the job order cost system, costs are accumulated by *job* or *lot*, rather than by departments as was illustrated under the process cost system. One advantage in the use of this system is that the accumulation of costs for a particular job facilitates the determination of its selling price, or, if the job was done on contract with a set price, the profit or loss on this particular job is readily determinable by comparing cost with contract price. At the same time, those costs that have been accumulated for a certain type of work will assist management in the preparation of bids for similar jobs in the future.

To illustrate the use of the job order cost accounting system, assume that the Patio Products Company accepts two orders to manufacture certain items during the month of February. These special orders are as follows:

(1) From the Space-Age Distributing Co.: to manufacture 2,000 benches to their specifications. Contract price, $26,000.
(2) From the Grand Merchandising Center: to manufacture 3,000 tables to their specifications. Contract price, $19,650.

After accepting these orders and planning the job requirements as to materials, labor, and overhead, the cost accounting department sets up a **job cost sheet** for each job. An example of this form is shown in Illustration 1-1. All of the costs applicable to each job will be accumulated on these forms. The job numbers 101 and 102, respectively, are assigned to these orders.

Assume that the following transactions take place during the month of February. The entries after each item are recorded using the job order cost system. In order to highlight job order cost accounting procedures, only those entries relating to the manufacture

ILLUSTRATION 1-1

Job Cost Sheet

PATIO PRODUCTS COMPANY

Job Cost Sheet

Customer Name: _____ Job No.: _____
Address:
_____ Date Started: _____
_____ Date Requested: _____
_____ Date Completed: _____
Quantity: _____
Product: _____
Description: _____

DIRECT MATERIALS			DIRECT LABOR			FACTORY OVERHEAD		
Date	Mat'l. Req. No.	Amount	Date	Time Ticket No.	Amount	Date	Basis Applied	Amount
Total								

Summary:		Selling price	$	Remarks:
Direct materials . . .	$	Mfg. cost		
Direct labor		Gross margin on sales	$	
Factory overhead . .		Selling expense . .		
Total cost	$	Administrative expense		
Unit cost	$	Profit	$	

of goods will be illustrated. Routine entries, such as those for purchases of materials, for recording of nonmanufacturing expenses, or for payment of vouchers, will be ignored, as these entries are made in the same way as previously illustrated regardless of the cost system being used.

1. Indirect materials with a cost of $2,620 are issued to the factory, and direct materials are issued as follows:

	Job 101	Job 102
Lumber	$11,000	$ 8,000
Paint	1,200	1,000
	$12,200	$ 9,000

The entry to record the issues is:

Work in Process — 101	12,200	
Work in Process — 102	9,000	
Factory Overhead (Indirect Materials)	2,620	
Materials		23,820

If the indirect materials were directly and easily traceable to a specific job, the cost could be charged directly to that job; however, it is often difficult to determine which particular job may have benefited from the use of the various supplies. Thus, indirect materials costs are usually charged to Factory Overhead and later distributed to all of the jobs.

2. Indirect labor costs of $2,180 are incurred, and direct labor costs are incurred as follows:

	Job 101	Job 102
Direct Labor	$6,000	$3,750

The entry to record these costs is:

Work in Process — 101	6,000	
Work in Process — 102	3,750	
Factory Overhead (Indirect Labor)	2,180	
Payroll		11,930

3. Monthly depreciation expense for the building is recorded as follows:

Factory Overhead (Depreciation of Building)	630	
Selling and Administrative Expense (Depreciation of Building)	70	
Accumulated Depreciation — Building		700

4. The entry to record monthly depreciation for machinery and equipment is:

Factory Overhead (Depreciation of Machinery and Equipment)	600	
Accumulated Depreciation — Machinery and Equipment		600

5. The cost of utilities for the month of February is $1,300 and is recorded as follows:

Factory Overhead (Utilities) 1,170
Selling and Administrative Expense................. 130
    Vouchers Payable 1,300

6. Total charges to Factory Overhead for the month are:

Indirect materials.. $2,620
Indirect labor.. 2,180
Depreciation of building.. 630
Depreciation of machinery and equipment 600
Utilities.. 1,170
    Total... $7,200

Assume that factory overhead is allocated 60% to Job 101 and 40% to Job 102.

Total Factory Overhead	60% Job 101	40% Job 102
$7,200	$4,320	$2,880

The distribution would be recorded as follows:

Work in Process — 101 4,320
Work in Process — 102 2,880
    Factory Overhead 7,200

At the end of the month, the work in process and factory overhead accounts would appear as follows:

WORK IN PROCESS — 101

(1) Direct materials	12,200	
(2) Direct labor	6,000	
(6) Factory overhead	4,320	
	22,520	

WORK IN PROCESS — 102

(1) Direct materials	9,000	
(2) Direct labor	3,750	
(6) Factory overhead	2,880	
	15,630	

FACTORY OVERHEAD

(1) Indirect materials	2,620	(6) Transfer to work	
(2) Indirect labor	2,180	in process	7,200
(3) Depr. — building	630		
(4) Depr.—mach. and equip.	600		
(5) Utilities	1,170		

The costs shown in the work in process accounts are the result of summary entries for the month. These same costs would be shown on the job cost sheets in more detail.

7. Assuming both jobs were completed by the end of the month, the costs of the completed jobs would be transferred to the finished goods inventory control account:

Finished Goods	38,150	
Work in Process — 101		22,520
Work in Process — 102		15,630

8. When the goods are shipped to the customers and billed, the following entries are made to record the sale and the cost of the jobs:

Accounts Receivable	45,650	
Sales		45,650
Cost of Goods Sold	38,150	
Finished Goods		38,150

The costs of producing the two jobs can be summarized as follows:

	Job 101 (2,000 units)		Job 102 (3,000 units)	
	Total Cost	Unit Cost	Total Cost	Unit Cost
Direct materials	$12,200	$ 6.10	$ 9,000	$3.00
Direct labor	6,000	3.00	3,750	1.25
Factory overhead...............	4,320	2.16	2,880	.96
Total.............................	$22,520	$11.26	$15,630	$5.21

The gross profit realized on each job is determined as follows:

	Job 101 (2,000 units)		Job 102 (3,000 units)	
	Total	Per Unit	Total	Per Unit
Selling price	$26,000	$13.00	$19,650	$6.55
Cost..................................	22,520	11.26	15,630	5.21
Gross profit.......................	$ 3,480	$ 1.74	$ 4,020	$1.34

The job cost sheets would reflect the above information in more detail, so that a short time after each job is completed, the gross profit can be determined. In addition, if management should have an opportunity to bid on similar jobs in the future, an accurate record of all costs would be available to assist in determining contract prices.

Many companies use both the job order cost and process cost systems concurrently. A situation where this might occur would be one in which the company manufactures goods on specific order but produces a number of small parts on a continuous basis that can be used in most job orders. The costs for making these small parts would be accumulated on a process cost basis, while the costs for each job would be gathered on a job cost sheet.

Work in Process Control Account

As jobs or departments become too numerous to designate a specific work in process account for each, a work in process control account in the general ledger will be used. In a job order cost system, the details on the job cost sheets support the balance in Work in Process in the general ledger. If a process cost system is being used, the balance in the work in process control account will be supported by detailed departmental cost analysis sheets. The use of the control accounts and supporting data will be discussed in more depth in subsequent chapters.

Work in Process Shown in the Manufacturing Statement

If there is work in process at the beginning and at the end of the month, it will be shown as follows in the statement of cost of goods manufactured:

ABC MANUFACTURING COMPANY
Statement of Cost of Goods Manufactured
For the Month Ended June 30, 19--

Direct materials used	$29,000
Direct labor	24,000
Factory overhead	13,000
Total manufacturing cost	$66,000
Add work in process inventory, June 1	8,500
Total	$74,500
Less work in process inventory, June 30	12,500
Cost of goods manufactured during the month	$62,000

$66,000 represents the cost of direct materials, direct labor, and factory overhead incurred during the month of June. $8,500 is the cost of materials, labor and overhead incurred the previous month for goods that were not completed at the end of that month. The total of $74,500, therefore, represents manufacturing cost that must be accounted for. Work in process at the end of June is represented by the cost of $12,500 incurred for those items that are not yet finished. Therefore, the cost of goods completed in June, of which some were started in production the previous month, is $62,000. The work in process ledger account, in "T" account form, would appear as follows at the end of the month:

WORK IN PROCESS

6/1 Balance	8,500	To Finished Goods	62,000
Direct materials	29,000		
Direct labor	24,000		
Factory overhead	13,000		
12,500	74,500		

If a job order cost system is being used, the balance of $12,500 in the account represents the manufacturing cost incurred to date on jobs that have not yet been completed. If a process system is in use, the balance represents the cost to date, in one or more departments, of goods still to be finished.

STANDARD COST SYSTEM

The job order and process cost accounting systems are the principal systems used by manufacturing organizations; however, as useful as they are in providing cost data, there is still a limitation with these systems with regard to the control of costs. These systems make it possible to determine what a product actually cost but not what it *should* have cost. By comparing current costs with those of the past, management can determine if manufacturing operations and costs are under control, but the efficiency of operation is an unknown factor. This is an after-the-fact approach to cost control. The **standard cost accounting system**, which is not a third system but is superimposed on either a job order or a process cost system, is designed to furnish management with a measurement that will help in making decisions regarding the efficiency of operations.

Standard costs are those costs that would be incurred under the most efficient operating conditions and are forecast before the manufacturing process begins. During operations, comparisons are made between the actual costs incurred and these predetermined standard costs, and **variances**, or differences, are calculated. These variances will reveal performances which deviate from standard and thus give management a basis on which they can take appropriate action to eliminate inefficient operating conditions. Standard cost accounting will be discussed in depth in Chapters 8 and 9.

ORGANIZATIONS INFLUENCING COST ACCOUNTING PRINCIPLES AND PROCEDURES

Cost accounting principles and procedures have developed because of the need of managers for the information provided. Certain professional organizations and governmental agencies have significantly affected this development. Most of these organizations are more directly concerned with general accounting principles and external financial reporting rather than with cost accounting. However, cost accounting principles and procedures are an extension of general accounting and are thus influenced by these organizations.

Private Organizations

The **American Institute of Certified Public Accountants (AICPA)** is the national professional organization for certified public accountants. The Institute is involved in a wide range of activities relating to the practice of public accounting, including professional certification, continuing education and professional development, and professional ethics. The AICPA also establishes auditing standards, and until 1973 was responsible for establishing generally accepted accounting principles (GAAP). The Institute conducts extensive research in accounting and auditing and publishes the *Journal of Accountancy*, a monthly publication which addresses contemporary accounting and reporting issues and professional responsibilities.

The **American Accounting Association (AAA)** is primarily an organization of accounting educators, but its members include practicing accountants and others as well. The AAA encourages and sponsors research in accounting theory and publishes selected research projects and a quarterly journal, *The Accounting Review*.

The **National Association of Accountants (NAA)** is primarily an organization for management accountants in industry and is thus directly concerned with cost accounting and internal information systems. The NAA publishes a monthly journal, *Management Accounting*, which deals mainly with cost accounting and the uses of internal information. However, since information systems within an enterprise generate data for both internal and external reporting purposes, the NAA is also concerned with principles of accounting in general.

The **Financial Accounting Standards Board (FASB)**, established in 1973 by the AICPA-sponsored Financial Accounting Foundation, is responsible for developing and issuing standards of financial reporting for businesses and other organizations. The Board issues *Statements of Financial Accounting Standards* which are recognized as generally accepted accounting principles and must be followed unless unusual circumstances justify departure from a standard. The FASB also issues *Statements of Financial Accounting Concepts*, which deal with the fundamental objectives and concepts of accounting and are intended to guide organizations in financial accounting and reporting, but are not accounting principles which must be followed.

Governmental Agencies

The **Securities and Exchange Commission (SEC)** was created by an Act of Congress in 1934 to regulate the public trading of securities. The SEC does not attempt to prohibit the trading of risky securities, but attempts to ensure full and fair disclosure of information so that buyers and sellers of securities can make informed investment decisions. Since much of the information disclosed is financial information, the SEC is vitally concerned with accounting and reporting practices. The Commission issues *Accounting Series Releases (ASRs)* which establish accounting and reporting requirements for corporations which are subject to SEC regulation. With few exceptions, this includes all corporations that issue securities for sale to the public.

The **Internal Revenue Service (IRS)** administers the provisions of the federal income tax law and issues regulations which require or permit certain methods of accounting for tax purposes. In most cases, the accounting methods required for tax purposes do not have to be used for financial reporting purposes. Nevertheless, the IRS has been influential in the development of financial accounting principles, particularly in the areas of depreciation and inventories.

The **Cost Accounting Standards Board (CASB)** was created by the U.S. Congress in 1970 for the purpose of establishing standards for cost accounting procedures to be followed by firms dealing with the federal government on certain contracts. Pronouncements of the Board are of considerable importance in accounting for nongovernmental contracts and other noncontractual manufacturing activities as well. Although the CASB was dissolved effective October 1, 1980, due to a lack of funding, its rules and regulations remain in force.

QUESTIONS

1. How does the cost accounting function assist in the management of a business?

2. In what ways does a typical manufacturing business differ from a merchandising concern? In what ways are they similar?

3. How are cost accounting data used by management?

4. Why is unit cost information important to management?

5. For a manufacturer, what does the planning process involve and how are cost accounting data used in planning?

6. How is effective control achieved in a manufacturing concern?

7. Define responsibility accounting.

8. What is a cost center?

9. How is cost accounting related to financial accounting?

10. How does the computation of cost of goods sold for a manufacturer differ from that of a merchandiser?

11. Describe the accounts, Finished Goods, Work in Process, and Materials.

12. What are the basic elements of production cost?

13. Define the following costs — direct materials, indirect materials, direct labor, indirect labor, and factory overhead.

14. Define prime cost and conversion cost. Does prime cost plus conversion cost equal the cost of manufacturing?

15. In what way does the accounting treatment of factory overhead differ from that of direct materials and direct labor costs?

16. Distinguish between cost of goods sold and cost of goods manufactured.

17. How are nonfactory costs and costs which benefit both factory and nonfactory operations accounted for?

18. When is process costing appropriate and how are costs accumulated in a process cost system?

19. When is job order costing appropriate and how are costs accumulated in a job order cost system?

20. What are the advantages of accumulating costs by departments or jobs rather than for the factory as a whole?

21. What are standard costs and what is the purpose of a standard cost system?

EXERCISES

1. Classify the following as direct materials, direct labor, or factory overhead.

DM **(a)** Lumber used in a furniture factory.
DM **(b)** Cloth used in a shirt factory.
DM **(c)** Steel used in a shipyard.
FO **(d)** Lubricating oils used on machines in a box factory.
DL **(e)** Wages of a press operator employed in a printing plant.
FO **(f)** Insurance on factory machines.
FO **(g)** Rent of factory buildings.
FO **(h)** Wages of elevator operators employed in a factory.
DM **(i)** Leather used in a shoe factory.
FO **(j)** A factory supervisor's wages.
FO **(k)** Electric power consumed in operating factory machines.
FO **(l)** Depreciation of factory machinery.
FO **(m)** Fuel used in heating a factory.
DM **(n)** Paint used in the manufacture of airplanes.
DL **(o)** A carpenter's wages paid in the construction business.
FO **(p)** Electricity used in lighting a factory.

2. Explain in narrative form the flow of direct materials, direct labor, and factory overhead costs through the accounts.

3. Following is a list of manufacturing costs incurred by the Redwood Products Co. during the month of May:

Direct materials used	$12,000
Indirect materials used	2,000
Direct labor employed	18,000
Indirect labor employed	4,000
Rent expense	3,000
Utilities	750
Repairs	450
Depreciation expense	1,200

Prepare in general journal form, the entries necessary to record the preceding information and the entry transferring factory overhead to Work in Process.

4. The following data are taken from the general ledger and other records of the Dolan Manufacturing Co. at January 31, the end of the first month of operations in the current fiscal year.

Sales	$50,000
Materials inventory (January 1)	25,000
Work in process inventory (January 1)	20,000
Finished goods inventory (January 1)	30,000
Materials purchased	15,000
Direct labor cost	12,500
Factory overhead (including $500 of indirect materials used and $2,500 of indirect labor cost)	9,000
Selling and administrative expense	8,000
Inventories at January 31:	
Materials	22,000
Work in process	24,000
Finished goods	32,000

Prepare a statement of cost of goods manufactured.

5. The Apex Manufacturing Co. is engaged in the manufacture of candy bars and uses a process cost accounting system. At the end of April, the cost accountant obtains the following information from the cost records:

	No. 1 Bar	No. 2 Bar
Direct materials used	$ 5,000	$ 8,000
Direct labor cost	3,000	4,000
Factory overhead	2,000	3,600
Total manufacturing costs	$10,000	$15,600
Number of boxes produced	12,500	20,000

During May, The Apex Manufacturing Co. records disclose the following data:

	No. 1 Bar	No. 2 Bar
Direct materials used	$ 6,000	$ 9,250
Direct labor cost	3,750	6,000
Factory overhead	2,700	5,000
Total manufacturing costs	$12,450	$20,250
Number of boxes produced	15,000	25,000

(a) Prepare a comparative statement showing the costs of materials, direct labor, and factory overhead applicable to each box and the total cost per box for each product for the months of April and May. (b) Give possible reasons for the changes in unit costs and the significance of each possibility.

6. The Cummings Company manufactures a single product and uses

the process cost system. There are two production departments. During the month, the following transactions took place for Department 1:

Direct materials issued	$45,000
Direct labor incurred	60,000
Factory overhead allocated	42,000

Work in process for Department 1 at the beginning of the period was $15,000 and at the end of the period, $18,000.

Prepare general journal entries to record **(a)** the flow of costs into Department 1 and **(b)** the transfer of manufacturing costs to Department 2.

7. The Revco Supply Co. uses the job order cost system of accounting. The following information was taken from the books of the company after all posting had been completed at the end of August:

Jobs Completed	Direct Materials Cost	Direct Labor Cost	Factory Overhead	Units Completed
No. 501	$1,800	$2,000	$800	100
No. 502	1,190	1,250	500	60
No. 503	900	850	340	50

(a) Prepare the journal entries to allocate the costs of materials, labor, and factory overhead to each job and to transfer the costs of jobs completed to Finished Goods. **(b)** Compute the total production cost of each job. **(c)** Compute the unit cost of each job.

8. Galaxie Products Co. manufactures goods on a job order basis. During the month of April, three jobs were started in process. (There was no work in process at the beginning of the month.) Jobs 401 and 402 were completed during the month; Job 403 was still in process at the end of April.

Shown below are data from the job cost sheets for each job. These costs include a total of $600 of indirect materials and $900 of indirect labor. One work in process control account is used.

	Job 401	Job 402	Job 403
Direct materials	$3,000	$4,500	$2,000
Direct labor	2,500	4,000	1,500
Factory overhead	1,250	2,000	750

Prepare an entry, in general journal form, to record each of the following: **(a)** materials used, **(b)** factory wages and salaries earned, **(c)** factory overhead transferred to Work in Process, and **(d)** jobs completed.

9. The following inventory data relate to the Shirley Company.

	Inventories	
	Ending	Beginning
Finished goods	$95,000	$110,000
Work in process	80,000	70,000
Direct materials	95,000	90,000

Costs Incurred During the Period

Cost of goods available for sale	$684,000
Total manufacturing costs	584,000
Factory overhead	167,000
Direct materials used	193,000

Calculate the following for the year: **(a)** direct materials purchased, **(b)** direct labor costs incurred, and **(c)** cost of goods sold.

(AICPA adapted)

PROBLEMS

1-1. Basic cost system; journal entries; financial statements. The post-closing trial balance of The Grand Manufacturing Co. at September 30 is reproduced below.

THE GRAND MANUFACTURING CO.
Post-Closing Trial Balance
September 30, 19--

Cash	15,000	
Accounts Receivable	18,000	
Finished Goods	25,000	
Work in Process	4,000	
Materials	8,000	
Building	156,000	
Accumulated Depreciation — Building		23,400
Factory Equipment	108,000	
Accumulated Depreciation — Factory Equipment		54,000
Office Equipment	12,000	
Accumulated Depreciation — Office Equipment		2,000
Vouchers Payable		30,000
Capital Stock		175,000
Retained Earnings		61,600
	346,000	346,000

During the month of October, the following transactions took place:

(a) Raw materials at a cost of $40,000 and general factory supplies at a cost of $5,000 were purchased and vouchers prepared (materials and supplies are recorded in the materials account).

(b) Raw materials to be used in production costing $36,000 and miscellaneous factory supplies costing $4,400 were issued.

(c) A voucher was prepared for wages and salaries earned for the month as follows: factory wages (including $1,600 indirect labor), $28,000, and selling and administrative salaries, $3,000. (Ignore payroll withholdings and deductions.)

(d) Depreciation was recorded for the month at an annual rate of 3% on the building and 10% on the factory equipment and office equipment. The sales and administrative staff uses approximately one fifth of the building for its offices.

(e) During the month, various other expenses totaling $3,024 were incurred and the vouchers prepared. It is determined that one fourth of this amount is allocable to the office function.

(f) Total factory overhead costs were transferred to Work in Process.

(g) During the month, goods with a total cost of $73,000 were completed and transferred to the finished goods storeroom.

(h) Vouchers totaling $75,000 were paid.

(i) Sales for the month totaled $88,000 for goods costing $78,000. (Assume all sales were made on account.)

(j) Accounts receivable in the amount of $90,000 were collected.

Required: (1) Prepare general journal entries to record the transactions. **(2)** Set up "T" accounts. Post the beginning trial balance and the journal entries prepared for (1) above to the accounts and determine the balances in the accounts on October 31. **(3)** Prepare a statement of cost of goods manufactured, an income statement, and a balance sheet.

1-2. Process cost; two departments; work in process. Assuming the same transactions as presented in Problem 1-1, also assume that The Grand Manufacturing Co. has two production departments, A and B, and uses a process cost system. Additional data are as follows:

(a) Materials are processed first in Department A and are then transferred to Department B for finishing.

(b) Materials, labor, and factory overhead costs are incurred in the ratio of three to one in Departments A and B, respectively.

(c) Work in process inventories were as follows:

	October 1	October 31
Department A...	$3,000	$2,000
Department B...	1,000	880

Required: Prepare the general journal entries to record the transactions which affect the work in process accounts. (All other entries would be the same as in Problem 1-1.)

1-3. Job order cost; journal entries; profit analysis. The King Manufacturing Co. obtains the following information from its records for the month of August:

	Jobs Completed		
	Job 161	**Job 162**	**Job 163**
Direct materials cost......................	$ 1,500	$1,000	$ 2,500
Direct labor cost...........................	5,000	5,000	5,000
Factory overhead...........................	3,000	3,000	3,000
Units manufactured.......................	500 units	400 units	1,000 units
Selling prices	$10,000	$8,000	$17,000

Required: (1) Prepare, in summary form, the journal entries that would have been made during the month to record the above. **(2)** Prepare schedules showing the gross profit or loss for August:

- **(a)** For the business as a whole.
- **(b)** For each job completed and sold.
- **(c)** For each unit manufactured and sold.

(3) Explain the significant facts and possible causes brought out by the analysis in (2) above.

1-4. Job cost; journal entries; inventory analysis; manufacturing statement. The Pack Manufacturing Co. is engaged in the manufacture of engines which are made only on customers' orders and to their specifications. During July, the company worked on Jobs Nos. 901, 902, 903, and 904. The following figures summarize the cost records for the month.

	Job No. 901 (100 units)	Job No. 902 (60 units)	Job No. 903 (25 units)	Job No. 904 (100 units)
Direct materials put into process:				
July 2	$15,000	$ 5,000	——	——
18	20,000	16,000	$ 500	——
22	15,000	1,000	1,000	$ 6,000
28	——	——	3,500	2,000
Direct labor cost: week ending				
July 2	$ 1,000	$ 1,000	——	——
9	27,000	9,000	——	——
16	32,000	27,000	——	——
23	20,000	3,000	$5,000	$ 500
30	——	——	3,000	11,500
Factory overhead	$60,000	$32,000	$7,500	$ 9,000
Engines completed	100	60	——	——

Job No. 901 has been completed and delivered to the customer at a selling price of $228,000. Job No. 902 is finished but has not yet been delivered. Jobs Nos. 903 and 904 are still in process. There was no work in process at the beginning of the month.

Required: (1) Prepare the summary general journal entries for the month to record the preceding information. (Assume a work in process account is maintained for each job.) **(2)** Prepare a summary showing the total cost of each job completed during the month or in process at the end of month. Also state the valuation of the inventories of completed engines and engines in process at end of month. **(3)** Prepare a statement of cost of goods manufactured.

1-5. Job order cost; journal entries; ending work in process; inventory analysis. The Allen Company manufactures goods to special order and uses a job order cost system. During its first month of operations, the following selected transactions took place:

(a) Materials purchased on account................................... $25,000
(b) Materials issued to the factory:
    Job No. 101 .... $ 1,500
    Job No. 102 3,800
    Job No. 103 4,700
    Job No. 104 1,100
    For general use in the factory................................ 900
(c) Factory wages and salaries earned:
    Job No. 101 .... $ 1,800
    Job No. 102 4,700
    Job No. 103 6,100
    Job No. 104 1,400
    For general work in the factory 1,500
(d) Factory overhead costs vouchered.............................. $ 1,600
(e) Depreciation of $1,600 on the factory machinery was recorded.
(f) Factory overhead allocated as follows:
    Job No. 101 .... $ 720
    Job No. 102 1,880
    Job No. 103 2,440
    Job No. 104 560
(g) Jobs Nos. 101, 102, and 103 were completed.
(h) Jobs Nos. 101 and 102 were shipped to the customer and billed at $21,600.

Required: (1) Prepare a schedule reflecting the cost of each of the four jobs. **(2)** Prepare entries in general journal form to record the transactions above. (One control account is used for Work in Process.) **(3)** Prove the balance in the work in process account. **(4)** Prove the balance in the finished goods account.

1-6. Cost flow; journal entries; account analysis. Selected account balances and transactions of The Jenks Manufacturing Co. are as shown below.

	Account Balances	
	October 1	October 31
Materials:		
Raw Materials...	$ 5,000	$ 6,500
Factory Supplies...	800	900
Work in Process...	6,000	5,300
Finished Goods..	12,000	13,200

October Transactions

(a) Purchases of raw materials and factory supplies were made on account at costs of $38,000 and $3,000 respectively. (One inventory account is maintained).
(b) Wages earned during the month totaled $60,000 of which $5,000 was for indirect labor.
(c) Factory overhead costs in the amount of $8,500 were vouchered.
(d) Entries to record $4,200 of factory overhead were made in the general journal.

Required: Prepare, in general journal form, all of the entries necessary to show the complete flow of all costs through the accounts.

1-7. Data analysis; manufacturing statement. The Helper Corporation manufactures one product and accounts for costs by a job order cost system. You have obtained the following information for the year ended December 31 from the corporation's books and records:

(a) Total manufacturing cost added during the year was $1,000,000 based on actual direct materials, actual direct labor, and actual factory overhead.

(b) Cost of goods manufactured was $970,000, also based on actual direct materials, actual direct labor, and actual factory overhead.

(c) Factory overhead charged to work in process was 75% of direct labor dollars and 27% of the total manufacturing cost.

(d) Beginning work in process inventory, January 1, was 80% of ending work in process inventory, December 31.

Required: Prepare a statement of cost of goods manufactured for the year ended December 31 for Helper Corporation.

(AICPA adapted)

2

Accounting for Materials

The total cost of a finished product is composed of the expenditures made for the raw materials used, the direct labor incurred, and the factory overhead generated by the manufacturing activities. The principles and procedures for controlling and accounting for these cost elements are the major subjects of Chapters 2, 3, and 4. In each chapter, the specific controls and accounting procedures which apply to that particular element will be discussed. However, there are common controls and practices that pertain to all cost control systems. The major function, in general, of any cost control system is to keep expenditures within the limits prescribed by a preconceived plan. The control system should also encourage cost reductions by eliminating waste and operational inefficiencies. An effective system of cost control is designed to control the people responsible for the expenditures because people control costs, costs do not control themselves.

An effective cost control system should include:

(1) Specific assignments of duties and responsibilities for the approval of cost expenditures.
(2) An established plan of objectives and goals to be achieved.
(3) Regular reports and analyses of differences between goals and the actual performance.
(4) Initiation of corrective action to prevent a recurrence of unfavorable differences.

(5) Follow-up procedures to insure that corrective measures are being effectively applied.

Responsibility accounting is an integral part of a cost control system because it focuses attention on specific individuals who have been designated to maintain the established goals. Often, of the three major objectives of cost accounting — cost control, product costing, and inventory pricing — cost control is the most difficult to achieve. A remedy for this weakness is to place more emphasis on responsibility accounting.

CONTROLLING MATERIALS

There are two basic aspects of materials control: (1) physical control or safeguarding of materials and (2) control of the investment in materials. Physical control is necessary to protect materials from misuse or misappropriation. Controlling the investment in materials is requisite for maintaining appropriate levels of materials inventories.

Physical Control of Materials

Every business requires a system of internal control which includes procedures for the safeguarding of assets. Highly liquid assets, such as cash and marketable securities, are particularly susceptible to misappropriation, and the protection provided for such assets is usually more than adequate. However, other assets, including inventories, must also be protected from unauthorized use or theft.

Because inventories usually represent a significant portion of a manufacturer's current assets, materials must be controlled from the time they are ordered until the time they are shipped to customers in the form of finished goods. In general, effective control of materials involves:

(1) Limited access
(2) Segregation of duties
(3) Accuracy in recording

Limited Access. Only authorized personnel should have access to materials storage areas. Materials should be issued for use in production only if requisitions for materials are properly documented and approved. Finished goods should also be safeguarded in limited access storage areas and not released for shipment in the absence of appropriate documentation and authorization. Procedures should be established within each production area or department for safe-guarding work in process.

Segregation of Duties. A basic principle of internal control is the segregation of duties to minimize opportunities for misappropriation of assets. With respect to materials control, the following functions should be segregated: purchasing, receiving, storage, use, and recording. The independence of personnel assigned to these functions does not eliminate the danger of misappropriation or misuse, since the possibility of collusion still exists. However, appropriate segregation of duties limits an individual employee's opportunities for misappropriation and concealment. In smaller organizations, it is frequently not possible to achieve optimum segregation due to limited resources and personnel. In such cases, specially designed control procedures must be relied upon to compensate for the lack of independence of assigned functions.

Accuracy in Recording. An effective materials control system requires the accurate recording of purchases and issuances of materials. Inventory records should permit the determination of inventory quantities on hand upon request, and cost records should provide the data for the valuation of inventories for preparation of financial statements. Periodically, recorded inventories should be compared with a physical inventory count. Significant discrepancies between recorded and actual amounts should be investigated. Differences may be due to recording errors or may result from inventory losses from theft or spoilage. Once the cause has been determined, corrective action should be taken when appropriate.

Controlling the Investment in Materials

Maintaining the proper balance of materials on hand is one of the most important objectives of materials control. An inventory of sufficient size and diversity for efficient operations must be maintained, but the size should not be excessive in relation to scheduled production needs.

Since funds invested in inventories are unavailable for other uses, management must consider other working capital needs in determining the amount of funds to be invested in inventories and alternative uses of funds which might yield a greater return. In addition to the usage of funds, consideration should be given to the costs of materials handling, storage, and insurance against fire, theft, or other casualty. Also, higher than needed inventory levels could increase the possibility of loss from damage, deterioration, and obsolescence. The planning and control of the materials inventory investment requires careful study of all these factors in determining **(1)** when orders should be placed and **(2)** how many units should be ordered.

Order Point. A minimum level of inventory should be determined for each article of raw material, and inventory records should indicate how much of each article is on hand. This requires the establishment of a subsidiary ledger in which a separate account is maintained for each individual item of raw material used in the manufacturing process.

The point at which an item should be ordered, called the **order point**, occurs when the predetermined minimum level of inventory on hand is reached. Calculation of the order point is based on the following data:

(1) *Usage* — the anticipated rate at which the material will be used.
(2) *Lead time* — the estimated time interval between the placement of an order and receipt of the material.
(3) *Safety stock* — the estimated minimum level of inventory needed to protect against **stockouts** (running out of stock). Stockouts may occur due to inaccurate estimates of usage or lead time or various other unforeseen events, such as the receipt of damaged or inferior materials from the supplier.

Assume that the expected daily usage of an item of material is 100 units, the anticipated lead time is 4 days, and it is estimated that a safety stock of 500 units is needed. The following calculation shows that the order point is reached when the inventory on hand reaches 900 units:

100 units (daily usage) × 4 days (lead time)	400 units
Safety stock required	500 units
Order point	900 units

If estimates of usage and lead time are accurate, the level of inventory when the new order is received would be equal to the safety stock of 500 units. If, however, a 3-day delay is encountered in receiving the new order, it would be necessary to issue 300 units of material from the safety stock in order to maintain the production level.

Economic Order Quantity. The order point establishes the time when an order is to be placed, but does not indicate the most economical number of units that should be ordered. In determining the quantity to be ordered, the costs of placing an order and the costs of carrying inventory must be considered. **Order costs** generally include such factors as:

(1) Salaries and wages of employees engaged in purchasing, receiving, and inspecting materials.

(2) Communications costs associated with ordering, such as telephone, postage, and forms or stationery.

(3) Accounting and record keeping for materials.

Factors to be considered in determining **carrying costs** typically include:

(1) Materials storage and handling costs.

(2) Interest, insurance, and property taxes.

(3) Loss due to theft, deterioration, or obsolescence. ⌐security (labor)

(4) Records and supplies associated with the carrying of inventories.

Order costs and carrying costs move in opposite directions — order costs decrease when order size increases, while carrying costs increase with increases in order size. The optimal quantity to order at one time, called the **economic order quantity**, is the order size which minimizes total order and carrying costs over a period of time, e.g., one year.

The factors to be considered in determining order and carrying costs for a particular company vary with the nature of operations and organizational structure. Special analyses are usually required to identify relevant costs, since these data are not normally accumulated in an accounting system. Care must be exercised in determining which costs are relevant. For example, a company may have adequate warehouse space to carry a large additional quantity of inventory. If the space cannot be used for some other profitable purpose, the cost of the space is not a relevant factor in determining carrying costs. If, however, the space in the company warehouse could be used for a more profitable purpose, or if additional warehouse space must be leased or rented to accommodate increased inventories, then the costs associated with the additional space are relevant in determining carrying costs.

The interest cost associated with carrying an inventory in stock should be considered whether or not funds are borrowed to purchase the inventory. If these funds were not used for inventory, they could have been profitably applied to some alternate use. The rate of interest to be used in the computations will vary depending upon the cost of borrowing, the average cost of capital, or the rate that could be earned by the funds if they were used for some other purpose.

Quantitative models or formulas have been developed for calculating the economic order quantity. One formula that can be used is:

$$EOQ = \sqrt{\frac{2CN}{K}}$$

where:

EOQ = economic order quantity
C = cost of placing an order
N = number of units required annually
K = carrying cost per unit of inventory

To illustrate application of the formula, assume that the following data have been determined by analysis of the factors relevant to materials inventory:

Number of units of material required annually	10,000
Cost of placing an order	$10.00
Annual carrying cost per unit of inventory	$.80

Using the EOQ formula:

$$EOQ = \sqrt{\frac{2 \text{ (cost of order) (number of units required annually)}}{\text{(carrying cost per unit)}}}$$

$$= \sqrt{\frac{2 \ (\$10) \ (10,000)}{\$.80}}$$

$$= \sqrt{\frac{\$200,000}{\$.80}}$$

$$= \sqrt{250,000}$$

$$= \quad 500 \text{ units}$$

The EOQ can also be determined by constructing a table using a range of order sizes. A tabular presentation of the data from the previous example follows:

(1) Order Size	(2) Number of Orders	(3) Total Order Cost	(4) Average Inventory	(5) Total Carrying Cost	(6) Total Order & Carrying Costs
100	100	$1,000	50	$ 40	$1,040
200	50	500	100	80	580
300	33	330	150	120	450
400	25	250	200	160	410
500	20	200	250	200	400
600	17	170	300	240	410
700	14	140	350	280	420
800	13	130	400	320	450
900	11	110	450	360	470
1,000	10	100	500	400	500

(1) Number of units per order
(2) 10,000 annual units ÷ order size
(3) Number of orders × $10 per order
(4) Order size ÷ 2 = average inventory on hand during the year
(5) Average inventory × $.80 per unit carrying cost for one year
(6) Total order cost + total carrying cost

The data presented graphically (Illustration 2-1) show the order cost decreasing as the order size increases. Meanwhile, the carrying costs are increasing as the order size increases because of the necessity to maintain a large quantity of inventory in stock. At the 500-unit level, the carrying and order costs are at their minimum point.

ILLUSTRATION 2-1

Costs of ordering and carrying inventory

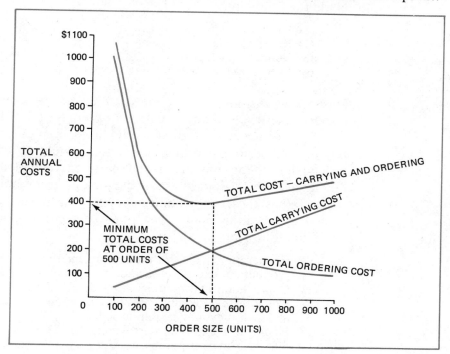

Limitations of Order Point and EOQ Calculations. The techniques illustrated for determining when to order (order point) and how much to order (EOQ) may give a false impression of exactness. However, because these calculations are based on estimates of factors such as production volume, lead time, and order and carrying costs, they are really approximations which serve merely as a guide to planning and controlling the investment in materials.

In addition, other factors may influence the time for ordering or the quantity ordered. Such factors include the availability of materials from suppliers, fluctuations in the purchase price of materials, and trade (volume) discounts offered by suppliers.

MATERIALS CONTROL PROCEDURES

Specific internal control procedures should be tailored to a company's needs. However, materials control generally involves the following functions: **(1)** purchase and receipt of materials, **(2)** storage of materials, and **(3)** requisition and consumption of materials.

Materials Control Personnel

Although actual job titles and duties may vary from one company to another, the personnel involved in materials control usually include the following:

    (1) Purchasing agent
    (2) Receiving clerk
    (3) Storeroom keeper
    (4) Production department supervisors

Purchasing Agent. The responsibility for buying the materials needed for the manufacturing enterprise should rest on the shoulders of one person. In a small plant the employee who does the buying may also perform other duties, while in a large plant the purchasing agent may head a department established to perform buying activities. Regardless of the size of an organization, it is important that the responsibility for the purchasing function be assigned to one individual. The duties of a purchasing agent may include the following:

    (1) Cooperation with the production manager to prevent delays in production because of lack of materials.
    (2) Compilation and maintenance of information as to sources from which the desired materials may be obtained and the lowest prices at which they may be purchased.
    (3) Placing of purchase orders for materials needed.
    (4) Supervision over purchase order until materials are received.

Receiving Clerk. The receiving clerk is charged with the responsibility of supervising the receipt of incoming shipments. All incoming materials must be checked as to quantity and quality and sometimes as to price.

Storeroom Keeper. The storeroom keeper, who has charge of the materials after they have been received, must see that the materials are properly stored and maintained. The materials must be placed in stock and issued only on properly authorized requisitions. The purchasing agent should be informed of the quantities on hand as a guide to the purchasing of additional materials.

Production Department Supervisor. Each production department has a person who is responsible for supervising the operational functions within the department. This individual may be given the title of the department supervisor or another similar designation. One of the assigned duties of a department supervisor is to prepare or approve the requisitions designating the quantities and kinds of material needed for the work to be done in the department.

Control During Procurement

Materials are ordered to maintain adequate levels of inventory to meet scheduled production needs. The storeroom keeper is responsible for monitoring quantities of materials on hand. When the order point is reached for a particular item of raw material, the procurement process is initiated. In many companies, electronic data processing (EDP) equipment is used to store data pertaining to inventories on hand, predetermined order points, and economic order quantities. The use of EDP equipment can simplify the task of maintaining appropriate inventory levels when the equipment is properly programmed, and the purchasing agent is adequately informed.

Supporting documents are essential to maintaining control during the procurement process. In general, the documents should be prenumbered and protected from unauthorized use. The documents commonly used in procuring materials include: (1) purchase requisitions, (2) purchase orders, (3) vendor's invoices, (4) receiving reports, and (5) debit-credit memoranda.

Purchase Requisitions. The form used to notify the purchasing agent that additional materials are needed is known as a **purchase requisition**. This requisition is an important part of the materials control process, because it is the agent's authority to buy. Purchase requisitions should originate with the storeroom keeper or some other individual with similar authority and responsibility.

Purchase requisitions should be prenumbered serially to help detect the loss or misuse of any of these forms. They are generally prepared in duplicate. The first copy goes to the purchasing agent; the second copy is retained by the storeroom keeper. A purchase requisition form is shown in Illustration 2-2 on page 52.

Purchase Order. The purchase requisition gives the purchasing agent authority to order the materials described in the requisition. The purchasing agent should maintain or have access to an up-to-date list of vendors, which includes prices, available discounts, estimated delivery time, and any other relevant information. From this list, a

```
┌─────────────────────────────────────────────────────────────────────┐
│                    PURCHASE REQUISITION              No. 3246         │
│                                                                       │
│  Date ___January 3_____ 19 -- ____                                 │
│                                                                       │
│  Date wanted ___February 1____ 19 -- ____                             │
│                                    ⎧ Job. No.      220                │
│                              For ⎨                                    │
│                                    ⎩ Account No.  1237                │
│                                         Authorization No.   4317      │
├───────────────────────┬───────────────────────────────────────────── │
│      QUANTITY         │               DESCRIPTION                     │
│                       │                                               │
│     41 500 L          │   Superglu - Triple AAA                       │
│                       │                                               │
│                       │                                               │
├───────────────────────┴───────────────────────────────────────────── │
│  Approved by  G. Sarnof          Signed by  A. Norman                 │
│                                                                       │
│  Purchase order No. 1131           Date ordered   January 6           │
│                                                                       │
│  Ordered from  The Goodeenuff Company                                 │
└─────────────────────────────────────────────────────────────────────┘
```

ILLUSTRATION 2-2

Purchase Requisition
(Notifies purchasing agent that additional materials should be ordered)

vendor is selected from whom the materials can be obtained at the lowest cost and with the least delay. If this information is not available from the list for a particular item of material, the purchasing agent may communicate with several prospective vendors and request quotations on the materials needed.

A **purchase order**, as shown in Illustration 2-3, is then completed and addressed to the chosen vendor, describing the materials wanted, stating price and terms, and fixing the date and method of delivery. This purchase order should be prenumbered serially and prepared in quadruplicate. The first copy goes to the vendor, one copy is sent to the accounting department, one copy goes to the receiving clerk, and a copy is retained by the purchasing agent.

The purchasing agent's copy of the order should be placed in an unfilled orders file. Before the order is filed, the purchase requisition on which it is based should be attached to the order. This last step is important, for it is the beginning of the assembly of a complete set of all the forms pertaining to the purchase transaction. In order to identify each document relating to a transaction with all others of

```
┌─────────────────────────────────────────────────────────────────┐
│                                                                   │
│              PURCHASE ORDER              Order No.  1131           │
│                                                                   │
│  To:  The Goodeenuff Company        Mark Order No. on invoice     │
│       Akron, Ohio  44313               and on all packages        │
│                                                                   │
│                               Date    January 6, 19--             │
│                               Terms   3/10 eom n/60               │
│                               Ship Via Truck (to arrive           │
│                                        January 25, 19--)          │
│  Please enter our order for the following:                        │
├──────────────┬───────────────────────────────┬──────────────────┤
│   QUANTITY   │          DESCRIPTION           │      PRICE        │
├──────────────┼───────────────────────────────┼──────────────────┤
│  41 500 L    │  Superglu - Triple AAA         │  $2,490   00     │
│              │                                │                  │
│              │                                │                  │
└──────────────┴───────────────────────────────┴──────────────────┘
   Deliver no goods without a written order on this form.
            THE CLARKSON MFG. COMPANY
                By  Alice Lauren
                                        Purchasing Agent
```

ILLUSTRATION 2-3

Purchase Order (Prepared by purchasing agent and sent to vendor to order additional materials)

the same set, the purchase order number should be shown on each of the documents. The sets can then be compiled according to the respective purchase order numbers.

Vendor's Invoice. The **vendor's invoice** should be received before the materials arrive at the factory. As soon as it is received, it goes to the purchasing agent, who compares it with the purchase order, noting particularly that the description of the materials is the same, that the price and the terms agree, and that the method of shipment and the date of delivery conform to the instructions on the purchase order. When satisfied that the invoice is correct, the purchasing agent initials or stamps the invoice indicating that it has been reviewed and agrees with the purchase order. The invoice is then filed together with the purchase order and the purchase requisition in the unfilled orders file until the materials are received.

An objection may be made to the practice of leaving the invoice in the hands of the purchasing agent until the goods are received because it delays the recording of this liability in the books of the buyer. However, the benefit to be derived from the preparation of the complete file on the transaction more than offsets this disadvantage, particularly since the delay will be very slight. Also, if there is any adjustment needed because of a discrepancy between the materials received and those ordered, there will not be the problem of correcting or rewriting the voucher for the order. However, care must be exercised at the end of the accounting period to add the invoices in the hands of the purchasing agent to the accounts payable in order not to understate the liabilities. Invoices received for goods in transit are classified as current liabilities if title passes to the purchaser at the time of shipment. An adjusting entry, debiting the appropriate accounts and crediting accounts payable for the total of the goods-in-transit invoices for which title has passed, should be made at the end of the period.

Receiving Report. As noted previously, a copy of the purchase order is sent to the receiving clerk to give advance notice of the arrival of the materials ordered. This is done to facilitate planning work and allotting space to incoming materials. The receiving clerk is in charge of the receiving department where all incoming materials are received, opened, counted or weighed, and tested for conformity with the order. If the materials received are of too technical a nature to be tested by the receiving clerk, the inspection may be undertaken by an engineer from the production manager's office, or the materials may be sent to the plant laboratory for testing.

As the receiving clerk counts and identifies the materials, a **receiving report** should be prepared similar in form to the one reproduced in Illustration 2-4. Each report is numbered serially and shows from whom the materials were received, when they were received, what the shipment contained, and the number of the purchase order that identifies the shipment. The report should be prepared in quadruplicate. Two copies go to the purchasing agent; one copy goes with the materials or supplies to the storeroom keeper to ensure that all of the materials that come to the receiving department are put into the storeroom; and one copy is retained by the receiving clerk. In some plants, the receiving clerk is given a copy of the purchase order with the quantity ordered omitted. This omission of the quantity assures that the items received will be counted.

The purchasing agent compares the receiving report with the vendor's invoice and the purchase order to determine that the materials received are those ordered and billed. If the documents agree, the purchasing agent initials or stamps the two copies of the receiving report. One copy is then attached to the other forms already in the file, and the entire set of forms is sent to the accounting depart-

**ILLUSTRATION 2-4
Receiving Report**

(incoming materials opened, counted, weighed, or tested for conformity with purchase order)

RECEIVING REPORT

No. 496   Date ___January 21___ 19 _ _

To the purchasing agent:

RECEIVED FROM ___The Goodeenuff Company___

Via ___Ace Trucking___   Transportation Charges ___$78.74___

QUANTITY	DESCRIPTION
41 500 L	Superglu - Triple AAA

Counted by ___R.S.___   Inspected by ___H.P.___

Purchase order No. ___1131___

---

ment, where a voucher is prepared and recorded in the voucher register. The other copy of the receiving report is sent to the person in the accounting department who maintains inventory records. The procedures for recording materials purchases are discussed in a subsequent section of this chapter.

Debit-Credit Memorandum. Occasionally, a shipment of materials does not match the order and the invoice. When this situation occurs, comparing the receiving report with the purchase order and the invoice will disclose the discrepancy to the purchasing agent. Whatever the cause of the difference, it will lead to correspondence with the vendor, and copies of the letters should be a part of the file of forms relating to the transaction. If a larger quantity has been received than has been ordered and the excess is to be kept for future use, a credit memorandum is prepared notifying the vendor of the amount of the increase in the invoice. One form of the **debit-**

credit memorandum is shown in Illustration 2-5. This memo shows that the vendor has delivered materials that do not meet the buyer's specifications. The purchasing agent will prepare a **return shipping order** and return the materials to the vendor.

ILLUSTRATION 2-5

Debit-Credit
Memorandum
(Discrepancy
between order,
shipment, and
vendor invoice.
Price adjustment
request shown on
debit/credit memo)

	DEBIT / CREDIT MEMORANDUM			
			Date January 3 _____ 19 --	
To:	The Iron and Brass Machine Company Cleveland, Ohio 44118			
	We have today Debited / Credited your account for the following:			
	Explanation wrong size _____			

QUANTITY	DESCRIPTION	UNIT PRICE	AMOUNT	
5 boxes	Brass machine screws, 8/32" x 1", flat head	$27.50	$137	50

Purchase order No. ___1029_____

Your invoice date ___December 27_____ 19 --

THE CLARKSON MFG. COMPANY

By _Alice Lauren_____
                              Purchasing Agent

If, on the other hand, the shipment is short, one of two courses of action may be taken. If the materials received can be used, they may be retained and a debit memorandum prepared notifying the vendor of the amount of the shortage. If the materials received cannot be used, a return shipping order is prepared and the materials returned. A return shipping order form is shown in Illustration 2-6.

The return shipping order is usually made out in triplicate. The first copy goes to the vendor, the second copy goes to the receiving or shipping clerk, and the third copy is filed with other forms relating to the transaction. Debit or credit memorandums should be prepared in duplicate. The first copy goes to the vendor and the second copy is filed with other documents relating to the transaction.

ILLUSTRATION 2-6

Return Shipping Order

(When material shipment is returned to vendor)

```
                        RETURN SHIPPING ORDER

                                        Date    January 4        19 --

        To the shipping clerk:
        Send the following to:      Martin Manufacturing Company
                                    Grand Rapids, Michigan 49501


 QUANTITY  |          DESCRIPTION           | UNIT PRICE | AMOUNT

    10       Laminated plywood boards,          $8.25      $82 50
             4 x 8 x 3/4




        Shipper's invoice date    December 14        19 --

        Purchase order No.   1011


                            THE CLARKSON MFG. COMPANY

                            By  Alice Lauren
                                                    Purchasing Agent
```

Not until all differences have been resolved will the transaction be complete. When they are resolved, the purchasing agent sends the documents to the accounting department for recording.

Control During Storage and Issuance

The preceding discussion applies to the control of materials during the process of procurement. The routine that has been suggested and the forms described have traced the ordering and the arrival of the materials and their transfer to the storeroom. The next problem to be considered is the storage and issuance of the materials and supplies.

Materials Requisition. As discussed earlier materials should be protected from unauthorized use. No materials should be issued from the storeroom except on written authorization so that there is less chance of theft, carelessness, or misuse. The form used to provide this control is known as the **materials requisition** or **stores requisition** (see Illustration 2-7) and is prepared by the person or persons in the factory authorized to withdraw materials from the storeroom. The individuals who are authorized to perform this function may differ from company to company, but such authority must be given to someone of responsibility. The most satisfactory arrangement would be to have the production manager prepare all of the materials requisitions, but this is usually not feasible. Another arrangement is to require that the supervisor of the department approve (sign) all materials requisitions. When a properly signed requisition is presented to the storeroom keeper, the requisitioned materials are released. Both the storeroom keeper and the employee to whom materials are issued should be required to sign the requisition.

MATERIALS REQUISITION

Date _January 19_____ 19 _--_   No. 632

To the storeroom keeper: Don Graham

   Deliver the following materials:

QUANTITY	DESCRIPTION	UNIT PRICE	AMOUNT
415 L	Superglu - Triple AAA	$.06	$24	90

Approved by _____   Issued by _____

Received by _____

Charge to Job/Dept. No. _319_____   Factory Overhead Expense Account No. _____

ILLUSTRATION 2-7

Materials Requisition (Authorization to withdraw materials from storeroom)

The materials requisition is usually prepared in quadruplicate. Two copies go to the accounting department for recording; one copy is forwarded to the storeroom keeper and serves as the authority for issuing the materials requisitioned; and one copy is retained by the production manager or supervisor who prepared it.

Identification is an important factor in the control of materials. For this reason, the materials requisition should indicate the job number (job order costing) or department (process costing) for which the materials are issued. When indirect materials, such as cleaning materials, lubricants, and paint are issued, the requisition will indicate the name or number of the factory overhead account to be charged.

Returned Materials Report. After materials are requisitioned, occasionally some or all of the materials must be returned to the storeroom. Perhaps more were taken out than were needed; or an accident occurred and spoiled some of the materials; or the manufacturing process is such that scrap materials (for example, metal shavings from the making of brass tubing) are recovered in the factory periodically and put back into the storeroom. Whatever the reason, a written report describing the materials and the reason for the return must accompany these materials to the storeroom.

Assume that after an order is started in the factory, it is discovered that more materials were taken out of the storeroom than were needed. The excess materials should be returned at once, accompanied by a **returned materials report** (Illustration 2-8). The report, except for price data, should be prepared by the supervisor of the

ILLUSTRATION 2-8

Returned Materials Report

(Materials requisitioned but unused by production and returned to storeroom)

RETURNED MATERIALS REPORT			No. **232**	
Date _January 21_ 19 --				
To the storeroom keeper: D. Graham				
The following excess materials are being returned to the storeroom from Job No. 319				
QUANTITY	DESCRIPTION	UNIT PRICE	AMOUNT	
200 L	Superglu - Triple AAA	$.06	$12	00

Date of original issue _January 19_ 19--

Post to:

Stores ledger by _F.C.N._

Job cost ledger by _G.H._

Returned by:

H. Beatley
Department Supervisor

Reason: _Production cutback_

Received by:

D. Graham
Storeroom Keeper

department returning the materials. One copy is sent to the storeroom keeper along with the returned materials. A copy is forwarded to the accounting department where the unit price and the total cost are entered. The return of the materials to the storeroom is then recorded in the appropriate accounting records as discussed in the following section. A third copy of the report is retained by the preparer, the production supervisor.

ACCOUNTING FOR MATERIALS

A company's inventory records should show (1) the number of units of each kind of materials on hand and (2) their cost. The most desirable method of achieving this result is to integrate the materials accounting system with the general ledger accounts. All purchases of materials are recorded through the voucher register as a debit to Materials in the general ledger (the corresponding credit is to Vouchers Payable). The materials account is a control account supported by a subsidiary **stores** (or **materials**) **ledger** in which there is an individual account for each item of material carried in stock. Periodically the balance of the control account and the total of the individual accounts are compared and any significant variation between the two investigated.

Each of the individual materials accounts in the subsidiary stores ledger shows (1) the quantity on hand and (2) the cost of the materials. In order to keep this information current, it is necessary to record in each individual account the quantity and the cost of materials received, issued, and on hand. The stores ledger accounts are usually kept on cards similar in design to the one shown in Illustration 2-9.

As explained previously, copies of the purchase order and receiving report are approved by the purchasing agent and sent to the accounting department. Upon receipt of the purchase order, the stores ledger clerk enters the quantity in the "On Order" columns of the appropriate stores ledger card. When materials are delivered, the ledger clerk's copy of the receiving report serves as the basis for posting the receipt of the materials to the stores ledger card. The posting shows the date of receipt, the number of the receiving report, and the number of units received and their cost. The cost may be expressed in terms of both unit cost and total cost, or in totals only.

When materials are issued, two copies of the materials requisition go to the accounting department. One copy is used in posting the cost of requisitioned materials to the appropriate accounts in the job cost and factory overhead ledgers. Direct materials are charged

Date	ON ORDER		RECEIVED				ISSUED				BALANCE		
	Purchase Order No.	Quantity	Receiving Report No./ (Returned Shipping Order No.)	Quantity	Unit Price	Amount	Materials Requisition/ (Returned Materials Report No.)	Quantity	Unit Price	Amount	Quantity	Unit Price	Amount

Description ___White Lead___   Location in Storeroom ___Bin 8___

Maximum ___15,000 lbs.___   Minimum ___1,000 lbs.___   Stores Ledger Acct. No. ___1411___

ILLUSTRATION 2-9 Stores Ledger Card

to the proper job (or department) and indirect materials are charged to the proper factory overhead accounts.

The other copy of the requisition is sent to the stores ledger clerk and becomes the basis for posting to the appropriate ledger cards. The posting shows the date of issue, the number of the requisition, and the number of units issued and their cost. The cost may be expressed in terms of both unit cost and total cost, or in totals only.

When materials are returned to the storeroom, a copy of the returned materials report is sent to the accounting department. The stores ledger clerk determines the cost of the returned materials, enters the information on the report, and posts the amount to the appropriate stores ledger card. The cost assigned to the returned materials should be the same as that recorded when the materials were issued to the factory.

The copy of the returned materials report is then routed to the cost accountant in charge of the job cost and factory overhead ledgers. Direct materials returned are credited to the appropriate job or department, and indirect materials returned are credited to the appropriate factory overhead account.

As the stores ledger clerk posts receipts and issues of materials to the stores ledger accounts, the balance is extended after each entry. These extensions could be made at the end of the accounting period when inventories are to be determined. However, to wait until that time would defeat one of the advantages of this method of materials control, because it would not be possible to determine from the stores ledger when the stock of any article of materials is falling below the set minimum requirements.

Determining the Cost of Materials Issued

One of the most difficult areas of accounting for materials is the costing of materials requisitioned from the storeroom for factory use. The unit cost of materials when purchased is known for each purchase. The date of each purchase is also known, but the materials on hand typically include items purchased on different dates and at different prices. Items which are alike in appearance usually are comingled in the storeroom. As a result, it may be difficult or impossible to identify an issue of materials with a specific purchase when determining what unit cost should be assigned to the materials being issued.

Several practical methods of solving this problem are available. In selecting the method to be employed, the accounting policies of the firm and the federal and state income tax regulations are important factors to be considered. As the methods are discussed, it should be remembered that the flow of materials does not necessarily dictate the flow of costs. The **flow of materials** is the order in which materials are actually issued for use in the factory. The **flow of costs** is the order in which unit costs are assigned to materials issued.

First-In, First-Out Method. The **first-in, first-out (fifo) method** of costing has the advantages of simplicity and wide adoption. The fifo method is based on the assumption that materials issued are taken from the oldest materials in stock. The materials are thus costed at the prices paid for the oldest materials. In some industries the flow of costs using fifo closely parallels the physical flow of materials. For example, if materials have a tendency to deteriorate in storage, the oldest materials would be issued first. However, as noted previously, the flow of costs does not have to be determined on the basis of the flow of materials. As a result, fifo may be used by any organization.

Application of the fifo method can be illustrated using the following data:

Dec. 1 Balance, 1,000 units @ $20.
     10 Issued 500 units.
     15 Purchased 1,000 units @ $24.
     20 Issued 250 units.
     26 Issued 500 units.
     28 Purchased 500 units @ $26.
     30 Issued 500 units.
     31 Balance, 750 units.

Using fifo, costs would be assigned to materials issued during the month and to materials on hand at the end of the month as follows:

Dec. 10 Issued from the December 1 balance: 500 units @ $20, total cost, $10,000.
     20 Issued from the December 1 balance: 250 units @ $20, total cost, $5,000.
     26 Issued from the December 1 balance: 250 units @ $20, total cost, $5,000.
         Issued from the December 15 purchase: 250 units @ $24, total cost, $6,000.
         Total cost of materials issued: $5,000 + $6,000 = $11,000.
     30 Issued from the December 15 purchase: 500 units @ $24, total cost, $12,000.
     31 The balance of materials on hand, 750 units, consists of the following:

Date of Purchase	Units	Unit Cost	Total Cost
December 15	250	$24	$ 6,000
December 28	500	26	13,000
	750		$19,000

As illustrated in the example, ending inventories using fifo are costed at the prices paid for the most recent purchases. Thus, 500 of the units on hand are assigned a unit cost of $26, the unit cost of the December 28 purchase. The remaining 250 units on hand are costed at $24 per unit, reflecting the unit cost of the next most recent purchase on December 15.

Last-In, First-Out Method. The **last-in, first-out (lifo) method** of costing materials, as the name implies, is based on the assumption that materials issued for use in manufacturing are the most recently purchased materials. Thus, materials issued are costed at the most recent purchase prices, and inventories are costed at prices paid for the earliest purchases. The lifo method of costing closely approximates the physical flow of materials in some industries. For example, in the smelting of iron ore, the raw material is stored in mountainous piles. As ore is needed for production, it is drawn from the pile in such a way that the material being used is the last ore to have been received.

Using the same data given to illustrate the fifo method, costs under the lifo method would be determined as follows:

Dec. 10 Issued from the December 1 balance: 500 units @ $20, total cost, $10,000.

20 Issued from the December 15 purchase: 250 units @ $24, total cost, $6,000.

26 Issued from the December 15 purchase: 500 units @ $24, total cost, $12,000.

30 Issued from the December 28 purchase: 500 units @ $26, total cost, $13,000.

31 The balance of materials on hand, 750 units, consists of the following:

Date of Purchase	Units	Unit Cost	Total Cost
Balance, December 1	500	$20	$10,000
December 15	250	24	6,000
	750		$16,000

Moving Average Method. The **moving average method** is based on the assumption that the materials issued at any time are simply withdrawn from the mixed group in the storeroom without any definite attempt being made to identify the materials as being from the earliest or the latest purchases. This method has the disadvantage of requiring more frequent and more difficult computations than the other methods. However, with the availability of the computer and electronic calculators, this disadvantage has been overcome and many firms are adopting this method. The basic requirement of this method is that an average unit price be computed every time a new lot of materials is received and that this average unit price be used to cost all issues of materials made until another lot is purchased. Thus, the issues in the illustration would be computed as follows:

Dec. 10 Issued from the December 1 balance: 500 units @ $20, total cost, $10,000.

15 The balance of materials on hand on December 15 consists of 500 units from December 1 and 1,000 units acquired on December 15, for a total of 1,500 units which cost $34,000. The average cost is $22.66⅔ per unit ($34,000 ÷ 1,500).

20 Issued 250 units @ $22.66⅔, total cost, $5,666.67.

26 Issued 500 units @ $22.66⅔, total cost, $11,333.33.

28 The balance of materials on hand on December 28 consists of 750 units which cost $17,000 (purchased prior to December 28) and 500 units @ $26 (purchased on December 28) costing $13,000. The total cost is $30,000 for 1,250 units, representing an average cost of $24 per unit ($30,000 ÷ 1,250).

30 Issued 500 units @ $24, total cost, $12,000.

31 The balance of materials on hand consists of:

Units	Unit Cost	Total Cost
750	$24	$18,000

Analysis of Fifo, Lifo, and Moving Average. Fifo, lifo, and moving average are the most commonly used methods of inventory costing. Any of these methods may be adopted for use in the keeping of the stores ledger as shown in Illustration 2–10.

Since no one method is best suited to all situations that may be encountered in manufacturing, the method chosen should be the one that most accurately reflects the income for the period in terms of the current economic conditions. One factor to be considered is the effect the costing method has on reported net income. Overstating net income will cause a firm to be subject to higher taxes than those of a competitor who is using a different costing method.

Under economic conditions in which prices are constantly rising, lifo is sometimes adopted so that the higher prices of materials may be charged against the increasingly higher sales revenue. The resulting gross margin, under these conditions, is assumed to reflect a more accurate picture of earnings. Also, the lower gross margin, brought about by use of the lifo method, results in a smaller tax assessment for the firm. This lifo benefit, however, does not mean that all companies should adopt lifo.

Before selecting any method for costing materials, a firm should give consideration to the size and dollar valuation of the inventory to be maintained, the inventory turnover rate, and the frequency, direction, and magnitude of price changes. If manufacturing opera-

FIRST-IN, FIRST-OUT METHOD

Date	Received Quantity	Unit Price	Amount	Issued Quantity	Unit Price	Amount	Balance Quantity	Unit Price	Amount
Dec. 1							1,000	20 00	20,000 00
10				500	20 00	10,000 00	500	20 00	10,000 00
15	1,000	24 00	24,000 00				{ 500 { 1,000	20 00 24 00	34,000 00
20				250	20 00	5,000 00	{ 250 { 1,000	20 00 24 00	29,000 00
26				{ 250 { 250	20 00 24 00	11,000 00	750	24 00	18,000 00
28	500	26 00	13,000 00				{ 750 { 500	24 00 26 00	31,000 00
30				500	24 00	12,000 00	{ 250 { 500	24 00 26 00	19,000 00

LAST-IN, FIRST-OUT METHOD

Date	Received Quantity	Unit Price	Amount	Issued Quantity	Unit Price	Amount	Balance Quantity	Unit Price	Amount
Dec. 1							1,000	20 00	20,000 00
10				500	20 00	10,000 00	500	20 00	10,000 00
15	1,000	24 00	24,000 00				{ 500 { 1,000	20 00 24 00	34,000 00
20				250	24 00	6,000 00	{ 500 { 750	20 00 24 00	28,000 00
26				500	24 00	12,000 00	{ 500 { 250	20 00 24 00	16,000 00
28	500	26 00	13,000 00				{ 500 { 250 { 500	20 00 24 00 26 00	29,000 00
30				500	26 00	13,000 00	{ 500 { 250	20 00 24 00	16,000 00

MOVING AVERAGE METHOD

Date	Received Quantity	Unit Price	Amount	Issued Quantity	Unit Price	Amount	Balance Quantity	Unit Price	Amount
Dec. 1							1,000	20 00	20,000 00
10				500	20 00	10,000 00	500	20 00	10,000 00
15	1,000	24 00	24,000 00				1,500	22 66⅔	34,000 00
20				250	22 66⅔	5,666 67	1,250	22 66⅔	28,333 33
26				500	22 66⅔	11,333 33	750	22 66⅔	17,000 00
28	500	26 00	13,000 00				1,250	24 00	30,000 00
30				500	24 00	12,000 00	750	24 00	18,000 00

ILLUSTRATION 2-10   Comparison of Inventory Valuation Methods

tions require only a small inventory that turns over rapidly, the materials costing method may have only a small effect on the profit margin, because the price changes are quickly absorbed in the current cost of goods sold. For such firms, the fifo method would be the most appropriate, because it is the method which usually minimizes the clerical costs associated with inventory maintenance.

To illustrate the effect that the popular costing methods have on profit determination, assume that competing companies — A, B, and C — use fifo, average cost, and lifo, respectively. The companies have no beginning inventories, and they purchase identical materials at the same time as follows (assume also that each purchase is for one unit):

> Purchase No. 1 @ $.20 per unit
> Purchase No. 2 @ $.50 per unit
> Purchase No. 3 @ $.80 per unit

Assuming that one unit of materials is used after the last purchase, the net income is determined as shown below.

	Company A (Fifo) (per unit)	Company B (Average Cost) (per unit)	Company C (Lifo) (per unit)
Net sales...	$1.00	$1.00	$1.00
Less cost of goods sold.............................	.20	.50*	.80
Gross margin on sales.................................	$ .80	$ .50	$ .20
Operating expenses...................................	.10	.10	.10
Income before provision for income taxes	$ .70	$ .40	$ .10
Less income tax (50%)	.35	.20	.05
Net income after provision for income taxes...	$ .35	$ .20	$ .05

$.20 + $.50 + $.80 = $1.50 ÷ 3 units = $.50 per unit.

This illustration shows that under conditions of rapidly rising prices, Company C has an advantage over its competitors. Although Company C shows a profit of only $.05 on each unit of sales, it pays only $.05 per unit for taxes, whereas Company A pays $.35 and Company B pays $.20 per unit for taxes. Therefore, of each $1.00 sales, Company C retains $.95 for the firm, while Company B retains $.80 and Company A retains $.65. Since the replacement cost of materials is now $.80, Company A will be short of cash by $.15 when it replaces the unit sold, and Company B will have to invest all of the $.80 it retained. Only Company C will be able to replace the materials used, pay operating expenses, and retain its $.05 per unit net income.

The methods leave the companies with the following ending materials inventory balances:

Company A (fifo)   — $1.30 ($.50 + $.80)
Company B (average) — $1.00 ($.50 + $.50)
Company C (lifo)   — $ .70 ($.20 + $.50)

Company C has the most conservatively valued inventory at $.70, followed by Company B with $1.00, and Company A at $1.30. The higher inventory valuation may, under some conditions, be advantageous; however, the inventory would probably be subject to state and local inventory or property taxes. Thus, Companies A and B will have an additional tax burden that Company C will partially avoid because of its lower inventory valuation.

Many companies have adopted the lifo method in order to match current materials costs with current revenue as well as to minimize the effect of income taxes in periods of rising prices. For companies which are considering the adoption of the lifo method, however, it is important to carefully analyze economic conditions, and to examine the tax regulations that pertain to lifo. If there should be a downward trend of prices, these companies would probably desire to change to the fifo method in order to have the same competitive advantages that were gained by using lifo when prices were rising. However, the lifo election cannot be rescinded unless authorized or required by the Internal Revenue Service.

Other Inventory Costing Methods. There are other inventory methods in addition to those previously discussed which are used for pricing inventory and costing materials issued. However, these methods are less frequently used because the firm's operational requirements must be carefully coordinated with the designed inventory system in order to make such methods feasible to use and to maintain.

Weighted or Month-End Average Method. The **weighted or month-end average** method is used normally with a periodic inventory system where a periodic physical count of items establishes the quantity of units on hand at the end of a designated period. Then, the quantity of inventory used is calculated by subtracting the ending quantity on hand from the total inventory that was available for use during the period. The unit cost of the inventory is calculated by dividing the total inventory cost incurred for the period by the total units available.

To illustrate, assume the same transactions as on page 63.

		Units	Unit Cost	Total Cost
Dec. 1	Balance	1,000	$20	$20,000
15	Purchase	1,000	24	24,000
28	Purchase	500	26	13,000
		2,500		$57,000

Weighted average cost per unit: $57,000 ÷ 2,500 = $22.80
Cost of ending inventory: $22.80 × 750 units = $17,100

Cost of inventory used:

Total available, 2,500 units..............................	$57,000
Less ending inventory, 750 units......................	17,100
Total inventory used, 1,750 units	$39,900

Market Price at Date of Issue. The **market price at date of issue** can be used for costing materials traded on commodity exchanges, such as cotton, wheat, copper, and crude oil. This method substitutes replacement cost for the actual price paid for the material. Currently, this method is used exclusively for internal reporting purposes. However, the popularity of using the market price at date of issue in costing materials can be expected to grow because the interest in current-value and replacement-value costing is increasing.

Standard Cost Method. A company that uses a **standard cost system** predetermines the cost of each unit of material, then charges production with the predetermined unit costs when materials are requisitioned. One advantage of this method is that only the quantity of the materials is maintained in the records since all units of the same class of materials have the same price per unit. The details of standard costing are discussed in Chapters 8 and 9.

Accounting Procedures

The purpose of materials accounting is to provide a summary from the general ledger of the total costs of materials purchased and used in manufacturing. The forms commonly used in assembling the required data have already been discussed. The purchase invoices provide the information needed in preparing the vouchers. The vouchers should then be recorded in a voucher register in which a special column is provided for recording materials purchased. At the end of the month, the total materials purchased during the month is posted by debiting Materials and by crediting Vouchers Payable or Accounts Payable. The materials account in the general ledger serves as a control account for the stores ledger.

All materials issued during the month and materials returned to stock are recorded on a **summary of materials issued and returned** form (see Illustration 2-11). When the summary is completed at the end of the month, the total cost of direct materials requisitioned is recorded by debiting Work in Process and by crediting Materials. The total of indirect materials requisitioned is recorded by debiting the appropriate factory overhead account and by crediting Materials. The work in process account in the general ledger serves as a control account for the factory cost ledger.

SUMMARY OF MATERIALS ISSUED AND RETURNED

Month Ending _____ 19___

| | | Materials Issued | | | | Materials Returned to Storeroom | | | | |
| | | Direct Materials | | Indirect Materials | | | Direct Materials | | Indirect Materials | |
Date	Req. No.	Job No.	Amount	Overhead Acct. No.	Amount	Report No.	Job No.	Amount	Overhead Acct. No.	Amount
Mar. 5	825	315	$2,150 00							
8	826	316	3,210 00						3121	$ 12 50
11	827	317	280 00	3121	$ 440 00					
14	828	317	415 00	3121	132 50					
17	829	316	340 00							
17	830	317	820 00						3121	15 00
18	831	318	290 00	3121	135 00					
19	832	319	224 20			232	319	$ 12 10		
20	833	319	975 90			233	320	448 90		
24	834	320	4,350 00	3121	432 00	234	321	318 20		
27	835	321	6,500 00							
29	836	322	550 00							
30	837	321	785 40							
31	838	320	870 00							
			$21,760 50		$ 1,139 50			$ 779 20		$ 27 50

ILLUSTRATION 2-11 Summary of Materials Issued and Returned

Any undamaged materials returned to the storeroom from the factory should also be recorded on the summary of materials issued and returned in order that the totals may be recorded at the end of the month. The entries required to record undamaged materials returned are the reverse of the entries required to record materials requisitioned. Thus, the total cost of direct materials returned to the storeroom is recorded by debiting Materials and by crediting Work in Process, while the total cost of indirect materials returned is recorded by debiting Materials and by crediting the proper factory overhead account.

Any materials in stores returned to the vendors from whom they were originally purchased should be recorded by debiting Vouchers Payable or Accounts Payable and by crediting Materials. Unless a special journal is provided for recording such returns, the entries may be made in the general journal. All transactions relating to materials should be recorded so that the balance of the materials account in the general ledger will represent the cost of materials on hand at the end of a period. The balance of the materials account may be proved by listing the stores ledger account balances.

A summary of the procedures involved in accounting for materials is shown in Illustration 2-12. This is a presentation of the recordings required for the more typical materials transactions, both at the time of the transaction and at the end of the period. At the time of the transaction, the recordings to be made affect the subsidiary ledgers such as the stores ledger and the job cost ledger. At the end of the period, the recordings to be made affect the control accounts for materials, work in process, and factory overhead in the general ledger.

The Voucher System. Throughout this discussion it has been assumed that the voucher system of accounting is in use. The voucher system, due to its many advantages, is more widely used than the simpler but less efficient purchases journal system, particularly in large manufacturing enterprises.

The two systems differ only in the effect they have on general accounting procedures. For example, when a purchase transaction is completed, the set of forms pertaining to the purchase is sent to the accounting department. If the voucher system is in use, a voucher is prepared, entered in the voucher register, and filed in the unpaid vouchers file. If the purchases journal system is in use, the invoice is entered in the purchases journal, posted to the accounts payable ledger, and filed under the vendor's name.

	Entry at Time of Transaction			Entry at End of Accounting Period		
Transaction	Source of Data	Book of Original Entry	Subsidiary Ledger Posting	Source of Data	Book of Original Entry	General Ledger Posting
Purchase of materials	Vendor's Invoice Receiving Report	Voucher Register	Stores Ledger	Voucher Register	None	Materials / Vouchers Payable
Materials returned to vendor	Return Shipping Order	General Journal	Stores Ledger	General Journal	None	Vouchers Payable / Materials
Payment of invoices	Approved Voucher	Check Register	None	Check Register	None	Vouchers Payable / Cash (or Bank)
Direct materials issued	Materials Requisitions	None	Stores Ledger / Job Cost Ledger	Materials Summary	General Journal	Work in Process / Materials
Indirect materials issued	Materials Requisitions	None	Stores Ledger / Factory Overhead Ledger	Materials Summary	General Journal	Factory Overhead / Materials
Direct materials returned from factory to storeroom	Returned Materials Report	None	Stores Ledger / Job Cost Ledger	Materials Summary	General Journal	Materials / Work in Process
Indirect materials returned from factory to storeroom	Returned Materials Report	None	Stores Ledger / Factory Overhead Ledger	Materials Summary	General Journal	Materials / Factory Overhead
Inventory adjustment: (a) Materials on hand less than stores ledger balance	Inventory Report	General Journal	Factory Overhead Ledger / Stores Ledger	General Journal	None	Factory Overhead / Materials
(b) Materials on hand more than stores ledger balance	Inventory Report	General Journal	Factory Overhead Ledger / Stores Ledger	General Journal	None	Materials / Factory Overhead

ILLUSTRATION 2-12   Summary of Materials Transactions

Inventory Verification. The stores ledger contains an account for each material used in the manufacturing process. Each account shows the number of units on hand and their cost. In other words, the stores ledger provides a perpetual inventory of the individual items of material in the storeroom. From the information in the store ledger, the necessary materials inventory data can be obtained for preparation of a balance sheet, an income statement, and a manufacturing statement.

However, it is always possible that errors may occur in recording receipts or issues of materials in the stores ledger accounts. Such errors affect the reliability of the inventory totals. To guard against error, the materials on hand should be periodically checked against the figures shown in the individual stores ledger accounts. The usual practice is to count one lot of materials at a time, spacing the time of the counts so that a complete check of all inventories in the storeroom can be made within a fixed period of time, such as three months. These periodic checks have the advantage of eliminating the costly and time consuming task of counting all the materials at one time. To guard against carelessness or dishonesty, the count should be made by someone other than the storeroom keeper or the stores ledger clerk.

The person making the count should prepare an **inventory report** similar to the one shown in Illustration 2-13. If the total indicated in

ILLUSTRATION 2-13

Inventory Report (Compares book inventory and physical inventory quantities)

INVENTORY REPORT	
Material	3/4" valves
Location in storeroom	Bin L123
Stores ledger acct. No.	12345
Date of verification	January 27, 19--
Units in storeroom	590
Units in receiving department	300
Total number units on hand	890
Balance per stores ledger	910
Difference	20
Counted by	P. Valence
Supervised by	W. Cory
Variance entered in stores ledger	
By	A. Numan

the report differs from the balance in the stores ledger account, an immediate correcting entry should be made in the proper stores ledger account. The entries in the general ledger accounts may be made in total at the end of the month. If the materials on hand exceed the balance in the control account, the balance in that account should be increased by the following entry:

Materials.. xxx
       Factory Overhead (Inventory Over and Short) xxx

If the amount of materials on hand is less than the control account balance, the balance should be decreased by the following entry:

Factory Overhead (Inventory Over and Short) xxx
       Materials.. xxx

Such inventory differences are almost always a shortage and arise from carelessness in handling materials, the shrinkage in goods which is the result of handling or, infrequently, from issuing excess quantities of materials to the factory. Because such errors are usually unavoidable, they constitute a proper part of the cost of operating a manufacturing plant and should be charged (or credited, if in excess) to the proper factory overhead account, usually entitled Inventory Over and Short.

Visual Aid. If a cost accounting system is to function properly, it is important that each employee has a clear understanding of assigned duties and the function of each form to be prepared and of each record to be kept. Illustration 2-14 emphasizes the importance of internal control in the manufacturing operations. It shows the interrelationship of the accounts and how internal control procedures can be established.

SCRAP, SPOILED GOODS, AND DEFECTIVE WORK

Manufacturing operations usually produce some imperfect units that cannot be sold as regular items by the company. The controls over imperfect items and operations which waste materials are important elements of inventory control. Scrap or waste materials may result naturally from the production process, or they may be spoiled or defective units that result from avoidable or unavoidable mistakes during production. Quality control techniques are usually introduced by a company, so that imperfect items will not be sold, thereby damaging the reputation of the company. Since scrap, spoiled

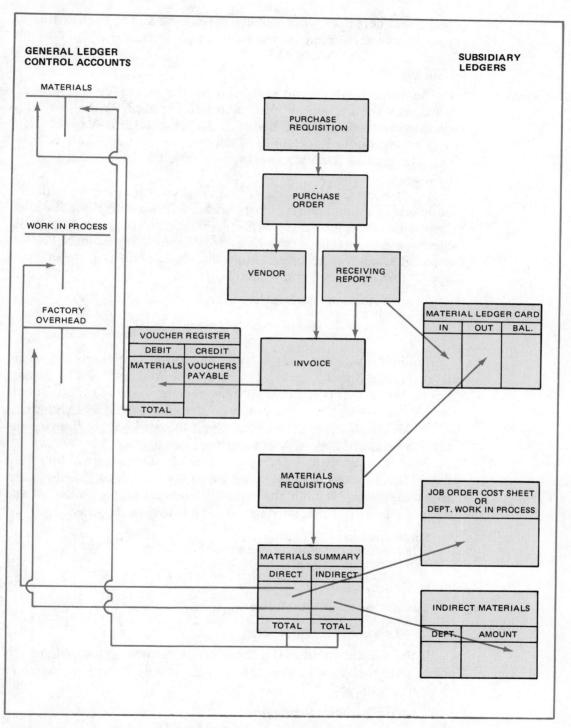

ILLUSTRATION 2-14 Interrelationship of Materials Documents and Accounts

goods, and defective work usually have some value, each is treated separately in accounting for their costs.

Scrap Materials

The value of the scrap produced by the manufacturing process determines the accounting procedures to be used. When the scrap value is small, no entry is made for the scrap until it is sold. Then, Cash or Accounts Receivable is debited, and Scrap Sales is credited. The income from scrap sales is reported as "Other income" in the income statement.

As an alternative, income from scrap sales may be treated as a reduction in manufacturing costs. If the scrap can be readily identified with a specific job or department, income generated from the sale is credited to the appropriate work in process account. For example, if scrap was generated in producing Job No. 123, the entry to record the sale of the scrap would be:

Cash (or Accounts Receivable).................................. xxx
    Work in Process — Job No. 123   xxx
        To record the sale of scrap generated by Job No.
     123.

Realistically, under normal manufacturing conditions, it would be extremely difficult to identify scrap materials by jobs or departments. When that is the case, if management wishes to treat income from scrap sales as a reduction in cost, the income may be credited to the factory overhead account. Using this procedure, the cost reduction would be spread over all jobs or departments.

When the value of the scrap is relatively high, an inventory card should be prepared, and the scrap transferred to a controlled materials storage area. If both the quantity and the market value of the scrap are known, the following journal entries are recorded:

Scrap Materials xxx
    Scrap Sales (or Work in Process or Factory
      Overhead)   xxx
        To record the scrap value transferred to scrap
        inventory.
Cash (or Accounts Receivable)................................. xxx
    Scrap Materials   xxx
        To record the sale of scrap.

If the market value of the scrap is not known, no journal entry is made until the scrap is sold. At the time of sale, the following entry is then recorded:

Cash (or Accounts Receivable)................................. xxx
    Scrap Sales (or Work in Process or Factory
      Overhead)   xxx

Spoiled and Defective Work

Scrap is an expected byproduct that results from the production of the primary product. Spoiled or defective goods are not by-products, but imperfect units of the primary product. **Spoiled units** have imperfections that a company believes cannot be economically corrected. They are sold as items of inferior quality or "seconds." **Defective units** have imperfections that are considered correctable, because the additional cost that must be incurred to make the items perfect is less than the market value of the perfected finished item.

Spoiled Work. The loss associated with spoiled goods may be treated as part of the cost of the job or department which produced the spoiled units, or the loss may be charged to Factory Overhead and allocated among all jobs or departments. Generally, Factory Overhead is charged, unless the loss results from a specific job which is a special order, and the spoilage is due to the type of work required on that particular order. In both cases, the spoiled goods are recorded in a spoiled goods inventory account at their expected sales price.

To illustrate, assume a garment manufacturer using job order costing completes an order for 1,000 sport jackets (Job No. 201) at the following unit costs:

Materials	$20
Labor	10
Factory overhead	10
Total cost per unit	$40

The journal entry to record the costs of production is:

Work in process	40,000	
Materials		20,000
Payroll		10,000
Factory Overhead		10,000
To record the production costs for Job No. 201.		

At the point of final inspection, 50 jackets are found to be inferior and are classified as irregulars or seconds. They are expected to sell for $10 each. If the unrecovered costs of spoilage are to be charged to Factory Overhead, the following entry is recorded:

Spoiled Goods	500	*reduced cost*
Factory Overhead	1,500	*lose*
Work in Process — Job No. 201	2,000	*full cost*
To record spoiled goods at market value (50 jackets @ $10) and charge Factory Overhead for the loss of $30 per unit.		

If the loss from spoilage is considered a cost of the specific job, the entry to record the market value is:

Spoiled Goods 500
   Work in Process — Job No. 201 500
      To record spoiled goods at market value.

When spoilage costs are charged to Factory Overhead, the costs are allocated among all jobs in production. When spoilage is attributed to a specific job, however, the entire cost of spoilage is reflected in the cost of that job. In the example, Job No. 201 will be charged with only a portion of the $1,500 loss from spoilage when Factory Overhead is allocated to the various jobs. When Factory Overhead is not charged for the spoilage costs, however, the entire $1,500 loss is included in the total cost of Job No. 201.

Defective Work. The procedures for handling the cost associated with defective work are similar to those employed in accounting for spoiled work. There are, however, additional costs for correcting the imperfections on defective units. If these costs are incurred on orders regularly produced by the company, they are charged to Factory Overhead. For special orders, the additional costs are charged to the job. An inventory account is not established for goods that are classified as defective, because the defects are corrected and the units become first-quality merchandise.

As in the previous illustration, assume it costs $40 to manufacture each jacket. Upon final inspection of the 1,000 jackets completed, 50 jackets are considered defective because one sleeve on each jacket is a slightly different shade of blue than the other parts of the jacket. Management decides to recut the sleeves from a bolt of material which is identical in color to the rest of the jacket. The costs of correcting the defects are $400 for materials, $300 for labor, and $300 for factory overhead, representing a total cost of $1,000.

If the additional costs are charged to Factory Overhead, the cost of correcting defective work is spread over all jobs that go through the production cycle. The journal entry is:

Factory Overhead (Costs to Correct Defective
   Work) 1,000
     Materials 400
     Payroll 300
     Factory Overhead 300
      To record costs of correcting defective units.

If the order for 1,000 jackets was a special order and the defects resulted from the specifications of the order, the additional costs would be charged to the job as follows:

Work in Process — Job No. 201 1,000
    Materials 400
    Payroll 300
    Factory Overhead... 300
        To charge Job No. 201 with the cost of
      correcting defective work.

The total cost of Job No. 201 will be higher if the costs of correcting the defective work are charged to the job rather than to Factory Overhead. If the $1,000 additional costs are charged to Factory Overhead, only a portion of the total will be allocated to Job No. 201.

Classifying Imperfect Units as Spoiled or Defective. The amount of net revenue that can be obtained from an irregular versus a perfected unit determines whether the item will be classified as spoiled or defective. For example, assume that if the 50 jackets are classified as spoiled, they can then be sold as seconds for $10 per jacket. However, if the defects are corrected at a cost of $1,000, these same jackets can be sold for $40 per jacket.

	Spoiled	Defective
Revenue from sales (50 units)	$500	$2,000
Cost to correct defects		1,000
Net revenue	$500	$1,000

In this situation, the correction of the imperfections appears warranted because the net revenue is $1,000 when the goods are classified as defective, and only $500 when they are considered spoiled and are sold as seconds.

SUMMARY

The control and accounting for material costs of a manufacturing organization benefits the company by helping to achieve previously established goals. The responsibility for material acquisition and usage must be clearly delineated. The investment in materials should be adequate to meet production requirements while minimizing the costs of carrying the required inventory.

In summary, an effective material control system should be designed to:

(1) Specifically assign duties and responsibilities for material cost expenditures and usage.

(2) Provide periodic reports and analyses of differences between actual performances and management goals pertaining to materials.

(3) Take corrective action to prevent a recurrence of unfavorable differences.

(4) Maintain an adequate quantity of material, at the lowest prices, so that the manufacturing operation can be performed at an optimum level.

QUESTIONS

1. What are the two major objectives of materials control?

2. Describe the control procedures for safeguarding materials.

3. What factors must management consider in determining the amount of investment in materials?

4. What is an order point?

5. What types of data and information are needed to calculate an order point?

6. Define economic order quantity (EOQ).

7. What are the factors that need to be considered to determine the cost of an order?

8. What are the costs of carrying materials in stock?

9. Outline briefly the usual duties of the following employees of a manufacturer:
   (a) Purchasing agent
   (b) Receiving clerk
   (c) Storeroom keeper
   (d) Production department supervisor

10. Distinguish between a purchase requisition and a purchase order.

11. Why does the purchasing agent review and approve incoming vendors' invoices?

12. Several forms are illustrated in the chapter which are used to requisition, order, and account for materials. If you went to work for a manufacturing company, would you expect to see exactly the same forms being used in their operations as are illustrated? Discuss.

13. What internal control procedures are used for incoming shipments of materials purchased?

14. What is the purpose of a debit-credit memorandum?

15. From whom do the following forms usually originate?
   (a) Purchase requisition
   (b) Purchase order
   (c) Receiving report
   (d) Return shipping order
   (e) Materials requisition
   (f) Returned materials report

16. Explain the relationship between the stores ledger and the general ledger account, Materials.

17. Describe briefly the following methods of pricing materials issued.
   (a) First-in, first-out method
   (b) Last-in, first-out method
   (c) Moving average method

18. Why are many companies with sizable inventories adopting the lifo method of materials costing? In your discussion include the effects on both the income statement and the balance sheet.

19. Which of the forms described in Chapter 2 constitute the source of each of the following entries to subsidiary ledger accounts?

(a) Debits to record materials purchased in stores ledger.
(b) Credits to record materials requisitioned in stores ledger.
(c) Debits to record materials placed in process in job cost ledger.
(d) Credits to record materials returned to storeroom in job cost ledger.
(e) Debits to record materials returned to storeroom in stores ledger.
(f) Credits to record materials returned to vendor in stores ledger.

20. Which book of original entry constitutes the source of each of the following entries in the general ledger (assume that a general journal, voucher register, and check register are used)?

(a) Debits to materials account to record materials purchased.
(b) Credits to materials account to record materials placed in process.
(c) Debits to vouchers payable account to record vouchers paid.
(d) Debits to work in process account to record materials placed in process.
(e) Credits to work in process account to record materials returned to storeroom.

21. What methods can be used to account for the sale value of scrap material?

22. Distinguish between spoiled and defective work.

23. On what basis does management determine whether goods are to be classified as spoiled or defective?

EXERCISES

1. The Stem Corporation predicts that 2,000 units of material will be used during the year. It anticipates that the material will cost $2 per unit. From an analysis of its ordering costs, the company has determined that the clerical cost for each order placed is $20. The annual carrying cost is $.32 per unit. Determine (a) the most economical order quantity by use of the formula; (b) the total cost of ordering and carrying at the EOQ point.

2. The Goalbe Corporation records the following use of materials during the month of September:

| | | | Materials Requisitions | |
| | Req. | | Direct | Indirect |
Date	No.	Use	Materials	Materials
1	110	Material A, Job 10	$10,000	
5	111	Material B, Job 11	8,000	
9	112	Material B, Job 12	6,000	
12	113	Factory supplies		$800
18	114	Material C, Job 10	3,000	
21	115	Material D, Job 10	9,000	
23	116	Material E, Job 13	2,000	
28	117	Factory supplies		300
30	118	Factory supplies		700

Prepare a summary general journal entry for the materials requisitions.

3. The Enstate Electric Motor Company manufactures small electric motors to be used in electric windshield wiper assemblies. Balances for selected accounts for September show:

Finished Goods, beginning of month	$ 80,500
Work in Process, beginning of month	161,200
Raw Materials, beginning of month	45,600
Raw Materials Purchases	425,300
Direct Labor	315,200
Indirect Materials	21,200
Repairs and Maintenance	40,150
Utilities	18,210
Indirect Labor	33,330
Supervisors' Salaries and Wages	62,250
Finished Goods, end of month	70,200
Work in Process, end of month	142,200
Raw Materials, end of month	22,200

Compute the cost of direct materials used during September.

4. Indicate the effect of each of the following materials transactions on the general ledger accounts by means of a general journal entry:

(a) Total materials purchased during the month, per voucher register, $180,000.

(b) Total direct materials requisitioned during the month, $150,000.

(c) Total indirect materials requisitioned during the month, $15,000.

(d) Excess direct materials returned to storeroom by factory during the month, $1,100.

(e) Total materials returned to vendor during the month, $1,200.

(f) Vouchers, for materials purchases only, paid during the month, $60,000 less 2% discount.

5. Using the first-in, first-out method of perpetual inventory costing, determine the cost of materials used and the cost of the May 31 inventory, based on the following information:

May   1 Balance on hand, 1,100 units (Bearings, $3 each).
        3 Issued 250 units.
        5 Received 500 units at $3.20 each.
        6 Issued 150 units.
     10 Issued 110 units.
     11 Factory returned 10 units to the storeroom that were issued on the 10th.
     15 Received 500 units at $3.50 each.
     20 Returned 300 units to vendor that were received on the 15th.
     26 Issued 100 units.

6. Using the last-in, first-out method of perpetual inventory costing, determine the cost of materials used and the cost of the May 31 inventory, based on the information in Exercise 5.

7. Using the moving average method of inventory costing, determine the cost of materials used and cost of the May 31 inventory, based on the information in Exercise 5.

8. In tabular form, compare the total cost transferred to Work in Process and the cost of the ending inventory for each method used in Exercises 5, 6, and 7.

9. The New Company was incorporated as of January 1, 19A. At the end of its third year of operations, December 31, 19C, a study was undertaken to determine what effect different materials inventory costing methods would have had on its net income during the three-year period.

The materials inventory account, using lifo, fifo, and moving average cost, had the following ending balances:

	Materials Inventory Balances		
December 31	Lifo	Fifo	Average
19A..............................	$10,000	$12,000	$11,000
19B..............................	12,000	14,000	13,000
19C..............................	16,000	20,000	18,000

(a) In what direction did the costs move for the items from 19A to 19C?

(b) Using these figures, which costing method would show the highest net income for 19A?

(c) Which method would show the highest net income for 19C?

(d) Which method would show the lowest net income for the three years combined?

(e) For the year 19B, how would the profit using lifo compare to the profit if average cost was used?

10. The Adams Manufacturing Company maintains the following accounts in the general ledger: Materials, Work in Process, Factory Overhead, Vouchers Payable. At the beginning of June, the materials account had a debit balance of $10,000. A summary of materials transactions for the month follows:

(1) Materials purchased, per voucher register, $56,750.

(2) Direct materials issued on requisitions, $43,150.

(3) Direct materials returned to storeroom, $1,500.

(4) Indirect materials issued on requisitions, $1,865.

(5) Indirect materials returned to storeroom, $125.

(a) Prepare in general journal form the entries required to record the materials transactions and post them to "T" accounts. **(b)** Foot the materials account and ascertain the balance which represents the inventory of materials on hand at the end of the month.

11. A machine shop manufactures part of an assembled product which is made of stainless steel. Materials charged to the job amounted to $500. It was discovered at the point of final inspection that the material used was not up to the required specifications and all units had to be scrapped.

Record the general journal entries required for scrap only under each of the following conditions: **(a)** The revenue received for scrap is to be spread over all jobs. The value of scrap stainless steel is stable and this scrap is sold two months later for $85. **(b)** Revenue received for scrap is to be spread over all jobs, but a firm price is not determinable for the scrap until it is sold. It is finally sold for $65. **(c)** The job worked on was a special job and the $75 received for the scrap is to be credited to the job. **(d)** Only $25 was received for the scrap when it was sold in the following fiscal period.

12. The Driver Company manufactured 12,000 golf jackets, of which 100 were considered seconds and were to be sold at $10 per jacket instead of the regular retail price of $39.95. The work in process account was charged $132,000: $36,000 for materials, $48,000 for labor, and $48,000 for factory overhead.

Record the required journal entries under each of the following conditions: **(a)** The loss due to spoiled work is spread over all jobs in the department. **(b)** The loss due to spoiled work is charged to this job because it is a special order.

13. The X-T-Y Company manufactures an integrated transistor circuit for regular customers and also accepts special orders. Job No. 10A1 incurred the following unit costs for 1,000 circuits manufactured:

Materials	$ 8.00
Labor	1.00
Factory overhead	1.00
Total cost per unit	$10.00

When the completed products were tested, 20 circuits were found to be defective, and the additional costs of correcting the defects per unit were:

Materials	$2.00
Labor	4.00
Factory overhead	4.00

Record the journal entry required **(a)** if the cost of the defective work is charged to factory overhead, and **(b)** if the cost of the defective work is charged to the job.

PROBLEMS

2-1. Economic order quantities. The Model Corporation is unable to establish, with certainty, the number of units of material that it will use in the coming fiscal period. Since the price paid is somewhat dependent upon the quantity purchased, three possible usage levels have been under study. The company believes that it will cost $25 for each order placed and the carrying cost will be $.75 per unit.

Required: Determine the most economical order quantity under each of the following conditions: **(1)** The expected annual usage of material is 2,000 units. **(2)** The expected annual usage of material is 5,000 units. **(3)** The expected annual usage of material is 10,000 units.

2-2. Inventory costing methods. The records of the Sundown Company reveal the following purchases and issues of copper flanges, one of the raw materials used in their manufacturing process:

			Units		
Nov.	1	Beginning inventory	30,000	@	$2.09
	4	Received, Receiving Report No. 112	10,000	@	$2.13
	5	Issued, Materials Requisition No. 49	30,000		
	8	Received, Receiving Report No. 113	50,000	@	$2.58
	15	Issued, Materials Requisition No. 50	20,000		
	22	Received, Receiving Report No. 114	25,000	@	$2.63
	28	Issued, Materials Requisition No. 51	50,000		

Required: (1) Using the above information, complete stores ledger account forms ruled similar to the form illustrated on page 61, pricing the materials using:

(a) Fifo costing
(b) Lifo costing
(c) Moving average costing

(2) Prepare a schedule showing the total cost of materials transferred to Work in Process and the cost of the ending inventory for each method. **(3)** In a period of rising prices, would you favor fifo or lifo costing for your company? Why? **(4)** In a period of rising prices, what is the effect of fifo versus lifo on the inventory valuation in the balance sheet?

2-3. Inventory costing methods. The following transactions were made in December:

Dec. 1 Balance on hand, 1,200 units @ $2.76, $3,312.00 (Copper Wire — 100 ft. units).
    5 Issued 60 units on Materials Requisition No. 108.
  11 Issued 200 units on Materials Requisition No. 210.
  14 Received 800 units, Receiving Report No. 634, price $2.8035.
  15 Issued 400 units, Materials Requisition No. 274.
  16 Returned for credit 90 units purchased on December 14 which were found to be defective.
  18 Received 1,000 units, Receiving Report No. 712, price $2.82712.
  21 Issued 640 units, Materials Requisition No. 318.

Required: Using **(1)** fifo, **(2)** lifo, and **(3)** moving average, record the above transactions on stores ledger account forms.

2-4. Inventory costing methods. The Frate Company was formed on December 1, 1982. The following information is available from Frate's inventory records for Product Ply:

	Units	Unit Cost
January 1, 1983, beginning inventory	800	$ 9.00
Purchases:		
January 5, 1983	1,500	$10.00
January 25, 1983	1,200	10.50
February 16, 1983	600	11.00
March 26, 1983	900	11.50

A physical inventory on March 31, 1983, shows 1,600 units on hand.

Required: Prepare schedules to compute the ending inventory at March 31, 1983, under each of the following inventory methods:

(1) Fifo
(2) Lifo
(3) Weighted average

Show supporting computations in good form.

(AICPA adapted)

2-5. *Comparison of inventory costing methods.* The controller of the Investor Corporation retail company made three different schedules of gross margin for the first quarter ended September 30. These schedules appear below.

		Sales ($10 per Unit)	Cost of Goods Sold	Gross Margin
Schedule A	Lifo	$280,000	$118,550	$161,450
Schedule B	ave.	280,000	116,900	163,100
Schedule C	fifo	280,000	115,750	164,250

The computation of cost of goods sold in each schedule is based on the following data:

	Units	Cost per Unit	Total Cost
Beginning inventory, July	10,000	$4.00	$40,000
Purchase, July 25	8,000	4.20	33,600
Purchase, August 15	5,000	4.13	20,650
Purchase, September 5	7,000	4.30	30,100
Purchase, September 25	12,000	4.25	51,000

The president of the corporation cannot understand how three different gross margins can be computed from the same set of data. As controller, you have explained that the three schedules are based on three different assumptions concerning the flow of inventory costs: first-in, first-out; last-in, first-out; and weighted average. Schedules A, B, and C were not necessarily prepared in the sequence of cost-flow assumptions.

Required: Prepare three separate schedules computing cost of goods sold and supporting schedules showing the composition of the ending inventory under each of the three cost-flow assumptions.

(AICPA adapted)

2-6. *Journalizing materials transactions*. The Mack Machine Tool Company uses the job order cost system of accounting. Following is a partial list of accounts taken from the general ledger with their November 1 balances indicated.

Cash, debit balance	$32,250
Materials, debit balance	29,500
Work in Process, debit balance...................	27,000
Vouchers Payable, credit balance	21,000
Factory Overhead.....................................	none

The following transactions were completed during the month of November:

(a) Total materials purchased during the month, per voucher register, $25,500.

(b) Total materials requisitioned during the month:
    (1) Direct materials, $23,750.
    (2) Indirect materials, $1,830.

(c) Direct materials returned to storeroom by factory during month, $1,870.

(d) Total materials returned to vendors during the month, $750.

(e) Total vouchers paid during the month, $24,350.

Required: (1) Draft the entries in general journal form required to record these transactions and post them to "T" accounts. **(2)** Foot the accounts and report the following information as of November 30:

(a) Cash balance
(b) Inventory of materials on hand
(c) Vouchers payable

2-7. *Analyzing materials and other transactions*. The Wilson Manufacturing Company uses the job order cost system of accounting. The following accounts are reproduced from the books of the company:

Materials

19--			19--		
Oct. 1	Inventory	7,000	Oct. 31	Requisitions for month	21,200
31	Purchases for month	18,000			

Work in Process

19--			19--		
Oct. 1	Inventory	3,600	Oct. 31	To finished goods	45,000
31	Materials requisitioned	21,200			
31	Direct labor	15,600			
31	Factory overhead	11,500			

Finished Goods

19--			19--		
Oct. 1	Inventory	11,650	Oct. 31	Cost of goods sold	50,000
31	Goods finished	45,000			

Required: (1) Analyze the accounts and tell in narrative form what transactions took place. **(2)** List all supporting documents or forms, if any, necessary for each transaction. **(3)** Ascertain the amount of the book inventories for materials, work in process, and finished goods on October 31.

2-8. Comprehensive analysis of materials accounting procedures. Listed below are the decisions made and the transactions completed by The Bay Metals Company in accounting for materials costs for April.

Mar. 31 The factory superintendent notifies the storeroom keeper that production for the month of April will require 2,000 sheets of aluminum. At the end of the day, the storeroom keeper checks the stock and finds 500 of the required aluminum sheets on hand at a cost of $23 each. A minimum stock of 300 aluminum sheets must be maintained at all times, so the purchasing agent is notified of the need for 1,800 sheets. This quantity will cover April production requirements and, at the same time, maintain the minimum inventory level.

Apr. 1 The purchasing agent, after checking with various suppliers, orders the requested number of aluminum sheets at $25 each.

   6 The shipment of aluminum sheets arrives; they are inspected and found to be in good condition. The order is short 200 sheets which are "back ordered" and will be shipped in five days.

   6 The vendor's invoice covering the aluminum sheets received arrives and is approved for payment.

  11 The balance of the order is received in good condition.

  11 The vendor's invoice for the latest shipment is received and approved.

  16 The invoice dated April 6 is paid, less a cash discount of 2%.

  30 During the month, 1,900 sheets of aluminum are issued to the factory. (The company uses the fifo inventory pricing method.)

  30 Twenty unused sheets of aluminum are returned to stores from the factory. (Assume the returned sheets have a cost of $25 each.)

  30 At the end of the day, 398 sheets are on hand in the storeroom.

Required: (1) In tabular form, show the answers to the following questions as they apply to *each* of the preceding decisions and transactions:

   (a) What forms, if any, were used?
   (b) What journal entries, if any, were made?
   (c) What books of original entry, if any, were used to record the data?
   (d) What subsidiary records were affected?

(2) Calculate (show your computations):

   (a) The materials inventory balance at April 30.
   (b) The cost of materials placed in production during April.

2-9. Materials control, order point, and EOQ. Long, CPA has been engaged to examine and report on the financial statements of Maylou Corporation. During the review phase of the study of Maylou's system of internal accounting control over purchases, Long was given the following document flowchart for purchases.

Maylou Corporation
DOCUMENT FLOWCHART FOR PURCHASES

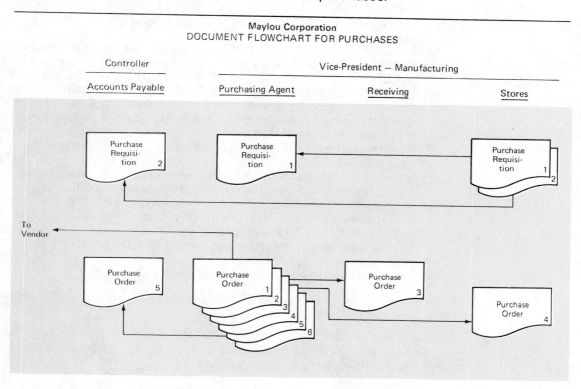

Required: (1) Identify the procedures relating to purchase requisitions and purchase orders that Long would expect to find if Maylou's system of internal accounting control over purchases is effective. For example, purchase orders are prepared only after giving proper consideration to the time of order and quantity to order. Do not comment on the effectiveness of the flow of documents as presented in the flowchart or on separation of duties. (2) What are the factors to consider in determining:

(a) The time to order?
(b) The quantity to order?

(AICPA adapted)

2-10. Materials inventory shortage; returns; scrap; spoiled goods. An examination of the records of the GIGO Manufacturing Company revealed the following transactions:

(a) The physical inventory of raw materials on December 31 was 9,970 units. The book quantity, using the moving average method, showed 11,000 units @ $.485 per unit.

(b) Excess materials worth $727.50 were returned to the storeroom from production.

(c) Materials amounting to $970 were charged to Factory Overhead (Repairs and Maintenance) but should have been charged to Work in Process.

(d) Defective material was returned to the vendor. The material returned cost $194 and the shipping charges (our cost) of $25 were paid in cash.

(e) Goods sold to a customer for $4,000 (cost $2,500) were returned. The goods were returned because of a misunderstanding of the quantity ordered. The customer stated that the goods returned were in excess of the quantity needed.

(f) Materials requisitioned totaled $21,230, of which $1,830 represented supplies used.

(g) Materials purchased totaled $22,350, of which $2,100 were supplies. Freight on the direct materials purchased amounted to $185.

(h) Direct materials returned to the storeroom amounted to $850.

(i) Scrap materials sent to the storeroom valued at selling price, from direct materials, $520; from supplies, $55.

(j) Spoiled work sent to the storeroom valued at sales price of $50 had production costs of $200 charged to it.

(k) The scrap materials (in (i) above) were sold for $575 cash.

Required: Record the entries, in general journal form, for each transaction.

2-11. Spoiled goods: loss charged to factory overhead; loss charged to job. The Fordalong Company manufactures holligigs which sell for $.95 each. The cost elements for each holligig are:

Materials	$.25
Labor	.15
Factory overhead	.20
Total	$.60

Job No. 1001 produced 10,000 holligigs of which 600 units were spoiled and were classified as seconds. Seconds are sold to a chain of department stores for $.30 each.

Required: Record the general journal entries under each of the following assumptions: **(1)** The loss from spoilage will be distributed to all jobs for the period. **(2)** The loss due to spoilage will be charged to Job No. 1001. The entries should include:

(a) Putting spoiled goods into inventory.

(b) Sale for cash of the spoiled units.

2-12. Spoiled goods and defective work. The Circuits Company manufactures electrical equipment based on specifications received from customers. Job No. X-1234 was for 1,000 specially designed motors. The following costs were determined for each motor:

Materials	$ 92.00
Labor	135.00
Factory overhead	100.00
Total	$327.00

At the point of final inspection, it was discovered that 33 motors did not meet the specifications established by the customer. A detailed examination indicated that 15 motors were beyond repair and should be sold as scrap for $55 each, and the remaining 18, although defective, could be reconditioned as first quality units by the addition of $1,420.00 for materials, $1,950 for labor, and $1,610 for factory overhead.

Required: Prepare the journal entries to record: **(1)** The scrapping of the units. **(2)** The correction of the defective units. **(3)** The additional cost of replacing the 15 scrapped motors. **(4)** The sale of the scrap motors.

2-13. Review problem; transactions and statements. The Hoists Company manufactures chain hoists. The inventories of raw materials on hand on January 1 were:

Chain	12,000 pounds, $24,000
Pulleys	4,000 units, $20,000
Bolts and taps	10,000 sets, $5,000
Steel plates	4,000 units, $2,000

The balances in the ledger accounts on January 1 were as follows:

Cash	$ 9,200	
Work in Process	10,000	
Materials	51,000	
Prepaid Insurance	2,500	
Machinery	125,000	
Office Equipment	30,000	
Office Furniture	20,000	
Accounts Payable		$ 25,000
Capital Stock		200,000
Retained Earnings		22,700
	$247,700	$247,700

Transactions during January were:

(a) Payroll recorded during the month: direct labor, $28,000; indirect labor, $3,000.

(b) Factory supplies purchased for cash, $1,000.

(c) Materials purchased on account: chain — 4,000 pounds, $8,800; pulleys — 2,000 units, $10,200; steel plates — 5,000 units, $3,000.

(d) Sales on account for the month, $126,375.

(e) Accounts receivable collected, $72,500.

(f) Materials used during January (fifo costing): chain, 14,000 pounds; pulleys, 4,400 units; bolts and taps, 4,000 sets; steel plates, 3,800 units.

(g) Payroll paid, $31,000.

(h) Factory supplies on hand, January 31, $350.

(i) Factory heat, power, and light costs for January $3,000 (not yet paid).

(j) Office salaries paid, $6,000.

(k) Advertising paid, $2,000.

(l) Factory superintendence paid, $1,800.

(m) Expired insurance — on office equipment, $100; on factory machinery, $300.

(n) Factory rent paid, $2,000.

(o) Depreciation on office equipment, $400; on office furniture, $180; on machinery, $1,200.

(p) Factory overhead charged to jobs, $11,950.

(q) Work in process, January 31, $6,000.

(r) Cost of goods sold during the month, $84,250.

(s) Accounts payable paid, $33,750.

Required: (1) Set up "T" accounts and enter the balances as of January 1. **(2)** Prepare general journal entries to record each of the above transactions. **(3)** Post the journal entries to the accounts, setting up any new ledger accounts necessary. Only controlling accounts are to be maintained; however, show the calculation for the cost of materials used. **(4)** Prepare a statement of cost of goods manufactured for January. **(5)** Prepare an income statement. **(6)** Prepare a balance sheet showing the classifications of current assets, plant and equipment, current liabilities, and stockholders' equity.

3

Accounting for labor

A manufacturer's factory payroll consists of two major categories: direct labor and indirect labor. **Direct labor** is the portion of payroll which is allocated directly to the product by a debit to the work in process account. **Indirect labor** consists of all other "types" of labor used in the manufacturing process, such as salaries and wages of the factory superintendent, supervisors, janitors, clerks, and timekeepers. Indirect labor is charged to the factory overhead account.

Accounting for labor involves the following procedures:

(a) Recording the time worked by the employee, in total and by job, process, or department, or recording the quantity of the worker's output.

(b) Analyzing the employee's working time to determine how the time was utilized.

(c) Allocating the factory labor cost to jobs, processes, departments, or factory overhead accounts.

(d) Preparing the payroll which involves computing and recording employee gross earnings, withholdings and deductions, and net earnings.

Most cost systems incorporate many of the procedures discussed in this chapter in accounting for labor costs. However, other procedures, which may be more or less elaborate, can also be used. Therefore, the illustrations, procedures, and forms, as presented, will apply to the majority of companies, while other manufacturers will find it necessary to make some modifications in order to meet their specific operational requirements.

WAGE PLANS

An hourly-rate plan, a piece-rate plan, or a combination of the two is used by most companies for computing the wages earned by factory employees. Each plan has advantages and limitations relating to production and quality control which should be evaluated by management in selecting the appropriate plan.

The **hourly-rate plan** is widely accepted and is technically simpler to apply and use than the piece-rate plan. An hourly-rate employee is paid a set rate per hour for the time spent on the assigned job. Earnings are computed by multiplying the number of hours worked by the established rate per hour.

If an employee earns $4 per hour for an assignment and works a total of 40 hours for the week, the week's gross earnings would amount to $160.

$$40 \text{ hours} \times \$4 \text{ per hour} = \$160$$

A serious limitation of the hourly-rate plan is that no incentive is provided by the plan design to maintain a high degree of productivity on the part of the employee. An employee is tempted to merely "put in time" because there is no reward for the extra effort of being a conscientious employee. However, neither does the plan encourage sacrificing the quality of the product by speeding up production to earn a higher wage.

Under a **piece-rate plan**, earnings are based on the worker's quantity of production. To illustrate, assume a machine operator earns $.20 for each part that is finished. If, in a week, 2,000 parts are produced, the operator will earn $400 for the week.

$$\$.20 \text{ per part} \times 2,000 \text{ parts} = \$400$$

An advantage of the plan is that it provides an incentive for the worker to produce a high quantity of output, thereby maximizing the employee's earnings and increasing the company's net income. However, a serious disadvantage of such plans is that they encourage the worker to sacrifice the quality of production in order to maximize earnings by producing a large quantity each working day. To overcome the plan's limitation, additional expense must be incurred for more supervision over the quality of product being manufactured. Also, the plan requires more record-keeping and continuous study if up-to-date piece rates are to be set and maintained.

There are other wage plans, often referred to as **modified wage plans**, which combine some features of these two basic plans. A modification may be to set a minimum wage which will be paid by the company even if an established quota of production is not attained by the employee.[1] If, however, the established quota is exceeded, an additional payment for each extra piece, above the quota, is added to the minimum wage. A plan with these specifications will direct management's attention to the employees who are unable to meet the established quotas.

The management and union negotiation process creates many variations of the hourly-rate and piece-rate plans. These variations occur because management wishes to minimize costs and maximize profits, while the labor union is attempting to maximize the employee's earnings and welfare.

To illustrate a modified wage plan, assume an employee earns $.20 per finished unit. However, the employee is guaranteed a minimum of $4 per hour. If the established daily quota of 160 units is not attained, the employee will be guaranteed $32 (8 hours × $4) for the day's work. When less than 160 units are produced, Factory Overhead is charged for the difference, which is often referred to as a **make-up guarantee**.

The production and earnings for one week are as follows:

	Hours Worked	Pieces Finished (Quota = 160)	Earnings @ $4 per Hour	Earnings @ $.20 per Unit	Make-Up Guarantee	Payroll Earnings
Mon.	8	170	$ 32	$ 34		$ 34
Tues.	8	150	32	30	$2	32
Wed.	8	140	32	28	4	32
Thurs.	8	180	32	36		36
Fri.	8	200	32	40		40
			$160	$168	$6	$174

Only $168 was earned from the number of units produced. However, the guarantee of a minimum daily wage of $32 requires a make-up-guarantee charge of $6 for the work performed on Tuesday ($2) and Wednesday ($4). When the payroll earnings are distributed, the journal entry will be:

Work in Process.. 168
Factory Overhead 6
Payroll 174
    To distribute payroll earned for the week.

Wage plans which feature **incentive-wage systems** are frequently introduced by management over the opposition of labor unions. Ba-

---

[1] Effective January 1, 1981, the Fair Labor Standards Act set a minimum hourly wage of $3.35 for workers covered by the Act.

sically, the new management creations in wage plans are attempts to increase output and maximize profits.

To illustrate an incentive-wage plan, assume a production quota is established that expects each employee to produce 100 units per hour. A study shows that the factory overhead fixed costs are $4 per hour per employee.[2] The significance of $4 fixed cost per hour is that the higher the employee's output, the smaller the fixed cost charge per unit. The employee rate per hour is $4 for each 8-hour day; when an employee meets or exceeds the quota (100 units), an incentive bonus is added to the regular wage rate per hour as shown below:

(1)	(2)	(3)	(4)	(5)	(6)	(7)	(8)
						Fixed	Total Labor and Fixed Overhead
				Fixed	Labor	Overhead	per Unit
Units	Wage		Total Wage	Overhead	per Unit	per Unit	per Unit
per Hour	per Hour	Bonus Rate	per Hour	per Hour	(4) ÷ (1)	(5) ÷ (1)	(6) + (7)
80	$4		$4.00	$4	$.050	$.050	$.100
90	4		4.00	4	.044	.044	.088
100	4	$1.00	5.00	4	.050	.040	.090
110	4	1.20	5.20	4	.047	.036	.083
120	4	1.40	5.40	4	.045	.033	.078

The employee will receive $160 per week ($4 × 8 hours × 5 days), even when the established quota of 100 units per hour is not attained. For a worker who is able to produce 120 units per hour, the gross earnings will amount to $216 for the week.

$$\$5.40 \text{ (per hour)} \times 8 \text{ (hours)} \times 5 \text{ (days)} = \$216$$

When an employee reaches the bonus quota level of 100 units and $1 is added to the $4 per hour wage rate, the labor cost per unit increases to $.05, and the total labor and fixed overhead per unit increases to $.09. After the 100 units per hour is surpassed, the total labor and fixed overhead per unit declines rapidly. This decline is extremely attractive to management, because the spreading of fixed costs over a larger volume of production results in increased profits.

CONTROLLING LABOR COST

The responsibility for maintaining required labor records is assigned to the departments of timekeeping and payroll. In some cases, the timekeeping and payroll functions may be organized as subdivisions of a single department rather than as separate depart-

---

[2] Fixed overhead represents a portion of the total overhead cost which remains constant for a given period, such as depreciation expense on equipment calculated using the straight-line method.

ments. In either case, they should function as independent units to provide an internal check on the accuracy of personnel who are assigned the responsibilities of computing, recording, and paying the costs for labor.

The **timekeeping department** is responsible for determining the time spent in the factory by the hourly employees. The overall objective of timekeeping is to determine the number of hours that the company should pay for and also the type of work the employees performed during the working day.

The **payroll department** is assigned the responsibility of computing each employee's gross earnings, the amount of withholdings and deductions, and the remainder or net earnings that will be paid directly to the employee on payday.

The departmental responsibilities of timekeeping and payroll are carried out by completing and maintaining the following forms and records:

Timekeeping	Payroll
Clock cards	Payroll records
Time tickets	Employees earnings records
Production reports	Payroll summaries

Clock Cards and Time Tickets

A clock card is maintained for each company employee who is required to punch a time clock. The card is used to account for the total amount of time the employee spends in the plant. The pre-printed card contains such information as the employee's name, clock number, and the week or pay period. The clock number is also used to identify the employee in the payroll records. An example of a clock card is shown in Illustration 3-1.

A time clock is placed at each entrance to a building. A rack of clock cards is placed next to each time clock. An employee who enters or leaves the building is required to use a designated entrance and to punch a clock card.

When reporting to a work station, the employee is given a time ticket (Illustration 3-2) on which the hours worked on assigned jobs are to be recorded. A timekeeper or a mechanical time-recording device may be used to record the time spent on each job. The labor recorded on the time ticket should be approved by a supervisor, because the ticket becomes the source document for allocating the labor costs to jobs or departments in the cost ledger or to accounts in the factory overhead ledger.

For the employee, the time ticket shows the time started and stopped on each job, the rate of pay, the amount of earnings, and the numbers of jobs worked on. When the employee continues to

ILLUSTRATION 3-1

Employee Clock Card

NAME	RICHARD GROVES

SOCIAL SEC. NO.   410-80-7865

DEPT. NO.	CLOCK NO.
04	2316

WEEK ENDING   2/16

AUTHORIZED   *Ann Runyon*

DAY	IN	OUT	IN	OUT	TOTAL	FOR PAYROLL USE ONLY
M	7:56	12:01	12:59	5:03	8	46.40
T	8:28	12:03	12:58	5:07	7½	43.50
W	7:54	12:01	12:57	5:00	8	46.40
TH	7:58	12:05	1:00	5:05	8	46.40
F	7:55	12:00	12:55	5:02	8	46.40
S						
S						

	RATE		HOURS	AMOUNT
REGULAR	5.80/hr.	REGULAR	39½	229.10
OVERTIME		OVERTIME		

ILLUSTRATION 3-2

Time Ticket (Daily)

Name   Richard Groves   Clock No.   2316

Dept.   Grinding (04)

Job No. or Type of Work	Time Started	Time Stopped	Hours Worked		Payroll Use Only			
			Reg.	O.T.	Rate Reg.	O.T.	Amount Earned	
402	8:00	11:00	3		5.80		17	40
437	11:00	4:00	4		5.80		23	20
Machine repair	4:00	5:00	1		5.80		5	80

Date   2/14   Signed   *Richard Groves*
                                                              Employee
                     Approved   *Celia Johnson*
                                                              Supervisor

work on the same job for the full working day, only the time of starting and stopping work needs to be recorded. However, if a transfer to another job occurs during a working day, the time of leaving the first job and the time of starting to work on the next job must be recorded. The ticket also shows working time which cannot be charged to any specific job. For example, Illustration 3-2 shows three hours assignable to Job No. 402, four hours to Job No. 437, and one hour for machine repairs charged to factory overhead.

After employees have clocked in, the timekeeper collects the previous day's time tickets from the department supervisors and then compares the time tickets to the clock cards. All time spent in the factory should be accounted for. Total time worked as shown on each employee's clock card should correspond to the time reported on the time ticket. If a discrepancy between a ticket and a card is discovered, the cause should be immediately investigated.

Even though some intangible factors are involved, the value of a worker's services should be compensated for by the employer on the basis of the time and performance of the employee on the job. When the services are not completely utilized, the employer suffers a loss just as if a theft of some tangible good had occurred. Therefore, if the time spent has been unproductive, the idle time, along with the reason for it, should be recorded.

After the comparison of the clock cards and time tickets, the time tickets are forwarded to the payroll department. The pay rates are entered, and the employee's gross earnings are calculated and recorded on the time tickets. The cards are returned to the clock-card racks next to the time clock. At the end of the week, the total hours worked are calculated for each employee and recorded on the clock card. The cards are then forwarded to the payroll department, where each employee's authorized pay rate and gross earnings are entered on the clock cards and recorded in the payroll records. The cards are then filed by employee name or number.

Some manufacturers require the preparation of separate or unit time tickets for each job or operation on which an employee works (Illustration 3-3). The color of these tickets may differ to facilitate the sorting of the tickets for direct labor and indirect labor charges.

ILLUSTRATION 3-3

Time Ticket (Unit)

DEPT.	CLOCK NO.	NAME			
04	2316	Richard Groves			
JOB NO.	DESCRIPTION OF WORK 3 HP gear				
402	Semi-finishing housings				
			PAYROLL USE ONLY		
			HOURS	AMOUNT	TOTAL
STOP 11:00		OVERTIME			
START 8:00		REGULAR	3	5.80	17.40
Date 2/14					
Signed Richard Groves					Employee
Approved Celia Johnson					Supervisor

Individual Production Reports for Piece-Rate Systems

Individual production reports (Illustration 3-4) are used in place of time tickets when a company determines its labor costs using a piece-rate system. A daily report is prepared for each employee. The report shows the assignments by job number or by the type of work performed and also the total number of units completed. After approval by the supervisor, the report is forwarded to the payroll department for the earnings computation.

ILLUSTRATION 3-4

Individual
Production Report

INDIVIDUAL PRODUCTION REPORT			
Employee's Name _Dolores Evers_			
Clock No. _1070_ Dept. _Finishing_ Date _February 3_ 19--			
Job No. or Type of Work Performed	Number of Units Completed	Rate	Amount
3149	40	.35	14.00
3152	60	.40	24.00
			38.00
Total			
Signed _Dolores Evers_ Employee			
Approved _CMF_ Supervisor			

Payroll Department

The payroll department is responsible for accurately computing the wages and salaries earned by the employees of the company. The computation involves combining the daily wages of each employee, determining the total earnings, and calculating the employee's deductions and withholdings.

Federal legislation requires that a statutory percentage of employees' wages be withheld for social security purposes. In addition, the accepted "pay-as-you-go" concept requires that a graduated percentage of earnings be withheld for federal, state, and local income taxes. Additional deductions, with the approval of the employee, can be taken for group insurance premiums, union dues, supplies purchased from the company store, U.S. Savings Bonds, pay advances, and so on.

Payroll Records. Although a variety of forms may be used to assemble the total earnings, all forms possess common characteristics. A typical **payroll record** sheet, as shown in Illustration 3-5, provides the following essential information pertaining to each employee:

(a) Marital status
(b) Number of withholding allowances
(c) Rate of pay
(d) Time worked — number of hours per day
(e) Regular earnings — hours and amount
(f) Overtime earnings — hours and amount
(g) Total earnings
(h) FICA taxable earnings
(i) Deductions — FICA tax, income tax, health insurance, etc.
(j) Net amount paid — check number and amount

Employee Earnings Records. In addition to the payroll record, which is a summary listing of employees' earnings, employers usually keep an auxiliary record of the earnings for each employee. Illustration 3-6 shows one type of **employee earnings record**. These records provide the following information, which varies according to whether an employee is entitled to extra compensation for overtime work:

EMPLOYEES ENTITLED TO EXTRA COMPENSATION FOR OVERTIME WORK
(a) Name in full
(b) Date of birth
(c) Occupation in which employed
(d) Regular hourly rate of pay and basis on which wages are paid
(e) Total hours worked each workweek
(f) Total daily or weekly straight-time earnings or wages
(g) Total weekly overtime excess compensation
(h) Total additions to or deductions from wages paid each pay period
(i) Total wages paid each pay period
(j) Date of payment and pay period covered by the payment

EMPLOYEES EXEMPT FROM OVERTIME PAY
(a) Name in full
(b) Date of birth
(c) Occupation in which employed
(d) Basis on which wages are paid
(e) Total additions to or deductions from wages paid each pay period
(f) Total wages paid each pay period
(g) Date of payment and pay period covered by the payment

FOR PERIOD ENDING February 16, 19--

NAME	Clock No.	Marital Status	No. of Allow.	Rate	M	T	W	T	F	S	S	Regular Hours	Regular AMOUNT	Overtime Hours	Overtime AMOUNT	TOTAL EARNINGS
Bonham, Patricia	1987	M	0	5.50	8	8	8	8	8			40	220 00			220 00
Fry, Robert	2483	M	2	5.00	8	8	9	9	8			40	200 00	2	15 00	215 00
Stevens, Richard	2316	S	1	5.80	8	7½	8	8	8			39½	229 10			229 10

(Left-hand page)

FICA Taxable Earnings	FICA Tax	Federal	State	Local	Health Insurance	OTHER Item	OTHER Amount	Check No.	AMOUNT	REMARKS
220 00	15 40	30 20	3 30	2 20	5 00			8441	163 90	
215 00	15 05	21 00	3 23	2 15	5 00	advance	25 00	8442	143 57	
229 10	16 04	33 80	3 44	2 30	5 00			8443	168 52	

(Right-hand page)

ILLUSTRATION 3-5 Payroll Record

	19— Period Ending	EARNINGS Regular Rate	Hours	Amount	Overtime Hours	Amount	Total Earnings	Accum. Total	WITHHOLDINGS FICA Tax	Income Taxes Federal	State	Local	DEDUCTIONS Health Ins.	Other	NET PAID Check No.	Amount
1	1/5	5.30	40	212 00			212 00	212 00	14 84	31 20	3 18	2 12	5 00		7971	155 66
2	1/12	5.30	40	212 00	4	31 80	243 80	455 80	17 07	37 00	3 66	2 44			8046	181 63
3	1/19	5.30	40	212 00	4	31 80	243 80	699 60	17 07	39 00	3 66	2 44	5 00		8129	178 63
4	1/26	5.30	40	212 00			212 00	911 60	14 84	31 20	3 18	2 12		18 75	8203	141 91
5	2/2	5.80	40	232 00	6	52 20	284 20	1175 80	19 59	49 40	4 26	2 84	5 00		8228	202 81
6	2/9	5.80	40	232 00			232 00	1427 80	16 24	36 40	3 48	2 32			8371	173 56
7	2/16	5.80	39½	229 10			229 10	1656 90	16 04	33 80	5 44	2 30	5 00		8443	168 52
8																
9																
10																
11																
12																
13																
Quarter Total																

Sex	Department	Occupation	Social Security No.	Marital Status	No. of Allow.	Name	Clock No.
Ⓜ F	Grinding	Machinist	410-80-7865	S	1	Richard A. Groves Date of Birth 4/4/47	2316

ILLUSTRATION 3-6 Employee Earnings Record

Payroll Summary. A schedule summarizing gross earnings, withholdings and deductions, and net earnings is prepared for each payroll period and sent to the accounting department. This schedule, frequently called a **payroll summary**, serves as the basis for recording the payroll in the voucher register.

Payment of Net Earnings. Copies of the payroll record sheets (Illustration 3-5) prepared by the payroll department are sent to the treasurer's department, which is responsible for the payment of net earnings or "take-home pay" to the employees. These earnings may be paid in the form of cash or check. In either case, a check for the total amount to be paid is drawn by the treasurer to create a special payroll fund from which the employees will be paid.

When checks are issued to the individual employees, the check drawn by the treasurer for the total payroll net earnings is deposited in a separate payroll account in the bank. This special account is only for payroll. The individual payroll checks, when cashed, are charged to this account. It is not unusual to establish a new payroll account for each pay period, numbering the accounts sequentially. The checks drawn for the pay period can then be identified as belonging to a particular payroll period. This number identification system facilitates the reconciliation of bank statements.

If cash is used to pay the individual wage earner, the treasurer's check is cashed, and the proceeds are sorted into the amount required for each employee. These cash amounts are placed in envelopes and distributed, usually by a member of the treasurer's department, to the employees. Frequently, a receipt in some form from the employee acknowledges each payment.

ACCOUNTING FOR LABOR COSTS

All working time of each nonsalaried employee should be accounted for on the employee's time ticket or individual production report. Each day the time tickets and production reports are sent to the payroll department. After pay rates and gross earnings have been entered on the tickets and production reports, they are forwarded to the accounting department. Cost accounting personnel sort the time tickets and production reports into those chargeable to jobs and those chargeable to factory overhead. Tickets and reports that contain both direct and indirect labor or regular time and overtime are analyzed to determine the amount of each, and the resulting breakdown is written on each ticket. This information is then transferred to a **labor cost summary** form, similar to the one shown in

Illustration 3-7, and to a job cost ledger or to an appropriate factory overhead ledger.

ILLUSTRATION 3-7

Labor Cost Summary

	LABOR COST SUMMARY			
Dept. _____ Month Ending _____ 19__				
Date	Dr. Work in Process (Direct labor-regular time)		Dr. Factory Overhead (Indirect labor and overtime premium)		Cr. Payroll (Total)

Employees whose wages are exempt from overtime pay are not required to prepare daily time tickets. The payroll department, however, will send to accounting a salaried-employee list, showing names, nature of work performed, and salary. The accounting department will post the earnings to the proper factory overhead ledger accounts and the labor cost summary.

From the information on the labor cost summary, a general journal entry is made to distribute payroll to the appropriate accounts. The entry is then posted to the control accounts, Work in Process and Factory Overhead, in the general ledger. Since the time tickets and individual production reports have been used as the posting media for recording the labor costs in the subsidiary job cost and factory overhead ledgers as well as in the labor cost summary, the debit posted to Work in Process must equal the direct labor cost charged to the jobs in the job cost ledger. Likewise, the debit posted to Factory Overhead must equal the labor costs recorded in the factory overhead ledger.

In preparing the labor cost summary from the time tickets, it is important to separate any overtime from an employee's regular time, because the accounting treatment may be different for each type of pay. Regular time is chargeable to jobs. Overtime, however, may be chargeable to jobs or it may be chargeable partly to jobs and partly to factory overhead, depending on conditions that can vary in any manufacturing process.

Employees may be requested to work longer than an eight-hour day. In such an event, the amount earned for the extra hours worked at the employee's regular rate of pay is called **overtime pay**. An additional rate, called an **overtime premium**, is added to the regular rate of pay for time worked in excess of eight hours. The premium pay rate is often one-half of the regular rate of pay. It could, however, be equal to or even twice the regular rate, in which case it would generally be referred to as double-time or triple-time pay.

If an employee who regularly earns $8 an hour works 12 hours in one day and earns time-and-a-half for overtime, the earnings for the day would be calculated as follows:

Direct labor — 8 hours @ $8		$ 64
Direct labor — 4 hours @ $8	$32	
Factory overhead — overtime premium — 4 hours @ $4	16	48
Total earnings		$112

If the above employee is paid double-time for the extra hours, the earnings for the day would be:

Direct labor — 8 hours @ $8		$ 64
Direct labor — 4 hours @ $8	$32	
Factory overhead — overtime premium — 4 hours @ $8	32	64
Total earnings		$128

By separating the overtime premium from the regular direct labor cost, the jobs in process can be charged for all hours worked at the regular rate of pay, and the premium can be charged to Factory Overhead. Charging the overtime premium to Factory Overhead spreads the additional cost for extra labor to all jobs in production rather than to one specific job. If, however, a job contract includes a provision which necessitates the use of overtime, that job should be charged for the overtime premium paid. It would be unfair to spread the cost to other jobs when a contract, as written, clearly indicates the need for overtime in order to complete the work according to the customer's special requirements.

Decisions regarding the charging of overtime premiums either to Factory Overhead or to specific jobs should not be made without giving consideration to the consequences that could result if the charges distort the accuracy of the job cost accumulations. For example, assume that a product requires four hours to complete. During a 12-hour day, 2 units are completed during the regular 8-hour period at a labor rate of $8 per hour, and 1 unit is completed during the 4-hour overtime period at a labor rate of $12, one-and-a-half times the regular pay rate.

If the overtime premium is charged to the third unit, each of the first two units would be charged with only $32 of labor cost at the regular rate of pay, whereas the third unit would be charged with $48. The conditions that created the need for overtime must be analyzed to determine whether the difference in unit labor cost is justified. An analysis of the conditions raises such questions as: Did employee inefficiency cause the third unit to be a rush job? Is the composition of the third unit different from the first two units? Did poor scheduling require more production for the day than could be produced during regular working hours? Was there a rush to complete the third unit due to an emergency demand from the customer?

If the conclusion reached, after analysis, is that the overtime is not attributable directly to the third unit, the overtime premium should be charged to Factory Overhead. Otherwise, the cost of the third unit will be overstated.

Employers' Payroll Taxes

Payroll taxes imposed on employers include social security tax and federal and state unemployment taxes. Employers are responsible for periodically reporting and paying the taxes to the appropriate government agencies. Employers who fail to file required reports or pay taxes due are subject to civil, and in some cases, criminal penalties.

The **Federal Insurance Contributions Act (FICA)** requires employers to pay social security tax on wages and salaries equal to the amount withheld from employees' earnings. Thus, employers and employees share equally the cost of the social security program. Legislation which governs FICA is frequently amended, changing the wage base subject to FICA tax and the percentage rate of tax. The FICA wage bases and tax rates for 1980–1982 and projected wage bases and rates through 1984 are as follows:

Year	Tax Rate for Employer and Employee	Wage Base Subject to FICA Tax
1980	6.13%	$25,900
1981	6.65%	29,700
1982	6.70%	32,400
1983	6.70%	35,700
1984	6.70%	37,800

Because of the uncertainty connected with frequently revised rates and wage bases, an arbitrary FICA tax rate of 7 percent applied to the first $40,000 of annual earnings is used in this text.

The **Federal Unemployment Tax Act (FUTA)** requires employers to pay an established rate of tax on wages and salaries to provide for compensation to employees if they should be laid off from their regular jobs. Employers are currently required under FUTA to pay tax at a rate of 3.4% on the first $6,000 of wages or salaries paid to each employee in the calendar year.

Unemployment benefits are actually paid by the individual states, and the employer's contributions are apportioned between the federal and state governments as follows: (a) 0.7 percent to the federal government for administering the program and (b) 2.7 percent to the state government to accumulate funds for paying unemployment compensation. Most state unemployment laws provide for a merit plan which permits employers with a history of stable employment to pay less than 2.7 percent to the state unemployment fund.

Although FUTA taxes are subject to amendment, in the past they have not changed as frequently or as dramatically as FICA taxes. Examples in the text are based on the current rate of 3.4 percent (2.7 percent for state taxes and 0.7 percent for the federal portion) applied to the first $6,000 of an employee's annual earnings.

Payroll taxes which the employer is required to pay are directly related to the costs of direct labor and indirect labor and in theory should be charged to these categories of labor cost. However, it is usually more practical to record all factory-related payroll taxes as factory overhead.

Illustration of Accounting for Labor Costs

The Courier Manufacturing Company pays its employees every two weeks. Monday, May 1, is the beginning of a new payroll period. The company maintains the following records:

(a) Payroll record
(b) Employees' earnings records
(c) Voucher register
(d) Check register
(e) General journal
(f) General ledger
(g) Job cost ledger
(h) Factory overhead ledger

The following general ledger accounts are used in accounting for labor costs:

(a) Cash
(b) Work in Process
(c) Vouchers Payable
(d) FICA Tax Payable
(e) Employees Income Tax Payable
(f) Federal Unemployment Tax Payable
(g) State Unemployment Tax Payable
(h) Health Insurance Premiums Payable
(i) Accrued Payroll
(j) Payroll
(k) Factory Overhead
(l) Administrative Salaries

(m) Sales Salaries
(n) Payroll Taxes Expense —
Administrative Salaries

(o) Payroll Taxes Expense —
Sales Salaries

Applicable withholding and payroll tax rates and wage bases are as follows:

| | Rates | | Annual |
	Employee Withholdings	Employer Payroll Taxes	Wages/Salaries Subject to Tax
Federal income tax.........	Graduated*		100%
FICA...........................	7.0%	7.0%	$40,000
Federal unemployment...		0.7%	$ 6,000
State unemployment......		2.7%	$ 6,000

*Federal income tax withholdings are determined from tables or statutory formulas. State and local income taxes are not shown in this illustration.

The following payroll summary is prepared by the payroll department and sent to general accounting for recording:

PAYROLL SUMMARY
For the Payroll Period May 1–14

	Factory Employees	Sales and Administrative Employees	Total
Gross earnings..	$62,300	$21,200	$83,500
Withholdings and deductions:			
FICA tax..	$ 4,361	$ 1,484	$ 5,845
Income Tax..	6,853	2,332	9,185
Health insurance premiums	786	284	1,070
Total..	$12,000	$ 4,100	$16,100
Net earnings..	$50,300	$17,100	$67,400

After the payroll data are verified, authorization is given for a payroll voucher which is recorded in the voucher register as follows:

May 14   Payroll 83,500
        FICA Tax Payable....................... 5,845
        Employees Income Tax Payable...... 9,185
        Health Insurance Premiums Payable 1,070
        Vouchers Payable.......................... 67,400
          To record payroll for the period
          ending May 14.

To record the payment of the net earnings to employees, the following entry is required:

May 14   Vouchers Payable............................ 67,400
        Cash 67,400
          To record payment of payroll for
          the period ending May 14.

The following schedule provides the information necessary to distribute the total payroll of $83,500 to the appropriate accounts and to record the employer's payroll taxes for the period.

SCHEDULE OF EARNINGS AND PAYROLL TAXES For Payroll Period, May 1–14, 19––			Unemployment Taxes		Total Payroll Taxes
Nonfactory Employees	Gross Earnings	FICA 7%	Federal .7%	State 2.7%	
Sales	$10,000	$ 700.00	$ 70.00	$ 270.00	$1,040.00
Administrative	11,200	784.00	78.40	302.40	1,164.80
	$21,200	$1,484.00	$148.40	$ 572.40	$2,204.80
Factory Employees					
Direct labor:					
Regular.......................	$52,000	$3,640.00	$364.00	$1,404.00	$5,408.00
Overtime Premium	8,000	560.00	56.00	216.00	832.00
Indirect labor...............	2,300	161.00	16.10	62.10	239.20
	$62,300	$4,361.00	$436.10	$1,682.10	$6,479.20
Total...........................	$83,500	$5,845.00	$584.50	$2,254.50	$8,684.00

The distribution of the payroll and the employer's payroll taxes are recorded as follows:

```
May 14   Work in Process ..........................   52,000
         Factory Overhead.......................   10,300*
         Sales Salaries..............................   10,000
         Administrative Salaries.................   11,200
             Payroll.....................................              83,500
                 To distribute payroll for the
                 period ending May 14.
```

*Overtime premium ($8,000) + indirect factory labor ($2,300)

```
May 14  Factory Overhead.........................   6,479.20
        Payroll Taxes Expense — Sales
            Salaries.................................   1,040.00
        Payroll Taxes Expense —
            Administrative Salaries..............   1,164.80
            FICA Tax Payable .................               5,845.00
            Federal Unemployment Tax
                Payable...............................                584.50
            State Unemployment Tax
                Payable...............................              2,254.50
                 To record employer's
                 payroll taxes for the period
                 ending May 14.
```

The following general ledger accounts reflect the entries relating to the payroll for May 1–14.

PAYROLL				FICA TAX PAYABLE		EMPLOYEES INCOME TAX PAYABLE	
(1)	83,500.00	(3)	83,500.00	(1) 5,845.00 (4) 5,845.00		(1) 9,185.00	

HEALTH INSURANCE PREMIUMS PAYABLE		VOUCHERS PAYABLE		CASH	
	(1) 1,070.00	(2) 67,400.00	(1) 67,400.00		(2) 67,400.00

WORK IN PROCESS		FACTORY OVERHEAD		SALES SALARIES	
(3) 52,000.00		(3) 10,300.00 (4) 6,479.20		(3) 10,000.00	

ADMINISTRATIVE SALARIES		PAYROLL TAXES EXPENSE SALES SALARIES		PAYROLL TAXES EXPENSE ADMINISTRATIVE SALARIES	
(3) 11,200.00		(4) 1,040.00		(4) 1,164.80	

FEDERAL UNEMPLOYMENT TAX PAYABLE		STATE UNEMPLOYMENT TAX PAYABLE	
	(4) 584.50		(4) 2,254.50

(1) To record payroll.
(2) To record payment of payroll.
(3) To record distribution of payroll.
(4) To record employer's payroll taxes.

The second payroll period in May begins on May 15. At the end of the two-week period, the payroll computations are made, and the following schedule is prepared:

PAYROLL SUMMARY
For the Payroll Period May 15–28

	Factory Employees	Sales and Administrative Employees	Total
Gross earnings	$72,000	$21,200	$93,200
Withholdings and deductions:			
FICA tax	$ 5,040	$ 1,484	$ 6,524
Income tax	7,920	2,332	10,252
Health insurance premiums	864	284	1,148
Total	$13,824	$ 4,100	$17,924
Net earnings	$58,176	$17,100	$75,276

After the payroll data are verified, authorization is given for a payroll voucher which is recorded in the voucher register as follows:

May 28   Payroll 93,200
        FICA Tax Payable..........................   6,524
        Employees Income Tax Payable......   10,252
        Health Insurance Premiums Payable   1,148
        Vouchers Payable..........................   75,276
           To record payroll for the period
           ending May 28.

To record the payment of the net earnings to employees, the following entry is required:

May 28   Vouchers Payable........................... 75,276
        Cash   75,276
           To record payment of payroll for
           the period ending May 28.

The following schedule provides the information necessary to distribute the total payroll of $93,200 to the appropriate accounts and to record the employer's payroll taxes for the period.

SCHEDULE OF EARNINGS AND PAYROLL TAXES For Payroll Period, May 15–28, 19——					
			Unemployment Taxes		
Nonfactory Employees	Gross Earnings	FICA 7%	Federal .7%	State 2.7%	Total Payroll Taxes
Sales	$10,000	$ 700.00	$ 70.00	$ 270.00	$1,040.00
Administrative	11,200	784.00	78.40	302.40	1,164.80
	$21,200	$1,484.00	$148.40	$ 572.40	$2,204.80
Factory Employees					
Direct labor:					
Regular......................	$60,000	$4,200.00	$420.00	$1,620.00	$6,240.00
Overtime Premium	9,000	630.00	63.00	243.00	936.00
Indirect labor...............	3,000	210.00	21.00	81.00	312.00
	$72,000	$5,040.00	$504.00	$1,944.00	$7,488.00
Total......................	$93,200	$6,524.00	$652.40	$2,516.40	$9,692.80

The distribution of the payroll and the employer's payroll taxes are recorded as follows:

May 28   Work in Process 60,000
        Factory Overhead........................ 12,000*
        Sales Salaries.............................. 10,000
        Administrative Salaries................. 11,200
        Payroll...................................   93,200
           To distribute payroll for the
           period ending May 28.

*Overtime premium ($9,000) + indirect factory labor ($3,000)

May 28   Factory Overhead........................ 7,488.00
           Payroll Taxes Expense — Sales
              Salaries.................................... 1,040.00
           Payroll Taxes Expense —
              Administrative Salaries.............. 1,164.80
                  FICA Tax Payable................   6,524.00
                  Federal Unemployment Tax
                    Payable...........................   652.40
                  State Unemployment Tax
                    Payable...........................   2,516.40
                    To record employer's
                    payroll taxes for the period
                    ending May 28.

Payroll Accrual Procedures

The preparation of periodic financial statements requires the recording of payroll and payroll taxes expense accrued since the end of the preceding pay period. Employees' withholdings are generally not computed for the accrual period, since they do not affect the determination of the employer's income or total liabilities on the balance sheet. Payroll taxes are accrued, however, to avoid understating expenses and liabilities for the period.

Continuing the previous example, a new two-week payroll period for the Courier Manufacturing Company begins on Monday, May 29. In order to prepare month-end financial statements, payroll must be accrued for the three-day period May 29–31. Employee earnings and the employer payroll taxes for the accrual period are as follows:

			Unemployment Taxes		
SCHEDULE OF EARNINGS AND PAYROLL TAXES **May 29–31**					
Nonfactory Employees	Gross Earnings	FICA 7%	Federal .7%	State 2.7%	Total Payroll Taxes
Sales	$ 3,000	$ 210.00	$ 21.00	$ 81.00	$ 312.00
Administrative	3,400	238.00	23.80	91.80	353.60
	$ 6,400	$ 448.00	$ 44.80	$172.80	$ 665.60
Factory Employees					
Direct labor:					
Regular..........................	$14,900	$1,043.00	$104.30	$402.30	$1,549.60
Overtime Premium...........	3,200	224.00	22.40	86.40	332.80
Indirect labor.................	750	52.50	5.25	20.25	78.00
	$18,850	$1,319.50	$131.95	$508.95	$1,960.40
Total.................................	$25,250	$1,767.50	$176.75	$681.75	$2,626.00

The following entries are required to record and distribute the accrued payroll and to record the employer's payroll taxes.

May 31	Payroll....................................	25,250	
	Accrued Payroll		25,250
	To record the accrued payroll for May 29–31.		

	Work in Process	14,900	
	Factory Overhead........................	3,950*	
	Sales Salaries............................	3,000	
	Administrative Salaries................	3,400	
	Payroll...................................		25,250
	To distribute accrued payroll for the period May 29–31.		

*Overtime premium ($3,200) + indirect labor ($750)

May 31	Factory Overhead........................	1,960.40	
	Payroll Taxes Expense — Sales Salaries.................................	312.00	
	Payroll Taxes Expense — Administrative Salaries..............	353.60	
	FICA Tax Payable		1,767.50
	Federal Unemployment Tax Payable............................		176.75
	State Unemployment Tax Payable...........................		681.75
	To record employer's payroll taxes for the period May 29–31.		

Before June transactions are recorded, the entry for accruing payroll should be reversed:

June 1	Accrued Payroll	25,250	
	Payroll...................................		25,250
	To reverse May 31 adjusting entry for accrued payroll.		

Although the cost of the May 29–31 payroll is recognized as part of the May production, sales, and administrative costs, the payment to the employees will be included in the June 11 disbursement. The credit balance in the payroll account created by the reversing entry will assure that only the payroll costs accumulated during the June 1–11 period will be included in the production, sales, and administrative costs for the month of June.

The following general ledger accounts reflect all the entries relating to payroll for the month of May.

	PAYROLL				FICA TAX PAYABLE	
May 14	83,500.00	May 14	83,500.00		May 14	5,845.00
28	93,200.00	28	93,200.00		14	5,845.00
31	25,250.00	31	25,250.00		28	6,524.00
	201,950.00	June 1	25,250.00		28	6,524.00
			227,200.00		31	1,767.50
		25,250				26,505.50

EMPLOYEES
INCOME TAX PAYABLE

	May 14	9,185.00
	28	10,252.00
		19,437.00

HEALTH INSURANCE
PREMIUMS PAYABLE

	May 14	1,070.00
	28	1,148.00
		2,218.00

VOUCHERS PAYABLE

May 14	67,400.00	May 14	67,400.00
28	75,276.00	28	75,276.00

CASH

	May 14	67,400.00
	28	75,276.00

WORK IN PROCESS

May 14	52,000.00
28	60,000.00
31	14,900.00
	126,900.00

FACTORY OVERHEAD

May 14	10,300.00
14	6,479.20
28	12,000.00
28	7,488.00
31	3,950.00
31	1,960.40
	42,177.60

ACCRUED PAYROLL

June 1	25,250.00	May 31	25,250.00

SALES SALARIES

May 14	10,000.00
28	10,000.00
31	3,000.00
	23,000.00

ADMINISTRATIVE SALARIES

May 14	11,200.00
28	11,200.00
31	3,400.00
	25,800.00

PAYROLL TAXES EXPENSE—
SALES SALARIES

May 14	1,040.00
28	1,040.00
31	312.00
	2,392.00

PAYROLL TAXES EXPENSE—
ADMINISTRATIVE SALARIES

May 14	1,164.80
28	1,164.80
31	353.60
	2,683.20

FEDERAL UNEMPLOYMENT
TAX PAYABLE

	May 14	584.50
	28	652.40
	31	176.75
		1,413.65

STATE UNEMPLOYMENT
TAX PAYABLE

	May 14	2,254.50
	28	2,516.40
	31	681.75
		5,452.65

Summary of Labor Cost Accounting Procedures

Illustrations 3-8 and 3-9 show, in summary, the labor cost accounting procedures and forms that are commonly encountered in payroll systems. After a detailed study of labor costing, these brief summaries can be used to help recall when a specific technique and form should be used in accounting and reporting for payroll costs.

Additional Labor Cost Accounting Problems

There are various labor-related costs that an employer may incur, including shift premiums, pensions, guaranteed annual wages,

Transaction	Source of Data	Book of Original Entry	General Ledger Entry

Recording wages and salaries	Payroll summary	Voucher register	Payroll (gross earnings for payroll period)
			  FICA Tax Payable
			  Employees Income Tax Payable
			  Health Insurance Premiums Payable
			  Vouchers Payable (net amount payable to employees)

Paying wages and salaries	Voucher	Check register	Vouchers Payable Cash
Distributing wages and salaries	Labor cost summary	General journal	Work in Process (direct labor) Factory Overhead (indirect labor and overtime premium) Administrative Salaries Sales Salaries Payroll

Recording payroll taxes imposed on the employer	Schedule of earnings and payroll taxes	General journal	Factory Overhead (taxes on factory labor)
			Payroll Taxes Expense — Administrative Salaries
			Payroll Taxes Expense — Sales Salaries
			  FICA Tax Payable
			  Federal Unemployment Tax Payable
			  State Unemployment Tax Payable

ILLUSTRATION 3-8   Summary of Payroll Transactions

bonuses, and vacation and holiday pay. Each of these costs must be systematically recorded and recognized as part of the cost of production.

When a company operates more than one work shift, an additional rate of pay, called a **shift premium**, is usually added to the regular rate for employees who do not work during the regular day shift. For example, assume that a company operates three shifts: 8:00 a.m. to 4:00 p.m.; 4:00 p.m. to 12:00 a.m.; and 12:00 a.m. to 8:00 a.m. Employees who work during the second shift receive an additional $.75 per hour, and those working during the third shift receive an additional $1 per hour. The company does not expect an increase in productivity from these second and third shift workers. To the contrary, these employees are usually found to be less productive than day shift workers. Therefore, shift premiums are usually charged to factory overhead in order to avoid a substantial distortion of productivity per worker. However, due to their unproductive nature, shift premiums may be charged to a separate account and closed directly to Income Summary.

Shift premiums which are charged to Factory Overhead become a part of the cost of a manufactured product. If inventories remain at the end of an accounting period, the cost of such inventories,

Name of Form and Illustration Number	When Prepared	By Whom Prepared	Purpose	How Used
Clock Card Illus. 3-1	On entering and leaving factory.	Employees	To show length of time, regular and overtime, spent in factory or office.	Provides a check on the accuracy of the number of hours reported on time tickets and as a means of employee control. Used by payroll clerk for computing employees' earnings and recording the data in the payroll record and employee earnings record.
Time Ticket Illus. 3-2 or 3-3 Individual Production Report Illus. 3-4	During each working day.	Timekeeper or employees under supervisor	To show how employee spends time in factory.	Timekeeper reconciles with hours shown on clock card. Payroll clerk enters pay rates and gross earnings. Cost accountant uses as source of data for labor cost summary and for posting to the job cost ledger and factory overhead ledger.
Schedule of Fixed Salaries (for factory employees)	Usually once a year (unless salaries are changed during year).	Payroll clerk	To provide a ready source of the amount payable to those employees who do not prepare time tickets and clock cards.	Source of data on fixed salaries to be entered in the payroll record and in the employee earnings record. Cost accountant uses as source of data for labor cost summary and for posting to the factory overhead ledger.
Payroll Record Illus. 3-5	At end of payroll period from clock cards and schedule of fixed salaries.	Payroll clerk	To show by payroll periods, amounts earned, deductions, and net amounts payable.	Source of information for preparing payroll vouchers. Basis for preparing individual payroll checks or pay envelopes.
Employee Earnings Record. Illus. 3-6	At end of payroll period from payroll record	Payroll clerk	To show for each employee a permanent, continuous record of earnings while with company.	Provides permanent record of each employee's earnings. Satisfies requirement of FICA and income tax laws as to record keeping. Basis for preparing payroll tax returns.
Labor Cost Summary Illus. 3-7	Daily from time tickets and at end of payroll period from schedule of fixed salaries.	Cost accountants	To classify total factory wages between regular time and overtime and between direct and indirect.	Source of amounts to be charged to Work in Process and Factory Overhead in the general ledger.

ILLUSTRATION 3-9   Summary of Labor Cost Accounting Forms

which includes the shift premium, is deferred as a product cost to the next period. When shift premiums are closed directly to Income Summary, they are charged to the period in which they are incurred. The net income determination is affected by the method chosen. It appears logical, however, to charge shift premiums to factory overhead, because they result directly from manufacturing activities and are somewhat similar to overtime premium pay.

A common problem for many companies involves pensions for employees. **Pension costs** result from an agreement between a company and its employee group whereby the company promises to provide income to its former employees who have retired. The pension, which is usually paid on a monthly basis, is commonly determined using the employee's level of income and the length of service with the company. Some plans are completely paid for (funded) by the company, while others require an additional contribution from the employees. When a pension plan is initiated by a company, it is a common practice to permit retroactive coverage for previous years service with the company.

A basic provision included in all plans is to accrue, systematically, over the period of active service, the total estimated pension cost from the date the pension plan started to the date the employee retires. The periodic contributions for pensions or the accrual of current pension costs can be charged to general or administrative expenses rather than to manufacturing costs under the premise that the costs of the pensions are beneficial to the company as a whole. However, it is also appropriate to charge such costs directly to the individual employee's department or to apportion the pension costs as a percentage of the total payroll to all departments within the company. The percentage allocation plan seems to be the most desirable, because if a direct-departmental charge plan is used, the highest pension costs are charged to the departments employing the oldest workers, thereby distorting the departmental costs.

A problem which requires resolution when dealing with pensions, is the accrual of pension costs for an employee's past services when there is a provision for retroactive coverage in the pension plan. These costs, in order to update an employee's previous service coverage, should be classified as nonrecurring, extraordinary costs and should be charged to an expense account in the period they are incurred. In direct contrast, the current pension costs for factory employees are part of the cost of production and should be charged to factory overhead.

Guaranteed Annual Wage (GAW) plans are of relatively recent origin in the fringe benefit packages offered to employees. These plans assure the employees a guaranteed level of earnings over a stipulated period (weeks or months), even though the company experiences a shutdown. These plans vary widely and may include a combination of (**a**) unemployment compensation, (**b**) flexibility of hours (may permit overtime without penalty in certain periods), and (**c**) a guarantee that a minimum wage will be awarded. Most companies feel that sometime in its future, it will experience a layoff and, therefore, be required to pay the employees wages under a GAW plan. Due to the expectation that a layoff could occur, recognition of the potential contingency should be made in the records by establishing accounts for accumulating the liability. One plan requires that an amount be set aside for each hour an employee works. The factory overhead account is debited for the hourly cost and a GAW Liability account is credited.

To illustrate, assume a department's weekly payroll for 2,000 hours amounted to $14,000. If the established GAW plan requires $.35 per hour be recognized as a liability to cover the possibility of a layoff, the entry in the records would be:

Work in Process	14,000	
Factory Overhead	700	
Payroll		14,000
GAW Liability		700
To distribute the payroll and record the GAW liability for 2,000 hours at $.35 per hour.		

Further assume that the company continued adding to the liability for 10 years, and the liability amounted to $3,500,000 when a layoff occurred. The weekly payment for GAW was $30,000 and was recorded:

GAW Liability	30,000	
Cash		30,000
To pay employees as per GAW agreement.		

Bonuses are paid to employees for many different reasons, such as higher-than-usual company profits, exceeding departmental quotas for selling or production, or for any other reasons that management feels a bonus should be awarded. Bonus plans may include some employees or all employees. The cost of bonuses usually follows the employee's job classification within the company. Factory workers' bonuses are charged to factory overhead and sales persons' bonuses are charged to selling expense.

Vacation pay is an amount paid at the end of a designated period to a temporarily nonworking employee. The amount of time off and the pay for the vacation period was earned gradually, by the employee's previous daily service record on the job. Vacation plans usually stipulate that an employee must work a minimum of one year for the company before being entitled to a vacation with pay. Usually after one year's service, the employee is entitled to one week's paid vacation.

Holiday pay is based upon an agreement between the employees and management that certain holidays during the year will be no-work days but will be paid for by the company. These paid holidays are usually determined prior to beginning a new fiscal period.

Bonus payments, vacation, and holiday pay can be considered together as a group when accounting for their cost because they have many similar characteristics.

To illustrate accounting for these items, assume a factory worker earns $500 each week and a management bonus plan shows that the job station at which the work is performed should be entitled to a $1,000 year-end bonus. In addition, there will be a 4-week paid vacation and 8 paid holidays during the year. To record the payroll and the costs and liabilities associated with the bonus, vacation, and holiday pay for the employee, the entry would be as follows:

Work in Process	500.00	
Factory Overhead (Bonus)[1]	19.23	
Factory Overhead (Vacation)[2]	41.67	
Factory Overhead (Holiday)[3]	15.38	
Payroll		500.00
Bonus Liability		19.23
Vacation Pay Liability		41.67
Holiday Pay Liability		15.38

[1]Bonus — $1,000 ÷ 52 weeks = $19.23 per week
[2]Vacation Pay — $500 × 4 weeks = $2,000 ÷ 48 weeks worked = $41.67 per week.
[3]Holiday Pay — $500 week ÷ 5 days = $100 per day × 8 holidays = $800 ÷ 52 weeks = $15.38 per week.

The vacation pay is spread over the worker's time on the job — 48 weeks, because a contribution to production from the employee can be expected only during this period. If workers on vacation are not replaced by other workers, production should diminish.

QUESTIONS

1. Distinguish between direct and indirect labor.
2. State briefly the advantages and disadvantages of **(a)** the hourly-rate wage plan and **(b)** the piece-rate wage plan.

3. What are incentive wage plans?
4. Briefly state the functions of the timekeeping department and the payroll department.
5. Why should the timekeeping and

payroll departments be required to function with some degree of independence from each other?

6. (a) Explain the functions of a clock card and a time ticket. **(b)** How is the information on clock cards and time tickets used?

7. In what way do the clock cards and time tickets complement each other?

8. Although payroll records may vary somewhat in design, what data would almost all payroll records contain about employees?

9. What is the source of the posting of the direct labor cost to **(a)** the individual accounts in the job cost ledger and **(b)** the work in process account in the general ledger?

10. What is the source of the posting of indirect labor cost to the indirect labor account in the factory overhead ledger?

11. What is the distinction, for cost accounting purposes, between regular pay and overtime premium pay?

12. If cost accounting procedures for labor are carried out properly, what internal control feature exists regarding the charge to the work in process account and the credit to the payroll accounts in the general ledger?

13. What accounts are required to record the employees' withholdings and the employer's payroll taxes?

14. Summarize the four procedures involved in accounting for labor cost, and name the supporting forms used for each process.

15. What are the sources of data and the books of original entry for the following?

- **(a)** Recording the wages and salaries earned during the payroll period.
- **(b)** Paying the wages and salaries earned.
- **(c)** Recording the payroll taxes imposed on the employer.

16. What is a shift premium?

17. What is a basic requirement in all pension plans?

18. What is the major purpose of a guaranteed annual wage plan?

19. What accounting treatments do factory bonuses and vacation and holiday pay for employees have in common?

EXERCISES

> *Note: For the exercises and problems in this chapter, use the following tax rates:*
>
> *FICA – Employer and employee, 7% of the first $40,000 of earnings per employee per calendar year.*
>
> *State unemployment – 2.7% of the first $6,000 of earnings per employee per calendar year.*
>
> *FUTA – .7% of the first $6,000 of earnings per employee per calendar year.*
>
> *Federal income tax withholding – 10% of each employee's earnings, unless otherwise stated.*

1. The Incredible Company paid wages to its employees during the year as follows:

Alvarez	$ 8,900
Clark	11,300
Donald	6,800
Edom	10,300
Hall	19,000
Mack	10,800
O'Sullivan	41,000
Schmitt	42,500

(a) How much of the total payroll is exempt from FICA tax? **(b)** How much of the total payroll is exempt from federal and state unemployment taxes?

2. Marion Laurion, of the Chiona Manufacturing Co., is paid at the rate of $8 an hour for an 8-hour day, with time and one half for overtime and double time for Sundays and holidays. Regular employment is on the basis of 40 hours a week — five days a week. The regular workday is from 7:00 a.m. to 12:00 noon and from 12:30 p.m. to 3:30 p.m. At the end of a week the clock card shows:

	A.M.		P.M.		Overtime	
	In	Out	In	Out	In	Out
Sunday	8:00	12:00				
Monday	6:58	12:01	12:25	3:35		
Tuesday	7:00	12:03	12:28	3:32		
Wednesday	6:56	12:02	12:30	3:33		
Thursday	6:55	12:05	12:28	3:35	6:00	9:30
Friday	6:55	12:01	12:29			6:32
Saturday	6:55			1:30		

On Monday through Friday night, Laurion worked on the production line. The hours worked on Saturday and Sunday were used to repair machinery. **(a)** Compute Laurion's total earnings for the week. (Ignore odd minutes). **(b)** Present the general journal entry to distribute Laurion's total earnings.

3. Using the earnings data developed in Exercise 2, and assuming that this was the first week of employment for Marion Laurion with the Chiona Manufacturing Co., prepare the following entries in general journal form:

(a) Set up the voucher for the week's payroll.
(b) Pay the voucher for the payroll.
(c) Record the employer's payroll taxes.

Note: *These single journal entries are for the purpose of illustrating the principle involved. Normally the entries would be made for the total factory payroll plus the administrative and sales payroll.*

4. Using the earnings data developed in Exercise 2, and assuming that this was the tenth week of employment for Laurion and that the previous earnings to date were $5,900, prepare the following entries in general journal form:

(a) Set up the voucher for the week's payroll.
(b) Pay the voucher for the payroll.
(c) Record the employer's payroll taxes.

5. Using the earnings data developed in Exercise 2, and assuming that this was the fiftieth week of employment for Laurion and that the previous earnings to date were $39,800, prepare the following entries in general journal form:

(a) Set up the voucher for the week's payroll.
(b) Pay the voucher for the payroll.
(c) Record the employer's payroll taxes.

6. The C. A. Arlinger Co. requires all factory workers to record the time of arrival and of departure by means of a time clock. The company operates on a forty-hour basis, time and a half allowed for overtime. The regular work day is from 8:30 a.m. to 12:00 noon and from 1:00 p.m. to 5:00 p.m., Monday through Friday, and from 8:30 to 11:50 a.m. on Saturday.

The clock card record of a group of employees for Monday, is as follows:

Employee No.	Morning In	Noon Out	Noon In	Night Out	Extra In	Extra Out
51	8:19	12:10	12:51	4:57		
52	8:30	12:01	12:56	4:58		
53	8:21	12:05				
54	8:20	12:02	12:57	4:53		
55	8:24	12:04	12:57	4:50		
56	8:29	12:04	12:53	4:57		
57	8:25	12:04				
58	8:27	12:00	12:48	4:56		
59	8:28	12:01	12:57			6:50
60	8:26	12:03	12:56			5:20
61	8:26	12:05	12:59	4:58		
62	8:23	12:00	12:52	4:59	5:30	9:30

(a) Compute the regular and overtime hours for each employee for the day. (Ignore odd minutes). (b) Assuming that all of the above employees are paid at the rate of $4.10 an hour, compute the amount of each employee's earnings for the day.

7. The total wages and salaries earned by all employees of The Clevedale Manufacturing Co. during the month of June as shown in the labor cost summary and the schedule of fixed administrative and sales salaries are classified as follows:

Direct labor	$327,829
Indirect labor..	62,313
Administrative salaries..	41,217
Sales salaries..	53,452
Total wages earned..	$484,811

(a) Prepare a general journal entry to distribute the wages earned during June. (b) What is the total amount of payroll taxes that will be imposed on the employer for the above payroll, assuming that none of the employees has achieved the maximums for FICA and unemployment taxes?

8. The Archer Machine Tool Co. produces tools on a job order basis. During May, two jobs were completed, and the following costs were incurred:

	Job 401	Job 402
Direct materials..	$14,000	$18,500
Direct labor: regular...	9,000	11,500
overtime premium	——	3,000

Other factory costs for the month totaled $8,400. Factory overhead costs are allocated one-third to Job 401 and two-thirds to Job 402.

(a) Describe two alternative methods for assigning costs to Jobs 401 and 402 and explain how the appropriate method would be determined. (b) Compute the cost of Job 401 and Job 402 under each of the two methods described in (a).

9. A weekly payroll summary made from time tickets shows the following data:

Employee	Classification	Hourly Rate	Regular	Overtime
Goldsmith, A.	Direct	$5	40	2
Hackett, B.	Direct	5	40	3
Karl, C.	Direct	6	40	4
Ramos, D.	Indirect	3	40	
Thomas, E.	Indirect	3	40	

Overtime is payable at one and a half times the regular rate of pay for an employee.

(a) Determine the net pay of each employee. The income taxes withheld for each employee amount to 15% of their gross wages. (b) Prepare general journal entries for:

(1) Preparation of the payroll voucher.
(2) Payment of the payroll voucher.
(3) The factory ledger entry to distribute the payroll.
(4) The employer's share of taxes imposed on the payroll. Assume that none of the employees has achieved the maximums for FICA and unemployment taxes.

10. The payroll records of the Supergo Manufacturing Co. show the following information for the week ended August 17:

Employee	Classification	Hours Worked	Production (Units)	Hourly Rate	Piece Rate	Weekly Rate	Income Tax Withheld
Carter, A.	Direct	42		$4.50			$22
Doyle, B.	Direct	48		4.40			24
Johnson, C.	Direct	39	2,000		$.11		27
Pappas, D.	Direct	40	1,800		.11		25
Quinn, E.	Indirect	40				$125	15
Steven, F.	Indirect	40				300	40
Wang, G.	Indirect	40				160	18

Hourly workers are paid time-and-a-half for overtime.

(a) Determine the net earnings of each employee. (b) Prepare the journal entries for:

(1) Setting up the liability for the payroll.
(2) Paying the payroll.
(3) Distributing the payroll.
(4) Setting up the employer's liability for payroll taxes. Assume that none of the employees has achieved the maximums for FICA and unemployment taxes.

11. A partial summary of the payroll data for The Big Bay Manufacturing Co., for each week of June is as follows:

	June 7	June 14	June 21	June 28
Total earnings..	$24,100.00	$23,750.00	$24,750.00	$25,300.00
Deductions:				
FICA tax 7.0%	$	$	$	$
Income taxes	2,284.00	2,247.50	2,362.50	2,467.00
Health insurance..	460.00	460.00	460.00	460.00
Total deductions ...				
Net amounts payable........	$	$	$	$

(a) Compute the missing amounts in the summary. (b) By means of general journal entries, show the effect of the required entries (1) in the voucher register and (2) in the check register.

PROBLEMS

3-1. Computing and journalizing employer's payroll taxes. The following form is used by the The Danville Manufacturing Co. to compute payroll taxes incurred during the month of June.

Classification of Wages and Salaries	Total Earnings for Month	FICA Tax 7.0%	Unemployment Taxes		Total Payroll Taxes Imposed on Employer
			Federal Tax .7%	State Tax 2.7%	
Direct labor	69,720.00				
Indirect labor....................	13,115.00				
Total taxes on factory wages					
Administrative salaries........	6,200.00				
Sales salaries.....................	8,000.00				
Total payroll taxes					

Required: (1) Complete the above form to show the payroll taxes imposed on the employer at the end of June. Assume that none of the employees has achieved the maximums for FICA and unemployment taxes. (2) Assuming that the payroll taxes imposed on the employer covering factory wages are treated as factory overhead, the taxes covering administrative salaries as an administrative expense, and the taxes covering sales salaries as a selling expense, prepare a general journal entry to record the employer's liability for the June payroll taxes.

3-2. Payroll for piece-rate wage system. The Westville Manufacturing Company operates on a piece-rate wage system. During one week's operation, the following direct labor costs were incurred.

Employee	Piece Rate per 100 Units	Units Completed				
		M	T	W	T	F
A. Johnson	$.45	6,800	7,100	6,500	8,000	4,800
B. Jones....................	.55	6,300	6,400	2,900	2,800	7,000
C. Jenson	.65	6,200	6,100	7,100	6,000	2,800

Each of these employees is a machine operator. Piece rates vary with the kind of product being produced. A minimum of $20 per day is guaranteed each employee by union contract.

Required: (1) Compute Johnson's, Jones', and Jenson's earnings for the week. (2) Set up the voucher for the week's payroll. (3) Pay the voucher for the payroll. (4) Record the employer's share of payroll taxes. Assume that none of the employees has achieved the maximums for FICA and unemployment taxes.

3-3. Payment and distribution of payroll. The general ledger of the Sidell Manufacturing Company showed the following credit balances on July 15.

FICA Tax Payable	$ 443.38
Employees Income Tax Payable...	1,520.00
FUTA Tax Payable	22.17
State Unemployment Tax Payable	85.51

Factory employees earned direct wages of $5,100 from July 16 to July 31. Income tax of $1,285 was withheld from the wages. The sales and administrative salaries for the same period amounted to $1,500, from which $200 was withheld for income taxes.

Required: (1) Prepare the journal entries to:

(a) Record the payroll voucher.
(b) Pay the salaries and wages.
(c) Record the employer's payroll tax liability.
(d) Distribute the payroll for July 16 to 31.

(2) Prepare the journal entries to record the payment of the amounts due for the month for FICA and income tax withholdings. **(3)** Calculate the amount of total earnings for the period from July 1 to July 15.

3-4. Payroll computation with incentive bonus. Fifteen workers are assigned to a group project. The production standard calls for 500 units to be completed each hour to meet a customer's set deadline for the products. If the required units can be delivered before the target date on the order, a substantial premium for early delivery will be paid by the customer. The company, wishing to encourage the workers to produce beyond the established standard, has offered a bonus that will be added to each project employee's pay for excess production. The bonus is to be computed as follows:

(a) $\dfrac{\text{Group's excess production over standard}}{\text{Standard units for week}} \times 50\% = \text{bonus percentage}$

(b) Individual's hourly wage rate $\times$ bonus percentage = hourly bonus rate
(c) Hourly wage rate + hourly bonus rate = new hourly rate for week
(d) Total hours worked $\times$ new hourly rate = earnings for week

The average wage rate for the project workers is $5 per hour. The production record for the week shows:

	Hours Worked	Production (Units)
Monday	112	61,040
Tuesday	112	60,032
Wednesday	112	60,480
Thursday	112	65,632
Friday	108	57,344
Saturday	50	26,000
	606	330,528

Required: (1) Determine the rate and the total amount of the bonus for the week. **(2)** What are the total wages of Sidney Paul, who worked 40 hours at a base rate of $5 per hour? **(3)** What are the total wages of Claudia Jones, who worked 35 hours at a base rate of $6 per hour?

3-5. Payroll work sheet and journal entries. The payroll records of the Allerton Corporation for the week ending October 7, the fortieth week in the year, show the following:

Employee	Classification	Pay Rate per 40-Hour Week	Hours Worked	Income Tax Withheld	Gross Earnings up to Fortieth Week
Carlie	President	$1,200	40	$250	$46,800
Diaz	Vice-President	1,000	40	230	39,000
Eber	Supervisor	700	40	180	27,300
Fredo	Factory-Direct	500	48	150	19,820
George	Factory-Direct	400	46	160	17,200
Harrison	Factory-Direct	400	44	110	16,600
Potts	Factory-Direct	380	42	120	15,200
Schultz	Factory-Indirect	300	42	80	13,200
Stobbs	Factory-Indirect	300	42	60	12,950

Required: (1) Complete a columnar work sheet with the following headings on the columns:

> Employee —
> 3 columns for Earnings for Week:
>   Use Column 1 for Regular Pay
>   Use Column 2 for Overtime Premium Pay
>   Use Column 3 for Total for Week
> Total Earnings through Fortieth Week
> FICA Taxable Earnings
> FUTA and State Unemployment Taxable Earnings
> FICA — 7%
> Income Tax Withheld
> Net Earnings

(2) Prepare journal entries for:

(a) Payroll for fortieth week.
(b) Payment of payroll for week.
(c) Distribution of the payroll.
(d) Employer's payroll tax liability.

(3) The company carries a disability insurance policy for the employees at a cost of $4.75 per week for each employee. Journalize the employer's cost of insurance premiums for the week.

3-6. Piece-rates and incentive wage plan. The Oakwood Company employs seven workers in its factory. The union contract provides that the minimum wage for a worker is the base rate, which is also paid for any "down time" when the worker's machine is under repair. The standard work week is 40 hours. The union contract also provides that workers be paid time and a half for overtime. In addition to these provisions, the following incentive wage plans are in effect:

(a) Straight piece-rate. The worker is paid at the rate of $.40 per unit produced.
(b) Percentage bonus plan. Standard quantities of production per hour are established by the engineering department. The worker's average hourly production, determined from total hours worked and production, is divided by the standard hourly production to determine a percentage. This percentage (if greater than 100%) is then applied to the worker's base rate to determine hourly earnings for the period.
(c) Efficiency bonus. A minimum wage is paid for production up to 66⅔%

of the standard output or "efficiency." When the worker's production exceeds 66⅔% of the standard output, a bonus rate is paid. The bonus is determined from the following table:

Efficiency	Bonus
Under 66⅔%	0%
66⅔%–79%	10%
80%–99%	20%
100%–125%	45%

A weekly payroll for the workers shows the following:

Worker	Incentive Wage Plan	Total Hours	Down Time Hours	Units Produced	Standard Units	Base Rate
Jonas	Straight piece-rate	40	5	400	—	$2.50
Long	Straight piece-rate	46	—	455(1)	—	2.50
Biggs	Straight piece-rate	44	4	420(2)	—	2.50
Boro	Percentage bonus	40	—	250	200	2.90
Johns	Percentage bonus	40	—	180	200	2.60
Ortiz	Efficiency bonus	40	—	240	300	2.80
Small	Efficiency bonus	40	2	590	600(3)	2.70

(1) Includes 45 pieces produced during the 6 overtime hours.
(2) Includes 50 pieces produced during the 4 overtime hours. The overtime, which was brought about by the "down time," was necessary to meet a production deadline.
(3) Standard units for 40 hours production.

Required: Compute each individual's gross wages, applying the contract provisions and incentive wage plans.   *(AICPA adapted)*

3-7. Payroll calculation and distribution; overtime and idle time. A rush order was accepted by the Hi-Way Trailer Company for five trailers. The time tickets and clock cards for the week ended March 27 show the following:

		Time Tickets — Hour Distribution				
Employees	Clock Hours	Trailer #1	Trailer #2	Trailer #3	Trailer #4	Trailer #5
Able (Supervisor)	42					
Braun	45	10	10	10	10	5
Calvo	48	24	24			
Davy	48			24	24	
Swenson	45	15	15	15		
Tsai	42	24	8			
Voll	40	20	10			

All employees are paid $9.25 per hour, except Able, who receives $12 per hour. All overtime premium pay except Able's is chargeable to the job and all employees, including Able, receive time and a half for overtime hours.

Required: (1) Calculate the total payroll and total net earnings for the week. Assume that an 18% deduction for federal income tax is required in addition to FICA deductions. Assume that none of the employees has achieved the maximums for FICA and unemployment taxes. Hours not worked on trailers are idle time and are not charged to the job. (2) Prepare the general journal entries to record and pay the payroll. (3) Distribute the payroll to the appropriate accounts. (4) Determine the dollar amount of labor that is chargeable to each trailer, assuming the overtime costs are proportionate to the regular hours used on the trailers.

3-8. Allocating overtime premium and bonus costs. The Lindale Manufacturing Company uses a job order cost system to cost its products. It recently signed a new contract with the union that calls for time and a half for all work over 40 hours a week and double time for Saturday and Sunday. Also, a bonus of 1% of the employees' earnings for the year is to be paid to the employees at the end of the fiscal year. The controller, the plant manager, and the sales manager disagree as to how the overtime pay and the bonus should be allocated.

An examination of the first month's payroll under the new union contract provisions shows the following:

Direct labor:		
Regular — 40,200 hours @ $8		$321,600
Overtime:		
Weekdays — 1,700 hours @ $12	$20,400	
Saturdays — 400 hours @ $16	6,400	
Sundays — 300 hours @ $16	4,800	31,600
Indirect labor		14,800
		$368,000

Analysis of the payroll supporting documents revealed:

(a) More production was scheduled each day than could be handled in a regular work day, resulting in the need for overtime.

(b) The Saturday and Sunday hours resulted from rush orders with special contract arrangements with the customers.

The controller believes that the overtime premiums and the bonus should be charged to factory overhead and spread over all production of the accounting period, regardless of when the jobs were completed.

The plant manager favors charging the overtime premiums directly to the jobs worked on during overtime hours and the bonus to administrative expense.

The sales manager states that the overtime premiums and bonus are not factory costs chargeable to regular production but are costs created from administrative policies and, therefore, should be charged only to administrative expense.

Required: (1) Evaluate each position — the controller's, the plant manager's, and the sales manager's. If you disagree with all of the positions taken, present your view of the appropriate allocation. **(2)** Prepare the journal entries to illustrate the position you support.

3-9. Calculating payroll and correcting payroll and tax accounts. A company's controller has requested a review of the financial statements regarding wage and salary tax computations. The company's general ledger accounts for salary and payroll taxes are as follows:

EMPLOYEES' FICA AND INCOME TAXES PAYABLE	
	19A
	Jan. 1 Balance
	forward 6,200

EMPLOYER'S FICA AND UNEMPLOYMENT TAXES PAYABLE	
	19A
	Jan. 1 Balance
	forward 1,900

WAGES AND SALARY EXPENSE	
19A	
Dec. 31 Total of	
12	
monthly	
summary	
entries 65,884	

PAYROLL TAXES EXPENSE	
19A	
Jan. 10 Quarterly	
payment 7,348	
Apr. 20 Quarterly	
payment 10,525	
July 14 Quarterly	
payment 9,846	
Oct. 18 Quarterly	
payment 9,644	

An investigation reveals the following additional data:

(a) Copies of the quarterly tax returns are not available, because the typist did not understand that the returns were to be typed in duplicate. The pencil drafts of the tax returns were discarded.

(b) The payroll records reveal that the payroll clerk properly computed the payroll tax deductions and the amounts of quarterly remittances. The following summary is developed:

Quarter	Gross Wages and Salaries	Taxes Withheld		Net Wages and Salaries
		FICA 7%	Income Tax	
First	$23,600	$1,652	$6,600	$15,348
Second	22,000	1,540	6,280	14,180
Third	22,800	1,596	6,128	15,076
Fourth	28,700	1,050	7,122	20,528

(c) The company did not make monthly deposits of taxes withheld. The following remittances were made with respect to 19A payrolls:

	Apr. 20, 19A	July 14, 19A	Oct. 18, 19A	Jan. 12, 19B
FICA — 14%	$ 3,304	$3,080	$3,192	$2,100
Income tax	6,600	6,280	6,128	7,122
State unemployment tax — 2.7%	621	486	324	162
Total	$10,525	$9,846	$9,644	$9,384

(d) The federal unemployment tax rate for 19A is .7% on salaries and wages up to a maximum of $6,000.

Required: (1) Prepare a work sheet to determine the correct balances at December 31, 19A, for the general ledger accounts, Wages and Salary Expense, Payroll Taxes Expense, Employees' FICA and Income Taxes Payable, and Employer's FICA and Unemployment Taxes Payable. (Disregard accrued wages and salaries at year-end.) **(2)** Prepare an adjusting entry to correct the accounts at December 31, 19A.

(AICPA adapted)

3-10. Estimating labor costs for bids. The Laurien Manufacturing Company prepares cost estimates for projects on which it will bid. In order to anticipate the labor cost to be included in a request to bid on a contract for 1,200,000 units which will be delivered to the customer at the rate of 100,000 units per month, the company has compiled the following data related to labor:

(a) The first 100,000 units will require 5 hours per unit.
(b) The second 100,000 units will require less labor due to the skills learned on the first 100,000 units finished. It is expected that labor time will be reduced by 10% if an incentive bonus of one-half of the labor savings is paid to the employees.
(c) For the remaining 1,000,000 it is expected that the labor time will be reduced 15% from the original estimate (the first 100,000 units) if the same incentive bonus (½ of the savings) is paid to the employees.
(d) Overtime premiums are to be excluded when savings are computed.

The contract will require 2,500 employees at a base rate of $8.00 per hour with time and a half for overtime. The plant operates on a 5-day, 40-hour-per-week basis. Employees are paid for a two-week vacation in August and for eight holidays.

The scheduled production for the 50-week work-year shows:

January–June: 26 weeks with 4 holidays
July–December: 24 weeks with 4 holidays

Required: Prepare cost estimates for direct labor and labor related costs for the contract showing:

(1) Wages paid at the regular rate.
(2) Overtime premium payments.
(3) Incentive bonus payments.
(4) Vacation and holiday pay.
(5) Employer's payroll taxes (10.4% of wages).

3-11. Summary of payroll procedures. An analysis of the time tickets for the month of November of the Georgetown Manufacturing Co. reveals the information shown:

Employee Name	11/8	11/15	11/22	11/29
A. Duvall	$148	$130	$150	$160
B. Jacobs	140	130	120	140
C. Kissel	150	130	160	140
D. Moreno	950	950	950	950
X. Skelly	400	380	440	460

Gross Earnings* — Week Ending

*All regular time

Duvall, Jacobs, and Kissell are production workers, and Moreno is the supervisor of the group. Skelly is in charge of the office.

Cumulative earnings paid (before deductions) in this calendar year prior to the payroll period ending November 8 were as follows: Duvall, $5,920; Jacobs, $5,700; Kissel, $5,510; Moreno, $38,000; and Skelly, $17,000.

Required: (1) Draft the following forms, using the indicated column headings:

Payroll Record
  Employee's Name
  Gross Earnings
  Withholdings (2 columns):
    FICA Tax
    Income tax (10%)
  Net Amount Paid

Employee Earnings Record
  Week Ending
  Weekly Gross Earnings
  Accumulated Gross Earnings
  Weekly Earnings Subject to FICA
  Withholdings (2 columns):
    FICA Tax
    Income Tax
  Net Amount Paid

Labor Cost Summary
  Week Ending
  Dr. Work in Process (Direct Labor)
  Dr. Factory Overhead (Indirect Labor)
  Dr. Administrative Salaries (Office)
  Cr. Payroll (Total)

Using these forms prepare the following: **(2)** An employee's earnings record for each of the five employees; **(3)** A payroll record for each of the four weeks; and **(4)** A labor cost summary for the month. **(5)** Prepare the entry, in general journal form, to record:

  (a) The payroll for each of the four weeks.
  (b) The payment of wages for each of the four payrolls.
  (c) The distribution of the monthly labor costs per the labor cost summary.
  (d) The company's payroll taxes covering the four payroll periods.

3-12. Summary of payroll procedures. The Paxton Construction Co. uses the job order cost system. In recording payroll transactions, the following accounts are used:

Cash
Vouchers Payable
FICA Tax Payable
Federal Unemployment Tax Payable
State Unemployment Tax Payable
Employees Income Tax Payable
Payroll

Administrative Salaries
Miscellaneous Administrative
  Expense
Sales Salaries
Miscellaneous Selling Expense
Factory Overhead
Work in Process

Factory employees are paid weekly, while all other employees are paid semimonthly on the fifteenth and the last day of each month. Amounts withheld from the earnings of the employees, income taxes and FICA taxes, are recorded in special columns of the voucher register at the time of recording the payroll vouchers.

Following is a narrative of transactions completed during the month of March:

Mar. 7 Issued payroll voucher for the total earnings of factory employees amounting to $31,400 less deductions for employees' income taxes and FICA taxes.

     7 Issued check for payment of the payroll voucher.

   14 Issued payroll voucher for the total earnings of factory employees

amounting to $26,300 less deductions for employees' income taxes and FICA taxes.

14 Issued check for payment of the payroll voucher.

15 Issued voucher covering administrative salaries, $5,500, and sales salaries, $8,250, less deductions for employees' income taxes and FICA taxes.

15 Issued check for payment of the salary voucher.

21 Issued payroll voucher for the total earnings of factory employees amounting to $28,500 less deductions for employees' income taxes and FICA taxes.

21 Issued check for payment of the payroll voucher.

28 Issued payroll voucher for the total earnings of factory employees amounting to $29,600 less deductions for employees' income taxes and FICA taxes.

28 Issued check for payment of the payroll voucher.

31 Issued voucher covering administrative salaries, $5,500, and sales salaries, $8,250, less deductions for employees' income taxes and FICA taxes.

31 Issued check for payment of the salary voucher.

31 The following wages and salaries were earned or accrued during March:

Direct labor	$117,500
Indirect labor	10,250
Administrative salaries	11,000
Sales salaries	16,500
Total	$155,250

The following form is used by The Paxton Construction Co. to compute the amount of payroll taxes incurred:

Items	Taxable Earnings		FICA	FUTA	State Unemployment Tax	Total Taxes Imposed on Employer
	FICA	FUTA				
Factory wages	12,750 00	127,750 00				
Administrative salaries						
Sales salaries						
Total	155,250 00	155,250 00				

Required: (1) Complete the above form to show the payroll taxes imposed on the employer for the month of March. (Reproduce the above form and show your solution on loose-leaf stationery.) **(2)** Prepare the entries, in general journal form, to record the foregoing transactions and payroll taxes, assuming that the payroll taxes imposed on the employer for factory wages are to be charged to Factory Overhead; the taxes for administrative salaries are to be charged to Miscellaneous Administrative Expense; and the taxes for sales salaries are to be charged to Miscellaneous Selling Expense. **(3)** Assume the factory employees worked on March 29, 30, and 31. What was the amount of accrued wages on March 31?

4

Accounting for Factory Overhead

All costs incurred in the factory that are not chargeable directly to the finished product are generally termed **factory overhead**. These operating costs of the factory cannot be traced specifically to a unit of production. A variety of terms have been used to describe this type of cost, such as *supplementary costs, indirect expenses, indirect manufacturing costs, factory overhead expenses,* or *factory burden*. These costs are also referred to simply as "overhead" or "burden." One method used to determine whether a cost is a factory overhead cost is to determine whether it is a direct materials cost or a direct labor cost. If the cost cannot be charged to either of these two "direct" factory accounts, it must be charged to factory overhead. Factory overhead costs include (1) indirect materials consumed, such as cleaning materials and lubricants; (2) indirect labor, such as overtime premiums and the wages of janitors, elevator operators, and supervisors; and (3) all indirect manufacturing expenses such as rent, insurance, property tax, depreciation, and heat, light, and power.

Accounting for factory overhead involves the following:

(1) Identifying cost behavior patterns
(2) Budgeting factory overhead costs
(3) Accounting for actual factory overhead
(4) Applying factory overhead
(5) Calculating budget variances and volume variances

135

IDENTIFYING COST BEHAVIOR PATTERNS

Direct materials and direct labor tend to vary as production varies and, therefore, can be easily classified as variable costs. Factory overhead costs, however, include some items that vary directly with the volume of production, some items that remain constant even when production levels change, and some items that appear to be erratic because they change in irregular patterns as production increases or decreases. Factory overhead costs, therefore, create a difficult problem for most companies because it is essential in production forecasts to predict the costs that can be expected at the production levels anticipated. The factory overhead costs that behave in the <u>same behavior pattern</u> as direct materials and direct labor are classified as **variable overhead costs** and they can be readily forecast because they move up or down proportionate to production changes. The factory overhead costs that remain unchanged and are classified as **fixed overhead costs** can also be anticipated because they remain at a given level even though the level of production changes. It is the group of factory overhead costs that change in rather unpredictable patterns, which are usually referred to as **semi-variable overhead costs**, that require special attention when attempts to forecast costs are made.

These basic cost patterns, plotted against volume, are shown in Illustration 4-1.

ILLUSTRATION 4-1

Cost Behavior Patterns

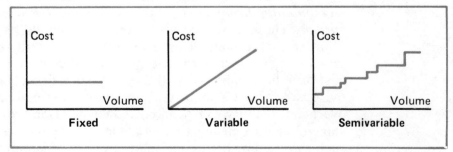

Examples of variable, fixed, and semivariable factory overhead costs are:

Variable: Power paid for in accordance with consumption, depreciation computed on a usage basis, repairs directly related to usage, supplies, spoilage, consumable small tools expense.

Fixed: Factory property taxes, depreciation computed on a straight-line basis, periodic rent payments, production executives' salaries, insurance.

Semivariable:

Type A: Will change at various levels of production. They remain constant until a certain level of production is reached, then will increase. The increase is not continuous but will plateau until another more advanced level of production is reached, then they will increase again.

Examples are: inspection and handling costs, factory supervision, indirect labor, indirect material, factory personnel costs.

Type B: Will vary continuously but not in proportion (ratio) to volume changes.

Examples are: fuel costs, power costs, maintenance of factory equipment.

The composition of semivariable costs makes predicting of a certain amount of semivariable cost at a given level of production very difficult. However, by isolating the fixed and variable components of the semivariable cost, forecasting overhead for expected levels of production within the usual operating (relevant) range removes, to a degree, some of the uncertainty involved with the prediction. There are several methods for isolating the fixed and variable elements of a semivariable expense. Many executives still rely on the **observation method**. The reaction of a semivariable expense to past changes in production is analyzed by reviewing the cost data for the semivariable item being studied. The relationship of the expense change to the production change is examined by observation. A decision is then made, subjectively, that the observed semivariable cost will be treated like a variable item because it was more proportional to the change in the level of production than a fixed cost or the decision could be to treat it like a fixed cost. The analyzed overhead expense will thereafter be treated like any other variable or fixed cost until another study is believed necessary. When this method is used, management does so in the belief that the discrepancy between the actual costs and the forecasted costs will be insignificant and will not affect management strategies of operations.

The observation method is probably still the most popular method for many companies but the present era, which emphasizes quantification of business data, has in recent years given more and more attention to mathematical methods. The two most widely discussed methods are **high-low** and **least squares**. Both methods isolate one of the elements, then suggest the remainder of the cost is the other element. Both use historic cost patterns to predict the future cost patterns, although adjustments can be made when obvious changes seem warranted. Before discussing the mathematical methods, it should be recognized that the limitations that apply to all "looking-to-the-future" techniques also apply to these methods. The fact that a great deal of time and energy may be put into the formulation of a forecast does not necessarily mean that a better forecast can be automatically expected. It is not the formula or the equation that insures accuracy, it is the input data used with the method that make the forecast accurate or inaccurate. The way a cost or expense reacted to a past change in production may or may not prove to be the same behavior pattern in the future. Usually the historic cost behavior patterns will carry forward into the future periods. It is for this reason the mathematical methods are often recommended instead of the more intuitive observation method.

High-Low Method

The **high-low method** compares a high volume and its related cost to a low volume with its related cost. The difference in volume between the two points is compared to the difference in costs. It is assumed that all costs between these two points are linear and will fall along a straight line.

To illustrate, assume the following costs were incurred at production levels of 1,000, 2,000, and 3,000 units:

	1,000 Units	2,000 Units	3,000 Units
Depreciation (fixed)	$1,000	$1,000	$1,000
Inspection costs (semivariable)	1,500	1,800	2,000
Factory supplies (variable)	1,000	2,000	3,000

Depreciation is a fixed cost and remained unchanged. Factory supplies varied proportionately with the change in volume. Inspection costs, however, were neither fixed nor did they change proportionately with volume. By using the high-low technique, part of the inspection cost will be considered variable and the remaining part fixed:

Variable Element:

		Units	Cost
High volume		3,000	$2,000
Low volume		1,000	1,500
Difference		2,000	$ 500

Variable cost per unit ($500 ÷ 2,000 units) = $.25

Fixed Element:

	1,000 Units	3,000 Units
Cost..	$1,500	$2,000
Variable element @ $.25 per unit....................	250	750
Fixed cost (remainder).................................	$1,250	$1,250

(handwritten margin notes: 2000 u, 1800, 500, 1300)

Least Squares Method

The **least squares method** is a more refined statistical technique that usually results in a more reliable separation of the variable and fixed elements than the high-low method. The least squares method is conceptually similar to a scatter-diagram method of estimating the straight line along which the semivariable costs will fall. In the **scatter-graph method** the observations of cost and production data are plotted on graph paper and only intuitive judgment is used to draw a line with an equal number of observations on either side. Then, two points are selected on the line, and the high-low method is used to determine the variable and fixed elements.

However, the least squares method uses a mathematical procedure, rather than intuitive judgment, to determine the cost of the element. As shown in Illustration 4-2, a straight line (regression line) is fitted to the observed data in a manner which minimizes the sum of the squared deviations between the observed data and the fitted line.

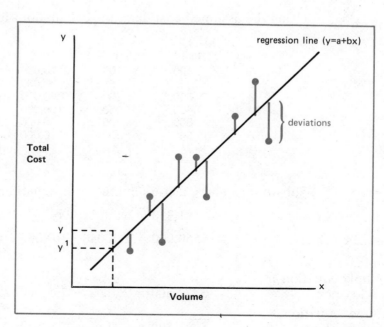

ILLUSTRATION 4-2

Least Squares
Method

The term *least squares* is derived from the process of minimizing the sum of the squares of the deviations. The line fitted to the calculated points represents an equation in which the sum of the squared deviations is a minimum.

One method of calculating the regression line is to solve two simultaneous equations to determine the fixed cost and the variable cost elements for each unit of activity.

The equations are:

$$\Sigma y = na + b\Sigma x$$
$$\Sigma xy = a\Sigma x + b\Sigma x^2$$
$$x = \text{number of units}$$
$$y = \text{total cost at a given production level}$$
$$n = \text{number of observations}$$
$$a = \text{fixed cost}$$
$$b = \text{variable cost per unit of production}$$

Assume the following cost data for a six month period:

Month	Units of Production	Semivariable Cost
1	100	$100
2	200	150
3	300	200
4	400	250
5	500	300
6	600	350

Using the assumed cost data, the calculations are as follows:

Month	x Units	y Cost	xy	x²
1	100	$ 100	$ 10,000	10,000
2	200	150	30,000	40,000
3	300	200	60,000	90,000
4	400	250	100,000	160,000
5	500	300	150,000	250,000
6	600	350	210,000	360,000
Total	2,100	$1,350	$560,000	910,000

Substitute *x* and *y* factors in the linear equations:

1 $\Sigma y = na + b\Sigma x$	$1,350 = 6a + 2,100b$	Equation 1
2 $\Sigma xy = a\Sigma x + b\Sigma x^2$	$560,000 = 2,100a + 910,000b$	Equation 2

To eliminate a:
multiply equation 1
by 350, then

$$\$472,500 = 2,100a + 735,000b \qquad \text{Equation 3}$$

subtract equation 3
from equation 2.

$$\$\ 87,500 = -0- + 175,000b \qquad \text{Equation 4}$$

Solve equation 4 for b:

$$\$175,000b = \$87,500$$
$$b = \$.50 \text{ variable cost}$$
$$\text{per unit of production}$$

Solve for a by substituting
$.50 for b in either
equation 1 or 2:

$$\$1,350 = 6a + 2,100(.50) \qquad \text{Equation 1}$$
$$\$1,350 = 6a + \$1,050$$
$$6a = \$1,350 - \$1,050$$
$$a = \$50 \text{ fixed cost}$$

The computations for a and b establish the values for the fixed and variable components in the semivariable costs. Using the calculated values, $a = \$50$ fixed cost per month and $b = \$.50$ variable cost per unit, the composition of the semivariable cost could be shown as follows:

$$2,100 \text{ units @ \$.50 per unit} = \$1,050 \text{ variable cost}$$
$$6 \text{ months @ \$50 per month} = \underline{300} \text{ fixed cost}$$
$$\text{Total semivariable cost} = \underline{\$1,350}$$

Using the same cost data, the fixed and variable components can be calculated in the following manner without using the equations:

	Column 1	Column 2	Column 3	Column 4	Column 5	Column 6
		Deviations from		Deviations from		Column 2
	Units (Volume)	Average of x	Cost	Average of y	Column 2	Times
	x	in Column 1	y	in Column 3	Squared	Column 4
	100	−250	$ 100	$−125	62,500	$31,250
	200	−150	150	− 75	22,500	11,250
	300	− 50	200	− 25	2,500	1,250
	400	+ 50	250	+ 25	2,500	1,250
	500	+150	300	+ 75	22,500	11,250
	600	+250	350	+125	62,500	31,250
Total	2,100	—0—	$1,350	—0—	175,000	$87,500
Average	350		$ 225			

The variable cost $b = \dfrac{\text{Column 6}}{\text{Column 5}} = \dfrac{\$\ 87,500}{175,000}$

$$b = \$.50 \text{ variable cost per unit of production}$$

The fixed element is calculated by substituting the average of x (Column 1) and the average of y (Column 3) in the equation for a straight line, $y = a + bx$, as follows:

$$y = a + bx$$
$$\$225 = a + 350(.50)$$
$$a = \$50 \text{ fixed cost}$$

Limitations of High-Low and Least Squares Methods

Both the high-low and least squares methods use historical cost patterns to predict future cost patterns, and are thus subject to the limitations that apply to all forecasting techniques. The use of mathematical techniques does not insure an accurate forecast. The accuracy of a forecast depends on the validity of the data used with the method.

Cost analysis requires that all costs be segregated into two categories: variable and fixed. The semivariable costs, therefore, must be analyzed and subdivided. The high-low method bases its solution on two observations and assumes that all other unanalyzed volumes will fall along a straight line between these observations. Such an assumption is highly unrealistic, however, because two observations from a group of data will not likely be representative. Nevertheless, the method may be considered reliable if additional observations are analyzed, two at a time, and the results are approximately the same as those given by the first observations.

The least squares method presents a solution that has been calculated with mathematical precision; however, caution must be used before accepting the results as being reliable because the method can fit a straight line to any set of cost data. The equations used in the calculations may give the impression of accuracy which may not be justified. If invalid data are used in the calculations, no known mathematical technique will produce a reliable solution.

Both methods stress the importance of the relationship of cost factors to volume; however, many other factors may affect cost behavior and should not be ignored. For example, consideration should also be given to price changes and changes in technological methods. Generalizations about cost patterns should be avoided because only a few costs have inherent characteristics; most costs are directly influenced by managerial policies.

BUDGETING FACTORY OVERHEAD COSTS

Budgets are management's operating plans expressed in quantitative terms — units of production and related costs. After management is satisfied that all factory overhead costs are properly classified as either fixed or variable, factory overhead costs can be projected or "budgeted" for expected levels of production. The isolation of fixed and variable cost components permits the company to prepare a **flexible budget** which shows the expected factory overhead at any anticipated level of production.

Assume that management wishes to budget expected factory overhead costs at three levels of production — 50,000, 60,000, and 70,000 units. Analysis indicates that variable factory overhead cost per unit is $5, and the total fixed factory overhead cost is $100,000. These data are reflected in a flexible budget as follows:

Units...	50,000	60,000	70,000
Variable cost @ $5/unit..................	$250,000	$300,000	$350,000
Fixed cost.....................................	100,000	100,000	100,000
Total factory overhead	$350,000	$400,000	$450,000
Factory overhead per unit..............	$7.00	$6.67	$6.43

The reduction in factory overhead cost per unit as production volume increases is caused by the spreading of the total fixed cost of $100,000 over an increasing quantity of units. The variable cost stays constant at $5 per unit throughout the range of production. At the 50,000-unit level of production, fixed cost will add $2 ($100,000 ÷ 50,000 units) to the total unit cost, but only $1.67 ($100,000 ÷ 60,000 units) and $1.43 ($100,000 ÷ 70,000) at the higher volumes.

Budgeting is a valuable tool for planning and controlling costs. A flexible budget aids management in establishing realistic production goals and in comparing actual costs with budgeted costs. Differences (variances) between actual and budgeted costs are discussed in a later section of this chapter.

ACCOUNTING FOR ACTUAL FACTORY OVERHEAD

Accounting systems are designed to accumulate and classify the factory overhead costs actually incurred. The specific procedures used to account for actual factory overhead costs depend on the nature and organization of the manufacturing firm.

In a small manufacturing company having only one production department, the factory overhead may be accounted for in much the same manner as the selling and administrative expenses. All the factory overhead accounts may be kept in the general ledger. However, separate accounts should be kept for indirect materials, indirect labor, and for each of the indirect manufacturing expenses.

The costs of indirect materials and indirect labor are first recorded in the general journal. The sources of these entries are the summary of materials issued and returned and the labor cost summary. If the voucher system is used, other factory overhead expenses are first recorded in the voucher register from which they are posted to the appropriate accounts in the general ledger. The sources of these entries are the invoices received by the company.

Schedules of fixed costs may be prepared and used as the source of general journal entries to record the amount of taxes, depreciation, insurance, and other similar expenses at the end of each accounting period.

A change in the accounting system is necessary when the factory overhead accounts are numerous. Rather than maintain individual accounts in the general ledger, a factory overhead subsidiary ledger is kept, with a control account in the general ledger. The subsidiary ledger is known as the **factory overhead ledger** and the control account in the general ledger is titled Factory Overhead. This system requires a special column in the voucher register in which all vouchered factory overhead expenses are entered. The column total is posted to the debit side of the control account at the end of each accounting period. All entries in the voucher register representing items of factory overhead are posted either individually or in total to the appropriate accounts in the subsidiary factory overhead ledger. At the end of each accounting period the balance of the factory overhead control account should be proved by comparing its balance to the total factory overhead account balances taken from the subsidiary ledger.

Individual accounts in the factory overhead ledger should be given titles that are clearly descriptive of the nature of the expense. Following are examples of some of the typical factory overhead expenses which might be encountered:

Defective workmanship	Overtime premium
Depreciation	Plant protection
First-aid service	Power
Fuel consumed	Property tax
Heat and light	Rentals
Indirect labor	Repairs
Indirect materials	Shop supplies used
Insurance	Spoilage
Janitorial service	Telephone
Lubricants	Trucking expense
Maintenance	Water
Materials handling	Worker's compensation insurance
Nondurable tools	

In addition to these expenses which are related to the operation of the factory and the manufacturing process, the factory overhead will include the company's cost of employee fringe benefits. These benefits include paid vacations and holidays, paid sick leave, pensions, bonuses, profit sharing plans, group life insurance, group medical and hospitalization insurance, credit unions, free physical examinations, payment of tuition for education, recreational activities, and other services. Fringe benefits may also include the employer's cost for FICA and state and federal unemployment taxes.

Departmentalizing Factory Overhead

In a relatively large manufacturing company with several departments, the accounting system is usually designed to accumulate costs by department. Separate budgets may also be prepared for each department and combined in a master budget. Actual costs can thus be readily compared with budgeted costs for each department.

Each factory overhead expense should be given careful consideration to determine the kind and amount of expense to charge to each department. For example, the total amount of depreciation for the entire factory must be determined; but it is also necessary to determine how much of the total depreciation should be charged to each department. This distribution requires more analysis; therefore, accounting methods must be developed which provide the required data promptly and accurately.

There are several methods which can be used to make the required analysis of factory overhead. One of these methods is to expand the factory overhead ledger to include a separate account for each department's share of each kind of expense. For example, instead of having one account for indirect materials, the ledger could contain the following accounts: Indirect Materials — Department A, Indirect Materials — Department B, Indirect Materials — Department C, Indirect Materials — Building Maintenance Department, and so on, for every department that uses indirect materials. The total number of accounts required is approximately equal to the number of types of expenses multiplied by the number of departments. This method is often used in a moderate size entity with few expense accounts and only three or four departments.

In a large enterprise this method of recording factory overhead would be unwieldy. Several hundred accounts would be required, so that valuable time would be lost in preparing analytical work sheets at the end of each accounting period.

Standing Orders. Instead of using conventional ledger sheets, **analysis ledger sheets** may be used to keep a subsidiary record of factory overhead expenses. A separate analysis ledger sheet is used to record each type of expense, with individual columns that show a departmental classification of the expense; or a separate analysis ledger sheet is used for each department with individual columns that show an expense classification. Factory overhead accounts kept in analysis sheet form are commonly referred to as **standing orders**. The term "standing order" probably originated from the fact that factory overhead is usually distributed among departments in accordance with standing instructions based on such things as time studies or area measurements. These orders remain unchanged until a new classification of accounts is prepared.

Illustration 4-3 shows a standard form of an analysis ledger sheet used to keep an individual record of each kind of factory overhead expense. The **expense-type** sheet is ruled to provide a separate amount column for each department, making it possible to distribute expenses on a departmental basis as expenses are recorded. Since each column represents a different department, each analysis sheet takes the place of as many separate accounts as there are departments in the factory. In the illustration, depreciation, a fixed expense, is distributed by multiplying the plant and equipment valuation in each department (A: $1,000; B: $875; C: $875; D: $2,000) by the rate of depreciation (20%) applicable to the property. The source of the posting is an entry in the general journal to record the estimated depreciation for the month of January.

Account No. *3111*						**Distribution Base:** *Valuation of Plant and Equipment*							
Account *Depreciation*													
DEPARTMENTAL ANALYSIS				Date		Description	Post. Ref.	Debit		Credit		Balance	
Dept. A	Dept. B	Dept. C	Dept. D										
200 00	175 00	175 00	400 00	Jan.	31	Depreciation for January	GJ	950 00				950 00

ILLUSTRATION 4-3   Factory Overhead Analysis Ledger Sheet — Expense Type

Illustration 4-4 shows a standard form of analysis ledger sheet used to keep a record of the operations of each department. The **department-type** sheet is ruled to provide a separate amount column for each kind of expense incurred, making it possible to distribute the expenses on a departmental basis as the expenses are recorded. Since each column represents a different kind of expense, each analysis sheet takes the place of as many separate accounts as there are expenses in the factory. All of the expenses incurred for the benefit of Department A during the month of January are shown recorded in the illustration. Only the totals are entered. Vouchered expenses are posted from the books of original entry either in total or as of the date they are incurred, and the fixed expenses are posted from the general journal at the end of the month.

FACTORY OVERHEAD — DEPARTMENT A						
Indirect Materials No. 311.1	Indirect Labor No. 311.12	Power No. 311.13	Depreciation No. 311.18	Factory Property Tax No. 311.20	Insurance No. 311.30	General Factory Expenses No. 311.50
100 00	200 00	125 00	200 00	190 00	160 00	115 00

(Left-hand page)

FACTORY OVERHEAD — DEPARTMENT A							
Misc. Factory Expenses							
Account No.	Amount	Date	Description	Post. Ref.	Debit	Credit	Balance
		Jan. 31	Total expenses – January Dept A		1,090 00		1,090 00

(Right-hand page)

ILLUSTRATION 4-4   Factory Overhead Analysis Ledger Sheet — Department Type

Regardless of whether separate analysis ledger sheets are used for each kind of factory overhead expense or for each department, either analysis sheet serves as a subsidiary ledger controlled by the factory overhead account in the general ledger. The advantage of using an analysis ledger sheet for each kind of expense, classified by departments, is to provide only as many amount columns as there are departments within the factory (see Illustration 4-3). However, a summary must be prepared at the end of each accounting period to determine the total expenses incurred for each department.

The advantage of using an analysis ledger sheet for each department, classified by kinds of expense, is that fewer sheets are required and it is not necessary to prepare a summary at the end of each accounting period (see Illustration 4-4). When the factory is departmentalized, the factory overhead must be recorded to determine the total cost of operating each department.

To illustrate a departmental analysis ledger sheet, assume that the Cortez Manufacturing Company has four departments: A, B, C, and D. A factory overhead control account is kept in the general ledger, and an overhead analysis ledger sheet is prepared at the beginning of each period for each department. In the voucher register, a special amount column is used for factory overhead.

Lubricating oil, an indirect material, is issued from the storeroom on a requisition form that shows the department to which the oil is issued. The requisition shows that lubricants costing $100 were issued to Department A. The amount is entered in the Indirect Materials column of the expense analysis ledger sheet for Department A (see Illustration 4-4).

Idle time, an indirect cost, occurs when a machine operator, for lack of work, remains idle for part of a day. For example, if a worker in Department B, whose hourly rate of pay is $4, was idle for two hours during the day, the idle time cost of $8 would be entered in the Indirect Labor column of the expense analysis ledger sheet for Department B.

Assume that an invoice for $50 is received from an outside company which was engaged to repair a machine in Department C. The repair cost is an indirect factory overhead expense. A voucher is prepared identifying the department in which the work was done, and the amount is entered in the voucher register in a column titled Factory Overhead. The voucher, or a memorandum, is then sent to the accountant in charge of the factory overhead ledger who enters the expense in the Misc. Factory Expenses column of the expense analysis ledger sheet for Department C.

In the manufacturing process, power is used in Departments A, B, C, and D and the total cost of the power, $500, is distributed evenly among the four departments according to standing orders. After a voucher is prepared, the amount is entered in the voucher register in the Factory Overhead column. The voucher, or a memorandum, is then sent to the accountant who records the expense of $125 for Departments A, B, C, and D in the column titled Power (See Illustration 4-4).

Cost accounting records should show factory overhead expenses by type and by department. Accounts are maintained to show the total amount of each type of overhead incurred in each department. By periodically studying these records of factory overhead, management should be able to keep overhead costs at minimum levels.

Schedule of Fixed Costs. The usual feature of fixed costs is that within limits, they do not vary in amount from month to month; furthermore, as in the case of insurance or property tax, most fixed costs are either prepaid or accrued. Since they do not vary greatly, it is possible to determine in advance what the amount of expense will be for items such as insurance, property tax, rent, and depreciation. Thus, a **schedule of fixed costs** similar to the one shown in Illustration 4-5, can be prepared in advance for several periods, usually a year. By referring to the schedule at the end of a period, the accoun-

SCHEDULE OF FIXED COSTS						
Item of Cost	January	February	March	April	May	June
Depreciation:						
Dept. A	$ 200.00	$ 200.00	$ 200.00	$ 200.00	$ 200.00	$ 200.00
Dept. B	175.00	175.00	175.00	175.00	175.00	175.00
Dept. C	175.00	175.00	175.00	175.00	175.00	175.00
Dept. D	400.00	400.00	400.00	400.00	400.00	400.00
Total................	$ 950.00	$ 950.00	$ 950.00	$ 950.00	$ 950.00	$ 950.00
Property tax:						
Dept. A	$ 190.00	$ 190.00	$ 190.00	$ 190.00	$ 190.00	$ 190.00
Dept. B	175.00	175.00	175.00	175.00	175.00	175.00
Dept. C	150.00	150.00	150.00	150.00	150.00	150.00
Dept. D	185.00	185.00	185.00	185.00	185.00	185.00
Total................	$ 700.00	$ 700.00	$ 700.00	$ 700.00	$ 700.00	$ 700.00
Insurance:						
Dept. A	$ 160.00	$ 160.00	$ 160.00	$ 160.00	$ 160.00	$ 160.00
Dept. B	145.00	145.00	145.00	145.00	145.00	145.00
Dept. C	115.00	115.00	115.00	115.00	115.00	115.00
Dept. D	180.00	180.00	180.00	180.00	180.00	180.00
Total................	$ 600.00	$ 600.00	$ 600.00	$ 600.00	$ 600.00	$ 600.00
Grand Total	$2,250.00	$2,250.00	$2,250.00	$2,250.00	$2,250.00	$2,250.00

ILLUSTRATION 4-5 Schedule of Fixed Costs

tant can obtain the figures for a journal entry to record the total fixed costs and at the same time post from the schedule to the departmental factory overhead analysis ledger sheets.

In illustration 4-5, the schedule of fixed costs shows that for the month of January, the expenses for depreciation of machinery total $950, divided among the four departments as follows: A, $200; B, $175; C, $175; D, $400. The schedule also shows the monthly departmental fixed costs for property tax and insurance.

At the end of January, the accountant would post from the schedule of fixed costs as follows:

To the factory overhead analysis sheet (Illustration 4-4) for Department A:

Depreciation (Col. 4)...	$200
Property Tax (Col. 5)	190
Insurance (Col. 6)..	160

To the factory overhead analysis sheet for Department B:

Depreciation (Col. 4)...	$175
Property Tax (Col. 5)	175
Insurance (Col. 6)..	145

A similar posting is made to the other departmental factory overhead analysis sheets. The following general journal entry is prepared from information shown in the schedule of fixed costs:

Jan. 31   Factory Overhead 2,250
              Accumulated Depreciation—Machinery.   950
              Accrued Property Tax   700
              Prepaid Insurance   600
              Fixed expenses for January.

General Factory Overhead Expenses. All factory overhead expenses are systematically recorded so that at the end of an accounting period all expenses chargeable to the period have been distributed among the various departments of the factory. The division is made in proportion to the measurable benefits received. However, certain items of factory overhead are such that no particular department can be said to receive a measurable amount of benefit from them. Instead, the factory as a whole is the beneficiary. An example is the salary of the superintendent, whose duty is to oversee all factory operations. Another example would be the wages of the company security guards.

Since factory overhead expenses of this general type cannot be clearly identified with a specific department, they are charged to the departments by a process of allocation. This allocation is usually made on some arbitrary basis such as each department's proportion of the total expenses identified as chargeable to the departments. The allocation may be made separately for each of the items of expense at the time it is incurred and recorded, or such expenses may be accumulated as they are incurred and the allocation of the total made at the end of the accounting period. If it is desired to make the allocation at the end of the period, a separate analysis ledger sheet is used to record each kind of general factory overhead expense incurred during the period. At the end of the period, the total is allocated to and recorded on the departmental analysis ledger sheets. The desirability of recording general factory overhead on a separate analysis ledger sheet depends on the frequency with which such expenses are incurred during the period.

Summary of Factory Overhead. All factory overhead expenses incurred during each accounting period, whether variable or fixed, are recorded both on the factory overhead analysis ledger sheets and in the factory overhead control account in the general ledger. After the posting is completed, the balance of the control account is proved by preparing a **summary of factory overhead** from the analysis ledger sheets. This summary may be prepared as shown in Illustration 4-6.

ILLUSTRATION 4-6

Summary of Factory
Overhead

SUMMARY OF FACTORY OVERHEAD For the Month Ended January 31, 19—					
Expenses	Departmental Classification				Total
	Dept. A	Dept. B	Dept. C	Dept. D	
Indirect materials	$ 100	$ 35	$ 25	$ 20	$ 180
Indirect labor	200	170	150	160	680
Power....................................	125	120	100	75	420
Depreciation	200	175	175	400	950
Factory property tax................	190	175	150	185	700
Insurance	160	145	115	180	600
General factory expenses.........	115	200	180	220	715
Total	$1,090	$1,020	$ 895	$1,240	$4,245

*subsid.
control*

Distributing Service Department Costs

A primary objective of all job order or process cost systems is to
determine the total cost of each completed job or unit of product. In
order to include factory overhead as part of the total cost, it is necessary first to ascertain the amount of expenses that each production
department incurred.

In a factory of any size, production consists of a series of operations performed in departments or cost centers. Departments are
usually divided into two classes, service and production. A **service
department** is essential to the functioning of the organization, but it
does not work on the product. The only function of a service department is to serve the needs of the production departments. The product thereby receives the benefit of the work performed by the service department. Examples of service departments are: a
department that generates power for the rest of the factory; a building maintenance department that is charged with the responsibility
of maintaining the buildings in good repair; or the cost accounting
department that maintains the factory accounting records.

A **production department** is one in which actual manufacturing
operations are performed, and the units being processed are physi-
cally changed. Since the production departments receive the benefit
of the work performed by the service departments, the total cost of
production must include not only the costs charged directly to the
production departments but also a share of the costs of operating the
service departments. The total product costs should therefore include a share of service department costs. One method of adding

these costs to the cost of the product is to distribute the service department costs to the production departments on some equitable basis.

Distributing the costs of the service departments involves analysis and apportionment. The cost of operating each service department should be distributed to the production departments in proportion to the benefit that each service department renders to each production department. The apportionment of service department costs is complicated because some service departments render service to other service departments as well as to the production departments. The cost of operating a service department should be divided fairly among the departments it serves.

The first step in making the distribution is to determine how the service department divides its services among the other departments. Sometimes a division can be determined accurately, but often the distribution must be based on an approximation. For example, the power department may be furnishing power for the operation of the machines and the lighting of the buildings and grounds. If the power used in each of the departments passes through a meter as it is received in the department, the meters can be read at the end of the period and the various departments charged with the exact amount of power used. These charges to the departments are **direct distributions**.

On the other hand, a department such as the building maintenance department which keeps the building clean and in repair cannot use an exact method to determine just how much benefit each of the other departments has received from it. The cost of operating the building maintenance department is therefore distributed on some basis that fairly divides its cost among the other departments, similar to the manner in which general factory overhead expenses are allocated to various departments.

Following is a list of some typical service departments and the common bases for distributing their costs to other departments:

Service Departments	Basis for Distribution
Building Maintenance	Floor space of other departments
Inspection and Packing	Amount of production
Machine Shop	Cost of machinery and equipment
Personnel	Total number of workers in the departments served
Purchasing	Cost of materials used
Shipping	Floor space of the other departments
Stores	Units of materials requisitioned
Tool	Total direct labor hours of all workers in the departments served

The type of work done by each department should be analyzed carefully, and a base should be selected that will increase or decrease in proportion to the increase or decrease in the benefits rendered. For example, in the preceding list, the suggested base for distributing the expense of operating the personnel department is the total number of workers in the department served. This is based on the assumption that the more workers there are in a department the more service that must be rendered to that department by the personnel staff. In the case of the tool room, the base suggested is the total direct labor hours of all workers in the department served. The theory for this basis is that usually only those who work directly on the manufactured product use tools. The cost of maintaining and repairing the tools used should therefore increase or decrease as the direct labor hours increase or decrease.

After selecting the basis of distribution for each service department, the next step is to distribute the total cost of each service department to the other departments. The following illustrates the problem:

(1) The maintenance department services the power plant building.
(2) The power department furnishes power for maintenance equipment used by the maintenance department.
(3) The power department and the maintenance department service the personnel department facilities.
(4) The personnel department services the power and maintenance departments through their functions of hiring personnel and maintaining the departments' personnel records.

Observations:

(1) Total maintenance department cost includes part of the total costs of the power department and the personnel department.
(2) Total power department cost includes part of the total costs of the maintenance and personnel departments.
(3) Total personnel department cost includes part of the total costs of the maintenance department and power department.

The first step is to compute the total cost of any one of these overlapping departments. At least three different methods may be used:

(1) Distribute service department costs to production departments only.
(2) Distribute service department costs regressively to remaining service departments, then to production departments. The sequence of service departments is established on the basis of:
(a) Service to other departments, or
(b) Magnitude of total costs in each service department.
(3) Distribute by algebraic procedures.

In the first method, no attempt is made to determine to what extent the service departments service each other. Instead of prorating the costs of the service department to other service departments as well as production departments, the service department costs are distributed directly to the production departments only. The results of using this method, while more easily attained, may not be as accurate as the other methods. The use of this method is justified on the basis that no material difference results in the total cost accumulated by the production departments.

The second method recognizes a partial interrelationship of the service departments. The Power Department costs are divided among the Personnel, Maintenance, and production departments. The Personnel Department costs (now including part of the Power Department costs) are divided among the Maintenance and production departments. Finally, the Maintenance Department costs are divided among the production departments. This method does not permit a transfer of costs to a service department once that department's costs have been divided.

The sequence in which the service department costs are distributed is a matter of great importance. The rule to follow is to distribute first the costs of that service department which renders the greatest amount of service to all the other departments. Next, distribute the costs of the department that renders the next greatest amount of service to all other departments, and so on, until all service department costs have been distributed. This method of distribution is comparatively long and laborious, for it necessitates a careful analysis of the services rendered by the service departments; but it has the advantage of being the more accurate of the two methods. Often there is some uncertainty as to which department's costs should be distributed first to the other departments. When such uncertainty cannot be resolved, the department with the largest total overhead is distributed first. This order of distribution is based on the assumption that the departments render services in direct proportion to the amount of expense they incur.

The algebraic method takes into consideration that some service departments not only may provide service to, but may also receive service from other service departments. If the power department provides power for the building maintenance department and the building maintenance department keeps the power department building in repair, the cost of the building maintenance department cannot be determined until part of the cost of the power department is added to it. Likewise, the cost of the power department cannot be determined until part of the cost of the building maintenance department is added to it. This type of distribution creates a circular flow of costs because two or more service departments render services to each other. When service department overhead distributions are made to other service departments on a reciprocal basis, the departments not included in the circle are distributed first. The method used may involve continued distribution back and forth among the service departments which service each other until the amount remaining for distribution is so infinitesimal that it does not merit another redistribution. Simultaneous equations can also be used to obtain the same results as continued distributions; however, the results are a direct factor of the equations, and therefore require less arithmetical effort. Since conditions rarely justify such an exact distribution, only a brief explanation of these methods is presented. The results obtained from the complicated arithmetical or mathematical calculations usually do not justify the effort.

The methods of distributing service department costs to production departments are shown in Illustration 4-7 (direct distribution to production departments only), Illustration 4-8 (distribution to service departments and production departments based on sequence of service to other departments), and Illustration 4-9 (distribution to service departments and production departments based on magnitude of total costs in service departments). The operations of one factory may differ from those of another factory so materially that the individual relationships within each firm would determine which method is the most desirable. If the variation from one method to another is not significant, the method that distributes the service department costs directly to production departments (method one) may be best, because it saves time and effort.

The following is a comparison of the results of the distributions according to the different methods of apportionment as shown in the work sheets on pages 156–158:

	Dept. A	Dept. B	Dept. C	Dept. D	Total
Method 1	$34,995.00	$33,905.00	$45,350.00	$79,750.00	$194,000.00
Method 2(a) — based on service	35,150.00	34,050.00	45,300.00	79,500.00	194,000.00
Method 2(b) — based on total costs	35,000.00	33,733.33	45,600.00	79,666.67	194,000.00
Difference between 1 and 2(a)	$−155.00	$−145.00	$+ 50.00	$+250.00	—0—
Difference between 1 and 2(b)	− 5.00	+171.67	−250.00	+ 83.33	—0—
Difference between 2(a) and 2(b)	+150.00	+316.67	−300.00	−166.67	—0—

When the overhead distribution work sheet is completed, the figures thereon become the basis for a series of entries in the general journal. The figures taken from the work sheet shown in Illustration 4-9 are used in the entries on page 159.

	Power	Personnel	Main-tenance	Dept. A	Dept. B	Dept. C	Dept. D	Total
Total from factory overhead analysis sheets	11,000 00	6,000 00	9,000 00	30,000 00	28,000 00	40,000 00	70,000 00	194,000 00
Power distribution — (kw. hours)								
A — 12,000 @ $.11*				1,320 00				
B — 18,000 @ $.11					1,980 00			
C — 20,000 @ $.11						2,200 00		
D — 50,000 @ $.11							5,500 00	
100,000								
Personnel distribution (number of employees served)								
A — 12 @ $100**				1,200 00				
B — 10 @ $100					1,000 00			
C — 18 @ $100						1,800 00		
D — 20 @ $100							2,000 00	
60								
Maintenance distribution — (square feet)								
A — 5,500 @ $.45***				2,475 00				
B — 6,500 @ .45					2,925 00			
C — 3,000 @ .45						1,350 00		
D — 5,000 @ .45							2,250 00	
20,000				34,995 00	33,905 00	45,350 00	79,750 00	194,000 00

*$11,000 ÷ 100,000 (kilowatt hours) = $.11 per kilowatt hour
**$6,000 ÷ 60 (number of employees served) = $100 per employee
***$9,000 ÷ 20,000 (square feet) = $.45 per square foot

ILLUSTRATION 4-7   Method 1 — Distribution of Service Department Costs Directly to Production Departments

already allocated
Indirect Labor + costs etc.

	Power	Personnel	Maintenance	Dept. A	Dept. B	Dept. C	Dept. D	Total
Total from factory overhead analysis sheets......	11,000 00	6,000 00	9,000 00	30,000 00	28,000 00	40,000 00	70,000 00	194,000 00
Power distribution (kilowatt hours)								
Personnel — 4,000 @ $.10*......		400 00						
Maintenance — 6,000 @ .10......			600 00					
A — 12,000 @ .10......				1,200 00				
B — 18,000 @ .10......					1,800 00			
C — 20,000 @ .10......						2,000 00		
D — 50,000 @ .10......							5,000 00	
110,000								
		6,400 00						
Personnel distribution (number of employees served)								
Maintenance — 4 @ $100**......			400 00					
A — 12 @ 100......				1,200 00				
B — 10 @ 100......					1,000 00			
C — 18 @ 100......						1,800 00		
D — 20 @ 100......							2,000 00	
64								
			10,000 00					
Maintenance distribution (square feet)								
A — 5,500 @ $.50***......				2,750 00				
B — 6,500 @ .50......					3,250 00			
C — 3,000 @ .50......						1,500 00		
D — 5,000 @ .50......							2,500 00	
20,000								
				35,150 00	34,050 00	45,300 00	79,500 00	194,000 00

*$11,000 ÷ 110,000 (kilowatt hours) = $.10 per kilowatt hour
**$6,400 ÷ 64 (number of employees served) = $100 per employee
***$10,000 ÷ 20,000 (square feet) = $.50 per square foot

ILLUSTRATION 4-8   Method 2(a) — Distribution of Service Department Costs in Sequence of Service to Other Departments

	Power	Main-tenance	Personnel	Dept. A	Dept. B	Dept. C	Dept. D	Total
Total from factory overhead analysis sheets............	11,000 00	9,000 00	6,000 00	30,000 00	28,000 00	40,000 00	70,000 00	194,000 00
Power distribution (kw hours)								
Maintenance — 6,000 @ $.10*..........		600 00						
Personnel — 4,000 @ .10..........			400 00					
A — 12,000 @ .10..........				1,200 00				
B — 18,000 @ .10..........					1,800 00			
C — 20,000 @ .10..........						2,000 00		
D — 50,000 @ .10..........							5,000 00	
110,000								
		9,600 00						
Maintenance distribution (square feet)								
Personnel — 4,000 @ $.40**..........			1,600 00					
A — 5,500 @ .40..........				2,200 00				
B — 6,500 @ .40..........					2,600 00			
C — 3,000 @ .40..........						1,200 00		
D — 5,000 @ .40..........							2,000 00	
24,000								
			8,000 00					
Personnel distribution (number of employees served)								
A — 12 @ $133⅓***..........				1,600 00				
B — 10 @ 133⅓..........					1,333 33			
C — 18 @ 133⅓..........						2,400 00		
D — 20 @ 133⅓..........							2,666 67	
60								
				35,000 00	33,733 33	45,600 00	79,666 67	194,000 00

*$11,000 ÷ 110,000 (kilowatt hours) = $.10 per kilowatt hour
**$9,600 ÷ 24,000 (square feet) = $.40 per square foot
***$8,000 ÷ 60 (number of employees served) = $133⅓ per employee

ILLUSTRATION 4-9   Method 2(b) — Distribution of Service Department Costs in Sequence of Magnitude of Total Costs in Service Departments

Factory Overhead—Power Department	11,000.00	
Factory Overhead—Maintenance Department.	9,000.00	
Factory Overhead—Personnel Department.....	6,000.00	
Factory Overhead—Department A...............	30,000.00	
Factory Overhead—Department B...............	28,000.00	
Factory Overhead—Department C...............	40,000.00	
Factory Overhead—Department D...............	70,000.00	
Factory Overhead		194,000.00
To close factory overhead expenses to service and production departments.		

The apportionment of the service department costs would be journalized as follows:

Factory Overhead—Maintenance Department	600.00	
Factory Overhead—Personnel Department	400.00	
Factory Overhead—Department A	1,200.00	
Factory Overhead—Department B	1,800.00	
Factory Overhead—Department C	2,000.00	
Factory Overhead—Department D	5,000.00	
Factory Overhead — Power Department		11,000.00
To close factory overhead expenses of the Power Department.		
Factory Overhead—Personnel Department	1,600.00	
Factory Overhead—Department A	2,200.00	
Factory Overhead—Department B	2,600.00	
Factory Overhead—Department C	1,200.00	
Factory Overhead—Department D	2,000.00	
Factory Overhead—Maintenance Department.		9,600.00
To close overhead expenses of the Maintenance Department.		
Factory Overhead—Department A	1,600.00	
Factory Overhead—Department B	1,333.33	
Factory Overhead—Department C	2,400.00	
Factory Overhead—Department D	2,666.67	
Factory Overhead—Personnel Department		8,000.00
To close overhead expenses of the Personnel Department.		

Using the distribution work sheet, the above entries may be combined into a compound entry to close the three service departments to the production departments as follows:

Factory Overhead—Maintenance Department	600.00	
Factory Overhead—Personnel Department	2,000.00	
Factory Overhead—Department A	5,000.00	
Factory Overhead—Department B	5,733.33	
Factory Overhead—Department C	5,600.00	
Factory Overhead—Department D	9,666.67	
Factory Overhead—Power Department		11,000.00
Factory Overhead—Maintenance Department.		9,600.00
Factory Overhead—Personnel Department		8,000.00
To close service departments to production departments.		

An accounting system can be designed which will reduce the number of factory overhead accounts that have to be maintained for the service departments. In such a system, after the distribution work sheet, Illustration 4-9, has been completed, a journal entry is made to close the factory overhead control account, and the charges are made directly and only to the production departments as follows:

Factory Overhead—Department A	35,000.00	
Factory Overhead—Department B	33,733.33	
Factory Overhead—Department C	45,600.00	
Factory Overhead—Department D	79,666.67	
Factory Overhead		194,000.00

To close overhead control account to various departments. The departmental totals include the apportioned costs of the service departments.

After the journal entries have been posted to the general ledger, the total of the balances of the departmental factory overhead accounts will be the same as the balance of the factory overhead control account before it was closed. The journal entries have not affected the total of the factory overhead expenses; however, the general ledger now shows the amount of factory overhead expense that is being charged to each of the production departments.

APPLYING FACTORY OVERHEAD

In previous chapters, the actual factory overhead costs were charged or applied to production. Since many of these costs will not be known until the end of an accounting period and management needs to know the cost of a job or process soon after completion, the jobs or processes must be charged with an *estimated* amount of factory overhead. This estimate is also used to value inventories and to measure operating efficiencies or inefficiencies which may cause month-to-month fluctuations of actual factory overhead costs. Assume, for example, that a factory receives a job on the first of April and completes it on the fifth of the same month. Although the direct materials and direct labor costs are known on the fifth of the month, the total factory overhead would not be known until sometime in the future. This uncertainty of the actual amount of overhead costs is often due to the irregular arrival of invoices. If, in this example, it is impossible to determine the selling price until the total production cost is finalized, the customer might not be billed until a month or more after the order has been filled. This loss of time in collecting accounts receivable would be quite costly to the company. Furthermore, if a company must submit bids to obtain contracts, a bid should include the expected actual costs of the job as accurately as possible. Fulfilling a contract awarded on the basis of a bid understated as to actual overhead costs would result in a loss of revenue. The approximation of the overhead costs assigned to bids and completed jobs is important in terms of charging a fair proportion of cost to each unit produced.

Predetermined Factory Overhead Rates

The flexible budget, which includes the anticipated factory overhead costs for the various departments at a given level of production, is used to establish a **predetermined factory overhead rate**. The rate is calculated by dividing the budgeted factory overhead by the budgeted production for the period. The accuracy of the estimated rate depends upon the accuracy of the cost and production estimates used in preparing the budget. In preparing the budgets, the fixed and variable components, past cost behavior patterns and how future economic and operational expectations may alter them, must be carefully considered. Specifically these factors include: the expected volume of production, the variability of the expenses, the fixed costs relevant to the anticipated level of production, the forecast activity of industry, and the possible price changes that may be encountered. Because a large number of unknowns must be anticipated, absolute accuracy cannot be expected; nevertheless, a relatively high degree of accuracy should be a management requirement.

For a manufacturing company that is departmentalized, the factory overhead should be budgeted for each department. The procedure to distribute the budgeted departmental expenses should be the same as that used to departmentalize the actual factory overhead expenses. The departmental overhead budgets should also include an allocation of the budgeted fixed expenses, such as depreciation, as well as a portion of the budgeted service department expenses.

After the factory overhead expense budget has been determined, a method for applying the estimated expenses to the departments, jobs, or processes must be selected. The usual application methods require that data from the period's production budget be obtained. These production budgets will show, among other things, the estimated quantity of product in terms of direct labor cost, direct labor hours, machine hours, and units of production.

Using these production estimates, either for the entire plant or for each individual department, a method is selected that will most accurately charge the product with a fair share of the factory overhead that is expected to be incurred by the company. Some influence on the method selected will be exerted by the departmental composition of manual laborers versus its degree of mechanization. A department with few machines will usually apply the predetermined overhead by either the direct labor cost or direct labor hour method, whereas, a more mechanized production department will use the machine hour method.

Direct Labor Cost Method

The **direct labor cost method** uses the amount of direct labor cost that has been charged to the product as the basis for applying factory overhead. The overhead rate to be used is predetermined by dividing the estimated (budgeted) factory overhead cost by the estimated (budgeted) direct labor cost. The relationship of the overhead to the direct labor cost is expressed as a percentage of direct labor cost (the base).

Using the information shown in Illustration 4-7 (page 156), but assuming that the data represent the budgeted rather than actual factory overhead costs, the Department A column shows that approximately $35,000 (rounded) of factory overhead is estimated for the period. By dividing the estimate of factory overhead ($35,000) by an assumed estimate of direct labor cost ($70,000), a direct labor cost rate of 50% results. This rate is interpreted to mean that for every $1 of direct labor cost charged to the product, $.50 for factory overhead will be applied. For example, if a job incurs $1,000 in direct labor cost, factory overhead of $500 ($1,000 × 50%) will be charged (applied) to the job. The same percentage of factory overhead will be used for all jobs produced in Department A during the period.

The departmental environment in which the direct labor ˙cost method is normally used should include a relatively stable direct labor cost charge from one product to another. If a labor force which generates the direct labor cost has a widely varying hourly-rate range or if there are many instances, because of absenteeism, that part-time workers must be brought in and paid materially different rates, another factory overhead method should be used. An environment which causes a fluctuation in the direct labor cost that is not reflected proportionately in factory overhead expenses causes a distortion in the product's total cost which can be detrimental to the company's ability to control costs.

Direct Labor Hour Method

The **direct labor hour method** overcomes the problem of varying wage rates by using only the number of direct labor hours spent on the job or process as the basis for applying factory overhead. This method requires that a record be kept of both the direct labor cost and the number of direct labor hours incurred.

To determine the direct labor hour rate, the estimated (budgeted) factory overhead cost is divided by the estimated (budgeted) number of direct labor hours. Again, using Illustration 4-7, assume that Department B uses the direct labor hour method. Management estimates that 17,000 direct labor hours will be needed. The estimated factory overhead of $34,000 (rounded) divided by the 17,000 direct labor hours, results in a direct labor hour rate of $2 for each hour. This means that for every direct labor hour worked in the department, it is anticipated that $2 of factory overhead will be incurred. For example, a job or process which required 250 direct labor hours will be charged $500 (250 hours × $2) for factory overhead.

An advantage of the direct labor hour method is that the amount of factory overhead which is applied to a job or process is not affected by the mix of labor rates comprising the direct labor cost. A disadvantage of the method is that the application base, the number of direct labor hours, is substantially smaller than if direct labor cost was used. Therefore a significant difference in the amount of applied factory overhead could occur when the direct labor hours used deviates only slightly from expectations.

Machine Hour Method

The machine hour method is appropriate when a department is highly mechanized. In such a department, the factory overhead cost should be more proportionate to the machine hours generated, than to the direct labor hours or cost incurred. It is not unusual, in a mechanized department, for one direct labor hour to generate five machine hours if the worker runs five machines from an assigned work station. It is the most difficult of the methods discussed, and requires substantial preliminary study before installation and more detailed records. The advantage of a more dependable factory overhead application rate, however, more than outweighs the additional records and costs involved. The machine hour rate is predetermined by dividing the estimated (budgeted) factory overhead cost by the estimated (budgeted) machine hours to be used.

Assume that Department C in Illustration 4-7 uses the machine hour method and that 5,000 hours are estimated for the period. The estimated factory overhead of $45,000 is divided by the 5,000 machine hours, resulting in a rate of $9 per machine hour. Therefore, for every machine hour used it is expected that $9 of factory overhead will be incurred. If a job or process requires 50 hours of machine time, it will be charged $450 ($9 × 50) in factory overhead costs.

Importance of Selecting the Proper Method

Each method will apply the estimated factory overhead to production. However, it is important to select the method for the department which allocates the estimated factory overhead in the same amounts as the actual factory overhead expenses are incurred within the department.

For example, assume two employees in a department are doing the same work at the same speed and same efficiency using identical tools and machines. One worker with longer seniority is paid $10 per hour, and the other receives $4 per hour. The more senior employee works on Job No. 100 and the other worker is assigned to Job No. 101. Both workers apply five hours of direct labor to their assigned jobs. Job No. 100 is charged $50 ($10 × 5 hours) for direct labor and Job No. 101, $20 ($4 × 5 hours). The actual factory overhead incurred in the department for each job is exactly the same. Yet, if the direct labor cost method is used and the rate was 50% of the direct labor cost, $25 ($50 × 50%) would be added to Job No. 100, while only $10 ($20 × 50%) would be charged to Job No. 101. The merit of using the direct labor cost method should be questioned because there is no supporting evidence which indicates that different amounts of expense should be charged when conditions clearly indicate that both jobs should have similar charges.

Factory overhead may not change in proportion to the changes in workers' rates of pay. An increase in an employee's wage does not mean more light, more heat, and more power will be consumed in the performance of the job. Neither does a worker's pay increase affect the depreciation expense of the machine or tools used. Under conditions where factory overhead does not vary in proportion to direct labor costs, the direct labor cost method may not be acceptable.

Using the same data to examine the acceptability of the direct labor hour method, since both employees worked the same number of hours (five) under identical conditions, the same dollar amount of factory overhead, $10 (5 × $2), would be added to each job. Therefore, the analysis would show the direct labor hour method to be an acceptable way to allocate the factory overhead cost to the jobs.

The amount of heat, light, and power used by the workers is not affected by the amount of wages earned but rather by the length of time worked. Neither will the total employee earnings affect the amount of depreciation, property taxes, rent, and most other factory overhead items. The payroll taxes, however, which are based on wages earned, will increase in proportion to the increase in employees' earnings.

In mechanized factories, the machine hour method is the most desirable technique for applying factory overhead costs. Assume, for example, that a factory has two departments. Department A punches out blanks on two high-cost machines, then transfers the blanks to Department B. The two machines are completely automatic and require only an occasional inspection to determine whether or not they are operating efficiently. However, in Department B there are no machines, and all work on the product is performed manually. The production data sheets for the two departments show that Department A has incurred actual factory overhead costs of $3,000, consisting mostly of power, depreciation, property taxes, insurance, repairs, and maintenance. Department B has incurred $2,000 of factory overhead, consisting of expenses for supervision, heat, light, property taxes, and depreciation.

If factory overhead costs were applied on a direct labor hour basis, Department A would not have any applied factory overhead because no direct labor hours or cost has been charged to the department. Therefore, if factory overhead is to be allocated to the jobs of Department A, another more appropriate overhead method must be used. The machine hour method would seem to be the most suited to the department's operational makeup. The direct labor hour method could serve Department B's requirements effectively.

This example of the use of machine hour rates may be considered extreme; however, it illustrates that under certain circumstances the direct labor hour method of application does not provide an accurate application of factory overhead to the individual job cost. The machine hour method is most useful when the greater part of a department's production is mechanized, since the factory overhead will likely increase or decrease as the hours of operation of the machines increase or decrease. As the trend accelerates toward the use of automatic machines in manufacturing operations, the use of the machine hour method for applying factory overhead will also increase in popularity.

Although the methods of direct labor cost, direct labor hours, and machine hours have been emphasized, other methods can be devised that will work just as well for some firms. For example, a firm may select units of production or materials cost as the base for applying overhead. A company is not limited to the methods described in this chapter, since a factory could have any number of operating conditions existing in its production departments. A factory may use one, two, or all of the methods described to apply overhead. However, all methods have one ingredient in common — the factory overhead expected to be incurred.

Applying Factory Overhead Using Predetermined Rates

After the application method is selected and the predetermined rate is calculated, all jobs or processes will be charged with the estimated overhead cost rather than with the actual factory overhead costs which are being incurred on a day-by-day, month-by-month basis. The estimated factory overhead is applied to production by a debit to Work in Process and a credit to an account entitled **Applied Factory Overhead**. For example, if the direct labor hour method was used, with a predetermined rate of $5 per direct labor hour, and a production job required 100 direct labor hours to complete, $500 of factory overhead would be applied to Work in Process as follows:

    Work in Process... 500
        Applied Factory Overhead   500
            To apply factory overhead to job (100 hours @
            $5).

At the end of the period, the applied factory overhead account is closed to the factory overhead control account:

    Applied Factory Overhead 500
        Factory Overhead   500
            To close the applied factory overhead account.

After the above entry is posted, if a balance (debit or credit) remains in the factory overhead account, it indicates that the actual factory overhead incurred did not equal the estimated factory overhead applied. A Factory Overhead debit balance indicates that a smaller amount of overhead was applied to production than was incurred during the period. The balance shows that factory overhead costs were **underapplied** or **underabsorbed**. A credit balance in Factory Overhead indicates that more overhead was applied than was actually incurred. The credit balance shows that factory overhead was **overapplied** or **overabsorbed**. An account entitled **Under- and Overapplied Factory Overhead** is created, and the debit or credit balance in the factory overhead control account is transferred to the special account at the end of each designated period, as follows:

    For a Factory Overhead debit balance (underapplied):
        Under- and Overapplied Factory Overhead   xx
            Factory Overhead   xx
    For a Factory Overhead credit balance (overapplied):
        Factory Overhead   xx
            Under- and Overapplied Factory Overhead   xx

The transfer of the balance from Factory Overhead balances the account at zero and when a new period begins only transactions for that period will be shown in the account. The under- and overapplied factory overhead account will continue to accumulate the differences between the actual and applied overhead, month-to-month, to the end of the year, when it will be closed to Cost of Goods Sold or prorated to Work in Process, Finished Goods, and Cost of Goods Sold. If interim statements are prepared during the year, the Under- and Overapplied Factory Overhead balance can be shown in the income statements as a debit or credit adjustment to the Cost of Goods Sold (depending on the net balance) or in the balance sheet as a deferred charge or a deferred credit.

The following figures show how under- and overapplied factory overhead costs often offset each other in succeeding months of the year as seasonal demands and production levels change:

UNDER- AND OVERAPPLIED FACTORY OVERHEAD

Month	Underapplied	Overapplied	Dr. (Cr.) Balance
January	$ 600	....	$ 600
February	300	....	900
March	....	$ 400	500
April	....	800	(300)
May	....	500	(800)
June	200	....	(600)
July	700	....	100
August	900	....	1,000
September	....	500	500
October	....	800	(300)
November	....	400	(700)
December	800	....	100
	$3,500	$3,400	

When the year-end balance in Under- and Overapplied Factory Overhead is a small amount and therefore will not materially change the year's calculated net income, it is closed in total to Cost of Goods Sold. If the balance is a large amount and will materially alter the year's net income if the total balance is closed to Cost of Goods Sold, a proration should be computed, charging some of the balance to Work in Process and Finished Goods.

Even though $100 is a small amount, for illustration purposes it will be used to show how the proration, when it is required, is accomplished. Assume that the year-end balances, before proration, for the following accounts are:

		Percent of Total
Work in Process	$ 1,000	10%
Finished Goods	2,000	20
Cost of Goods Sold	7,000	70
Total	$10,000	100%

The prorata amount chargeable to each account is calculated as follows:

Work in Process ($100 × 10%)... = $ 10
Finished Goods ($100 × 20%) .... =   20
Cost of Goods Sold ($100 × 70%) .... =   70
   Total $100

The journal entry to close the Under- and Overapplied Factory Overhead would be:

Work in Process... 10
Finished Goods.. 20
Cost of Goods Sold... 70
   Under- and Overapplied Factory Overhead   100
     To close year-end debit balance in Under- and
     Overapplied Factory Overhead.

The amount allocated to Cost of Goods Sold becomes a **current period cost** which will directly reduce the amount of net income for the period. The amounts prorated to Work in Process and Finished Goods become part of the **product cost** of the inventories and will be deferred, along with the other regular inventory costs, to the next period.

Factory Overhead Flow Charts

Illustrations 4-11 through 4-16 summarize the complete flow of costs for factory overhead, using the data from Illustration 4-10.

CALCULATING BUDGET AND VOLUME VARIANCES

Earlier in the chapter, it was stated that a company needs to forecast the factory overhead costs associated with different levels of production, or capacity. When costs are separated into fixed and variable elements, a company can establish a flexible budget for different levels of capacity. Such a budget permits a firm to analyze the over- and underapplied factory overhead in terms of the budgeted factory overhead at the capacity attained compared to the actual incurred costs. The result of this comparison is called a **budget** or **spending variance**. Usually, to calculate the budget variance, a comparison is made of the total budgeted overhead at actual capacity with the total overhead costs incurred. The budget variance, however, can be analyzed in greater depth to show the separate effects of the actual capacity on the fixed cost factor and the variable cost factor. The combination of these effects results in the overall budget variance, which is favorable (credit) when the actual overhead costs

	Power	Maintenance	Personnel	Dept. A	Dept. B	Dept. C	Dept. D	Total
Total actual expenses from factory overhead analysis sheets	11,000 00	9,000 00	6,000 00	30,000 00	28,000 00	40,000 00	70,000 00	194,000 00
Power distribution (kw hours)								
Maintenance — 6,000 @ $.10		600 00						
Personnel — 4,000 @ .10			400 00					
Dept. A — 12,000 @ .10				1,200 00				
B — 18,000 @ .10					1,800 00			
C — 20,000 @ .10						2,000 00		
D — 50,000 @ .10							5,000 00	
110,000		9,600 00						
Maintenance distribution (square feet)								
Personnel — 4,000 @ $.40			1,600 00					
Dept. A — 5,500 @ .40				2,200 00				
B — 6,500 @ .40					2,600 00			
C — 3,000 @ .40						1,200 00		
D — 5,000 @ .40							2,000 00	
24,000			8,000 00					
Personnel distribution (number of employees served)								
Dept. A — 12 @ $133⅓				1,600 00				
B — 10 @ 133⅓					1,333 33			
C — 18 @ 133⅓						2,400 00		
D — 20 @ 133⅓							2,666 67	
60				35,000 00	33,733 33	45,600 00	79,666 67	194,000 00
Applied factory overhead				35,100 00	35,000 00	44,100 00	78,200 00	192,400 00
(Over-) or underapplied factory overhead				(100 00)	(1,266 67)	1,500 00	1,466 67	1,600 00

ILLUSTRATION 4-10 Distribution of Service Department Costs in Sequence of Magnitude of Total Costs in Service Departments

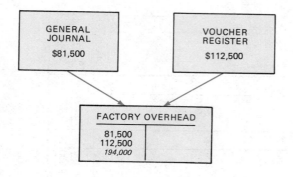

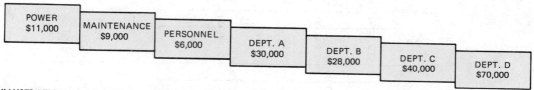

ILLUSTRATION 4-11   Summary of Flow of Factory Overhead Expenses

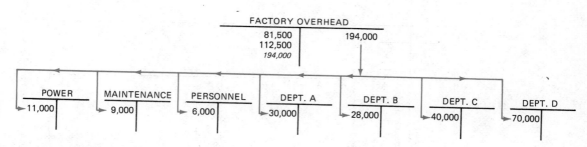

ILLUSTRATION 4-12   Distribution of Factory Overhead Account to Service and Production Departments

are less than the budget, and unfavorable (debit) when the actual costs exceed the budget.

A second variance that can be calculated to explain the over- or underapplied overhead is the **volume variance**. This variance measures the effect of a change in the volume of production. To calculate the volume variance, the total budget at actual capacity is compared with the overhead applied at actual capacity.

To illustrate the calculation of budget and volume variances, assume a company budgets for a 100% capacity level of 120,000 direct

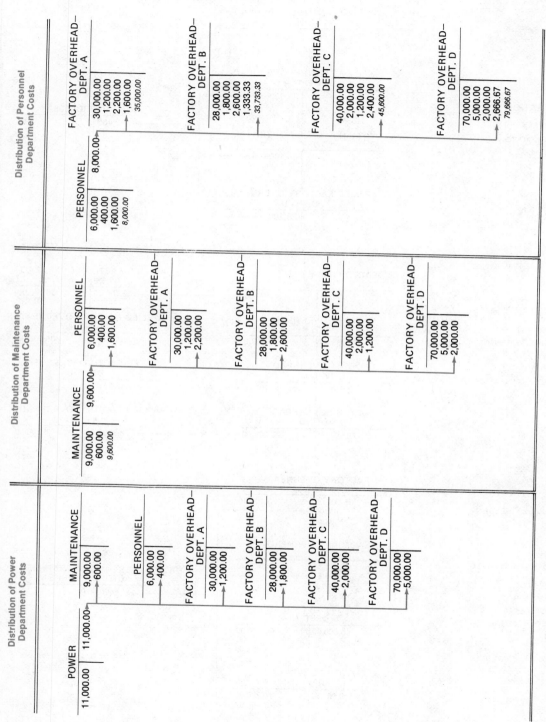

Distribution of Personnel Department Costs

PERSONNEL
6,000.00	8,000.00
400.00	
1,600.00	
8,000.00	

FACTORY OVERHEAD— DEPT. A
30,000.00
1,200.00
2,200.00
1,600.00
35,000.00

FACTORY OVERHEAD— DEPT. B
28,000.00
1,800.00
2,600.00
1,333.33
33,733.33

FACTORY OVERHEAD— DEPT. C
40,000.00
2,000.00
1,200.00
2,400.00
45,600.00

FACTORY OVERHEAD— DEPT. D
70,000.00
5,000.00
2,000.00
2,666.67
79,666.67

Distribution of Maintenance Department Costs

MAINTENANCE
9,000.00	9,600.00
600.00	
9,600.00	

PERSONNEL
6,000.00
400.00
1,600.00

FACTORY OVERHEAD— DEPT. A
30,000.00
1,200.00
2,200.00

FACTORY OVERHEAD— DEPT. B
28,000.00
1,800.00
2,600.00

FACTORY OVERHEAD— DEPT. C
40,000.00
2,000.00
1,200.00

FACTORY OVERHEAD— DEPT. D
70,000.00
5,000.00
2,000.00

Distribution of Power Department Costs

POWER
11,000.00	11,000.00

MAINTENANCE
9,000.00
600.00

PERSONNEL
6,000.00
400.00

FACTORY OVERHEAD— DEPT. A
30,000.00
1,200.00

FACTORY OVERHEAD— DEPT. B
28,000.00
1,800.00

FACTORY OVERHEAD— DEPT. C
40,000.00
2,000.00

FACTORY OVERHEAD— DEPT. D
70,000.00
5,000.00

ILLUSTRATION 4-13   Distribution of Service Department Costs

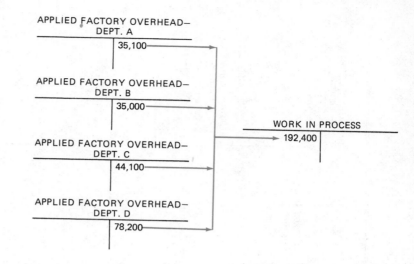

ILLUSTRATION 4-14

Departmental
Applied Factory
Overhead

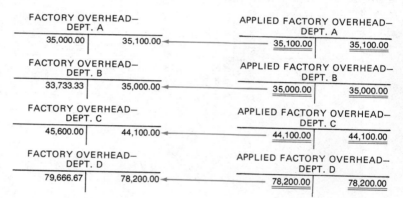

ILLUSTRATION 4-15

Closing Applied
Factory Overhead
Accounts to
Departmental
Control Accounts

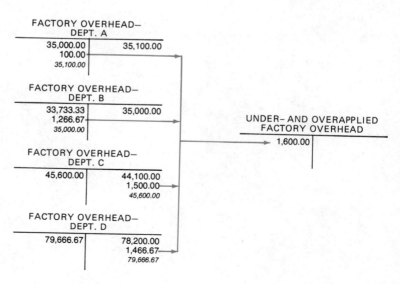

ILLUSTRATION 4-16

Transferring
Balances in
Departmental
Control Accounts

labor hours annually, a total fixed cost of $240,000 ($2 per direct labor hour), and a $3 per direct labor hour variable overhead cost rate. The total predetermined factory overhead rate, therefore, is $5 per direct labor hour ($2 fixed + $3 variable). The monthly budgets expect 10,000 direct labor hours to be used and $20,000 of fixed costs incurred.

Actual costs and labor hours and factory overhead applied for the first month of operations were as follows:

Actual factory overhead:		
Fixed costs...	$23,000	
Variable costs...	29,000	$52,000 *total*
Direct labor hours used	9,800	
Applied factory overhead (9,800 × $5).......................		$49,000 *applied*

After all the journal entries and postings for the month are made, Under- and Overapplied Factory Overhead has a $3,000 debit balance, indicating that factory overhead has been *under-applied*. The analysis of this balance requires determining whether the budgeted variable rate was more or less than was experienced. If the actual variable rate differed from the budgeted rate, a **budget variance** will result. The budget variance will show the total amount of the overexpenditure (unfavorable-debit) or the saving (favorable-credit). The **volume variance** shows whether or not all the fixed cost allocated to the month has been charged to the month's production by the predetermined overhead rate. If more direct labor hours were used in the month than were anticipated, the volume variance will be favorable (credit). When the hours used are less than budgeted hours, not all the expected fixed cost is applied to production, therefore, the variance is unfavorable (debit).

	Fixed Costs	Variable Costs	Total Factory Overhead Costs
Budgeted overhead.....................................	$20,000	$30,000	$50,000
Budget capacity — labor hours.....................	10,000	10,000	10,000
Predetermined overhead application rate.......	$2	$3	$5
Actual hours used.......................................	9,800	9,800	9,800
Actual factory overhead..............................	$23,000	$29,000	$52,000
Applied factory overhead:			
9,800 hours × $2.....................................	19,600		
9,800 hours × $3.....................................		29,400	
9,800 hours × $5.....................................			49,000
Underapplied overhead (debit)	$ 3,400		
Overapplied overhead (credit).................		$ (400)	
Net underapplied overhead (debit)..........			$ 3,000

Budget Variance — due to cost factors:

	Fixed Costs	Variable Costs	Total Factory Costs
Budget at capacity attained (9,800 hours)	$20,000	$29,400	$49,400
Actual factory overhead..............................	23,000	29,000	52,000
Variances due to costs:			
Favorable (credit)................................		$ (400)	
Unfavorable (debit)	$ 3,000		
Budget Variance — unfavorable (debit).......			$ 2,600
Volume Variance — due to production volume:			
Budget at attained capacity — 9,800 hours	$20,000	$29,400	$49,400
Applied factory overhead:			
9,800 hours × $2...................................	19,600		
9,800 hours × $3...................................		29,400	
9,800 hours × $5...................................			49,000
Volume variance — unfavorable (debit).......	$ 400	—0—	$ 400
Net underapplied overhead (debit)..........	$ 3,400	$ (400)	$ 3,000

The analysis of the $3,000 underapplied factory overhead balance indicates that $2,600 (the budget variance) was overexpended for variable costs at the 9,800 direct labor hours operating level. This budget variance would not have resulted if a higher ($3.265) rate had been used ($29,400 + $2,600 = $32,000 ÷ 9,800 = $3.265) or, if management had reduced its variable cost expenditures proportionately to the decreased use of direct labor hours, maintaining a $3 per direct labor hour variable cost, no budget variance would have resulted.

Another technique for examining the cause of the $3,000 underapplied factory overhead is to isolate the variable and fixed costs and then calculate the variances, as follows:

Actual factory overhead expenses	$52,000
Fixed cost — budgeted	20,000
Actual variable cost expenditures...	$32,000
Variable cost at 9,800 hours:	
9,800 × $3..	29,400
Budget variance (unfavorable)	$ 2,600

The fixed cost factor can be isolated as follows:

Fixed cost — budgeted	$20,000
Fixed cost applied: (9,800 × $2)	19,600
Volume variance (unfavorable)	$ 400

The volume variance is favorable (credit) when more direct labor hours are used than have been budgeted. The higher the volume of production and hours worked, the lower the fixed cost per unit of product. Therefore, at higher plant capacities the company should realize higher net income returns because the total product unit cost is reduced due to lower fixed cost charges per unit.

Budget and volume variances are measurements which provide management with information as to how well actual production met the standards set by the budget forecasts. The earlier notice is given to management concerning the deviations from the budget and their direction, the more time during an operating cycle there is to correct an undesirable tendency. When unwanted deviations are discovered only at the end of a fiscal period, the damage has been done and there is no time left in the period to change operational practices and revise the system. The regular calculation of variances serves as a management control over operations which makes them aware of period-to-period deviations from expected goals.

APPLICATION OF PRINCIPLES

On April 1, the accountant for the Sullivan Manufacturing Company found that Job No. 400 was completed on March 31, and there were no jobs being processed in the factory. Prior to April 1, the accountant estimated the predetermined overhead application rate for April using the following data:

Estimated factory overhead...	$13,750
Estimated direct labor hours..	55,000
Application rate per direct labor hour	$.25

The estimate showed fixed costs to be $8,250 and variable costs $5,500, totaling $13,750. The rate per hour ($.25) was $.15 for fixed costs and $.10 for variable costs.

There is one production department in the factory, and the direct labor hour method is considered best for applying overhead under the existing operating conditions.

During the month, three jobs are started and daily postings are made to the job cost sheets from the materials requisitions and the time tickets. The following summary shows the jobs and the amounts posted to the job cost sheets:

Job No.	Started	Materials	Direct Labor	Direct Labor Hours
401	April 1	$ 5,000	$10,000	15,000
402	April 12	15,000	20,000	32,000
403	April 15	5,000	4,000	7,000
		$25,000	$34,000	54,000

On April 11, Job No. 401 is completed. The materials and direct labor costs shown on page 175 have been recorded on the job cost sheet. To determine the total cost of the job, however, factory overhead must be applied. On the basis of the predetermined rate of $.25 per direct labor hour, $3,750 (15,000 hours × $.25) is added to the job cost sheet. The completed cost of Job No. 401 is therefore $18,750, consisting of direct materials, $5,000, direct labor, $10,000, and factory overhead, $3,750.

On April 24, Job No. 402 is completed and the accountant adds $8,000 (32,000 hours × $.25) for factory overhead to the job cost sheet. The cost of Job No. 402 is $43,000, consisting of $15,000 for direct materials, $20,000 for direct labor, and $8,000 for factory overhead.

On April 30, the accountant is informed by the factory superintendent that Job No. 403 is not completed. To determine the cost of the job as of the end of April, the accountant adds $1,750 (7,000 hours × $.25) for factory overhead to the uncompleted job. The total cost to date of Job No. 403 consists of direct materials, $5,000, direct labor, $4,000, and factory overhead, $1,750, totaling $10,750. This amount will be shown on the financial statements for work in process inventory at April 30.

The total amount of factory overhead charged to the three jobs processed during April is $13,500. At the end of April, the factory overhead control account in the general ledger has a debit balance of $14,000, representing the actual amount of factory overhead incurred during the month. The work in process account was debited in the general ledger for $25,000 of direct materials and $34,000 of direct labor. Since factory overhead of $13,500 has already been entered on the job cost sheets, the following journal entry is posted to the general ledger accounts to record the amount of factory overhead applied during the month:

Apr. 30   Work in Process............................. 13,500
                 Applied Factory Overhead   13,500

This entry brings the work in process control account into agreement with the subsidiary job cost ledger. If the factory has more than one production department and each department has a work in process account, it is necessary to debit each departmental work in process account and credit each applied factory overhead account for the amounts of the factory overhead applied.

The next step is to close the applied factory overhead account to Factory Overhead, and to transfer the $500 debit balance in the factory overhead account to the under- and overapplied factory overhead account as follows:

Apr. 30 Applied Factory Overhead 13,500
        Factory Overhead   13,500
          To close applied factory overhead
          account.

  30 Under- and Overapplied Factory
       Overhead..................................   500
         Factory Overhead   500
          To transfer the debit balance in
          factory overhead to the under-
          and overapplied factory
          overhead account.

The following entries were required to record the transactions completed during April:

Finished Goods 61,750
   Work in Process   61,750
      Job Nos. 401 and 402 were transferred to
      warehouse.

Accounts Receivable 25,000
   Sales   25,000
      To record the sale of Job No. 401.

Cost of Goods Sold 18,750
   Finished Goods   18,750
      To record the cost of Job No. 401.

The following diagram shows the work in process account and the flow of factory overhead costs:

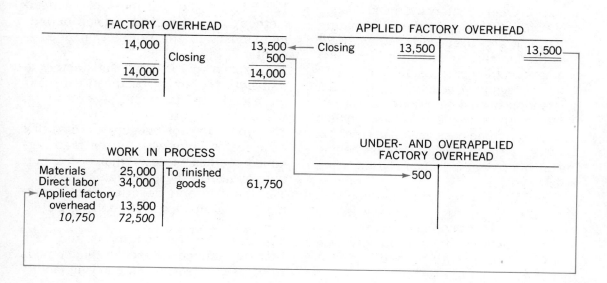

The analysis of the $500 debit balance in the under- and overapplied overhead account is as follows:

Actual factory overhead incurred..		$14,000
Budget at attained capacity:		
Fixed costs...	$8,250	
Variable costs (54,000 hours @ $.10)...............................	5,400	13,650
		$ 350
Budget variance — unfavorable (debit).....................................		
Budget at attained capacity (from above)	$13,650	
Applied factory overhead..	13,500	
Volume variance — unfavorable (debit).....................................		150
Net underapplied variance (debit)...		$ 500

Illustration 4-17 shows in summary form the transactions involved in accounting for factory overhead.

QUESTIONS

1. Define factory overhead expenses and distinguish them from other manufacturing costs. What other terms are used to describe this type of cost?

2. List the three categories of factory overhead expenses and give examples of each.

3. Distinguish between variable, fixed, and semivariable factory overhead costs.

4. Taking into consideration the nature of variable and fixed costs, what effect does the increase or decrease in production have on total unit costs?

5. In management accounting, is an understanding of cost behavior essential?

6. What effect does a change in volume have on the three basic cost patterns?

7. What is the basic assumption behind the high-low method of analyzing semivariable costs?

8. Does the least squares method give accurate, reliable results since it is a more mathematically sound procedure?

9. How does accounting for factory overhead in a small enterprise differ from that of a large enterprise?

10. In what way do the amounts posted to the factory overhead control account in the general ledger act as a check on the amounts posted to the individual factory overhead analysis sheets?

11. Explain the function and use of the two types of factory overhead analysis ledger sheets.

12. What are the two types of departments that are usually found in a factory? What is the function of each?

13. Explain the two most often used methods of distributing service department costs to the production departments.

14. Explain why it is not satisfactory to wait until the actual overhead expenses are ascertained to record such costs on the job cost sheets.

15. What types of budgets are essential to a cost system which uses predetermined overhead rates? What is the purpose of each of these budgets?

16. Identify and describe three commonly used methods for applying factory overhead to jobs.

17. Describe the conditions and data that are required for each of the methods to be used effectively in applying factory overhead.

18. A firm may use more than one method of applying factory overhead to

ACCOUNTING FOR FACTORY OVERHEAD

Transaction	Source of Data	Book of Original Entry	General Ledger Entry	Subsidiary Cost Records
Indirect materials requisitioned from storeroom for factory use	Materials issued summary	General Journal or Requisition Journal	Factory Overhead Materials	Factory overhead analysis ledger sheets Stores ledger cards
Indirect labor employed in factory	Labor cost summary	General Journal	Factory Overhead Payroll	Factory overhead analysis ledger sheets
Payroll taxes imposed on the employer	Payroll record	General Journal	Factory Overhead FICA Tax Payable FUTA Tax Payable State Unemployment Tax Payable	Factory overhead analysis ledger sheets
Vouchering factory overhead such as rent, power, and repairs	Invoices	Voucher Register	Factory Overhead Vouchers Payable	Factory overhead analysis ledger sheets
Adjustments for factory overhead such as expired insurance, accrued property tax, and depreciation	Schedules	General Journal	Factory Overhead Prepaid Insurance Accrued Property Tax Payable Accumulated Depreciation	Factory overhead analysis ledger sheets
Distribution of factory overhead to service and production departments	Schedules	General Journal	Departmental Factory Overhead Accounts Factory Overhead	None
Distribution of service department expenses to production department expense accounts	Schedules	General Journal	Production Department Factory Overhead Accounts Service Department Expense Accounts	Factory overhead analysis ledger sheets
Application of factory overhead to jobs	Schedule of predetermined departmental application rates	General Journal	Work in Process Production Department Applied Factory Overhead Accounts	Job cost sheets
Close applied factory overhead accounts to factory overhead control	Applied factory overhead accounts	General Journal	Applied Factory Overhead Accounts Factory Overhead	None
Close factory overhead control balances to under- and overapplied factory overhead account	Factory overhead control accounts	General Journal	Under- and Overapplied Factory Overhead Factory Overhead (If underapplied) Factory Overhead Under- and Overapplied Factory Overhead (If overapplied)	None

ILLUSTRATION 4-17   Summary of Factory Overhead Transactions

cost its production. Under what conditions would it be desirable to use one or more application methods?

19. The factory overhead control account has a credit balance of $1,000 at the end of June, the first month of the fiscal year. Has overhead been underapplied or overapplied for the month? Give possible reasons for the credit balance.

20. At the end of a fiscal period, describe two ways that an under- and overapplied factory overhead balance can be disposed of.

21. Into what two variances can under- and overapplied overhead be analyzed? How are they computed?

EXERCISES

1. Classify each of the following items of factory overhead as either a fixed or variable cost:

   (a) Indirect labor
   (b) Indirect material
   (c) Insurance on building
   (d) Overtime premium pay
   (e) Depreciation on building (straight-line)
   (f) Polishing compounds
   (g) Depreciation on machinery (based on hours used)
   (h) Employer's payroll taxes
   (i) Property taxes
   (j) Machine lubricants
   (k) Employees' hospital insurance (paid by employer)
   (l) Labor for machine repairs
   (m) Vacation pay
   (n) Patent amortization
   (o) Janitor's wages
   (p) Rent
   (q) Small tools

2. The Elite Company has accumulated the following data over a six-month period.

	Indirect Labor Hours	Indirect Labor Costs
January	400	$ 300
February	500	350
March	600	400
April	700	450
May	800	500
June	900	550
	3,900	$2,550

Separate the indirect labor into its fixed and variable components using **(a)** the high-low method, and **(b)** the least squares method.

3. The World Manufacturing Co. budgeted for 1,200 units of Product X during the month of May. The unit cost of Product X was $15, consisting of direct materials, $5; direct labor, $7; and factory overhead, $3 (fixed, $2 and variable, $1).

(a) What would be the unit cost if 800 units were manufactured? (b) What would be the unit cost if 1,500 units were manufactured? (c) Explain why there is a difference in the unit costs.

4. What would be the appropriate basis for distributing each of the following factory overhead expenses to departments?

(a) Depreciation on buildings
(b) Depreciation on machinery
(c) Taxes on the buildings
(d) Insurance on the machinery
(e) Heat
(f) Light

(g) Indirect materials
(h) Indirect labor
(i) FICA taxes
(j) Unemployment taxes
(k) Repairs to machinery

5. A manufacturing company has two service and two production departments. Building Maintenance and Factory Office are the service departments. The production departments are Department A and Department B. The following data have been estimated for next year's operations:

Direct labor hours: Department A, 80,000; Department B, 40,000
Floor space occupied: Factory Office 10%; Department A, 50%; Department B, 40%

The direct charges expected to be made to the departments are:

Building Maintenance	$ 60,000
Factory Office	168,000
Department A	378,000
Department B	328,000

The Building Maintenance Department services all departments of the company, while Factory Office costs are allocable to Departments A and B on the basis of direct labor hours. Determine the departmental direct labor hour application rate for each production department.

6. (a) If the direct labor cost method is used in applying factory overhead and the predetermined rate is 90%, what amount should be charged to Job No. 301, assuming that the direct materials used totaled $5,000 and the direct labor cost totaled $3,200?

(b) If the direct labor hour method is used in applying factory overhead and the predetermined rate is $1 an hour, what amount should be charged to Job No. 301, assuming that the direct materials used totaled $5,000, the direct labor cost totaled $3,200, and the number of direct labor hours totaled 2,500?

(c) If the machine hour method is used in applying factory overhead and the predetermined rate is $7 an hour, what amount should be charged to Job No. 301, assuming that the direct materials used totaled $5,000, the direct labor cost totaled $3,200, and the number of machine hours totaled 295?

7. The books of The Grover Products Co. revealed that the following

general journal entry had been made at the end of the current accounting period:

Factory Overhead...	200	
Under- and Overapplied Factory Overhead		200

The total direct materials cost for the period was $12,000. The total direct labor cost, at an average rate of $7.50 per hour for direct labor, was one and one-half times the direct materials cost. Factory overhead was applied on the basis of $.50 per direct labor hour. What was the total actual factory overhead incurred for the period?

8. The general ledger of The Sunset Manufacturing Co. contains the following control account:

WORK IN PROCESS

Materials	12,000	Finished goods	35,000
Labor	15,000		
Factory overhead	12,000		

If the materials charged to the one uncompleted job still in process amounted to $400, what amount of labor and factory overhead must have been charged to the job? (Assume overhead applied on the basis of direct labor cost.)

9. The following form represents an account taken from the general ledger of The Tryer Manufacturing Co.:

Indirect materials	50	Work in Process	820
Supervisor's salary	120	(50% of $1,640 direct labor)	
Power	380		
Building expenses	100		
Miscellaneous overhead	140		

Answer the following questions: **(a)** What is the title of the account? **(b)** Is this a departmentalized factory? **(c)** What does the balance of the account represent? **(d)** How was the 50% rate determined? **(e)** What disposition should be made of the balance?

10. The Lindy Manufacturing Company estimated its factory overhead expenses as follows:

Fixed expenses	$15,000
Variable expenses...	$45,000
Estimated direct labor hours..	60,000

The actual factory overhead expenses for the year amounted to $43,000 of which $10,750 were fixed costs. The production attained a capacity of 75% of that budgeted. **(a)** Compute the under- or overapplied factory overhead. **(b)** Determine the budget and volume variances.

11. The Fargo Company applies factory overhead to production using a predetermined rate based on a predicted number of direct labor hours. The number of direct labor hours estimated for the year is

400,000, and the estimates for factory overhead are $120,000 for fixed expenses and $220,000 for variable expenses. The actual production statistics for the year show that only 368,000 direct labor hours were used and the actual factory expenses totaled $305,000 of which $107,650 was fixed cost.

Determine the following: **(a)** the under- or overapplied expense for the year, **(b)** the budget variance, and **(c)** the volume variance.

PROBLEMS

4-1. Variable and fixed cost analysis: high-low and least squares methods. The Selecto Company manufactures a product which requires the use of a considerable amount of natural gas to heat it to a desired temperature. The process requires a constant level of heat, so the furnaces are maintained at a set temperature for 24 hours a day, although units are not continuously processed. Management desires that the variable cost be charged directly to the product and the fixed cost to the factory overhead. The following data have been collected for the year:

	Units	Cost		Units	Cost
January	2,400	$440	July	2,200	$420
February	2,300	430	August	2,100	410
March	2,200	420	September	2,000	400
April	2,000	400	October	1,400	340
May	1,800	380	November	1,900	390
June	1,900	390	December	1,800	380

Required: (1) Separate the variable and fixed elements using:

(a) High-low method   (b) Least squares method

(2) Determine the cost to be charged to the product for the year. **(3)** Determine the cost to be charged to factory overhead for the year.

4-2. Variable and fixed cost pattern analysis. The cost behavior patterns below are lettered A through L. The vertical axes of the graphs

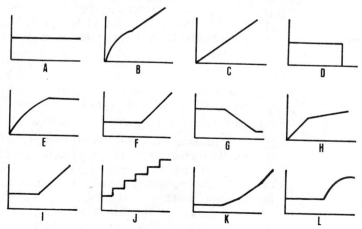

represent total dollars of expense and the horizontal axes represent production. In each case the zero point is at the intersection of the two axes. Each graph may be used more than once.

Required: Select the graph which matches the lettered cost described below.

(a) Depreciation of equipment — the amount of depreciation charged is computed by the machine hour method.

(b) Electricity bill — flat fixed charge, plus a variable cost after a certain number of kilowatt hours are used.

(c) City water bill — computed as follows:

First 1,000,000 gallons or less......	$1,000 flat fee
Next 10,000 gallons.....................	.003 per gallon used
Next 10,000 gallons.....................	.006 per gallon used
Next 10,000 gallons.....................	.009 per gallon used
etc., etc., etc.	

(d) Cost of lubricant for machines — cost per unit decreases with each pound of lubricant used (for example, if one pound is used, the cost is $10.00; if two pounds are used, the cost is $19.98; if three pounds are used, the cost is $29.94; with a minimum cost per pound of $9.25).

(e) Depreciation of equipment — the amount is computed by the straight-line method. When the depreciation rate was established, it was anticipated that the obsolescence factor would be greater than the wear-and-tear factor.

(f) Rent on a factory building donated by the city — the agreement calls for a fixed fee payment unless 200,000 work-hours are worked, in which case no rent need be paid.

(g) Salaries of repair workers — one repair worker is needed for every 1,000 hours of machine hours or less (i.e., 0 to 1,000 hours requires one repair worker, 1,001 to 2,000 hours requires two repair workers, etc.).

(h) Federal unemployment compensation taxes for the year — labor force is constant in number throughout year (average annual salary is $6,000 per worker).

(i) Cost of raw materials used.

(j) Rent on a factory building donated by the county — agreement calls for rent of $100,000, less $1 for each direct labor hour worked in excess of 200,000 hours, but minimum rental payment of $20,000 must be paid.

(AICPA adapted)

4-3. General journal entries for factory overhead. The Johnston Company uses a job order cost system. Selected transactions dealing with factory overhead for the month are as follows:

(a) Requisitioned indirect materials from storeroom, $1,400

(b) Purchased factory supplies for future needs, $2,000.

(c) Purchased parts for repairing a machine, $500.

(d) Requisitioned factory supplies from storeroom, $250.

(e) Returned defective factory supplies to vendor, $150.

(f) Rent accrued for the month, $1,000.

(g) Returned previously requisitioned factory supplies to storeroom, $75.

(h) Depreciation of machinery and equipment, $1,200.
(i) Payroll taxes liability for month, $1,400.
(j) Heat, light, and power charges payable for the month, $3,000.
(k) Expired insurance on inventories, $475.
(l) Factory overhead applied to production, $18,000.
(m) Indirect labor for the month, $1,100.
(n) Goods completed and transferred to finished goods: materials, $7,000; labor, $20,000; factory overhead, $15,000.

Required: Record the above transactions in general journal form assuming that the records include a control account and a subsidiary ledger for factory overhead to which the entries will be posted at some later date.

4-4. Distribution of service department costs to production departments. The Stillall Manufacturing Co. is divided into five departments, A, B, C, D, and E. The first three departments are engaged in production work. Departments D and E are service departments. During the month of August, the following factory overhead was incurred for the various departments:

Department A	$1,190	Department D	$ 810
Department B	775	Department E	640
Department C	1,335		

The bases for distributing service department expenses to the other departments are as follows:

Department E — On the basis of floor space occupied by the other departments as follows: Department A, 10,000 sq. ft.; Department B, 4,500 sq. ft.; Department C, 10,500 sq. ft.; and Department D, 7,000 sq. ft.

Department D — Divided: Dept. A — 30%; Dept. B — 20%; Dept. C — 50%.

Required: Prepare work sheets showing the distribution of the service departments' expenses to (1) the other service department and the production departments, and (2) to the production departments only (see Illustrations 4-7 and 4-8). (It is advisable to arrange the work sheets so that the service departments precede the production departments.)

4-5. Determining total job costs using predetermined overhead rate. The Cooper Manufacturing Co. uses the job order cost system of accounting. Shown below is a list of the jobs completed during the month of March showing the charges for materials requisitioned and for direct labor.

Job No.	Materials Requisitioned	Direct Labor
317	$ 30.00	$ 60.00
318	108.00	94.00
319	72.00	140.40
320	420.00	512.20

Required: Assuming that factory overhead is applied on the basis of direct labor costs and that the predetermined rate is 135%, compute **(1)** the amount of overhead to be added to the cost of each job completed during the month. **(2)** the total cost of each job completed during the month, and **(3)** the total cost of producing all the jobs finished during the month.

4-6. Determining job cost – calculation of predetermined rate for applying overhead by direct labor cost and direct labor hour methods. The Twistit Manufacturing Co. has its factory divided into three departments. In each department, all the operations are sufficiently alike for the department to be regarded as a cost center. The estimated monthly factory overhead for the departments are: Department A, $20,000; Department B, $18,000; and Department C, $7,140. The estimated production data are:

	Dept. A	Dept. B	Dept. C
Materials used	$20,000	$10,000	$10,000
Direct labor cost....................................	$16,000	$15,000	$ 8,400
Direct labor hours.................................	16,000	10,000	7,000

The job cost ledger shows the following data for Job No. 250, which was completed during the month:

	Dept. A	Dept. B	Dept. C
Materials used	$12.00	$14.00	$12.00
Direct labor cost....................................	$13.00	$13.50	$12.50
Direct labor hours.................................	11	9	10

Required: Determine the cost of Job No. 250, assuming that the factory overhead is applied to production orders on the basis of: **(1)** Direct labor cost. **(2)** Direct labor hours.

4-7. Determining overhead rates using direct labor cost, direct labor hour, and machine hour methods. The ENUFCO Manufacturing Company is studying the results of applying factory overhead to production. The following data have been used: estimated factory overhead $60,000; estimated materials costs, $50,000; estimated labor costs, $60,000; estimated direct labor hours, 40,000; estimated machine hours, 25,000; work in process at the beginning of the month, none.

The actual factory overhead incurred for the month of November was $55,000, and the production statistics at November 30 are:

Job No.	Materials Costs	Direct Labor Costs	Direct Labor Hours	Machine Hours	Date Jobs Completed
101	$ 6,000	$ 7,200	5,000	3,000	Nov. 10
102	8,000	10,000	6,000	3,200	Nov. 14
103	9,000	11,000	6,500	4,000	Nov. 20
104	7,000	9,000	5,600	3,400	In process
105	12,000	15,000	10,500	6,500	Nov. 26
106	3,000	4,200	3,000	1,500	In process
Total	$45,000	$56,400	36,600	21,600	

Required: (1) Calculate the predetermined rate based on:

    (a) Direct labor cost

    (b) Direct labor hours

    (c) Machine hours

(2) Using each of the methods, compute the total cost of each job at the end of the month. **(3)** Determine the under- or overapplied factory overhead at the end of the month under each of the methods. **(4)** Which method would you recommend? Why?

4-8. Determining overhead rate; using direct labor cost, direct labor hour, and machine hour methods. The following information was taken from the books of Tyit Company and represents the operations for the month of January:

	Dept. A	Dept. B	Dept. C
Materials used	$20,000	$10,000	$10,000
Direct labor cost	$ 6,400	$ 5,000	$ 7,000
Direct labor hours	16,000	10,000	20,000
Machine hours	3,200	5,000	2,800
Factory overhead	$ 8,000	$ 5,000	$ 5,600

The job cost system is used, and the February cost sheet for Job No. 100 shows the following:

	Dept. A	Dept. B	Dept. C
Materials requisitions	$2.00	$4.00	$2.00
Direct labor cost	$3.60	$3.00	$2.10
Direct labor hours	8	6	6
Machine hours	2	3	1

The following information was accumulated during February:

	Dept. A	Dept. B	Dept. C
Direct labor hours	15,000	9,800	20,000
Factory overhead	$ 7,000	$ 5,000	$ 5,500

Required: (1) Using the January data, ascertain the factory overhead application rates to be used during February on the basis of:

    (a) Direct labor cost

    (b) Direct labor hours

    (c) Machine hours

(2) Prepare a schedule showing the total production cost of Job No. 100 under each method of applying factory overhead. **(3)** Draft in general journal form the entries required to record the following operations:

    (a) Payment of total factory overhead.

    (b) Distribution of factory overhead to the departments.

    (c) Application of factory overhead to the jobs. (Use the predetermined rate calculated in (1) above.)

    (d) Closing of the applied factory overhead accounts.

    (e) Recording under- and overapplied factory overhead.

4-9. Determining the under- and overapplied overhead; budget variances; volume variances. The Omar Corporation has four departmental accounts: Building Maintenance, General Factory Overhead, Department A, and Department B. The direct labor hours method is used to apply factory overhead to the jobs being worked on in Departments A and B. The company expects each production department to use 30,000 direct labor hours during the year. The estimated overhead rates for the year are:

	Dept. A	Dept. B
Variable cost per hour	$ .70	$ .50
Fixed cost per hour	2.50	2.80
	$3.20	$3.30

During the year, both Departments A and B used 28,000 direct labor hours in their departments. Factory overhead costs incurred during the year were as follows:

Building maintenance	$20,000
General factory overhead	60,000
Department A	42,000
Department B	62,000

In determining application rates at the beginning of the year, cost allocations were made as follows:

Building maintenance to general factory overhead, 20%; to Department A, 50%; to Department B, 30%.

General factory overhead was distributed according to direct labor hours.

Required: (1) Determine the under- or overapplied overhead for each production department. **(2)** Calculate the budget variance and the volume variance for each production department.

4-10. Distribution of service department costs; reasons for allocations. Given below are the details pertaining to the Power Service Department.

SCHEDULE OF HORSEPOWER HOURS

	Production Departments		Service Departments	
	A	B	X	Y
Needed at capacity production.	10,000	20,000	12,000	8,000
Used during the month of April	8,000	13,000	7,000	6,000

During the month of April, the expenses of operating the Power Service Department amounted to $9,300; of this amount $2,500 was considered to be fixed costs.

Required: (1) What dollar amounts of the Power Service Department expense should be allocated to each production and service department?

(2) What are the reasons for allocating the costs of one service department to other service departments as well as to production departments?

(AICPA adapted)

4-11. Allocating service departments to production departments; determining overhead rates. The Tidal Manufacturing Company has decided to change its method of distributing factory overhead to its products, all of which are manufactured on special order.

The company's factory ledger for the six months ended on June 30, contains the following account balances (cents omitted):

	Debit	Credit
Materials and Factory Supplies	$ 85,321	
Work in Process — Materials	86,105	
Work in Process — Labor	82,872	
Work in Process — Factory Overhead	161,480	
Indirect Labor	41,740	
Factory Rent	2,400	
Insurance — Machinery and Equipment	4,216	
Compensation Insurance	2,486	
Superintendence	6,000	
Factory Clerical Salaries	4,950	
Machinery Maintenance and Repairs	31,010	
Depreciation Expense — Machinery and Equipment	42,800	
Fuel	3,172	
Electricity	2,178	
Factory Supplies Used	3,617	
Payroll Taxes Expense	9,210	
Factory Office Supplies Used	879	
Miscellaneous Factory Expense	1,212	
Applied Factory Overhead		$158,200

The manufacturing operations are carried on in three production departments, A, B, and C, with the aid of two service departments, numbered 1 and 2 respectively. Other data are as follows:

	Departments					
	1	2	A	B	C	Total
Plant floor space (square feet)	7,500	5,500	10,000	5,000	2,000	30,000
Number of employees	25	10	50	20	4	109
Number of labor hours	26,000	10,400	52,000	20,800	4,160	113,360
Number of machine hours	5,840	—0—	31,912	9,640	560	47,952
Salaries and wages	$ 37,230	$ 9,460	$ 76,180	$ 28,472	$ 9,975	$ 161,317
Cost of machinery and equipment	$112,862	$11,790	$623,225	$250,960	$20,210	$1,019,047
Annual depreciation rate	10%	20%	8%	8%	10%	

In developing overhead rates, expenses not distributed in the above table are distributed to departments as follows:

On the basis of floor space:

Factory rent, fuel, ¼ of electricity

On the basis of salaries and wages:

Compensation insurance, superintendence, factory supplies used, payroll taxes, factory office supplies used, miscellaneous factory expense

On the basis of investment in machinery and equipment:

Insurance on machinery and equipment, machinery maintenance and repairs, ¾ of electricity

Factory clerical salaries and $4,510 of indirect labor are charged to Department 2. The balance of indirect labor is charged to Department No. 1.

Expenses of Department 1 are to be distributed $1/10$ to Department 2, and the balance to all other departments on the basis of machine hours.

Expenses of Department 2 are to be distributed to Departments A, B, and C on the basis of labor hours.

The departmental overhead rates are to be based on machine hours for Departments A and B and on labor hours for Department C.

Data applicable to Job Order No. 987 are as follows:

Materials, $487.92; direct labor, $465.00
Machine hours: Department A — 50 hours
                Department B — 12 hours
Labor hours: Department C — 20 hours

Required: (1) Develop appropriate departmental rates based on the company's operations for the first half of the fiscal year. **(2)** Determine the cost of Job No. 987 by applying the rates developed. *Note: Carry distributions to three decimal places and round totals to the nearest dollar.*

(AICPA adapted)

4-12. Using overhead to determine gross profit rates. The Candoo Company sold 50 air conditioning units for $200 each in June. Costs included materials cost of $50 a unit and direct labor cost of $30 a unit. Factory overhead is computed at 100% of direct labor cost. Interest expense on a 14% bank loan is equivalent to $1 a unit. Federal income tax at a 30% rate is equivalent to $15 a unit.

Effective July 1, materials costs decreased 5% and direct labor costs increased 20%. Also effective July 1, the interest rate on the bank loan increased from 14% per annum to 18% per annum.

Required: (1) Assuming no change in the rate of overhead in relation to direct labor costs, compute the sales price per unit that will produce the same ratio of gross profit. **(2)** Assuming that $10 of the overhead consists of fixed costs, compute the sales price per unit that will produce the same ratio of gross profit.

(AICPA adapted)

5

Job Order Cost Accounting— Application of Principles

The principles and procedures involved in accounting for materials, labor, and factory overhead have been discussed in detail in the preceding chapters. The objectives of this chapter are to integrate the information previously developed and to illustrate the application of cost accounting procedures to the operations of a hypothetical manufacturing concern. The procedures illustrated are typical of those encountered in firms using the job order cost system.

To derive the maximum benefit from this chapter, it should be read carefully and thoughtfully. Each transaction should be followed through the accounting process, and each figure in the general ledger accounts should be analyzed in order to understand the origin of the figure and how it flows into the ledger account.

COMPREHENSIVE ILLUSTRATION OF JOB ORDER COST ACCOUNTING

The illustration which follows covers the accounting procedures for the Judson Manufacturing Corporation for the month of May. Following a description of the company's factory organization and accounting system, a complete accounting cycle is presented — from beginning-of-the-month balances through the recording of transactions for the month and end-of-month procedures including preparation of the trial balance, the work sheet, schedules, and financial statements.

Factory Organization

The Judson Manufacturing Corporation is engaged in the manufacture of commercial water softening equipment. The softeners are either built to order in accordance with customer specifications or manufactured according to standard specifications and carried in stock for sale in the usual course of business. Essentially, a water softening unit comprises two tanks: one contains the softening agent, the other rock salt. Rock salt provides the brine to rejuvenate the softening agent. Parts are also manufactured and carried in stock for sale or for use in the production of softeners. The job order cost system is used in accounting for the cost of production.

The factory is organized on a departmental basis. The departmentalization described here is not intended to be complete for a factory of this type. Two typical production departments and two typical service departments are used. Following is a brief description of the activities of each of these departments.

Department A — Welding. This production department fabricates the water softening unit tanks. First, prerolled and formed sheet steel purchased from a foundry is welded in a lengthwise direction to make the tank wall. Then the bottom and top plates, which have been cut in Department B, are fitted and welded to the tank wall.

Department B — Cutting and Assembling. This production department cuts sheet steel into circular pieces for the bottom and top of the tank; it also cuts galvanized iron pipe used in the assembly into various required lengths. This department also assembles, tests, and inspects the softeners.

Department C — Maintenance. This service department is responsible for the maintenance of the buildings, machinery, and other factory equipment as well as for the janitor service and the heating and lighting of the factory. The expenses of this department are apportioned to Departments A, B, and D on the basis of the floor space that each occupies.

Department D — Planning and Engineering. This service department is responsible for preparing the detailed specifications and plans for all softeners manufactured. The necessary blueprints are prepared in this department. The expenses of this department are apportioned to Departments A and B on a basis of two thirds to A and one third to B. This allocation is arbitrary but is based on the past experience of the company. It indicates that, in general, twice as much work is performed for Department A as for Department B and that no services are rendered to Department C.

Chart of Accounts

The chart of general ledger accounts for The Judson Manufacturing Corporation is reproduced below. Control accounts for subsidiary ledgers are maintained as described on page 194.

THE JUDSON MANUFACTURING CORPORATION

Chart of Accounts

Current Assets

Cash
1110 Cash
1120 Petty Cash

Temporary Investments
1200 Marketable Securities

Receivables
1310 Notes Receivable
1320 Interest Receivable
1330 Accounts Receivable
    1331 Allowance for
        Doubtful Accounts

Inventories
1410 Finished Goods
1420 Work in Process
1430 Materials

Prepayments
1510 Prepaid Insurance

Property, Plant, and Equipment
1610 Land
1620 Buildings
    1621 Accumulated Depreciation —
        Buildings
1630 Machinery
    1631 Accumulated Depreciation —
        Machinery
1640 Furniture and Fixtures
    1641 Accumulated Depreciation —
        Furniture and Fixtures
1650 Small Tools
    1651 Accumulated Depreciation —
        Small Tools

Intangibles
1710 Goodwill

Current Liabilities
2210 Notes Payable
2220 Vouchers Payable
2230 FICA Tax Payable
2240 Federal Unemployment Tax
    Payable

2250 State Unemployment Tax
    Payable
2260 Employees Income Tax Payable
2271 Property Tax payable
2272 Estimated Income Tax Payable
2273 Interest Payable
2274 Accrued Payroll

Long-Term Liabilities
2710 Bonds Payable

Stockholders' Equity
2910 Capital Stock
2980 Retained Earnings
2990 Income Summary

Factory Overhead
3100 Factory Overhead
3140 Factory Overhead — Department A
3150 Factory Overhead — Department B
3160 Factory Overhead — Department C
3170 Factory Overhead — Department D
3180 Under- and Overapplied Overhead

Sales and Cost of Goods Sold
4100 Sales
4600 Cost of Goods Sold

Payroll and General Expenses
5000 Payroll
5100 Salaries
5200 Payroll Taxes Expense — Salaries
5300 Office Expense
5500 Public Relations Expense
5800 Uncollectible Accounts Expense
5900 Miscellaneous General Expense

Additions to and Deductions from Operating Income
Additions to Income:
    6110 Purchases Discount
    6120 Interest Income
Deduction from Income:
    6220 Interest Expense
Deduction for Income Tax:
    6420 Provision for Income Tax

1330 Accounts Receivable. This is the control account for the accounts receivable ledger. The accounts receivable ledger is a loose-leaf ledger in which balance-column type ledger sheets of standard form are used for the customer accounts. These accounts are kept in alphabetic order.

1410 Finished Goods. This is the control account for the finished goods ledger. An account for each size softener or finished part is maintained on a card. Since most of the work done by the company is on specific order received from customers, the only items that will be recorded in the finished goods ledger will be softeners of standard sizes, for which there is a continuous demand, parts that may be either sold or used in the manufacture of softeners, or jobs completed and not delivered. During slack seasons, the employees and facilities of the company may be profitably employed in building up the stock of standard softeners and parts. The job cost sheets are the source of the information needed in recording the quantities and manufacturing costs of all softeners and parts manufactured for stock.

1420 Work in Process. This is the control account for the job cost ledger. The job cost ledger is a loose-leaf ledger in which a job cost sheet is used to keep an account of the cost of completing each job.

1430 Materials. This is the control account for the stores ledger. Cards are used to keep accounts of the various types of materials and factory supplies carried in stock. The purchase invoices and the receiving reports are the sources of the information needed in recording the quantities and costs of materials and factory supplies received, while the requisitions are the source of the information needed in recording the quantities and costs of materials and factory supplies issued.

2910 Capital Stock. This is the control account for the stockholders ledger. A separate account for each stockholder is kept in the stockholders ledger. The Judson Manufacturing Corporation has an authorized capital of $200,000 divided into 2,000 shares of common stock with par value of $100 per share. All of the stock has been issued and is outstanding.

3100 Factory Overhead. This is the control account for the factory overhead ledger. The factory overhead ledger is a loose-leaf ledger in which analysis ledger sheets, similar to those on pages 146 and 147, are used.

Following is a list of the individual accounts kept in the factory overhead ledger.

Fixed Costs

3111 Depreciation
3112 Property Tax
3113 Insurance

Variable Costs

3121 Indirect Materials
3122 Indirect Labor
3123 Fuel Consumed
3124 Water
3125 Light
3126 Power
3127 Payroll Taxes Expense
3128 Miscellaneous Factory Expense

Trial Balance

The company operates on a fiscal year ending April 30. Following is the post-closing trial balance as of April 30:

THE JUDSON MANUFACTURING CORPORATION
Post-Closing Trial Balance
April 30, 19__

Cash	21,500.00	
Petty Cash	100.00	
Marketable Securities	16,050.00	
Notes Receivable	10,000.00	
Interest Receivable	101.66	
Accounts Receivable	36,000.00	
Allowance for Doubtful Accounts		1,800.00
Finished Goods	18,000.00	
Work in Process	10,000.00	
Materials	25,000.00	
Prepaid Insurance	2,000.00	
Land	25,100.00	
Buildings	80,000.00	
Accumulated Depreciation — Buildings		12,000.00
Machinery	120,000.00	
Accumulated Depreciation — Machinery		25,000.00
Furniture and Fixtures	14,000.00	
Accumulated Depreciation — Furniture and Fixtures		4,480.00
Small Tools	14,000.00	
Accumulated Depreciation — Small Tools		8,520.00
Goodwill	5,300.00	
Notes Payable		7,000.00
Vouchers Payable		15,000.00
FICA Tax Payable		1,800.00
Federal Unemployment Tax Payable		315.00
State Unemployment Tax Payable		1,215.00
Employees Income Tax Payable		1,500.00
Property Tax Payable		2,000.00
Estimated Income Tax Payable		16,200.00
Interest Payable		102.22
Bonds Payable		25,000.00
Capital Stock		200,000.00
Retained Earnings		75,219.44
	397,151.66	397,151.66

Books of Account

The Judson Manufacturing Corporation uses an accounting system in which separate journals and books of account are kept to record each type of transaction. The books of account and other records consist of the following:

LEDGERS
   (1) General ledger
   (2) Subsidiary ledgers
      (a) Accounts receivable ledger
      (b) Stores ledger
      (c) Job cost ledger
      (d) Factory overhead ledger
      (e) Finished goods ledger
      (f) Stockholders ledger

JOURNALS
   (1) General journal
   (2) Voucher register
   (3) Check register
   (4) Sales journal
   (5) Cash receipts journal

AUXILIARY RECORDS
   (1) Clock card
   (2) Time ticket
   (3) Materials requisition
   (4) Petty cash disbursements record

The voucher register and check register used by Judson Manufacturing Corporation appear as follows:

VOUCHER REGISTER   Page

Materials Dr.	Payroll Dr.	Factory Overhead Dr.	Sundry Accounts				Vouchers Payable Cr.
			Acct. No.	Amount Dr.	Amount Cr.	✓	

CHECK REGISTER   Page

Vouchers Pay. Dr.		Day	Drawn to the Order of	Purchases Discount Cr.	Cash Cr.	
No.	Amount				Ck. No.	Amount

Narrative of Transactions

The following is a discussion of the transactions completed during May. The subsequent posting of the journal entries illustrated in each of the following transactions is presented on pages 209 to 215.

(a) Materials Purchased. As each purchase transaction is completed, the purchase invoice is verified and vouchered. The voucher is recorded in the voucher register in the columns headed Materials and Vouchers Payable and is posted to the proper accounts in the stores ledger. Since the voucher system is used, the file of unpaid vouchers takes the place of the creditors ledger.

At the end of the month, when the summary posting from the voucher register is completed, the total of the Materials column, amounting to $22,200 is posted as a debit to Materials (Account No. 1430). At the same time, the total of the Vouchers Payable column is posted as a credit to Vouchers Payable (Account No. 2220). The entry, in general journal form, to record these summary data appears as follows:

```
Materials.................................................... 22,200
        Vouchers Payable ...................................          22,200
```

(b) Factory Overhead. Invoices for factory overhead expenses are verified and vouchered, recorded in the voucher register in the columns headed Factory Overhead and Vouchers Payable, and are posted to the proper accounts in the factory overhead ledger. The factory overhead ledger contains individual accounts for each type of overhead expense, including indirect materials, indirect labor, and indirect manufacturing expenses.

At the end of the month, the total of the Factory Overhead column is posted as a debit to Factory Overhead (Account No. 3100). The amounts recorded in the Vouchers Payable column are included in the column total, which is posted as a credit to Vouchers Payable. The entry, in general journal form, to record these summary data appears as follows:

```
Factory Overhead....................................... 4,664
        Vouchers Payable ...................................          4,664
```

(c) Payroll. The wages of factory employees are paid weekly, while the salaries of all other employees are paid semimonthly. On each payday, a voucher is prepared for the amount of the wages and salaries earned during the pay period. The source of this information is a summary of the time tickets and a schedule of the fixed salaries.

The amounts to be withheld for FICA taxes and employees' income taxes and the net amount payable to all factory employees are indicated on the voucher. The payroll vouchers are recorded in the voucher register, where the total amount of the wages earned is entered in the column headed Payroll Dr. and the net amount of the total wages payable to employees is entered in the column headed Vouchers Payable Cr. The amounts credited to FICA Tax Payable and Employees Income Tax Payable are entered in the Sundry Accounts Cr. amount column and are posted individually to the proper general ledger accounts.

At the end of the month, the total of the voucher register column headed Payroll is posted as a debit to Payroll (Account No. 5000). The amounts recorded in the Vouchers Payable column are included in the column total, which is posted as a credit to Vouchers Payable. The entry, in general journal form, to record these summary data appears as follows:

Payroll	33,000	
FICA Tax Payable		2,310
Employees Income Tax Payable		3,300
Vouchers Payable		27,390

(d) Payroll Checks. The checks issued in payment of the payroll vouchers are recorded in the check register. At the end of the month, the total of the check register column headed Vouchers Payable is posted as a debit to Vouchers Payable, and the total of the Cash column is posted as a credit to Cash. The entry, in general journal form, to record the payment of wages and salaries is:

Vouchers Payable	27,390	
Cash		27,390

(e) Materials Requisitioned. During the month, materials requisitions are posted to the proper accounts in the subsidiary stores ledger, job cost ledger, and factory overhead ledger. At the end of the month, a summary of the materials requisitions is prepared. The summary for May provides the following information:

Direct materials requisitioned:	
For Job No. 308	$ 900
For Job No. 309	2,500
For Job No. 310	4,000
For Job No. 311	5,500
For Job No. 312	2,800
For Job No. 313	3,000
Total direct materials requisitioned	$18,700
Indirect materials requisitioned	2,700
Total materials requisitioned	$21,400

The entry, in general journal form, to record these summary data appears as follows:

Work in Process	18,700	
Factory Overhead	2,700	
Materials		21,400

Three control accounts are affected by this entry: Work in Process, the control account for the job cost ledger; Factory Overhead (Account No. 3100), the control account for the factory overhead ledger; and Materials, the control account for the stores ledger.

(f) Wages and Salaries Earned. The time tickets and schedule of fixed salaries are the sources of individual postings to the proper accounts in the subsidiary job cost ledger and factory overhead ledger. At the end of the month, the labor cost summary is prepared from the the time tickets, which show the amount of labor applied directly to jobs in process and the amount of indirect labor. The labor cost summary and a schedule of the fixed salaries provide the information for drafting a general journal entry to distribute the total wages and salaries earned during the month.

In distributing the total wages and salaries earned during the month, two control accounts are affected: Work in Process (Account No. 1420) is debited for the total of the direct labor cost; and Factory Overhead (Account No. 3100) is debited for the total indirect labor cost. Also, Salaries (Account No. 5100) is debited for the total of the salaries paid to all other employees. Payroll (Account No. 5000) is credited for the total wages and salaries earned during the month. The following general journal entry distributes the total wages and salaries earned during the month:

Work in Process	29,400	
Factory Overhead	4,000	
Salaries	5,000	
Payroll		38,400

In the subsidiary job cost ledger, the detail for the direct labor in Work in Process is as follows:

Job No. 303	$ 1,500
Job No. 308	1,200
Job No. 309	2,400
Job No. 310	6,850
Job No. 311	7,250
Job No. 312	4,100
Job No. 313	6,100
Total direct labor	$29,400

The total wages and salaries earned during the month will be the same as the total amount of the payroll vouchers issued during the month if all wages and salaries are paid on a monthly or semi-monthly basis. However, since some of the wages are paid on a weekly basis and the last payday for the month does not fall on the last day of the month, Judson Manufacturing Corporation must account for accrued wages. The amount of the accrued wages for May is $5,400, which is the credit balance of the payroll account.

If the payroll account is debited for the total wages and salaries paid during the month and is credited for the total wages and salaries earned during the month, the credit balance of the account should always represent the total amount of the wages and salaries accrued at the end of the month. This credit balance should be transferred to a liability account. Therefore, at the end of May, the following general journal entry is recorded:

Payroll..	5,400	
Accrued Payroll......................................		5,400

(g) Payroll Taxes Imposed on Employer. The payroll records provide the information for the schedule of wages earned and payroll taxes shown below. At the end of each payroll period, the payroll taxes imposed on the employer for FICA and federal and state unemployment taxes are recorded. At the end of May, the employer's payroll taxes on the accrued payroll are recorded.

SCHEDULE OF EARNINGS AND PAYROLL TAXES
For the Month Ended May 31, 19—

Classification of Wages and Salaries	Total Earnings	FICA 7%	Unemployment Taxes Federal .7%	State 2.7%	Total Payroll Taxes
Direct labor	$29,400.00	$2,058.00	$205.80	$ 793.80	$3,057.60
Indirect labor............	4,000.00	280.00	28.00	108.00	416.00
Total taxes on wages..		$2,338.00	$233.80	$ 901.80	$3,473.60
Salaries....................	5,000.00	350.00	35.00	135.00	520.00
Total.....................	$38,400.00	$2,688.00	$268.80	$1,036.80	$3,993.60

The combined general journal entry to record these summary data for May is as follows:

Factory Overhead	3,473.60	
Payroll Taxes Expense — Salaries...............	520.00	
FICA Tax Payable..................................		2,688.00
Federal Unemployment Tax Payable.........		268.80
State Unemployment Tax Payable		1,036.80

(h) Fixed Expenses. At the end of each month, the schedule of fixed costs is the source of a general journal entry debiting Factory Overhead (Account No. 3100) for the amount of all fixed manufacturing expenses, such as depreciation, property tax, and insurance applicable to the month. The schedule of fixed expenses is also the source of the posting of the proper amounts to the individual accounts in the subsidiary factory overhead ledger.

The depreciation of factory property is computed at the following annual rates:

Buildings — 4.875%	Furniture and Fixtures — 10%
Machinery — 8.25%	Small Tools — 20%

It should be noted that small tools are depreciated at the rate of 20 percent. It is rather difficult to determine a satisfactory rate of depreciation on small tools because there are so many of them and their life is so unpredictable. Instead of using the depreciation method, many firms use the fixed-sum system. Under this system, a definite amount, representing the average value of the tools on hand at all times, is set up as a plant asset and the amount of all replacements is treated as factory overhead. Other firms use the inventory system, in which all replacements are charged to the asset account, and at the end of the period the tools on hand are inventoried. The difference between the inventory value and the balance of the small tools account is then charged to Factory Overhead. Regardless of which method is used, the amount consumed in each accounting period should be treated as factory overhead.

The following general journal entry records these fixed expenses:

Factory Overhead	1,850.00	
Accumulated Depreciation — Buildings		325.00
Accumulated Depreciation — Machinery		825.00
Accumulated Depreciation — Furniture and Fixtures		116.67
Accumulated Depreciation — Small Tools		233.33
Property Tax Payable		150.00
Prepaid Insurance		200.00

(i) Factory Overhead Distributed to Departments. At the end of each month, a summary of factory overhead is prepared on a departmental basis. The summary for May is at the top of page 202.

The subsidiary factory overhead ledger accounts are the source of the information for this summary. The amounts charged to Payroll Taxes Expense (Account No. 3127) include the FICA tax of 7%, the federal unemployment tax of .7%, and the state unemploy-

Acct. No.	Account	Dept. A Welding	Dept. B Cutting and Assembling	Dept. C Maintenance	Dept. D Planning and Engineering	Total
	SUMMARY OF FACTORY OVERHEAD **For the Month Ended May 31, 19—**					
3111	Depreciation.....................	$ 625.00	$ 585.00	$ 200.00	$ 90.00	$ 1,500.00
3112	Property tax.....................	60.00	55.00	25.00	10.00	150.00
3113	Insurance........................	90.00	80.00	20.00	10.00	200.00
3121	Indirect materials.............	1,100.00	1,200.00	270.00	130.00	2,700.00
3122	Indirect labor..................	1,000.00	1,200.00	1,400.00	400.00	4,000.00
3123	Fuel consumed................	300.00	250.00	150.00	50.00	750.00
3124	Water............................	20.00	50.00	32.00	222.00	324.00
3125	Light.............................	500.00	400.00	200.00	100.00	1,200.00
3126	Power............................	900.00	500.00	150.00	200.00	1,750.00
3127	Payroll taxes	2,100.00	997.60	241.00	135.00	3,473.60
3128	Miscellaneous factory expenses...................	240.00	192.00	128.00	80.00	640.00
	Total...........................	$6,935.00	$5,509.60	$2,816.00	$1,427.00	$16,687.60

ment tax of 2.7% imposed on employers. From the summary, a general journal entry is prepared as follows:

Factory Overhead — Department A.......... 6,935.00
Factory Overhead — Department B.......... 5,509.60
Factory Overhead — Department C.......... 2,816.00
Factory Overhead — Department D.......... 1,427.00
　　Factory Overhead.............................. 16,687.60

After this entry is posted, the factory overhead control account has a zero balance. The individual accounts in the subsidiary factory overhead ledger are also assumed to have zero balances.

(j) Distribution of Maintenance Department Expenses. At the end of each month, the service departments' expenses are distributed on the basis of service rendered to the other departments. There are two service departments: Department C, the Maintenance Department; and Department D, the Planning and Engineering Department. The work sheet on page 203 was prepared to distribute the expenses of both service departments. The Maintenance Department expenses are distributed to the other departments on the basis of the number of square feet occupied by each department:

Department	Area Sq. Ft.	Rate per Sq. Ft.	Amount
A..................	16,000	$.0938666	$1,501.87
B..................	7,500	.0938666	704.00
D..................	6,500	.0938666	610.13
	30,000		$2,816.00

SERVICE DEPARTMENTS EXPENSE DISTRIBUTION WORK SHEET
For the Month Ended May 31, 19––

Description	Dept. C Maintenance	Dept. D Planning and Engineering	Dept. A Welding	Dept. B Cutting and Assembling	Total
Direct costs	$2,816.00	$1,427.00	$6,935.00	$5,509.60	$16,687.60
Department C — Distribution $.0938666 per sq. ft.					
Dept. D — 6,500 sq. ft. ...		610.13			
Dept. A — 16,000 sq. ft. .			1,501.87		
Dept. B — 7,500 sq. ft. ...				704.00	
		$2,037.13			
Department D — Distribution basis arbitrary					
Dept. A — ⅔			1,358.09		
Dept. B — ⅓				679.04	
Total			$9,794.96	$6,892.64	$16,687.60

The distribution is accomplished by the following general journal entry:

Factory Overhead — Department A............. 1,501.87
Factory Overhead — Department B............. 704.00
Factory Overhead — Department D............. 610.13
Factory Overhead — Department C......... 2,816.00

(k) Distribution of Planning and Engineering Department Expenses.
The Planning and Engineering Department expenses are distributed to the production departments on the basis of two thirds to Department A and one third to Department B. This arbitrary distribution is based on the past experience of the company. The amount to be distributed includes both the direct expenses from Department D and the apportioned expenses from Department C. The apportioned amounts are calculated as follows:

Dept. A — ⅔ × $2,037.13 = $1,358.09
Dept. B — ⅓ × $2,037.13 = $679.04

The distribution is accomplished by the following general journal entry:

Factory Overhead — Department A............. 1,358.09
Factory Overhead — Department B............. 679.04
Factory Overhead — Department D......... 2,037.13

(l) Distribution of the Production Departments' Expenses. During the month, direct materials and direct labor costs are charged to the proper accounts in the job cost ledger from the materials requisitions and time tickets. To ascertain the total cost of each job processed during the month, factory overhead must be added. The company has adopted the direct labor hour basis for applying factory overhead. To ascertain the current rates, the following annual estimates were prepared at the beginning of the fiscal year, May 1:

Department	Estimated Direct Labor Hours	Estimated Factory Overhead	Application Rate per Hour
A	64,500	$105,780	$1.64
B	36,600	77,592	2.12
	101,100	$183,372	

During the month, departmental overhead expenses are added to the cost of the jobs in process by applying the predetermined application rates to the actual number of direct labor hours used on each job. The amount of overhead applicable to each job finished during the month is recorded at the time of completion. The amount of overhead applicable to the jobs still in process at the end of the month is recorded on the last day of the month. To determine the amount of overhead applied to jobs processed during May, the following summary is prepared on May 31:

	SUMMARY OF APPLIED FACTORY OVERHEAD FOR MAY						
Job No.	Dept. A — Welding			Dept. B — Cutting and Assembling			Total Applied Factory Overhead
	Direct Labor Cost	Direct Labor Hours	Applied Factory Overhead	Direct Labor Cost	Direct Labor Hours	Applied Factory Overhead	
303				$1,500	350	$ 742.00	$ 742.00
308	$ 500	60	$ 98.40	700	90	190.80	289.20
309	1,400	500	820.00	1,000	250	530.00	1,350.00
310	3,350	1,350	2,214.00	3,500	1,050	2,226.00	4,440.00
311	5,000	1,750	2,870.00	2,250	800	1,696.00	4,566.00
312	3,250	775	1,271.00	850	175	371.00	1,642.00
313	6,100	1,250	2,050.00				2,050.00
	$19,600	5,685	$9,323.40	$9,800	2,715	$5,755.80	$15,079.20

The summary is the basis for the following general journal entry:

```
Work in Process....................................  15,079.20
    Factory Overhead — Department A........               9,323.40
    Factory Overhead — Department B........               5,755.80
        A — 5,685 DLH × $1.64 = $9,323.40
        B — 2,715 DLH × $2.12 = $5,755.80
```

On May 1, there were three jobs in process, represented in the general ledger by a debit balance of $10,000 in the work in process control account, with three subsidiary accounts to which materials and labor costs have been posted during April and factory overhead has been applied on April 30. Following is a summary of the jobs in process:

WORK IN PROCESS, APRIL 30

Job No.	Materials	Labor	Overhead	Total
303	$2,000	$1,500	$ 750	$ 4,250
308	500	1,000	500	2,000
309	1,500	1,500	750	3,750
	$4,000	$4,000	$2,000	$10,000

Job No. 303 is almost completed; the other two need considerable work before they will be completed. All three are worked on during May. In addition, work is started on Jobs Nos. 310, 311, 312, and 313. In all, seven jobs are being processed during May. In the case of the jobs in process on May 1, the costs incurred for their benefit during May are added to the costs already recorded in April. Following is a summary of the jobs in process during May.

SUMMARY OF FACTORY OPERATIONS FOR MAY

Job No.	Charges to Work in Process During May				Charges to Work in Process in Prior Periods	Total Charges to Work in Process
	Materials	Labor	Applied Overhead	Total		
303		$ 1,500.00	$ 742.00	$ 2,242.00	$ 4,250.00	$ 6,492.00
308	$ 900.00	1,200.00	289.20	2,389.20	2,000.00	4,389.20
309	2,500.00	2,400.00	1,350.00	6,250.00	3,750.00	10,000.00
310	4,000.00	6,850.00	4,440.00	15,290.00		15,290.00
311	5,500.00	7,250.00	4,566.00	17,316.00		17,316.00
312	2,800.00	4,100.00	1,642.00	8,542.00		8,542.00
313	3,000.00	6,100.00	2,050.00	11,150.00		11,150.00
	$18,700.00	$29,400.00	$15,079.20	$63,179.20	$10,000.00	$73,179.20

The charges of $73,179.20 must be accounted for as costs assigned to jobs remaining to be completed and to completed jobs that have been transferred out of Work in Process.

(m) Under- and Overapplied Overhead. After the departmental overhead expenses are applied to the costs of the jobs in process at the predetermined application rates, Factory Overhead — Department A has a debit balance of $471.56 ($9,794.96 − $9,323.40) and

Factory Overhead — Department B has a debit balance of $1,136.84 ($6,892.64 − $5,755.80). The debit balances represent an underapplication of overhead to the jobs in process during the month. It is common practice to transfer the balances of the departmental factory overhead accounts to an account entitled Under- and Overapplied Overhead. At the end of the year, this account is usually closed into Cost of Goods Sold, unless the balance of the account is unusually large.

The following general journal entry closes the departmental factory overhead accounts:

Under- and Overapplied Overhead	1,608.40	
Factory Overhead — Department A		471.56
Factory Overhead — Department B		1,136.84

(n) Finished Goods. Jobs Nos. 303, 308, 309, and 310 are completed during May. The following information is prepared from the summary on page 205.

Job No.		Total Cost
303		$ 6,492.00
308		4,389.20
309		10,000.00
310		15,290.00
Total cost of goods finished during May		$36,171.20

The following general journal entry transfers the cost applicable to jobs finished in May from Work in Process to Finished Goods:

Finished Goods	36,171.20	
Work in Process		36,171.20

After Finished Goods is debited and Work in Process is credited for the total cost of the jobs completed during May, the balance of the work in process account, $37,008, represents the amount of work in process on May 31.

(o) Sales. The sales for May are as follows:

Job No.	Manufacturing Cost	Selling Price
303	$ 6,492.00	$ 9,000.00
307	18,000.00	26,000.00
308	4,389.20	6,500.00
310	15,290.00	18,500.00
	$44,171.20	$60,000.00

Job No. 307 was completed during April at a total cost of $18,000. Reference to the post-closing trial balance for April 30 shows that this amount was the inventory of finished goods and indicates that this job was the only job completed and not delivered on that date. The sales during May are recorded in a sales journal in which separate amount columns are provided for recording both the selling price and the cost of goods sold. At the end of the month, the amount of total sales is posted to the general ledger as a debit to Accounts Receivable (Account No. 1330) and a credit to Sales (Account No. 4100). The total cost of goods sold is posted to the general ledger as a debit to Cost of Goods Sold (Account No. 4600) and a credit to Finished Goods (Account No. 1410).

The entries, in general journal form, to record these summary data, appear as follows:

Accounts Receivable	60,000.00	
Sales		60,000.00
Cost of Goods Sold	44,171.20	
Finished Goods		44,171.20

After the posting is completed, the finished goods account has a balance of $10,000. This amount represents the cost of Job No. 309, which is the only job completed but undelivered at May 31.

(p) Receipts from Customers. Cash received from customers to apply on account is recorded in the cash receipts journal, in which a separate amount column is provided for recording credits to Accounts Receivable. At the end of May, the total of this column, amounting to $53,000, is posted to the general ledger as a credit to Accounts Receivable. At the same time, the amount of cash received is included in the total deposits, which is posted as a debit to Cash.

The entry, in general journal form, to record these summary data is:

Cash	53,000	
Accounts Receivable		53,000

(q) Payments to Creditors. Checks issued to creditors in settlement of vouchers payable are recorded in the check register, in which a separate amount column is provided for recording debits to Vouchers Payable. At the end of May, the total of this column is posted to the general ledger as a debit to Vouchers Payable. At the same time, the total of the column headed Purchases Discount is posted to the general ledger as a credit to Purchases Discount (Account No. 6110), and the total of the Cash column is posted to the general ledger as a credit to Cash.

The entry, in general journal form, to record these summary data appears as follows:

Vouchers Payable 8,282
    Purchases Discount   82
    Cash...   8,200

(r) Vouchering FICA Taxes and Employees' Income Taxes. Periodically, the amounts withheld for employee FICA and income taxes plus the employer's share of FICA tax are paid to a depository (bank). Therefore, after the entries for the employer's and employees' taxes are made, vouchers are prepared to pay the taxes.

During May, vouchers were prepared for the taxes which were recorded for the last week of April and the first three weeks of May. These vouchers were recorded in the voucher register as a debit to FICA Tax Payable, a debit to Employees Income Tax Payable, and a credit to Vouchers Payable. The debits are posted individually to Accounts Nos. 2230 and 2260, while the amount credited to Account No. 2220 is included in the total of the column headed Vouchers Payable, which is posted at the end of the month.

The entry, in general journal form, to record these summary data appears as follows:

FICA Tax Payable 4,200
Employees Income Tax payable 3,600
    Vouchers Payable   7,800

(s) Payment of FICA Taxes and Employees' Income Taxes. The check for $7,800, issued to the depository in payment of the taxes, is recorded in the check register as a debit to Vouchers Payable and as a credit to Cash. At the end of the month, the total of the column headed Vouchers Payable is posted as a debit to Account No. 2220, while the total of the Cash column is posted as a credit to Account No. 1110.

The entry, in general journal form, to record these summary data appears as follows:

Vouchers Payable 7,800
    Cash...   7,800

(t) General Expenses. The general expenses incurred during the month include the following:

Office expenses, $1,200
Miscellaneous general expense, $1,300
Public relations expense, $1,700.

Vouchers are issued for the expense invoices as they are received. The entry, in general journal form, to record these summary data appears as follows:

Office Expense	1,200	
Public Relations Expense	1,700	
Miscellaneous General Expense.....................	1,300	
Vouchers Payable		4,200

The End of the Month

Following is the General Ledger of the Judson Manufacturing Corporation showing the balances of the accounts on May 31 (including adjustments from the work sheet).

GENERAL LEDGER

CASH — Account No. 1110

19--			19--		
May 1 Balance		21,500.00	May 31 Payroll		(d) 27,390.00
31 Deposit		(p) 53,000.00	31 Creditors		(q) 8,200.00
	31,100.00	74,500.00	31 Taxes		(s) 7,800.00
					43,390.00

PETTY CASH — Account No. 1120

19--		
May 1 Balance	100.00	

MARKETABLE SECURITIES — Account No. 1200

19--		
May 1 Balance	16,050.00	

NOTES RECEIVABLE — Account No. 1310

19--		
May 1 Balance	10,000.00	

INTEREST RECEIVABLE — Account No. 1320

19--		
May 1 Balance	101.66	
31 Adjustment	48.34	
	150.00	

ACCOUNTS RECEIVABLE — Account No. 1330

19--			19--		
May 1 Balance		36,000.00	May 31 Receipts		(p) 53,000.00
31 Sales		(o) 60,000.00			
	43,000.00	96,000.00			

ALLOWANCE FOR DOUBTFUL ACCOUNTS — Account No. 1331

		19--		
		May 1 Balance		1,800.00
		31 Adjustment		500.00
				2,300.00

FINISHED GOODS   Account No. 1410

19--				19--			
May 1	Inventory		18,000.00	May 31	Cost of goods sold	(o)	44,171.20
31	Goods completed	(n)	36,171.20				
		10,000.00	*54,171.20*				

WORK IN PROCESS   Account No. 1420

19--				19--			
May 1	Inventory		10,000.00	May 31	Finished goods	(n)	36,171.20
31	Materials	(e)	18,700.00				
31	Labor	(f)	29,400.00				
31	Overhead	(l)	15,079.20				
		37,008.00	*73,179.20*				

MATERIALS   Account No. 1430

19--				19--			
May 1	Inventory		25,000.00	May 31	Requisitions	(e)	21,400.00
31	Purchases	(a)	22,200.00				
		25,800.00	*47,200.00*				

PREPAID INSURANCE   Account No. 1510

19--				19--			
May 1	Balance		2,000.00	May 31	Expired	(h)	200.00
		1,800.00					

LAND   Account No. 1610

19--			
May 1	Balance		25,100.00

BUILDINGS   Account No. 1620

19--			
May 1	Balance		80,000.00

ACCUMULATED DEPRECIATION — BUILDINGS   Account No. 1621

				19--			
				May 1	Balance		12,000.00
				31	Addition	(h)	325.00
							12,325.00

MACHINERY   Account No. 1630

19--			
May 1	Balance		120,000.00

ACCUMULATED DEPRECIATION — MACHINERY   Account No. 1631

				19--			
				May 1	Balance		25,000.00
				31	Addition	(h)	825.00
							25,825.00

FURNITURE AND FIXTURES   Account No. 1640

19--		
May 1 Balance		14,000.00

ACCUMULATED DEPRECIATION —
FURNITURE AND FIXTURES   Account No. 1641

		19--		
		May 1 Balance		4,480.00
		31 Addition	(h)	116.67
				4,596.67

SMALL TOOLS   Account No. 1650

19--		
May 1 Balance		14,000.00

ACCUMULATED DEPRECIATION — SMALL TOOLS   Account No. 1651

		19--		
		May 1 Balance		8,520.00
		31 Addition	(h)	233.33
				8,753.33

GOODWILL   Account No. 1710

19--		
May 1 Balance		5,300.00

NOTES PAYABLE   Account No. 2210

		19--	
		May 1 Balance	7,000.00

VOUCHERS PAYABLE   Account No. 2220

19--			19--		
May 31 Payroll	(d)	27,390.00	May 1 Balance		15,000.00
31 Creditors	(q)	8,282.00	31 Materials	(a)	22,200.00
31 U.S. Depository	(s)	7,800.00	31 Overhead	(b)	4,664.00
		43,472.00	31 Payroll	(c)	27,390.00
			31 FICA taxes and		
			employees'		
			income taxes	(r)	7,800.00
			31 Misc. general		
			expense	(t)	4,200.00
			37,782.00		81,254.00

FICA TAX PAYABLE   Account No. 2230

19--			19--		
May 31 Vouchered	(r)	4,200.00	May 1 Balance		1,800.00
			31 Employees	(c)	2,310.00
			31 Employer	(g)	2,688.00
			2,598.00		6,798.00

FEDERAL UNEMPLOYMENT TAX PAYABLE   Account No. 2240

	19—			
	May 1	Balance		315.00
	31	Employer	(g)	268.80
				583.80

STATE UNEMPLOYMENT TAX PAYABLE   Account No. 2250

	19—			
	May 1	Balance		1,215.00
	31	Employer	(g)	1,036.80
				2,251.80

EMPLOYEES INCOME TAX PAYABLE   Account No. 2260

19—				19—			
May 31 Vouchered	(r)	3,600.00		May 1	Balance		1,500.00
				31	Withheld	(c)	3,300.00
			1,200.00				4,800.00

PROPERTY TAX PAYABLE   Account No. 2271

	19—			
	May 1	Balance		2,000.00
	31	Accrued	(h)	150.00
				2,150.00

ESTIMATED INCOME TAX PAYABLE   Account No. 2272

	19—		
	May 1	Balance	16,200.00
	31	Adjustment	1,930.00
			18,130.00

INTEREST PAYABLE   Account No. 2273

	19—		
	May 1	Balance	102.22
	31	Adjustment	31.53
			133.75

ACCRUED PAYROLL   Account No. 2274

	19—			
	May 31	Accrued	(f)	5,400.00

BONDS PAYABLE   Account No. 2710

	19—		
	May 1	Balance	25,000.00

CAPITAL STOCK   Account No. 2910

	19—		
	May 1	Balance	200,000.00

RETAINED EARNINGS   Account No. 2980

	19--		
	May 1	Balance	75,219.44
	31	Net income	2,169.21
			77,388.65

INCOME SUMMARY   Account No. 2990

19--			19--		
May 31	Closing	57,961.13	May 31	Closing	60,130.34
	Retained Earnings	2,169.21			
		60,130.34			60,130.34

FACTORY OVERHEAD   Account No. 3100

19--				19--			
May 31	Manufacturing expenses	(b)	4,664.00	May 31	Distributed	(i)	16,687.60
31	Indirect materials	(e)	2,700.00				
31	Indirect labor	(f)	4,000.00				
31	Payroll taxes	(g)	3,473.60				
31	Fixed expense	(h)	1,850.00				
			16,687.60				16,687.60

FACTORY OVERHEAD — DEPARTMENT A   Account No. 3140

19--				19--			
May 31	Distributed	(i)	6,935.00	May 31	Applied	(l)	9,323.40
31	Department C	(j)	1,501.87	31	Trans. to Acct.		
31	Department D	(k)	1,358.09		No. 3180	(m)	471.56
			9,794.96				9,794.96

FACTORY OVERHEAD — DEPARTMENT B   Account No. 3150

19--				19--			
May 31	Distributed	(i)	5,509.60	May 31	Applied	(l)	5,755.80
31	Department C	(j)	704.00	31	Trans. to Acct.		
31	Department D	(k)	679.04		No. 3180	(m)	1,136.84
			6,892.64				6,892.64

FACTORY OVERHEAD — DEPARTMENT C   Account No. 3160

19--				19--			
May 31	Distributed	(i)	2,816.00	May 31	Distributed	(j)	2,816.00

FACTORY OVERHEAD — DEPARTMENT D   Account No. 3170

19--				19--			
May 31	Distributed	(i)	1,427.00	May 31	Distributed	(k)	2,037.13
31	Department C	(j)	610.13				
			2,037.13				2,037.13

UNDER- AND OVERAPPLIED OVERHEAD   Account No. 3180

19--				19--		
May 31	Underapplied overhead	(m)	1,608.40	May 31	Cost of goods sold	1,608.40

SALES   Account No. 4100

19--			19--		
May 31	Income Summary	60,000.00	May 31	On account	(o) 60,000.00

COST OF GOODS SOLD   Account No. 4600

19--			19--		
May 31	Finished goods	(o) 44,171.20	May 31	Income Summary	45,779.60
31	Under- and over-applied overhead	1,608.40			
		45,779.60			45,779.60

PAYROLL   Account No. 5000

19--			19--		
May 31	Vouchered	(c) 33,000.00	May 31	Distributed	(f) 38,400.00
31	Accrued	(f) 5,400.00			
		38,400.00			38,400.00

SALARIES   Account No. 5100

19--			19--		
May 31	(f)	5,000.00	May 31	Income Summary	5,000.00

PAYROLL TAXES EXPENSE — SALARIES   Account No. 5200

19--			19--		
May 31	(g)	520.00	May 31	Income Summary	520.00

OFFICE EXPENSE   Account No. 5300

19--			19--		
May 31	(t)	1,200.00	May 31	Income Summary	1,200.00

PUBLIC RELATIONS EXPENSE   Account No. 5500

19--			19--		
May 31	(t)	1,700.00	May 31	Income Summary	1,700.00

UNCOLLECTIBLE ACCOUNTS EXPENSE   Account No. 5800

19--			19--		
May 31	Adjustment	500.00	May 31	Income Summary	500.00

MISCELLANEOUS GENERAL EXPENSE   Account No. 5900

19--			19--		
May 31	(t)	1,300.00	May 31	Income Summary	1,300.00

PURCHASES DISCOUNT   Account No. 6110

19--			19--			
May 31	Income Summary	82.00	May 31		(q)	82.00

INTEREST INCOME   Account No. 6120

19--			19--		
May 31	Income Summary	48.34	May 31	Adjustment	48.34

INTEREST EXPENSE   Account No. 6220

19--			19--		
May 31	Adjustment	31.53	May 31	Income Summary	31.53

PROVISION FOR INCOME TAX   Account No. 6420

19--			19--		
May 31	Adjustment	1,930.00	May 31	Income Summary	1,930.00

Work Sheet

A work sheet, properly designed, is an aid in preparing monthly financial statements. The work sheet for May is presented on pages 216 and 217.

Trial Balance. The first step in preparing the work sheet is to prepare a trial balance of the general ledger accounts as of May 31. This unadjusted trial balance appears in the first two amount columns.

The balances of the accounts for work in process, accounts receivable, and vouchers payable are verified by preparing schedules of the subsidiary work in process and accounts receivable accounts, and a schedule of the unpaid vouchers. These schedules are reproduced below and on page 218.

SCHEDULE OF WORK IN PROCESS, MAY 31, 19--

Job No.	Name	Amount
311	Patterson Textiles	$17,316
312	Plasco Dye and Chemical Corp.	8,542
313	International Bleaching	11,150
	Total	$37,008

SCHEDULE OF ACCOUNTS RECEIVABLE, MAY 31, 19--

Name	Amount
Chemical Bleachers & Dyers, Newark	$ 9,175
Glen Rock Plumbing Supplies, Glen Rock	5,455
Manufacturers Supplies, Dayton	5,860
Moline, The City of, Moline	7,400
Pinehurst Dairies, Inc., Marysville	7,610
Plasco Dye & Chemical Corp., New Milford	7,500
Total	$43,000

THE JUDSON
Work
For the Month

Account	Acct. No.	Trial Balance	
		Debit	Credit
Cash	1110	31,110.00	
Petty Cash	1120	100.00	
Marketable Securities	1200	16,050.00	
Notes Receivable	1310	10,000.00	
Interest Receivable	1320	101.66	
Accounts Receivable	1330	43,000.00	
Allowance for Doubtful Accounts	1331		1,800.00
Finished Goods	1410	10,000.00	
Work in Process	1420	37,008.00	
Materials	1430	25,800.00	
Prepaid Insurance	1510	1,800.00	
Land	1610	25,100.00	
Buildings	1620	80,000.00	
Accumulated Depreciation — Buildings	1621		12,325.00
Machinery	1630	120,000.00	
Accumulated Depreciation — Machinery	1631		25,825.00
Furniture and Fixtures	1640	14,000.00	
Accumulated Depreciation — Furniture and Fixtures	1641		4,596.67
Small Tools	1650	14,000.00	
Accumulated Depreciation — Small Tools	1651		8,753.33
Goodwill	1710	5,300.00	
Notes Payable	2210		7,000.00
Vouchers Payable	2220		37,782.00
FICA Tax Payable	2230		2,598.00
Federal Unemployment Tax Payable	2240		583.80
State Unemployment Tax Payable	2250		2,251.80
Employees Income Tax Payable	2260		1,200.00
Property Tax Payable	2271		2,150.00
Estimated Income Tax Payable	2272		16,200.00
Interest Payable	2273		102.22
Accrued Payroll	2274		5,400.00
Bonds Payable	2710		25,000.00
Capital Stock	2910		200,000.00
Retained Earnings	2980		75,219.44
Under- and Overapplied Overhead	3180	1,608.40	
Sales	4100		60,000.00
Cost of Goods Sold	4600	44,171.20	
Salaries	5100	5,000.00	
Payroll Taxes Expense — Salaries	5200	520.00	
Office Expense	5300	1,200.00	
Public Relations Expense	5500	1,700.00	
Uncollectible Accounts Expense	5800		
Miscellaneous General Expense	5900	1,300.00	
Purchases Discount	6110		82.00
Interest Income	6120		
Interest Expense	6220		
		488,869.26	488,869.26
Provision for Income Tax	6420		
Net Income (to Retained Earnings)			

MANUFACTURING CORPORATION
Sheet
Ended May 31, 19——

Adjustments		Income Statement		Balance Sheet	
Debit	Credit	Debit	Credit	Debit	Credit
				31,110.00	
				100.00	
				16,050.00	
48.34				10,000.00	
				150.00	
	500.00			43,000.00	2,300.00
				10,000.00	
				37,008.00	
				25,800.00	
				1,800.00	
				25,100.00	
				80,000.00	12,325.00
				120,000.00	
				14,000.00	25,825.00
					4,596.67
				14,000.00	8,753.33
				5,300.00	7,000.00
					37,782.00
					2,598.00
					583.80
	1,930.00				2,251.80
	31.53				1,200.00
					2,150.00
					18,130.00
					133.75
					5,400.00
					25,000.00
					200,000.00
		1,608.40			75,219.44
		44,171.20	60,000.00		
		5,000.00			
		520.00			
		1,200.00			
500.00		1,700.00			
		500.00			
		1,300.00			
	48.34		82.00		
			48.34		
31.53		31.53			
		56,031.13	60,130.34	433,418.00	431,248.79
1,930.00		1,930.00			
		2,169.21			2,169.21
2,509.87	2,509.87	60,130.34	60,130.34	433,418.00	433,418.00

SCHEDULE OF VOUCHERS PAYABLE, MAY 31, 19—

Voucher No.	To Whom Issued	Amount
17	Rockford Pipe Co., Inc.	$ 2,365
32	Acme Steel Corp.	1,735
35	Synthetic Resins, Inc.	3,850
53	Baker Roller Mills Co.	1,870
58	Acme Steel Corp.	3,700
60	Buckeye Steel Co.	7,350
61	Arco Plastics	2,570
62	Synthetic Resins, Inc.	1,950
64	Automation, Inc.	2,730
66	The Globe Valve Co.	6,250
67	Rockford Pipe Co., Inc.	3,412
	Total	$37,782

Adjustments. It is usually necessary to adjust certain accounts before financial statements can be prepared. The adjustments required on May 31 are as follows:

Increase in accrued interest receivable, $48.34.
Increase in accrued interest payable, $31.53.
Increase in allowance for doubtful accounts, 1% of the account sales for May, $500.
Provision for estimated income tax, $1,930.

The proper adjustments are entered in the third and fourth amount columns on the work sheet.

Income Statement. The adjusted balances of the temporary or nominal accounts are extended to the fifth and sixth amount columns on the work sheet, after which these columns provide the information for preparing the income statement for May.

Balance Sheet. The adjusted balances of the assets, liabilities, and capital, or real accounts, are extended to the seventh and eighth amount columns on the work sheet; these columns provide the information for preparing the balance sheet as of May 31.

Financial Statements

It is generally desirable to prepare monthly financial statements for the use of the principal executives of the company. These statements can be prepared only if inventories are taken monthly or if a system of cost accounting is made a part of the accounting procedure of the company. Ordinarily, it is impractical to take monthly physical inventories of materials, work in process, and finished goods. A properly developed cost accounting system, however, makes a monthly physical inventory unnecessary, inasmuch as it provides for recording the cost of work in process and finished goods and the maintenance of book inventories of materials, work in process, and finished goods.

The Judson Manufacturing Corporation follows the practice of preparing a monthly balance sheet, income statement, and manufacturing statement. The statements prepared at the end of May are reproduced on pages 220 and 221.

Balance Sheet. It will be noted that the accounts are listed in the balance sheet in the order of their arrangement in the chart of accounts. Thus, the current assets appear first in the assets section of the balance sheet followed by plant assets and goodwill. In the liabilities section, the current liabilities are listed first, followed by the long-term liabilities and capital. In practice, the arrangement of items will depend on the uses for which the balance sheet is intended. If it is to be submitted to a bank with application for a loan, the form of balance sheet to which the particular bank is accustomed would be desirable. If it is prepared at the end of the year for inclusion in the report to stockholders, it should be arranged so as to be most informative to them. If it is prepared monthly for the use of the principal executives, the items may be expressed in more technical language than would be advisable if it were to be submitted to the stockholders.

Income Statement. The income statement reproduced on page 221 follows the usual form, with the gross margin on sales shown first, followed by the income from operations and finally the income both before and after deducting income tax. The provision for income tax is based on an estimate, since the actual amount of the tax cannot be ascertained until the income for the year is determined and the rates applicable to the year are known.

Statement of Cost of Goods Manufactured. In preparing the manufacturing statement for May, the costs of materials, labor, and applied factory overhead are first ascertained. The work in process account is the source of the information for these costs. Since the application rates are based upon estimates made at the beginning of the fiscal year, it is not unusual that the amount of applied overhead may differ from the actual overhead incurred during any month of the year. It is to be expected that there will be further fluctuations during succeeding months. In preparing the manufacturing statement for any part of the year, the amount of any underapplied overhead should be added in computing the actual cost of the goods

THE JUDSON MANUFACTURING CORPORATION
Balance Sheet
May 31, 19--

Current assets:

Cash		$ 31,110.00
Petty cash		100.00
Marketable securities		16,050.00
Notes receivable		10,000.00
Interest receivable		150.00
Accounts receivable	$43,000.00	
Less allowance for doubtful accounts	2,300.00	40,700.00
Finished goods		10,000.00
Work in process		37,008.00
Materials		25,800.00
Prepaid insurance		1,800.00
Total current assets		$172,718.00

Property, plant, and equipment:

Land		$ 25,100.00	
Buildings	$ 80,000.00		
Less accumulated depreciation	12,325.00	67,675.00	
Machinery	$120,000.00		
Less accumulated depreciation	25,825.00	94,175.00	
Furniture and fixtures	$ 14,000.00		
Less accumulated depreciation	4,596.67	9,403.33	
Small tools	$ 14,000.00		
Less accumulated depreciation	8,753.33	5,246.67	
Total property, plant, and equipment			201,600.00

Intangibles:

Goodwill	5,300.00
Total assets	$379,618.00

Liabilities

Current liabilities:

Notes payable	$ 7,000.00	
Vouchers payable	37,782.00	
FICA tax payable	2,598.00	
Federal unemployment tax payable	583.80	
State unemployment tax payable	2,251.80	
Employees income tax payable	1,200.00	
Property tax payable	2,150.00	
Estimated income tax payable	18,130.00	
Interest payable	133.75	
Accrued payroll	5,400.00	
Total current liabilities		$ 77,229.35

Long-term liability:

Bonds payable	25,000.00
Total liabilities	$102,229.35

Stockholders' Equity

Capital stock		$200,000.00
Retained earnings, May 1	$ 75,219.44	
Net income for month	2,169.21	
Retained earnings, May 31		77,388.65
Total stockholders' equity		277,388.65
Total liabilities and stockholders' equity		$379,618.00

THE JUDSON MANUFACTURING CORPORATION
Income Statement
For the Month Ended May 31, 19——

Net sales		$60,000.00
Less cost of goods sold:		
Finished goods inventory, May 1....................	$18,000.00	
Add cost of goods manufactured	37,779.60	
Goods available for sale	$55,779.60	
Less finished goods inventory, May 31...........	10,000.00	
Cost of goods sold......................................		45,779.60
Gross margin on sales......................................		$14,220.40
Operating expenses:		
Salaries	$ 5,000.00	
Public relations expense...............................	1,700.00	
Office expense...	1,200.00	
Uncollectible accounts expense	500.00	
Payroll taxes expense — salaries......................	520.00	
Miscellaneous general expense.......................	1,300.00	
Total operating expenses		10,220.00
Income from operations....................................		$ 4,000.40
Other revenue:		
Purchases discount.......................................	$ 82.00	
Interest income	48.34	130.34
		$ 4,130.74
Other expense:		
Interest expense..		31.53
Income before provision for income tax		$ 4,099.21
Less income tax (estimated)...........................		1,930.00
Net income		$ 2,169.21

THE JUDSON MANUFACTURING CORPORATION
Statement of Cost of Goods Manufactured
For the Month Ended May 31, 19——

Direct materials used	$18,700.00
Direct labor..	29,400.00
Applied factory overhead	15,079.20
Total manufacturing cost...	$63,179.20
Add work in process inventory, May 1...................................	10,000.00
Total	$73,179.20
Less work in process inventory, May 31	37,008.00
Cost of goods manufactured during the month at predetermined application rates...	$36,171.20
Add underapplied factory overhead..	1,608.40
Cost of goods manufactured during the month.........................	$37,779.60

manufactured during the period, while any overapplied overhead should be subtracted in computing the actual cost of the goods manufactured.

Adjusting Entries

After the financial statements have been prepared, the adjustments entered on the work sheet are journalized as shown below and are posted to the accounts to bring them into agreement with the statements.

ADJUSTING ENTRIES, MAY 31

Interest Receivable...................................	48.34	
Interest Income......................................		48.34
Increase in accrued interest receivable.		
Interest Expense	31.53	
Interest Payable		31.53
Increase in accrued interest payable.		
Uncollectible Accounts Expense	500.00	
Allowance for Doubtful Accounts............		500.00
Increase in allowance for doubtful accounts.		
Provision for Income Tax..........................	1,930.00	
Estimated Income Tax Payable		1,930.00
Providing for estimated income tax applicable to the income for May.		

Closing Entries

The Judson Manufacturing Corporation prepares monthly financial statements but does not close the temporary accounts until the end of the fiscal year. However, to illustrate the procedure in closing the accounts of a manufacturing company, the closing entries that would be required if the accounts were to be closed at the end of May are journalized below and on page 223 and are posted to the accounts on pages 209 to 215.

CLOSING ENTRIES, MAY 31

Cost of Goods Sold ....:	1,608.40	
Under- and Overapplied Overhead		1,608.40
Underapplied overhead transferred to Cost of Goods Sold.		
Sales	60,000.00	
Purchases Discount.............................	82.00	
Interest Income	48.34	
Income Summary		60,130.34
Closing the income accounts into Income Summary.		

Income Summary	57,961.13	
Cost of Goods Sold		45,779.60
Salaries..		5,000.00
Payroll Taxes Expense — Salaries		520.00
Office Expense.................................		1,200.00
Public Relations Expense		1,700.00
Uncollectible Accounts Expense		500.00
Miscellaneous General Expense		1,300.00
Interest Expense		31.53
Provision for Income Tax		1,930.00

> Closing the cost of goods sold and expense accounts into Income Summary.

| Income Summary .... | 2,169.21 | |
| Retained Earnings............................. | | 2,169.21 |

> Balance of the income summary account transferred to Retained Earnings.

QUESTIONS

This chapter reviews subjects discussed in previous chapters. These chapters should be referred to for answers to some of the following questions, exercises, and problems.

1. Explain the difference between direct costs and indirect costs.

2. A manufacturer of an electronic component ran short of a part needed to complete an assembly. The reason for the shortage was that the purchasing department inaccurately estimated the materials requirements. The required parts were shipped by air freight at a cost of $3,750. When these materials are shipped by regular transportation methods, these items cost $3,600. How would you recommend recording the amount paid for these rush-order materials?

3. Due to an improperly adjusted machine, 80 of the 200 units produced during the day on a job order are damaged beyond repair. How should these units be accounted for?

4. A company that is using departmental predetermined rates is considering changing to a blanket predetermined rate for all departments. The controller believes the change will substantially reduce accounting costs, because only one

rate will have to be developed and applied to all production. Do you believe the "saving" is justifiable?

5. The Judson Manufacturing Corporation is organized on a departmental basis. Name the departments and indicate which are service departments and which are production departments.

6. What subsidiary ledgers are maintained for the Judson Manufacturing Corporation and what are the numbers and titles of their control accounts in the general ledger?

7. Name the books of original entry used by The Judson Manufacturing Corporation.

8. Are the deductions for FICA tax and employees' income tax entered in the voucher register at the time of recording the voucher, or in the check register at the time of recording the payroll check?

9. List and describe the purpose of each form used in accounting for materials.

10. Name the control accounts affected and explain how they are affected by the general journal entry required at the end of each month to record materials requisitioned during the month.

11. List and describe the purpose of each form used in accounting for labor.

12. Explain how the control account for factory overhead is closed at the end of each month.

13. Assume that the direct labor hour method is used to apply factory overhead and that the following estimates were made for each department:

	Total Direct Labor Hours for the Year	Total Factory Overhead for the Year
Department A.........	170,400	$86,904 = .51
Department B.........	117,600	85,848 .48
Department C.........	40,800	11,016 .27

What amount should be charged to the work in process account for the month of June if the departments used the following number of direct labor hours?

Department A — 14,200 hours × .51 = 7242
Department B — 9,800 hours   4704
Department C — 3,400 hours   1134

14. Refer to the ledger of the Judson Manufacturing Corporation and ascertain the amounts of the inventories of finished goods, work in process, and materials at the end of May.

15. Refer to the ledger of the Judson Manufacturing Corporation and ascertain the amount of the under- and overapplied overhead for each production department at the end of May.

16. Refer to the financial statements of The Judson Manufacturing Corporation prepared at the end of May and ascertain the following:

(a) Cost of goods manufactured during May.

(b) Cost of goods sold during May.

(c) Net income for May.

(d) Retained earnings as of the end of May.

EXERCISES

1. Certain selected accounts from the general ledger of the Drysdale Manufacturing Co. are shown below.

WORK IN PROCESS				MATERIALS		
14,700	35,800		1/1	2,850.00		16,250
14,250				1915.0.*		
9,120			1/31 Bal.	5,750.00		

PAYROLL			FACTORY OVERHEAD		UNDER- AND OVERAPPLIED OVERHEAD	
15,600.00	15,600.00		1,550.00	9120.*	175.00	
			1,350.00	175.00		
			1,622.40			
		4522.40 ......*		9295		

*To be calculated.

From an analysis of these accounts, complete the following requirements: **(a)** Draft all entries, in general journal form, that were made during the month to the various manufacturing accounts. (For recording payroll taxes, use the arbitrary rates of: FICA, 7%; federal income tax, 10%; federal unemployment tax, .7%; and state unemployment tax, 2.7%.) **(b)** Prepare a statement of cost of goods manufactured. **(c)** If the ending work in process balance has the same proportion of materials, labor, and factory overhead as the goods processed during the month, how much of each cost is included in the ending balance? **(d)** If the average cost of direct labor per hour was $5.00, what is the overhead application rate based on direct labor hours?

2. The Bartone Machine Tool Company uses the job order cost system of accounting. Following is a summary of the factory overhead incurred during the month of January. The information needed to prepare this summary was obtained from the accounts in the subsidiary factory overhead ledger. Draft an entry in general journal form to distribute the factory overhead expenses to the proper departments.

SUMMARY OF FACTORY OVERHEAD FOR JANUARY

Acct. No.		Dept. A Machine Shop	Dept. B Assembly	Dept. C Mainte-nance	Dept. D Engi-neering	Total
51	Depreciation..............................	$1,400.00	$1,250.00	$ 700.00	$ 250.00	$3,600.00
52	Property tax..............................	75.00	50.00	25.00	12.00	162.00
53	Insurance..............................	100.00	75.00	20.00	10.00	205.00
54	Power	100.00	50.00	35.00	10.00	195.00
55	Indirect materials..........................	1,000.00	600.00	90.00	40.00	1,730.00
56	Indirect labor..............................	900.00	500.00	600.00	300.00	2,300.00
57	Heat, light, and power....................	200.00	150.00	85.00	25.00	460.00
58	Payroll taxes.............................	245.00	110.00	95.00	70.00	520.00
	Total...	$4,020.00	$2,785.00	$1,650.00	$ 717.00	$9,172.00

3. Departments C and D of the Bartone Machine Tool Company are service departments, while Departments A and B are production departments. Department C expenses are distributed to Departments A, B, and D on the basis of the number of square feet occupied by each department, as follows:

Department	Area Square Feet
A.....................................	15,000
B.....................................	10,000
D.....................................	8,000

Department D expenses are distributed to the production departments on a basis of 60% to A and 40% to B.

Prepare a work sheet showing the proper distribution of the service department expenses and draft the required entries in general journal form to record the distribution of the service department expenses to the production departments.

4. The A-Hey Company, using a job order cost system, has compiled the following data on work started during the week:

Job	Direct Materials	Direct Labor Hours
101	$ 2,750	180
102	3,100	210
103	2,500	170
104	1,500	100
105	1,850	120
106	2,100	160
107	800	40
108	1,000	50
109	600	30
	$16,200	1,060

The direct labor rate is $6 an hour. The overhead rate is $8 per direct labor hour (fixed cost — $5,000; variable cost — $3 an hour). The actual factory overhead costs for the week were $9,015. Jobs Nos. 101, 102, 103, and 106 were completed.

(a) Determine the total cost of each job for the week. (b) Compute the under- or overapplied factory overhead for the week. (c) Determine the volume and budget variances. (d) Calculate the work in process at the end of the week. (e) Prepare a general journal entry to transfer the completed goods to finished goods.

PROBLEMS

5-1. Scrap material. The Gettem Company manufactures a product that is started in Department A and is finished in Department B. All materials required for the product are issued in Department A. When the materials are introduced in Department A, about 10% are usually spoiled and have to be sold as scrap. The receipts from the sale of scrap are credited to the department.

The following costs were incurred for one month's production:

	Department A	Department B
Materials.....................................	$ 35,800	—0—
Direct labor	62,400	$21,300
Factory overhead.........................	78,000	21,450
	$176,200	$42,750

Receipts from the sale of scrap during the month amounted to $700.

Production data for the month were as follows:

	Department A	Department B
Units started or received from preceding department	5,000	4,500
Units spoiled (material only).......................	500	
Units completed and transferred	4,500	4,500

Required: (1) Prepare a schedule that shows the unit cost of production in Department A, Department B, and in total. (2) Suppose that Department B, at the point of final inspection before the goods are transferred to finished goods, discards 135 units as spoiled with no salvage value. How much will the total cost per unit increase if this spoilage is not charged to factory overhead?

5-2. *Effect of change in capacity on unit costs.* The Fastpan Company has just negotiated a new labor contract which increases direct labor costs by 10%. The company is already experiencing a serious decline in sales and profit. As a consequence, the president has requested production and sales statistics which include the following:

(a) The maximum capacity the plant can achieve is 100,000 units per year. At this capacity, the production costs will be:

Materials..		$ 500,000
Direct labor		1,000,000
Factory overhead:		
Fixed cost	$1,000,000	
Variable cost...	1,000,000	2,000,000
Total...		$3,500,000

(b) Sales are not expected to exceed 80,000 units per year, nor can the units be sold for more than $50 per unit because of market competition.

(c) To maintain its position in the industry, a 40% gross margin on sales should be realized on a volume of 80,000 units per year.

(d) A cost study shows that at 80,000 units per year, fixed costs can be reduced by 60% and there is some possibility of reducing the variable factory overhead costs.

Required: (1) What are the unit costs for materials, labor, and overhead at the 100,000 unit level? What is the gross margin per unit? (2) If direct labor costs increase by 10% but only 80,000 units are produced and sold, what is the gross margin per unit? (3) What unit cost will result if at the 100,000 unit capacity, the fixed costs are reduced by 60%, labor cost increases 10%, and 80,000 units are produced and sold? (4) At the 80,000 unit level for production and sales, with a 60% fixed cost reduction and 10% labor cost increase, how much per unit must variable factory overhead be reduced to achieve a 40% gross margin?

5-3. *Calculation of budget and volume variances.* The Alcalie Company has accumulated the following data pertaining to factory overhead costs for the year. Each department is budgeted for $15,000 of fixed costs for the year. The company uses the direct labor hour method of applying factory overhead to the jobs.

	Department A	Department B	Department C
Total budgeted factory overhead..........	$50,000	$75,000	$105,000
Budgeted direct labor hours................	10,000	15,000	15,000
Total actual factory overhead	$55,000	$70,000	$105,000
Actual direct labor hours....................	12,000	14,000	16,000

Required: (1) Compute the under- or overapplied factory overhead for each department. **(2)** Compute the budget variances due to cost factors and indicate whether they are favorable or unfavorable. **(3)** Compute the volume variances and indicate whether they are favorable or unfavorable.

5-4. Comprehensive review problems of job order procedures. The Holt Chrome Products Co. manufactures special chromed parts made to the order and specifications of the customer. It has two production departments, Stamping and Plating, and two service departments, Power and Maintenance. In any production department, the job in process is wholly completed before the next job is started.

The company operates on a fiscal year which ends March 31. Following is the post-closing trial balance as of March 31:

HOLT CHROME PRODUCTS CO.
Post-Closing Trial Balance
March 31, 19--

Cash	19,000	
Accounts Receivable	24,200	
Finished Goods	8,400	
Work in Process	2,400	
Materials	5,000	
Prepaid Insurance	2,700	
Factory Building	60,000	
Accumulated Depreciation — Factory Building		20,000
Machinery and Equipment	30,000	
Accumulated Depreciation — Machinery and Equipment		15,000
Office Equipment	16,000	
Accumulated Depreciation — Office Equipment		8,000
Vouchers Payable		3,700
FICA Tax Payable		1,560
Federal Unemployment Tax Payable		182
State Unemployment Tax Payable		702
Employees Income Tax Payable		2,600
Capital Stock		100,000
Retained Earnings		15,956
	167,700	167,700

1. The balance of the materials account represents the following:

Materials	Units	Unit Cost	Total
A	100	$12	$1,200
B	300	6	1,800
C	150	10	1,500
Factory Supplies			500
			$5,000

The company uses the fifo method of accounting for all inventories. Material A is used in the Stamping Department and Materials B and C in the Plating Department.

2. The balance of the work in process account represents the following costs which are applicable to Job No. 312. (The customer's order is for 1,000 units of the finished product.)

Direct materials....................... $1,000
Direct labor............................ 800
Factory overhead 600
$2,400

3. The finished goods account reflects the cost of Job No. 311, which was finished at the end of the preceding month and is awaiting delivery orders from the customer.

4. At the beginning of the year, factory overhead application rates were based on the following data:

	Stamping Dept.	Plating Dept.
Estimated factory overhead for the year...........	$67,500	$63,000
Estimated direct labor hours for the year	25,000	7,000

NARRATIVE OF TRANSACTIONS FOR APRIL

(a) Purchased the following materials and supplies on account:

Material A ....1,500 units @ $13
Material B ....1,400 units @ $ 7
Material C ....1,200 units @ $10
Factory Supplies $1,400

(b) The following materials were issued to the factory:

	Job No. 312	Job No. 313	Job No. 314
Material A.....................................		600 units	400 units
Material B.....................................		400 units	200 units
Material C.....................................	200 units	400 units	

Factory Supplies — $1,300

Customer's orders covered by Jobs Nos. 313 and 314 are for 1,000 and 500 units of finished product, respectively.

(c) Factory wages and office, sales, and administrative salaries are paid at the end of each month.

The following data, provided from an analysis of labor time tickets and salary schedules, will be sufficient for the preparation of the entries to voucher the payroll (assume FICA and federal income tax rates of 7% and 10%, respectively.); record the company's liability for state and federal unemployment taxes (assume rates of 2.7% and .7%, respectively); and record the payroll distribution for the month of April.

	Stamping Dept.	Plating Dept.
Job No. 312	100 hrs. @ $4	300 hrs. @ $5
Job No. 313	1,200 hrs. @ $4	300 hrs. @ $5
Job No. 314	800 hrs. @ $4	

Wages of the supervisors, custodial personnel, etc., totaled $4,600; sales and administrative salaries were $9,600.

(d) Miscellaneous factory overhead incurred during the month totaled $2,965. Miscellaneous selling and administrative expenses were $1,700. Vouchers were prepared for these items as well as for the FICA tax and federal income tax withheld for March. (See account balances on the post-closing trial balance for March 31.)

(e) Annual depreciation on plant assets is calculated using the following rates:

Factory buildings — 2%
Machinery and equipment — 10%
Office equipment — 10%

(f) The balance of the prepaid insurance account represents a three-year premium for a fire insurance policy covering the factory building and machinery. It was paid on the last day of the preceding month and became effective on April 1.

(g) The summary of factory overhead prepared from the factory overhead ledger is reproduced below:

SUMMARY OF FACTORY OVERHEAD FOR APRIL

Trans-action	Account	Stamping	Plating	Power	Mainte-nance	Total
(b)	Factory supplies	$ 520.00	$ 390.00	$ 260.00	$130.00	$ 1,300.00
(c)	Indirect labor...................	1,920.00	1,690.00	760.00	230.00	4,600.00
(c)	Payroll taxes	789.60	442.00	310.00	122.40	1,664.00
(d)	Miscellaneous..................	1,286.00	1,089.50	393.00	196.50	2,965.00
(e)	Depreciation....................	140.00	105.00	70.00	35.00	350.00
(f)	Insurance.......................	30.00	25.00	10.00	10.00	75.00
	Total...........................	$4,685.60	$3,741.50	$1,803.00	$723.90	$10,954.00

(h) The total expenses of the Maintenance Department are distributed on the basis of floor space occupied by the Power Department (8,820 sq. ft.), Stamping Department (19,500 sq. ft.), and Plating Department (7,875 sq. ft.). The Power Department expenses are then allocated equally to the Stamping and Plating Departments.

(i) After the actual factory expenses have been distributed to the departmental accounts and the applied factory overhead has been recorded and posted, any balances in the departmental accounts are transferred to Under- and Overapplied Overhead.

(j) Jobs Nos. 312 and 313 were finished during the month. Job No. 314 is still in process at the end of the month.

(k) During the month, Jobs Nos. 311 and 312 were sold at a markup of 95% on cost.

(l) Received $31,500 from customers in payment of their accounts.

(m) Checks were issued during the month in the amount of $33,500 for payment of vouchers.

(n) The estimated provision for federal income tax applicable to the earnings for April was $800.

Required: (1) Set up the beginning trial balance in "T" accounts. **(2)** Prepare materials inventory ledger cards and enter April 1 balances. **(3)** Set up job cost sheets as needed. **(4)** Record all transactions and related entries in general journal entry form for the month of April and post to "T" accounts. **(5)** Prepare a service department expense distribution work sheet for April. **(6)** At the end of the month:

(a) Analyze the balance in the materials account, the work in process account, and the finished goods account.

(b) Prepare the statement of cost of goods manufactured, income statement, and balance sheet for April 30.

5-5. Review of job order cost procedures. The Airie Manufacturing Company uses a job order cost system. The balances in the inventory accounts on September 1 were:

Finished Goods	$210,000
Work in Process	94,100
Materials	100,000

The job cost sheets on September 1 contained the following data:

Job No.	Materials	Labor	Overhead	Total
1234	$ 1,200	$ 2,000	$ 2,500	$ 5,700
1235	3,000	3,300	3,900	10,200
1238	4,100	5,100	6,100	15,300
1244	2,500	3,000	3,200	8,700
1250	12,000	15,000	17,000	44,000
1251	2,800	3,400	4,000	10,200
Total	$25,600	$31,800	$36,700	$94,100

The transactions for September were:

(a) Materials purchased, $74,000.

(b) Materials requisitioned by the factory were as follows:

Job No. 1234	$ 2,200
Job No. 1235	1,200
Job No. 1244	1,500
Job No. 1252	5,300
Job No. 1253	3,700
Job No. 1254	4,800
Job No. 1255	12,000
Indirect Materials — Dept. A	4,700
Indirect Materials — Dept. B...	3,000
Indirect Materials — Dept. C...	2,500
Total	$40,900

(c) Actual labor costs incurred were as follows:

Job No.	Dept. A	Dept. B	Dept. C	Total
1234		$ 700	$ 500	$ 1,200
1235	$ 100	300	700	1,100
1238	800	1,100	2,800	4,700
1244	900	800	400	2,100
1250	1,000	2,200	1,800	5,000
1251	1,100	800	1,300	3,200
1252	2,300	1,800	800	4,900
1253	1,700	1,300	1,000	4,000
1254	2,700	1,600	700	5,000
1255	7,000	6,000	300	13,300
Indirect	5,000	2,700	4,200	11,900
Total	$22,600	$19,300	$14,500	$56,400

(d) Other factory overhead costs were:

	Dept. A	Dept. B	Dept. C	Total
Supervision	$ 1,600	$ 1,200	$ 800	$ 3,600
Heat, light, and water..............	1,500	1,400	1,900	4,800
Maintenance	700	600	900	2,200
Payroll taxes, vacation pay, etc.	8,600	8,100	6,200	22,900
Depreciation..........................	4,400	2,600	3,600	10,600
Miscellaneous........................	600	400	500	1,500
Total.................................	$17,400	$14,300	$13,900	$45,600

(e) The direct labor cost method is used to apply factory overhead to the jobs. The rates for the departments are:

> Dept. A — 150%
> Dept. B — 130%
> Dept. C — 180%

(f) The jobs completed and transferred to finished goods were: Jobs Nos. 1234, 1235, 1250, 1252, and 1255.

(g) Finished goods sold totaled $235,000.

Required: (1) Set up individual job cost sheets and record the September costs for each job. **(2)** Record the beginning balances in the inventory accounts and record the September transactions in inventory, overhead, and cost of goods sold accounts. Each department has a factory overhead account. **(3)** Compute the under- or overapplied overhead for each department. **(4)** Prepare a statement of cost of goods manufactured.

5-6. Service department allocations and determining overhead rates. The Flop-Top Manufacturing Company has two production departments (Fabrication and Assembly) and three service departments (General Factory Administration, Factory Maintenance, and Factory Cafeteria). A summary of overhead costs and other data for each department prior to allocation of service department costs is as follows:

	General Factory Admin.	Factory Mainte- nance	Factory Cafeteria	Fabrication	Assembly	Total
Indirect labor	$90,000	$82,100	$87,000	$1,950,000	$2,050,000	$4,259,100
Indirect material.............	——	65,000	91,000	3,130,000	950,000	4,236,000
Other factory overhead....	70,000	56,100	62,000	1,650,000	1,850,000	3,688.100
Direct labor hours...........				562,500	437,500	1,000,000
Number of employees......	12	8	20	280	200	520
Square footage occupied .	1,750	2,000	4,800	88,000	72,000	168,550

The costs of the general factory administration department, factory maintenance department, and factory cafeteria are allocated on the basis of direct labor hours, square footage occupied, and number of employees, respectively.

Required: (1) Allocate the service departments' costs directly to production without interservice department cost allocation and calculate an overhead rate for each production department based on direct labor hours. **(2)** Allocate the service departments' costs sequentially, starting with the service department with the greatest total costs, to other service departments as well as to the production departments. Calculate an overhead rate for each production department based on direct labor hours. *(AICPA adapted)*

5-7. Determining overhead variances. The Boolu Company is a manufacturer of heavy machinery. It applies factory overhead to production on the basis of an average percentage of direct labor cost. At the time the rate was established, it was based on the following information as to expected operations:

Direct labor hours...		136,000
Direct labor cost...		$571,200.00
Average rate per hour		$4.20
Fixed overhead...	$202,776.00	
Variable overhead..	454,104.00	
Total overhead		$656,880.00

At December 31, the end of the first accounting period, the records disclosed the following information:

Direct labor hours...		130,000
Direct labor cost...		$573,040.00
Average rate per hour		$4.408
Fixed overhead..	$225,400.00	
Variable overhead...	475,100.00	$700,500.00
Underapplied overhead...................................		$41,504.00

Management is concerned that the year's operations failed to absorb overhead of $41,504.

Required: (1) Calculate the application rates for fixed cost, variable cost, and total overhead. **(2)** Show the computation of the underapplied overhead as determined by the company. **(3)** Compute the budget variances due to cost factors. **(4)** Compute the volume variances. **(5)** Analyze the volume variance in additional detail by giving consideration to the effect of the increase in labor rate and the decrease in the number of labor hours used on the factory overhead. **(6)** Compute the budget and volume variances if the company had used the direct labor hour method. **(7)** Show a reconciliation between the direct labor cost and direct labor hour variances calculated. *(AICPA adapted)*

5-8. Analysis of under- and overapplied factory overhead. The A Company, engaged in production of heavy equipment, has applied factory overhead to its product on the basis of an average rate of 115% of direct labor cost. This rate, at the time it was established, was based on the following information as to expected operations:

Direct labor hours		13,600
Direct labor cost		$163,200
Average rate per hour		$12
Fixed overhead	$ 57,936	
Variable overhead	129,744	
Total overhead...		$187,680

At December 31, the end of the first accounting period, the records disclosed the following information:

Direct labor hours		13,000
Direct labor cost		$183,040
Average rate per hour		$14.08
Fixed overhead	$ 75,400	
Variable overhead	145,600	
Total overhead (actual expense)		$221,000
Underapplied overhead		10,504

The management is concerned with the fact that it failed to apply overhead of $10,504 in the year's operations.

Required: (1) Evaluate the system currently being used to apply overhead. **(2)** Prepare an explanation for management showing why the $10,504 underapplication existed. Compute and show the effect of variation in direct labor rates and direct labor hours on the application of both fixed and variable overhead. Support your conclusions with computations and explanatory comments setting forth the significance of each item in the analysis. (Computations should be rounded to the nearest dollar.)   *(AICPA adapted)*

6

Process Cost Accounting— General Procedures

The basic purpose of cost accounting is the accumulation of data designed to provide management with accurate information on the cost of manufacturing a product. The appropriate cost accounting system for a particular entity depends on the nature of manufacturing operations. The preceding chapter focused on the job order cost system. This chapter and Chapter 7 focus on procedures applicable in a process cost system.

COMPARISON OF BASIC COST SYSTEMS

As explained in Chapter 1, a job cost system is appropriate when products are manufactured on a special order basis. Process costing is appropriate when goods are manufactured in a continuous or mass production operation.

The focal point of job order costing is the "job," even though the factory may be departmentalized. The costs of materials, direct labor, and factory overhead are gathered for each job and divided by the number of units produced to determine the unit cost for that particular job. The primary objective is to ascertain the costs of producing each job completed during the accounting period as well as the cost incurred on each job in process at the end of the period. Management uses this information not only for inventory valuation but also for planning, control, and measurement of performance.

The focus of process cost is the **cost center**, which is usually a department, but which could be a process or an operation. Costs are accumulated for a particular cost center or function and divided by the number of units produced to determine the average cost per unit in that cost center for the period. The primary objective, like that of the job order system, is to ascertain the unit cost of the products manufactured during the period and of those in process at the end of the period and to promote efficiency within the factory.

Many of the procedures studied for job order cost accounting are also applicable to process cost accounting. The main difference in the two methods is the manner in which costs are accumulated.

Materials and Labor Costs

Under the job order cost system, the costs of materials and labor, as determined from the summaries of materials requisitions and time tickets, are charged to specific jobs or to factory overhead. Under the process cost system, the costs of materials and labor are charged to the departments in which they are incurred. However, the indirect materials and indirect labor costs which cannot be directly associated with a particular department are charged to Factory Overhead. Examples of such costs would include custodial supplies for the factory and the salary of a supervisor who is responsible for several departments.

Less clerical effort is required in a process system than in a job order system, because some of the direct and indirect materials and labor are not separated, and also because costs are charged to a few departments rather than to many jobs. For example, in accounting for labor costs, detailed time tickets might be eliminated completely in a process cost system. While a typical factory employee under the job order cost system might work on several jobs, requiring allocation of labor to each job, the employee in a process cost system usually works only in one department so that only a simple time record is required.

Other than the differences discussed above, the procedures for acquiring, controlling, accounting for, and paying for materials and labor are similar in both systems. At the end of each month, the materials requisitions summary provides the data for the journal entry debiting Work in Process and Factory Overhead and crediting Materials. Similarly, the labor cost summary provides the data for the journal entry debiting Work in Process and Factory Overhead and crediting Payroll.

Factory Overhead Costs

In a process cost system, overhead costs are accumulated from the various journals in the same manner as in a job order cost accounting system. The actual costs for the period are gathered in a control account in the general ledger to which postings are made from the general journal (for certain indirect materials, indirect labor, and fixed costs), from the voucher register, and from other appropriate journals. This control account is supported by a subsidiary ledger which consists of factory overhead analysis sheets showing the detailed allocation of costs to the departments. At the end of the month, based on the data reflected in the analysis sheets, the total actual factory overhead is distributed to the departmentalized overhead accounts.

Service Departments. As with job order cost accounting, the applicable factory overhead is charged to the service departments. These service department expenses are distributed to the production departments. A distribution work sheet is prepared showing the allocation of each service department's expenses to other service departments and to production departments. A journal entry also records the distribution of the service departments' expenses to production departments and thus closes the service departments' accounts for factory overhead. Service department costs will not be considered in the following discussion because the fundamentals were developed in Chapter 4.

Application of Factory Overhead. In the job order cost system, overhead is applied to the jobs through the use of predetermined rates. The use of predetermined rates is also quite common in a process cost system but overhead is applied on the basis of departments rather than jobs. As in the job order cost system, the amount of overhead applied is determined by multiplying the predetermined rate by the appropriate base. This base might be labor hours, machine hours, or any other method that will equitably distribute overhead to the departments in reasonable proportion to the benefit received by each department. Under- or overapplied overhead is treated in the same manner as discussed in Chapter 4.

PRODUCT COST IN A PROCESS COST SYSTEM

The basic principle established in this comparison of the two cost accounting systems is that all costs of manufacturing must eventually be charged to production departments, either directly or indirectly, in a process cost system. The unit cost in each department is the total cost charged to that department for the period divided by the number of units produced in the department during the same period. The total cost of each item produced is the combined unit costs from each department.

Nondepartmentalized Factory

When the factory is operated as a single department producing a single product in a continuous output, the process cost system is particularly appropriate and simple. The costs of operating the factory are summarized at the end of each accounting period. Then the total of these costs is divided by the quantity of units produced to determine the cost of each unit manufactured during the period.

The following cost of production summary illustrates this procedure:

Materials	$ 50,000
Labor	75,000
Factory overhead	35,000
Total cost of production..	$160,000
Unit output for period	40,000 units

Unit cost for period: $160,000 ÷ 40,000 units = $4.

Departmentalized Factory

In other than the simplest type of manufacturing operation, a company has several production and service departments. Products accumulate costs as they pass through each successive production department. Costs are recorded by departments according to the following procedure: (1) the costs of the service departments are allocated to the production departments; (2) the costs added in prior departments are carried over to successive departments; and (3) the costs of materials and labor directly identifiable with a department, as well as applied overhead, are charged to that department. The unit cost within a department is determined by dividing the sum of these costs by the number of units produced during the period.

WORK IN PROCESS INVENTORIES

If there is no work in process at the end of an accounting period, ascertaining the unit cost under the process cost system is relatively simple; divide total cost by number of units produced. Usually, however, each department will have work in process at the end of each accounting period. The valuation of work in process inventories presents one of the most important and difficult problems in process cost accounting. Normally, a factory will have (1) units started and finished during the current period; (2) units started in a prior period and completed during the current period; and (3) units started during the current period but not finished at the end of the period. Since materials, labor, and overhead may have been applied to each of the unfinished items, such charges cannot be ignored in computing the cost of the units finished during the accounting period. Therefore, consideration must be given to not only the number of items finished during the period but also the units in process at the beginning and at the end of the period. The primary problem is the allocation of total cost between (1) units finished during the period and (2) units still in process at the end of the period.

Two procedures are commonly used for assigning costs to the ending inventories: the **average cost** method and the **first-in, first-out (fifo)** method. The average cost method is discussed and illustrated in the remainder of this chapter. The first-in, first-out method is discussed in Chapter 7.

Average Cost Method

Under the **average cost method**, the cost of the work in process at the beginning of the period is added to the production costs for the current period. Average unit cost for the period is then determined by dividing the total of these costs by the total equivalent production. **Equivalent production** represents the number of units which could be completed as determined by the production costs incurred during a period. To illustrate, assume that the production costs of a department during a certain period are as follows:

Materials..	$12,000
Labor...	18,000
Factory overhead	6,000
Total cost of production	**$36,000**

If 18,000 units were produced during the period and there was no work in process at the beginning or at the end of the period, the unit cost of production is easily calculated to be $2, and $36,000 would be transferred to the finished goods account in the general ledger.

Assume, instead, that the production report for the period shows that there was no beginning work in process, that 17,000 units were finished during the period, and that there are 2,000 units in process at the end of the period. The problem that now arises is allocating the production cost for the period, $36,000, between the goods that were finished and the goods that are still in process. What portion of the total production cost was incurred to start the remaining 2,000 units in process?

If the 2,000 units are almost finished, clearly more cost has been incurred to bring them to that stage of completion than would have been incurred if they had just been started in process. In order to make a rational measurement, the **stage of completion** of the units still in process must be taken into consideration. An estimate of the stage of completion, expressed in fractions or percentages, is made by the department head. This estimate is obviously subject to the inaccuracies that may result with the use of any method of averaging. The possibility of error is minimized because the department head usually has the skills and the familiarity with the work to make reliable estimates.

At the end of the accounting period, the department head submits a **production report** showing: **(1)** the number of units in process at the beginning of the period, **(2)** the number of units completed during the period, and **(3)** the number of units in process at the end of the period and their estimated stage of completion.

Continuing the example, assume that the 2,000 units in process are half finished. If materials, labor, and overhead are applied evenly throughout the process, one half of the total cost for completing 2,000 units can be applied to these units. Expressed in another way, the cost to bring these 2,000 units to the halfway point of completion is equivalent to the cost of fully completing 1,000 units. Therefore, in terms of equivalent production, 2,000 units one-half completed are equal to 1,000 units fully completed. Unit cost is calculated as follows:

Units finished during the period......................................	17,000
Equivalent units of work in process at the end of the period (2,000 units one-half completed)	1,000
Equivalent production for the period..................................	18,000 units

$36,000 ÷ 18,000 = $2 unit cost for the month.

The inventory cost can now be calculated as follows:

Transferred to finished goods (17,000 units at $2)............	$34,000
Work in process (2,000 units × ½ × $2)..........................	2,000
Total production costs accounted for	$36,000

Determining equivalent units of work in process at the end of the period is frequently more complex than suggested in the example. For example, when it is not reasonable to assume that all production costs are incurred evenly throughout the production process, the amount of materials, labor, and overhead applicable to the work in process would have to be evaluated separately in estimating the stage of completion. In addition, the work in process at the end of the period may consist of a large number of units in widely varying stages of completion, thus requiring a more detailed analysis to determine equivalent units. This condition is discussed in Chapter 7.

Cost of Production Summary. In a process cost system, the reporting of production and related costs in each department involves:

(1) Accumulating costs for which the department is accountable.
(2) Calculating equivalent production for the period.
(3) Computing the unit cost for the period.
(4) Summarizing the disposition of the production costs.

These data are reported on a **cost of production summary** which presents the necessary information for inventory valuation and which can also serve as the source for summary journal entries. The procedures previously discussed are further developed through four illustrative problems that follow.

Illustrative Problem No. 1 — Computing the unit cost when there is no beginning inventory and only one department.

The Pyramid Toy Corp. manufactures a plastic toy. The small factory is operated as a single department and the finished goods are placed in stock to be withdrawn as orders are received. At the end of January, the factory supervisor submits the following production report. The estimate of the stage of completion indicates that the units in process at the end of the month were examined and found to be, on the average, about one-half completed.

PRODUCTION REPORT

For Month Ending _____ *January 31,* _____ 19__

In process, beginning of month _____ *none*

Finished during the month _____ *4,900 units*

In process, end of month _____ *200 units*

Estimated stage of completion of work in process, end of month ____ *one half*

Remarks

Signed *Bill Blank*
Supervisor

After receiving the production report, the cost accountant begins the preparation of the cost of production summary by collecting the period production costs from summaries of materials requisitions, payroll, and factory overhead analysis sheets. The units in process are then converted to equivalent units. In this case, the supervisor's estimate that the 200 units in process are one-half completed implies that approximately one half the total cost of the materials, labor, and factory overhead needed to produce 200 units has been incurred. On the basis of this reasoning, the equivalent of 200 units in process, one-half completed, is 100 units. In other words, the costs incurred in partially completing 200 units is considered to be the equivalent of the entire cost of producing 100 units. The cost of producing 4,900 fully completed units and 200 units one-half completed during the month is therefore the equivalent of the cost of producing 5,000 fully completed units.

PYRAMID TOY CORP.
Cost of Production Summary
For the Month Ended January 31, 19––

Cost of production for month:		
Materials		$ 5,000
Labor		3,000
Factory overhead		2,000
Total costs to be accounted for		$10,000
Unit output for month:		
Finished during month		4,900
Equivalent units of work in process, end of month (200 units, one-half completed)		100
Total equivalent production		5,000
Unit cost for month:		
Materials ($5,000 ÷ 5,000 units)		$1.00
Labor ($3,000 ÷ 5,000 units)		.60
Factory overhead ($2,000 ÷ 5,000 units)		.40
Total		$2.00
Inventory costs:		
Cost of goods finished during month (4,900 × $2)		$ 9,800
Cost of work in process, end of month:		
Materials (200 × ½ × $1)	$100	
Labor (200 × ½ × $.60)	60	
Factory overhead (200 × ½ × $.40)	40	200
Total production costs accounted for ...... $2.—/unit		$10,000

Since the work in process is estimated to be one-half completed, its value for inventory purposes is one half the unit cost of finished goods.

At the end of the month, the following journal entries record the factory operations for January:

Jan. 31	Work in Process	5,000	
	Materials		5,000
	Work in Process	3,000	
	Payroll		3,000

```
Jan. 31   Factory Overhead ........................   2,000
             Various accounts
             (Accumulated Depreciation,
             Prepaid Insurance, Accrued
             Taxes, Accounts Payable)...........          2,000

          Work in Process...........................   2,000
             Factory Overhead ......................          2,000
```

After preparing the cost of production summary, the accountant can make the following entry:

```
Jan. 31   Finished Goods..............................   9,800
             Work in Process..........................          9,800
```

After posting these entries, the work in process account, as shown below, has a debit balance of $200, representing the valuation of the work in process on January 31.

WORK IN PROCESS

Jan. 31		5,000	Jan. 31	9,800
		3,000		
		2,000		
	200	10,000		

The cost accountant can now prepare the January statement of the cost of goods manufactured, shown below.

PYRAMID TOY CORP.
Statement of Cost of Goods Manufactured
For the Month Ended January 31, 19—

Materials	$ 5,000
Labor	3,000
Factory overhead	2,000
Total	$10,000
Less work in process inventory, January 31..............	200
Cost of goods manufactured during the month...........	$ 9,800

Illustrative Problem No. 2 — Computing the unit cost when there is a beginning inventory and only one department.

At the end of February, the factory supervisor for the Pyramid Toy Corp. submits the following production report.

PRODUCTION REPORT

For Month Ending ___ *February 28* ___ 19—

In process, beginning of month ___	*200 units*
Finished during the month ___	*6,900 units*
In process, end of month ___	*600 units*
Estimated stage of completion of work in process, end of month ___	*one third*

The cost accountant prepares the following cost of production summary for February.

PYRAMID TOY CORP.
Cost of Production Summary
For the Month Ended February 28, 19––

Cost of work in process, beginning of month:		
Materials	$ 100	
Labor	60	
Factory overhead	40	$ 200
Cost of production for month:		
Materials	$7,000	
Labor	4,200	
Factory overhead	2,800	14,000
Total costs to be accounted for		$14,200
Unit output for month:		
Finished during month		6,900
Equivalent units of work in process, end of month (600 units, one-third completed)..		200
Total equivalent production		7,100
Unit cost for month:		
Materials ($7,100 ÷ 7,100)..		$1.00
Labor ($4,260 ÷ 7,100)...		.60
Factory overhead ($2,840 ÷ 7,100)................................		.40
Total		$2.00
Inventory costs:		
Cost of goods finished during month (6,900 × $2)		$13,800
Cost of work in process, end of month:		
Materials (600 × ⅓ × $1)	$200	
Labor (600 × ⅓ × $.60)	120	
Factory overhead (600 × ⅓ × $.40)...............................	80	400
Total production costs accounted for		$14,200

Note that the cost of the beginning work in process from the prior month is added to the total costs incurred during the current month because all costs must be accounted for. The calculation of unit output for the month takes into consideration the units finished during the month, including those that had been started in process during the prior month, as well as the stage of completion of the units in process at the end of the month. The fact that one half of the work had been completed on 200 units in the prior month does not have to be considered in this calculation, because the cost of doing that work is included with the current month's costs for the purpose of calculating unit costs. In determining the unit cost of materials, labor, and factory overhead, the accountant considers not only the current month's cost of each element, but also the cost carried over from the prior month. This procedure is the identifying characteristic of the average costing method.

Since the work in process is estimated to be one-third completed, its value for inventory purposes is one third the unit cost of finished goods, or $.66667. If a company does not carry out its unit costs to several decimal places, a common practice is to use a rounding procedure as shown below:

Item	Unit Cost	Rounded to Nearest Ten
Materials.....................................	$1.00 ÷ 3 = $.33 × 600 = $198	$200
Labor..	.60 ÷ 3 = .20 × 600 = 120	120
Factory overhead	.40 ÷ 3 = .13 × 600 = 78	80
Total.....................................		$400

From the data developed on the cost of production report, the accountant can now make this entry:

Feb. 28   Finished Goods.............................. 13,800
              Work in Process......................... 13,800

After posting this entry and the entries for the month's production costs, the work in process account has a debit balance of $400, as shown below.

WORK IN PROCESS

Jan. 31		5,000	Jan. 31	9,800
		3,000		
		2,000		
	200	10,000		
Feb. 28		7,000	Feb. 28	13,800
		4,200		23,600
		2,800		
	400	24,000		

The following statement of the cost of goods manufactured can now be prepared:

PYRAMID TOY CORP.
Statement of Cost of Goods Manufactured
For the Month Ended February 28, 19--

Materials	$ 7,000
Labor	4,200
Factory overhead	2,800
Total	$14,000
Add work in process inventory, February 1...............................	200
Total	$14,200
Less work in process inventory, February 28	400
Cost of goods manufactured during the month............................	$13,800

Illustrative Problem No. 3 — Computing the unit cost when there are no beginning inventories and two or more departments.

The business of the Pyramid Toy Corp. continued to grow until management decided to departmentalize the factory and reorganize the cost records. Accordingly, on January 1 of the following year the factory was divided into three departments as follows:

Department A — Cutting
Department B — Forming
Department C — Painting

Separate control accounts are maintained in the general ledger for recording the costs of operating each department. Departmental expense analysis sheets are used in recording the manufacturing expenses incurred. The departmental production reports for January are reproduced below and on page 249. Note that there were no beginning inventories of work in process in any department.

PRODUCTION REPORT

Dept. _____ A – Cutting _____ Month ___ January ___ 19--

In process, beginning of period _____ none

Stage of completion _____

Placed in process during period _____ 3,300 units

Received from Dept. _____ during period _____

Transferred to Dept. __B__ during period _____ 2,700 units

Transferred to stockroom during period _____ none

In process end of period _____ 600 units

Stage of completion _____ one half

After receiving the production reports from the department heads, the cost accountant prepares a cost of production summary for each department and prepares the journal entries to record the operations of each department and the transfer of costs.

Note that the costs accumulated in the department are transferred to the next department for those units completed during the period and sent on for further processing. Thus, costs follow the flow of goods through the manufacturing process.

PYRAMID TOY CORP.
Cost of Production Summary — Department A
For the Month Ended, January 31, 19--

Cost of production for month:

Materials	$15,000
Labor	8,000
Factory overhead	7,000
Total costs to be accounted for	**$30,000**

Unit output for month:

Finished and transferred to Dept. B during month	2,700
Equivalent units of work in process, end of month (600 units, one-half completed)	300
Total equivalent production	3,000

Unit cost for month:

Materials ($15,000 ÷ 3,000 units)	$ 5.000
Labor ($8,000 ÷ 3,000 units)	2.667
Factory overhead ($7,000 ÷ 3,000 units)	2.333
Total	$10.000

Inventory costs:

Cost of goods finished and transferred to Dept. B during month (2,700 × $10.00)		$27,000
Cost of work in process, end of month:		
Materials (600 × ½ × $5.00)	$1,500	
Labor (600 × ½ × $2.667)	800*	
Factory overhead (600 × ½ × $2.333)	700*	3,000
Total production costs accounted for		**$30,000**

*Rounded

After posting the usual end-of-the-month entries, the work in process account for Department A, as shown below, has a debit balance of $3,000.

WORK IN PROCESS — DEPT. A

Jan. 31			Jan. 31		
	15,000				27,000
	8,000				
	7,000				
	3,000	30,000			

The only difference in procedure between this problem and Illustrative Problem No. 1 is that the goods finished in Department A are transferred to Department B for further processing rather than being transferred to the stockroom as finished goods.

Although still in process, the transferred units and their related costs are treated as completed products in Department A and as raw materials added at the beginning of the process in Department B. The cost of the units includes the costs of materials, labor, and factory overhead incurred in Department A. However, the individual cost elements are combined and transferred in total to Department B.

In reviewing the cost of production summary for Department B below, note that the calculation of unit cost for the month in Department B takes into consideration only those costs incurred during the month in that department and the equivalent units produced in the department. The **transferred-in** or **prior department** costs and units are not included in the computation.

However, in determining the cost transferred to Department C and the cost of the work in process, the prior department costs must be considered. Also, in the calculation of the work in process valuation, the full cost from Department A is included, while only a fraction of cost from Department B, based on the stage of completion, is considered.

PYRAMID TOY CORP.
Cost of Production Summary — Department B
For the Month Ended January 31, 19--

Cost of goods received from Dept. A during month (2,700 units × $10.00)...		$27,000
Cost of production for month:		
Materials	$ 1,000	
Labor	3,000	
Factory overhead	2,000	$ 6,000
Total costs to be accounted for		$33,000
Unit output for month:		
Finished and transferred to Dept. C during month		2,200
Equivalent units of work in process, end of month (500 units, two-fifths completed)...........................		200
Total equivalent production		2,400
Unit cost for month:		
Materials ($1,000 ÷ 2,400 units)...............................		$ .417
Labor ($3,000 ÷ 2,400 units)....................................		1.250
Factory overhead ($2,000 ÷ 2,400 units)....................		.833
Total		$ 2.500
Inventory costs:		
Cost of goods finished and transferred to Dept. C during month:		
Cost in Dept. A (2,200 × $10.00)	$22,000	
Cost in Dept. B (2,200 × 2.50)	5,500	$27,500
$12.50		
Cost of work in process, end of month:		
Cost in Dept. A (500 × $10.00)................................		$ 5,000

Cost in Dept. B:			
Materials (500 × 2/5 × $.417)......................	$ 83		
Labor (500 × 2/5 × $1.25)...........................	250		
Factory overhead (500 × 2/5 × $.833)...........	167	500	5,500
Total production costs accounted for			$33,000

```
                    PRODUCTION  REPORT

      Dept. _____B – Forming_____  Month ____January___ 19__

      In process, beginning of period _____none_____

      Stage of completion _____

      Placed in process during period _____none_____

      Received from Dept. __A__ during period _____2,700 units_____

      Transferred to Dept. __C__ during period _____2,200 units_____

      Transferred to stockroom during period _____none_____

      In process, end of period _____500 units_____

      Stage of completion _____two fifths_____
```

After posting the end-of-the-month entries, the work in process account for Department B, as shown below, has a debit balance of $5,500.

WORK IN PROCESS — DEPT. B

Jan. 31			Jan. 31		27,500
		1,000			
		3,000			
		2,000			
		27,000			
	5,500	33,000			

```
                    PRODUCTION  REPORT

      Dept. _____C – Painting_____  Month ____January___ 19__

      In process, beginning of period _____none_____

      Stage of completion _____

      Placed in process during period _____none_____

      Received from Dept. __B__ during period _____2,200 units_____

      Transferred to Dept. _____ during period _____

      Transferred to stockroom during period _____2,000 units_____

      In process, end of period _____200 units_____

      Stage of completion _____one half_____
```

PYRAMID TOY CORP.
Cost of Production Summary — Department C
For the Month Ended January 31, 19--

Cost of goods received from Dept. B during month (2,200 units × $12.50)...		$27,500
Cost of production for month:		
Materials	$ 3,000	
Labor	2,400	
Factory overhead	3,000	8,400
Total costs to be accounted for		$35,900

Unit output for month:	
Finished and transferred to finished goods during month	2,000
Equivalent units of work in process, end of month (200 units, one-half completed).............................	100
Total equivalent production	2,100

Unit cost for month:	
Materials ($3,000 ÷ 2,100 units).............................	$ 1.429
Labor ($2,400 ÷ 2,100 units).................................	1.142
Factory overhead ($3,000 ÷ 2,100 units)..................	1.429
Total	$ 4.000

Inventory costs:			
Cost of goods finished and transferred to finished goods during month:			
Cost in Dept. A (2,000 × $10.00)		$20,000	
Cost in Dept. B (2,000 × 2.50)		5,000	
Cost in Dept. C (2,000 × 4.00)		8,000	$33,000
		$16.50	
Cost of work in process, end of month:			
Cost in Dept. A (200 × $10.00).............................		$ 2,000	
Cost in Dept. B (200 × $ 2.50)		500	
Cost in Dept. C:			
Materials (200 × ½ × $1.429)	$143		
Labor (200 × ½ × $1.142)	114		
Factory overhead (200 × ½ × $1.429)......	143	400	2,900
Total production costs accounted for			$35,900

(handwritten in margin: pg 258)

After posting the end-of-the-month entries, the work in process account for Department C, as shown below, has a debit balance of $2,900.

WORK IN PROCESS — DEPT. C

Jan. 31	3,000	Jan. 31	33,000
	2,400		
	3,000		
	27,500		
2,900	35,900		

As a means of classifying and summarizing the factory operations for January, the cost accountant prepares the work sheet reproduced on the next page. This work sheet provides the information for the following statement of cost of goods manufactured.

PYRAMID TOY CORP.
Statement of Cost of Goods Manufactured
For the Month Ended January 31, 19--

Materials	$19,000
Labor	13,400
Factory overhead	12,000
Total	$44,400
Less work in process inventories, January 31	11,400
Cost of goods manufactured during the month............................	$33,000

At the end of the month, the following general journal entries are made:

```
Jan. 31   Work in Process — Dept. A ..............   15,000
          Work in Process — Dept. B..............    1,000
          Work in Process — Dept. C..............    3,000
          Factory Overhead ..........................    1,000
              Materials ...................................           20,000
```

The amount charged to Factory Overhead for indirect materials is an arbitrary amount chosen to illustrate how the costs are gathered and distributed. This amount represents the cost of various expenses and supplies that were issued but could not be charged directly to a department.

```
Jan. 31   Work in Process — Dept. A ..............    8,000
          Work in Process — Dept. B..............    3,000
          Work in Process — Dept. C..............    2,400
          Factory Overhead ..........................    1,500
              Payroll .....................................           14,900
```

Again, the amount charged to Factory Overhead is an arbitrary amount chosen for purposes of illustration and represents payroll costs that could not be charged directly to any given department.

```
Jan. 31   Factory Overhead ..........................    9,000
              Various accounts
              (Accumulated Depreciation, Prepaid
              Insurance, Payroll Taxes) ..............            9,000
```

This entry is a summary of several entries that are made in the general journal and possibly other journals to reflect the current month's provision for depreciation, insurance, payroll taxes, and other expenses.

PYRAMID TOY CORP.
Departmental Cost Work Sheet
For the Month Ended January 31, 19——

Analysis	Cost per unit transferred		Units received in department	Units transferred or on hand	Amount charged to department		Amount credited to department	
Dept. A — Cutting:								
Started in process	....	....	3,300	....	....	....	....	....
Costs for month:								
Materials	....	....	....	....	15,000	00	....	....
Labor	....	....	....	....	8,000	00	....	....
Factory overhead	....	....	....	....	7,000	00	....	....
Finished and transferred to Dept. B...	10	00	....	2,700	....	....	27,000	00
Closing work in process	....	....	....	600	....	....	3,000	00
Total	10	00	3,300	3,300	30,000	00	30,000	00
Dept. B — Forming:								
Received during month from Dept. A .	....	....	2,700	....	27,000	00	....	....
Costs added during month:								
Materials	....	....	....	....	1,000	00	....	....
Labor	....	....	....	....	3,000	00	....	....
Factory overhead	....	....	....	....	2,000	00	....	....
Finished and transferred to Dept. C...	2	50	....	2,200	....	....	27,500	00
Closing work in process	....	....	....	500	....	....	5,500	00
Total	12	50	2,700	2,700	33,000	00	33,000	00
Dept. C — Painting:								
Received during month from Dept. B .	....	....	2,200	....	27,500	00	....	....
Costs added during month:								
Materials	....	....	....	....	3,000	00	....	....
Labor	....	....	....	....	2,400	00	....	....
Factory overhead	....	....	....	....	3,000	00	....	....
Finished and transferred to stock	4	00	....	2,000	....	....	33,000	00
Closing work in process	....	....	....	200	....	....	2,900	00
Total	16	50	2,200	2,200	35,900	00	35,900	00

					Amount		Total	
Summary:								
Materials:								
Dept. A	....	....	....	....	15,000	00	....	....
Dept. B	....	....	....	....	1,000	00	....	....
Dept. C	....	....	....	....	3,000	00	19,000	00
Labor:								
Dept. A	....	....	....	....	8,000	00	....	....
Dept. B	....	....	....	....	3,000	00	....	....
Dept. C	....	....	....	....	2,400	00	13,400	00
Factory overhead:								
Dept. A	....	....	....	....	7,000	00	....	....
Dept. B	....	....	....	....	2,000	00	....	....
Dept. C	....	....	....	....	3,000	00	12,000	00
Total production costs for January	....	....	....	....	....	....	44,400	00
Deduct work in process inventory, end of month:								
Dept. A	....	....	....	....	3,000	00	....	....
Dept. B	....	....	....	....	5,500	00	....	....
Dept. C	....	....	....	....	2,900	00	11,400	00
Cost of production, goods fully manufactured during January	....	....	....	....	....	....	33,000	00

Jan. 31	Factory Overhead — Dept. A	6,600	
	Factory Overhead — Dept. B	2,100	
	Factory Overhead — Dept. C	2,800	
	Factory Overhead		11,500

This entry distributes the actual overhead for the period to the departments. The basis for this entry would be the factory overhead analysis sheets which show in detail the allocation or apportionment of the actual expenses to the various departments.

Jan. 31	Work in Process — Dept. A	7,000	
	Work in Process — Dept. B...............	2,000	
	Work in Process — Dept. C..............	3,000	
	Factory Overhead — Dept. A		7,000
	Factory Overhead — Dept. B		2,000
	Factory Overhead — Dept. C		3,000

This entry records the application of factory overhead to work in process. The amounts are calculated by multiplying a predetermined overhead application rate by the base used for applying overhead to each department, such as labor hours or machine hours. A different base might be used for different departments, so that overhead would be equitably applied according to the benefit each department has received.

The cost of production summary is used to develop the entries to record the transfer of costs from one department to another and to Finished Goods, as shown below.

Jan.	31 Work in Process — Dept. B...............	27,000	
	Work in Process — Dept. A		27,000
	31 Work in Process — Dept. C...............	27,500	
	Work in Process — Dept. B............		27,500
	31 Finished Goods............................	33,000	
	Work in Process — Dept. C............		33,000

These journal entries are reflected in the "T" accounts below and on the following page. The balances remaining in the work in process accounts are reflected in total on the statement of cost of goods manufactured. The balances in the departmental factory overhead accounts represent under- or overapplied overhead and would usually be carried forward to future months; however, these balances can be transferred to an under- and overapplied factory overhead account. As discussed in previous chapters, these amounts of under- and overapplied overhead would be analyzed to determine if they are expected normal or seasonal variances, or if they represent inefficiences that must be corrected.

WORK IN PROCESS — DEPT. A				WORK IN PROCESS — DEPT. B			
Jan. 31	15,000	Jan. 31	27,000	Jan. 31	1,000	Jan. 31	27,500
	8,000				3,000		
	7,000				2,000		
3,000	30,000				27,000		
				5,500	33,000		

WORK IN PROCESS — DEPT. C								MATERIALS		
Jan. 31	3,000	Jan. 31	33,000						Jan. 31	20,000
	2,400									
	3,000									
	27,500									
2,900	35,900									

FINISHED GOODS			PAYROLL		
Jan. 31	33,000			Jan. 31	14,900

FACTORY OVERHEAD					FACTORY OVERHEAD — DEPT. A				
Jan. 31	1,000	Jan. 31	11,500		Jan. 31	6,600	Jan. 31	7,000	
	1,500							400	
	9,000								
	11,500								

FACTORY OVERHEAD — DEPT. B					FACTORY OVERHEAD — DEPT. C				
Jan. 31	2,100	Jan. 31	2,000		Jan. 31	2,800	Jan. 31	3,000	
100					200				

Illustrative Problem No. 4 – Computing the unit cost when there are beginning inventories and two or more departments.

The February production reports submitted by the department heads for the Pyramid Toy Corp. are reproduced below and on pages 256 and 258. These reports differ from the January production reports in that they show inventories of work in process in each department at the beginning of the month. Note that the number of

---

PRODUCTION REPORT

Dept. _____ *A – Cutting* _____ Month _____ *February* __19__

In process, beginning of period _____ *600 units*

Stage of completion _____ *one half*

Placed in process during period _____ *3,800 units*

Received from Dept. _____ during period _____ *none*

Transferred to Dept. _**B**_ during period _____ *3,900 units*

Transferred to stockroom during period _____ *none*

In process, end of period _____ *500 units*

Stage of completion _____ *four fifths*

units in process at the beginning of the period plus the units placed in process or received from another department during the period are equal to the number of units transferred to another department or to the stockroom during the period plus the units in process at the end of the period. After receiving the production reports for February, the cost accountant prepares a cost of production summary for each department and drafts the entries to record the operations of each department in the general ledger accounts.

It should be noted in the following cost of production summary that in determining unit cost, as with an earlier example, the cost of beginning work in process from the prior month is added to the total costs incurred during the current month. The calculation of unit output for the month takes into consideration all units finished during the month, including those that had been in process at the beginning

PYRAMID TOY CORP.
Cost of Production Summary — Department A
For the Month Ended February 28, 19——

Cost of work in process, beginning of month:		
Materials	$ 1,500	
Labor	800	
Factory overhead	700	$ 3,000
Cost of production for month:		
Materials	$20,000	
Labor	10,810	
Factory overhead	9,190	40,000
Total costs to be accounted for		$43,000
Unit output for month:		
Finished and transferred to Dept. B during month		3,900
Equivalent units of work in process, end of month (500 units, four-fifths completed)		400
Total equivalent production		4,300
Unit cost for month:		
Materials ($21,500 ÷ 4,300)		$ 5.00
Labor ($11,610 ÷ 4,300)		2.70
Factory overhead ($9,890 ÷ 4,300)...........................		2.30
Total		$10.00
Inventory costs:		
Cost of goods finished and transferred to Dept. B during month: (3,900 × $10.00).................................		$39,000
Cost of work in process end of month:		
Materials (500 × 4/5 × $5.00)	$ 2,000	
Labor (500 × 4/5 × $2.70)	1,080	
Factory overhead (500 × 4/5 × $2.30)....................	920	4,000
Total production costs accounted for		$43,000

as well as those in process at the end of the period. Although the total unit cost is the same as in January, the unit cost of labor has increased and the unit cost of factory overhead has decreased. Management would likely investigate the causes for these changes and take whatever action might be necessary.

At this time the following general journal entry can be made:

Feb. 28   Work in Process — Dept. B............... 39,000
               Work in Process — Dept. A   39,000

The work in process account for this department now appears as follows:

WORK IN PROCESS — DEPT. A

Jan. 31		15,000	Jan. 31	27,000
		8,000		
		7,000		
	3,000	30,000		
Feb. 28		20,000	Feb. 28	39,000
		10,810		66,000
		9,190		
	4,000	70,000		

```
                      PRODUCTION REPORT

Dept. ____B – Forming____        Month __February__ 19__

In process, beginning of period _____500 units_____

Stage of completion _____two fifths_____

Placed in process during period _____none_____

Received from Dept. __A__ during period _____3,900 units_____

Transferred to Dept. __C__ during period _____4,100 units_____

Transferred to stockroom during period _____none_____

In process, end of period _____300 units_____

Stage of completion _____one third_____
```

In determining the unit cost in Department B at the end of February, the amounts considered are the production costs incurred by the department during the month added to the departmental cost of work in process at the beginning of the month. The cost from Department A that is included in the beginning work in process valuation ($5,000) is not used in this calculation.

PYRAMID TOY CORP.
Cost of Production Summary — Department B
For the Month Ended February 28, 19—

Cost of work in process, beginning of month:
  Cost in Dept. A .... $ 5,000
  Cost in Dept. B:
    Materials .... $ 83
    Labor 250
    Factory overhead 167   500 $ 5,500
Cost of goods received from Dept. A during month 39,000

Cost of production for month:
  Materials .... $ 1,681
  Labor 5,000
  Factory overhead 3,319   10,000
    Total costs to be accounted for **$54,500**

Unit output for month:
  Finished and transferred to Dept. C during month 4,100
  Equivalent units of work in process, end of month
    (300 units, one-third completed) 100
    Total equivalent production 4,200

Unit cost for month:
  Materials ($1,764 ÷ 4,200) .... $ .42
  Labor ($5,250 ÷ 4,200) 1.25
  Factory overhead ($3,486 ÷ 4,200) .... .83
    Total .... $ 2.50

Inventory costs:
  Cost of goods finished and transferred to Dept. C dur-
    ing month:
    Cost in Dept. A (4,100 × $10.00) $41,000
    Cost in Dept. B (4,100 ×   2.50) 10,250 $51,250
                   $12.50

  Cost of work in process, end of month:
    Cost in Dept. A (300 × $10.00) .... $ 3,000
    Cost in Dept. B:
      Materials (300 × ⅓ × $.42) .... $ 42
      Labor (300 × ⅓ × $1.25) 125
      Factory overhead (300 × ⅓ × $.83) 83   250   3,250
  Total production costs accounted for **$54,500**

The following journal entry can now be made:

Feb. 28 Work in Process — Dept. C 51,250
         Work in Process — Dept. B 51,250

The general ledger account for work in process in Department B appears as follows:

WORK IN PROCESS — DEPT. B

Jan. 31	1,000	Jan. 31	27,500
	3,000		
	2,000		
	27,000		
5,500	33,000		
Feb. 28	1,681	Feb. 28	51,250
	5,000		78,750
	3,319		
	39,000		
3,250	82,000		

PRODUCTION REPORT

Dept. _____ **C – Painting** _____ Month _____ **February** _____ 19--

In process, beginning of period _____ **200 units**

Stage of completion _____ **one half**

Placed in process during period _____ **none**

Received from Dept. **B** during period _____ **4,100 units**

Transferred to Dept. _____ during period _____

Transferred to stockroom during period _____ **3,900**

In process, end of period _____ **400 units**

Stage of completion _____ **one half**

PYRAMID TOY CORP.
Cost of Production Summary — Department C
For the Month Ended February 28, 19--

Cost of work in process, beginning of month:			
Cost in Dept. A		$ 2,000*	
Cost in Dept. B		500*	
Cost in Dept. C:			
Materials	$143		
Labor	114		
Factory overhead	143	400	$ 2,900
Cost of goods received from Dept. B during month			51,250
Cost of production for month:			
Materials		$ 5,720	
Labor		4,560	
Factory overhead		5,720	16,000
Total costs to be accounted for			**$70,150**

Unit output for month:
Finished and transferred to finished goods during
month 3,900
Equivalent units of work in process, end of month
(400 units, one-half completed)............................ 200
        Total equivalent production 4,100

Unit cost for month:
Materials ($5,863 ÷ 4,100)..................................... $1.43
Labor ($4,674 ÷ 4,100)... 1.14
Factory overhead ($5,863 ÷ 4,100)........................... 1.43
        Total $4.00

Inventory costs:
Cost of goods finished and transferred to finished
goods during month:
Cost in Dept. A (3,900 × $10.00) $39,000
Cost in Dept. B (3,900 ×   2.50) 9,750
Cost in Dept. C (3,900 ×   4.00) 15,600 $64,350
                        $16.50

Cost of work in process, end of month:
Cost in Dept. A (400 × $10.00)................................ $ 4,000
Cost in Dept. B (400 × $ 2.50) 1,000
Cost in Dept. C:
    Materials (400 × ½ × $1.43) $286
    Labor (400 × ½ × $1.14)........................... 228
    Factory overhead (400 × ½ × $1.43).......... 286   800   5,800
Total production costs accounted for $70,150

*Not to be considered in calculating February unit cost in Department C.

The following journal entry can now be made:

Feb. 28   Finished Goods............................... 64,350
                Work in Process — Dept. C............   64,350

The general ledger account for work in process in Department C appears as shown below.

WORK IN PROCESS — DEPT. C

Jan. 31		3,000	Jan. 31	33,000
		2,400		
		3,000		
		27,500		
	2,900	35,900		
Feb. 28		5,720	Feb. 28	64,350
		4,560		97,350
		5,720		
		51,250		
	5,800	103,150		

The cost accountant can now prepare the work sheet, reproduced below and on page 261, which summarizes the factory operations for February and provides the data needed for preparing the statement of cost of goods manufactured.

PYRAMID TOY CORP.
Statement of Cost of Goods Manufactured
For the Month Ended February 28, 19--

Materials	$27,401
Labor	20,370
Factory overhead	18,229
Total	$66,000
Add work in process inventories, February 1	11,400
	$77,400
Less work in process inventories, February 28	13,050
Cost of goods manufactured during the month	$64,350

Departmental Cost Work Sheet
For the Month Ended February 28, 19--

Analysis	Cost per unit transferred		Units received in department	Units transferred or on hand	Amount charged to department		Amount credited to department	
Dept. A — Cutting:								
Opening inventory in process	....	....	600	....	3,000	00	....	....
Started in process	....	....	3,800	....	....	....	....	....
Costs for month:								
Materials	....		....	....	20,000	00	....	....
Labor	....		....	....	10,810	00	....	....
Factory overhead	....	....	....	....	9,190	00	....	....
Finished and transferred to Dept. B...	10	00	....	3,900	....	....	39,000	00
Closing work in process	....	....	....	500	....	....	4,000	00
Total	10	00	4,400	4,400	43,000	00	43,000	00
Dept. B — Forming:								
Opening inventory in process	....	....	500	....	5,500	00	....	....
Received during month from Dept. A .	....	....	3,900	....	39,000	00	....	....
Costs added during month:								
Materials	....		....	....	1,681	00	....	....
Labor	....		....	....	5,000	00	....	....
Factory overhead	....		....	....	3,319	00	....	....
Finished and transferred to Dept. C...	2	50	....	4,100	....	....	51,250	00
Closing work in process	....	....	....	300	....	....	3,250	00
Total	12	50	4,400	4,400	54,500	00	54,500	00
Dept. C — Painting:								
Opening inventory in process	....	....	200	....	2,900	00	....	....
Received during month from Dept. B .	....	....	4,100	....	51,250	00	....	....
Costs added during month:								
Materials	....		....	....	5,720	00	....	....
Labor	....		....	....	4,560	00	....	....
Factory overhead	....		....	....	5,720	00	....	....
Finished and transferred to stock	4	00	....	3,900	....	....	64,350	00
Closing work in process	....	....	....	400	....	....	5,800	00
Total	16	50	4,300	4,300	70,150	00	70,150	00

					Amount		Total	
Summary:								
Materials:								
Dept. A								
Dept. B					20,000	00		
Dept. C					1,681	00		
					5,720	00	27,401	00
Labor:								
Dept. A					10,810	00		
Dept. B					5,000	00		
Dept. C					4,560	00	20,370	00
Factory overhead:								
Dept. A					9,190	00		
Dept. B					3,319	00		
Dept. C					5,720	00	18,229	00
Total production costs for February							66,000	00
Add work in process, beginning of month:								
Dept. A					3,000	00		
Dept. B					5,500	00		
Dept. C					2,900	00	11,400	00
Total							77,400	00
Deduct work in process, end of month:								
Dept. A					4,000	00		
Dept. B					3,250	00		
Dept. C					5,800	00	13,050	00
Cost of production, goods fully manufactured during February							64,350	00

Occasionally, finished goods in a department at the end of the month may not be transferred to the next department until the following month. Because these units are still on hand in the first department at the end of the first month, they cannot be accounted for as being transferred even though they have been finished. They are accounted for as "goods completed and on hand" and priced out at the full unit price. However, it is important to remember that these goods are considered to be work in process for financial statement purposes. Although the goods are finished in the department, they are still in process as far as the factory is concerned.

Change in Unit Costs

In the preceding illustrative problem, it was assumed that the cost from prior departments was the same in the current month as it had been in the previous month. Often, however, the cost from prior departments will change from one month to the next, so that these costs must be averaged for purposes of assigning the total costs. The method is similar to that used for the cost of materials, labor, and factory overhead in the department.

To illustrate, assume that 2,000 units are in process in Department 2 at the beginning of the month with an accumulated cost of

$15,000. During the month, 10,000 units with a cost of $50,000 are received from Department 1; 11,000 units are finished and transferred to Department 3; and 1,000 units are in process in Department 2 at the end of the month, one-half completed. The following is a schedule of costs for Department 2 in such a situation.

	Units	Unit Cost	Cost from Dept. 1	Costs in Dept. 2 Materials	Costs in Dept. 2 Labor	Costs in Dept. 2 Overhead	Total Cost
In process, beginning of month.....	2,000	$5.30	$10,600	$ 2,000	$ 1,400	$ 1,000	$ 15,000
Received from Dept. 1 during month.....................................	10,000	$5.00	50,000				50,000
Cost incurred this month...............				21,000	14,700	10,500	46,200
Total units and costs to be accounted for	12,000		$60,600	$23,000	$16,100	$11,500	$111,200
Average cost of units from Dept. 1 ($60,600 ÷ 12,000)..................		$5.05					$5.05
Unit cost for month in Dept. B with equivalent production of 11,500 units............................				$2.00	$1.40	$1.00	4.40
Unit cost for finished goods..........							$9.45
Assignment of costs: Transferred to Dept. 3	11,000	$5.05	$55,550	$22,000	$15,400	$11,000	$103,950
In process end of month (½ complete).................................	1,000	$5.05	5,050	1,000	700	500	7,250
Total units and costs accounted for...	12,000	$5.05	$60,600	$23,000	$16,100	$11,500	$111,200

QUESTIONS

1. What are the two basic systems of cost accounting and under what conditions may each be used advantageously?

2. Following is a list of manufactured products. For each product, indicate whether a job order or a process cost system would be used to account for the costs of production.
   - (a) Lumber
   - (b) Buildings
   - (c) Airplanes
   - (d) Gasoline
   - (e) Cereal
   - (f) Textbooks
   - (g) Paint
   - (h) Women's hats

3. Is there any situation in which a manufacturing company might use both the job order cost system and the process cost system?

4. What is the primary difference between the two cost accounting systems regarding the accumulation of costs and the calculation of unit costs?

5. What is the difference between the term "unit cost" as commonly used in the process cost system and the term "job cost" as commonly used in the job order system of cost accounting?

6. How do the two cost accounting systems differ in accounting for: (a) materials, (b) labor, and (c) factory overhead?

7. What is the primary objective in accumulating costs by departments?

8. What is meant by the term "equivalent unit" as used in the process cost system?

9. Explain why it is necessary to estimate the stage or degree of completion of work in process at the end of the accounting period under the process cost system.

10. What would be the effect on the unit cost of finished goods if an inaccurate estimate of the stage of completion of work in process is made?

11. What information is reflected on a production report?

12. What are the four divisions of a cost of production summary?

EXERCISES

1. List in columnar form, the transactions and the accounts debited and credited to reflect the flow of costs through a process cost accounting system.

2. Compute the equivalent units of production (unit output) for the month for each of the following situations:

	Units Completed During Month	Units in Process End of Month	Stage of Completion
(a)	9,000	2,000	1/2
(b)	20,000	4,000	3/4
(c)	8,000	1,000	3/4
		500	2/5
(d)	18,000	4,000	1/2
		5,000	3/4
(e)	28,000	1,500	1/5
		4,000	3/4

3. Using the data presented below, compute the figures that should be inserted in the blank spaces.

	Beginning Units in Process	Units Started in Production	Units Transferred to Finished Goods	Ending Units in Process	Equivalent Units
(a)	600	8,000	8,600	0 ____	8600
(b)	900	6,500	7200	200 — ½ completed	7300
(c)	1,000	13100	12,900	1,200 — ¼ completed	13200
(d)	100	7,250	7,200	150 — ½ completed	7275
(e)	0	8,400	8,200	200 — ½ completed	8300
(f)	400	6,200	6,200	400 ¼	6,300

4. During the month, a company with no departmentalization incurred costs of $45,000 for materials, $30,000 for labor, and $20,625 for factory overhead. There were no units in process at the beginning or at the end of the month, and 3,750 units were completed. Determine the unit cost for the month for materials, labor, and factory overhead.

5. The Abel Manufacturing Co. recorded costs for the month of $15,750 for materials, $40,950 for labor, and $25,200 for factory overhead. There was no beginning work in process; 4,250 units were finished, and 1,000 units were in process at the end of the period, three-fourths completed. Compute the month's unit cost for each element of manufacturing cost.

6. The records of Ajax, Inc., reflect the following data:

Work in process, beginning of month — 2,000 units one-half completed at a cost of $1,250 for materials, $675 for labor, and $950 for overhead.

Production costs for the month — materials, $99,150; labor, $54,925; factory overhead, $75,050.

Units completed and transferred to stock — 18,500.

Work in process, end of month — 3,000 units one-half completed.

Calculate the unit cost for the month for materials, labor, and factory overhead.

7. The Realife Products Company has two production departments. The nature of the process is such that there are no units left in process in Department 2 at the end of the period. During the period, 8,000 units with a cost of $27,200 were transferred from Department 1 to Department 2. Department 2 incurred costs of $9,600 for materials, $6,400 for labor, and $8,000 for factory overhead, and finished 8,000 units during the month. Determine **(a)** the unit cost for the month in Department 2, and **(b)** the unit cost of the products transferred to finished goods.

8. The Como Manufacturing Co. had 500 units, three-fifths completed, in process at the beginning of the month. During the month 2,000 units were started in process and finished. There was no work in process at the end of the month. Unit cost of production for the month was $1.20. Costs for materials, labor, and factory overhead incurred in the current month totaled $2,655. Calculate the unit cost for the *prior* month.

PROBLEMS

6-1. Cost of production summary; one department; beginning and ending work in process. The Monroe Products Co. produces a household cleansing liquid and uses the process cost system. The following information was obtained from the accounts of the company at the end of August:

Production Costs

Work in process, beginning of period:		
Materials	$ 5,000	
Labor	3,750	
Factory overhead	3,750	$12,500
Costs incurred during month:		
Materials	$30,000	
Labor	22,500	
Factory overhead	22,500	75,000
Total		$87,500

Production Report	Units
Finished and transferred to stockroom during month......................	16,500
Work in process, end of period, one-fourth completed	4,000

handwritten notes: 16,500 × $5.— to goods 1000 × $5.5.— left Equiv 17,500 1000

Required: Prepare a cost of production summary for August.

6-2. *Cost of production summary; one department; beginning and ending work in process.* The Mallet company uses the process cost system. The following data taken from the books of the organization reflect the results of manufacturing operations during the month of March:

Production Costs

Work in process, beginning of period:		
Materials	$ 2,600	
Labor	2,300	
Factory overhead	1,000	$ 5,900
Costs incurred during month:		
Materials	$10,000	
Labor	7,500	
Factory overhead	6,000	23,500
Total		$29,400

Production Report	Units
Finished and transferred to stockroom during month.....................	6,000
Work in process, end of period, one-half completed.......................	2,000

Required: Prepare a cost of production summary.

6-3. *Cost of production summary; two departments.* Metro, Inc., which manufactures products on a continuous basis, had 800 units in process in Department 1, one-half completed at the beginning of July. The costs in June for processing these units were: materials, $1,200; labor, $900; and factory overhead, $1,000. During July, Department 1 finished and transferred 10,000 units to Department 2 with a cost of $77,500 and had 400 units in process at the end of July, one-half completed.

Department 2 had 200 units in process at the beginning of the month, one-half completed. June costs for these units were: from Department 1, $1,550, materials, $200, labor, $175, factory overhead, $225. During July, Department 2 completed 9,000 units and had 1,200 units in process at the end of the period, two-thirds completed.

Production costs incurred by the two departments during July were as follows:

	Department 1	Department 2
Materials.....................................	$29,400	$19,400
Labor...	22,050	16,975
Factory overhead.........................	24,500	21,825

Required: Prepare a cost of production summary for each department.

6-4. *Change in unit cost from prior department and valuation of inventory.* The Rose Products Co. has two departments — Mixing and Cooking. At the beginning of the month, the Cooking Department had 1,000 units in process with costs of $8,000 from the Mixing Department and its own departmental costs of $500 for materials, $1,000 for labor, and $2,500 for factory overhead. During the month, 9,000 units were received from the Mixing Department with a cost of $72,900. The Cooking Department incurred costs of $4,250 for materials, $8,500 for labor, and $21,250 for factory overhead, and finished 9,000 units. At the end of the month there were 1,000 units in process, one-half completed.

Required: Determine **(1)** the unit cost for the month in the Cooking Department; **(2)** the new average unit cost for all units received from the Mixing Department; **(3)** the unit cost of goods finished; **(4)** the accumulated cost of the goods finished and of the ending work in process. *Note: A schedule similar to the illustration on page 262 will be helpful.*

6-5. Cost of production summary; three departments; change in unit cost from prior department; departmental cost work sheet; journal entries; manufacturing statement. The Allied Manufacturing Co. uses the process cost system. The following information for the month of March was obtained from the books of the company and from the production reports submitted by the department heads:

Production Report	Dept. A	Dept. B	Dept. C
Units in process, beginning of period	2,500	1,500	3,000
Started in process during month	12,500	—	—
Received from prior department	—	13,000	10,000
Finished and transferred	13,000	10,000	11,000
Finished and on hand	—	500	—
Units in process, end of period	2,000	4,000	2,000
Stage of completion	1/4	4/5	1/2

Production Costs	Dept. A	Dept. B	Dept. C
Work in process, beginning of period:			
Cost in Dept. A		$ 3,075	$ 6,150
Materials	$ 1,470		
Labor	650		
Factory overhead	565		
Cost in Dept. B			3,660
Materials		240	
Labor		905	
Factory overhead		750	
Cost in Dept. C			
Materials			900
Labor			3,100
Factory overhead			3,080
Costs incurred during month:			
Materials	15,000	2,500	1,500
Labor	4,750	8,000	6,500
Factory overhead	5,240	6,100	7,000
Total	$27,675	$21,570	$31,890

Required: (1) Prepare cost of production summaries for Departments A, B, and C. **(2)** Prepare a departmental cost work sheet. **(3)** Draft the journal entries required to record the month's operations. **(4)** Prepare a statement of cost of goods manufactured for March.

6-6. Departmental cost work sheet analysis; cost of production summary; three departments; journal entries; manufacturing statement. The Leba Manufacturing Co. uses the process cost system of accounting. A portion of the departmental cost work sheet prepared by the cost accountant at the end of January is reproduced below.

Analysis	Cost per unit transferred	Units received in department	Units transferred or on hand	Amount charged to department	Amount credited to department
Departmental Cost Work Sheet					
For the Month Ended January 31, 19—					
Dept. A:					
Started in process	....	6,600	....	....	....
Costs for month:					
Materials	....	....	....	30,000 00	....
Labor	....	....	....	16,000 00	....
Factory overhead	....	....	....	14,000 00	....
Completed and transferred to Dept. B	10 00	....	5,400	....	54,000 00
Closing inventory in process.............	....	....	1,200	....	6,000 00
Total	10 00	6,600	6,600	60,000 00	60,000 00
Dept. B:					
Received during month from Dept. A .	....	5,400	....	54,000 00	....
Costs added during month:					
Materials	....	....	....	1,200 00	....
Labor	....	....	....	6,000 00	....
Factory overhead	....	....	....	4,800 00	....
Completed and transferred to Dept. C	2 50	....	4,400	....	55,000 00
Closing inventory in process.............	....	....	1,000	....	11,000 00
Total	12 50	5,400	5,400	66,000 00	66,000 00
Dept. C:					
Received during month from Dept. B .	....	4,400	....	55,000 00	....
Costs added during month:					
Materials	....	....	....	6,300 00	....
Labor	....	....	....	4,200 00	....
Factory overhead	....	....	....	6,300 00	....
Completed and transferred to stock ...	4 00	....	4,000	....	66,000 00
Closing inventory in process.............	....	....	400	....	5,800 00
Total	16 50	4,400	4,400	71,800 00	71,800 00

Required: (1) Prepare a cost of production summary for each department. The stage of completion of ending units in process must be computed. **(2)** Draft the necessary entries in general journal form to record the manufacturing costs incurred during the month of January. **(3)** Prepare a statement of cost of goods manufactured for the month ended January 31.

6-7. Ledger account analysis; cost of production summary. Analyze the information presented in the general ledger account of the XYZ Manufacturing Co. shown below.

WORK IN PROCESS — DEPT. B

Mar. 1		20,500	Mar. 31	100,000
31	Materials	8,000		
31	Labor	16,000		
31	Factory overhead	12,000		
31	Dept. A	72,000		
		28,500	*128,500*	

Additional facts:

(a) 2,000 units were in process at the beginning of the month one-half completed.

(b) 9,000 units were received from Department A during the month.

(c) 8,000 units were transferred to Department C during the month.

(d) The unit costs in Departments A and B were the same for March as for the prior month.

(e) The ratio of materials, labor, and factory overhead costs for Department B in the beginning and ending balances of Work in Process was in the same ratio as the costs incurred in Department B during the current month.

Required: Prepare a cost of production summary.

7

Process Cost Accounting—
Special Procedures

The illustrative problems presented in Chapter 6 are based on the assumption that materials, labor, and factory overhead are uniformly applied during the period of processing. If the work in process at the end of the accounting period was considered to be one-half completed, it was assumed that one half of the materials cost, one half of the labor cost, and one half of the factory overhead cost had been incurred.

EQUIVALENT PRODUCTION —
MATERIALS NOT UNIFORMLY APPLIED

In many industries where the process cost system is used, the materials may be put into production in irregular quantities and at varying points in the processing cycle.

For example, before any manufacturing process can begin, materials must be introduced into the first production department. This might be a sheet of metal which will be cut or trimmed to size, shaped, and formed through the application of labor and the use of machines. In this case, all of the materials are added at the start of the process and then labor and factory overhead are incurred to begin converting this material into the finished product. No matter what stage of completion the work is in at the end of the month in this department, it will have had all the materials costs added. If the work is unfinished in the department, it will have had only a portion of the labor and overhead costs applied to it.

In the second production department, this same material may be processed further through the application of other labor operations such as buffing and polishing, and then, at the end of the process in this department, have several coats of enamel applied to it. In this case, the units that are uncompleted in the department at the end of the month would have a part of the departmental labor and overhead costs applied to them but no materials cost in this department.

In the next department, other materials such as a knob, a handle, or pads may be added to the unit immediately, then a final polishing involving labor and equipment would be applied. After this process, in the same department, the unit may be placed in a plastic container which is additional material, and the package would be sealed, incurring more labor and overhead cost.

In this third department, the units not completed may have the first item of materials and some labor and overhead applied; they may have the first material, some labor and overhead, and the additional materials added; in any event, the stage of completion must be carefully determined to measure accurately how much of each element of cost to apply to these unfinished units.

Compared with the principles and procedures developed in the preceding chapter, the only new procedure presented here is that equivalent production must be computed for each element of production cost, rather than one equivalent production figure being determined for materials, labor, and overhead. In addition, the allocation of cost for each element must be carefully considered when valuing the ending work in process.

As an aid in explaining the problems involved in ascertaining unit costs under these conditions, three illustrative problems are presented. In these examples, materials are added at different stages in the process. Labor and factory overhead are assumed to be applied evenly throughout the process. This situation is typical in that the incurrence and application of overhead is usually so closely related to labor costs or hours that overhead is generally thought of as being incurred or applied in the same ratio as labor expense.

Illustrative Problem No. 1 – Computing the unit cost in Department A where all the materials are added at the beginning of processing.

The production report for the month, submitted by the department head, is shown on the following page. It is similar to those studied in the previous chapter.

```
┌─────────────────────────────────────────────────────────────┐
│                     PRODUCTION REPORT                        │
│                                                              │
│  Dept. ____A_____  Month ___April___ 19__ │
│                                                              │
│  In process, beginning of period _____  500 units     │
│                                                              │
│  Stage of competition _____     two fifths          │
│                                                              │
│  Placed in process during period _____  2,500 units    │
│                                                              │
│  Received from Dept. _____ during period _____          │
│                                                              │
│  Transferred to Dept. _B__ during period _____ 2,600 units │
│                                                              │
│  Transferred to stockroom during period _____          │
│                                                              │
│  In process, end of period _____   400 units       │
│                                                              │
│  Stage of completion _____     three fourths        │
│                                                              │
│                          Remarks                             │
└─────────────────────────────────────────────────────────────┘
```

The cost of production summary is illustrated on page 272. Note that it too is similar to the ones previously discussed, with the additional step of determining equivalent production for materials separately from that of labor and factory overhead.

In this department, because all materials are added at the start of processing, it is simple to determine the equivalent units for materials. The production report from the factory indicates that 500 units were in process at the beginning of the month with all materials added, and that 2,500 units were started in process; therefore, the equivalent production for materials is 3,000 units. Another way of calculating the figure by the method used in this chapter is: the 2,600 units finished during the month and the 400 units in process at the end of the month have all of the materials added. The total of these two figures is 3,000 units, which is the equivalent production for materials for the month.

The unit output for labor and factory overhead is calculated as shown in the preceding chapter: 2,600 completed units, plus the equivalent of 300 completed units (400 units three-fourths completed), gives a total of 2,900 for the unit output for the month for labor and overhead.

With the equivalent production figures determined for materials, labor, and overhead, the cost accountant can now calculate the unit cost for the month as illustrated in previous discussions. The cost of

MODERN MANUFACTURING CORP.
Cost of Production Summary — Department A
For the Month Ended April 30, 19--

Cost of work in process, beginning of month:		
Materials	$1,500	
Labor	250	
Factory overhead	150	$ 1,900
Cost of production for month:		
Materials	$7,500	
Labor	3,375	
Factory overhead	2,025	12,900
Total costs to be accounted for		$14,800
Unit output for month:		
Materials:		
Finished and transferred to Dept. B during month		2,600
Equivalent units of work in process, end of month		
(400 units, three-fourths completed, all materials) .		400
Total equivalent production		3,000
Labor and factory overhead:		
Finished and transferred to Dept. B during month		2,600
Equivalent units of work in process, end of month		
(400 units, three-fourths completed)....................		300
Total equivalent production		2,900
Unit cost for month:		
Materials ($9,000 ÷ 3,000)..		$3.00
Labor ($3,625 ÷ 2,900)..		1.25
Factory overhead ($2,175 ÷ 2,900).............................		.75
Total		$5.00
Inventory costs:		
Cost of goods finished and transferred to Dept. B dur-		
ing month (2,600 × $5)		$13,000
Cost of work in process, end of month:		
Materials (400 × $3)	$1,200	
Labor (400 × ¾ × $1.25)	375	
Factory overhead (400 × ¾ × $.75)........................	225	1,800
Total production costs accounted for		$14,800

each element in the beginning work in process is added to the cost of production for that element incurred in the current month; this total cost is then divided by the appropriate equivalent production figure to determine the unit cost for the month for each element of cost. In this example, the unit cost of materials is $3.00, of labor $1.25, and of overhead $.75, giving a total unit cost of $5.00.

The 2,600 units transferred to Department B are costed at $5.00 each, or a total of $13,000. In costing the ending work in process, the accountant must consider the stage of completion and the point at which materials are added. In this instance, because materials are put into production at the beginning of the manufacturing cycle, the 400 units in process at the end of the month have all of the materials added and are, therefore, costed at the full unit cost of $3.00 for materials. Because the goods are three-fourths completed, and labor and factory overhead are added evenly throughout the process, the 400 units are costed at three fourths of the month's unit cost for labor and overhead.

Illustrative Problem No. 2 – Computing the unit cost in Department B where all the materials are added at the close of processing.

In Department B, because the materials are added at the end of the manufacturing process, only those units finished will have materials cost applied; therefore, the equivalent production for the month for materials in this department is 2,500 units. The calculation for labor and factory overhead adds the 2,500 finished units to the equivalent production for the ending work in process, 350 units two-fifths completed, or 140, giving a total of 2,640 units as the output for the month.

As in Department A, the unit cost for each element of manufacturing cost is determined by adding the cost included in the beginning work in process to the cost for that element incurred during the

---

PRODUCTION REPORT

Dept. __B__   Month __April__ 19__

In process, beginning of period _____ **250 units**

Stage of completion _____ **one half**

Placed in process during period _____

Received from Dept. __A__ during period _____ **2,600 units**

Transferred to Dept. __C__ during period _____ **2,500 units**

Transferred to stockroom during period _____

In process, end of period _____ **350 units**

Stage of completion _____ **two fifths**

Remarks

month, and dividing this total by the unit output for the month. For Department B these unit costs for materials, labor, and factory overhead are $4, $3, and $3, respectively.

MODERN MANUFACTURING CORP.
Cost of Production Summary — Department B
For the Month Ended April 30, 19--

Cost of work in process, beginning of month:			
Cost in Dept. A		$ 1,250	
Cost in Dept. B:			
Materials	–0–		
Labor	$375		
Factory overhead......................................	375	750	$ 2,000
Cost of goods received from Dept. A during month.........			13,000
Cost of production for month:			
Materials		$10,000	
Labor		7,545	
Factory overhead		7,545	25,090
Total costs to be accounted for			$40,090
Unit output for month:			
Materials:			
Finished and transferred to Dept. C during month ...			2,500
Equivalent units of work in process, end of month ...			–0–
Total equivalent production			2,500
Labor and factory overhead:			
Finished and transferred to Dept. C during month ...			2,500
Equivalent units of work in process, end of month			
(350 units, two-fifths completed)........................			140
Total equivalent production			2,640
Unit cost for month:			
Materials ($10,000 ÷ 2,500).....................................			$ 4.00
Labor ($7,920 ÷ 2,640)..			3.00
Factory overhead ($7,920 ÷ 2,640).........................			3.00
Total			$10.00
Inventory costs:			
Cost of goods finished and transferred to Dept. C during month:			
Cost in Dept. A (2,500 × $5)		$12,500	
Cost in Dept. B (2,500 × $10)		25,000	$37,500
Cost of work in process, end of month:			
Cost in Dept. A (350 × $5)...................................		$ 1,750	
Cost in Dept. B:			
Materials...	–0–		
Labor (350 × 2/5 × $3).............................	$420		
Factory overhead (350 × 2/5 × $3)	420	840	2,590
Total production costs accounted for			$40,090

The units finished and transferred to Department C are valued at the full unit cost of $5, carried over from Department A, plus the unit cost of $10 added in Department B, giving a total cost transferred of $37,500.

The cost of the units in process at the end of the period includes the full cost of $5 from Department A. There is no materials cost for Department B to be considered because no materials have been added. If materials had been added, the units would have been finished. Because the units are two-fifths completed, two fifths of the current unit costs for labor and factory overhead is used in costing the units. The combination of these items results in a cost of $2,590 for the ending work in process.

Illustrative Problem No. 3 – Computing the unit cost in Department C where 60 percent of the materials cost is added to production at the beginning of processing and 40 percent when the processing is one-half completed.

In Department C, the calculation of equivalent production is more complex because materials are added at different stages throughout the process. The stage of completion of units in process cannot be averaged but must be reported in groups of units at varying points in the manufacturing process as shown in the following production report. In calculating the unit of output for the month, the stage of completion of each group must be carefully computed.

PRODUCTION REPORT

Dept. __C_____ Month __April__ 19—

In process, beginning of period _____ *500 units*

Stage of completion _*200 units ¾ completed – 300 units ⅓ completed*_

Placed in process during period _____

Received from Dept. _B_ during period _____ *2,500 units*

Transferred to Dept. ____ during period _____

Transferred to stockroom during period _____ *2,400 units*

In process, end of period _____ *600 units*

Stage of completion _*200 units ¼ completed – 400 units ¾ completed*_

Remarks

The equivalent production for the month for materials is determined as follows: 2,400 units were finished and therefore include all the materials. Two hundred units are one-fourth completed at the end of the period; since they are not yet at the halfway point of the process, they have had only 60 percent of the materials added, or the equivalent of 120 units. The 400 units that are three-fourths completed are past the halfway stage, and therefore have all of the materials added, or a total of 400 units. Combining these figures — 2,400, 120, and 400 — results in the unit output for materials of 2,920 units.

A simpler calculation is made for labor and factory overhead: 2,400 completed units, plus the equivalent of 50 completed units (200 units one-fourth completed), plus the equivalent of 300 completed units (400 units three-fourths completed) equals total equivalent production for the month for labor and overhead of 2,750 units.

The unit costs for the month are calculated as previously illustrated, and are determined to be $1.75, $1.20, and $.60 for materials, labor, and factory overhead respectively, for a total unit cost in Department C of $3.55. The cost of the units finished and transferred to the stockroom includes the unit costs from Department A of $5, from Department B of $10, and from Department C of $3.55.

In calculating the cost to be assigned to the ending work in process, the stage of completion must be considered. The 200 units that are one-fourth completed will have all of the costs from Departments A and B assigned to them. The costs in Department C are determined as follows: 60 percent of the materials cost has been added, and therefore the units will be costed at 60 percent of the unit cost for materials, or 200 units $\times$ 60% $\times$ $1.75 = $210; the costs allocated for labor and overhead are one fourth of the month's unit cost for each, or 200 units $\times$ 25% $\times$ $1.20 = $60 for labor and 200 units $\times$ 25% $\times$ $.60 = $30 for overhead.

The 400 units that are three-fourths completed are assigned all of the unit costs from Departments A and B. Although these units are still in process, they have all of the materials added, and therefore are charged for the full unit cost of materials in Department C — 400 units $\times$ $1.75 = $700. Three fourths of the unit costs for labor and factory overhead would be included in the cost of these units: 400 units $\times$ 75% $\times$ $1.20 = $360 for labor; 400 units $\times$ 75% $\times$ $.60 = $180 for overhead.

After the cost of production summaries have been prepared for each department, the journal entries, as illustrated in the previous chapter, can be made. Entries would be made to transfer costs from one department to another and finally to Finished Goods. The actual costs incurred during the month for materials, labor, and factory

MODERN MANUFACTURING CORP.
Cost of Production Summary — Department C
For the Month Ended April 30, 19—

Cost of work in process, beginning of month:			
Cost in Dept. A..		$ 2,500	
Cost in Dept. B..		5,000	
Cost in Dept. C:			
Materials..	$665		
Labor...	300		
Factory overhead	150	1,115	$ 8,615
Cost of goods received from Dept. B during month.....................			37,500
Cost of production for month:			
Materials..	$ 4,445		
Labor...	3,000		
Factory overhead..	1,500	8,945	
Total costs to be accounted for..			$55,060
Unit output for month:			
Materials:			
Finished and transferred to finished goods during month........			2,400
Equivalent units of work in process, end of month:			
200 units, one-fourth completed (60% of materials)...........			120
400 units, three-fourths completed (all materials)..............			400
Total equivalent production..			2,920
Labor and overhead:			
Finished and transferred to finished goods during month........			2,400
Equivalent units of work in process, end of month:			
200 units, one-fourth completed......................................			50
400 units, three-fourths completed			300
Total equivalent production..			2,750
Unit cost for month:			
Materials ($5,110 ÷ 2,920)			$1.75
Labor ($3,300 ÷ 2,750)			1.20
Factory overhead ($1,650 ÷ 2,750)...			.60
Total..			$3.55
Inventory costs:			
Cost of goods finished and transferred to finished goods during month:			
Cost in Dept. A (2,400 × $5)...		$12,000	
Cost in Dept. B (2,400 × $10)..		24,000	
Cost in Dept. C (2,400 × $3.55)...		8,520	$44,520
Cost of work in process, end of month:			
200 units, one-fourth completed:			
Cost in Dept. A (200 × $5)...		$ 1,000	
Cost in Dept. B (200 × $10)...		2,000	
Cost in Dept. C:			
Materials (200 × 60% × $1.75).........................	$210		
Labor (200 × 25% × $1.20)................................	60		
Factory overhead (200 × 25% × $.60)	30	300	
400 units, three-fourths completed:			
Cost in Dept. A (400 × $5)...		2,000	
Cost in Dept. B (400 × $10)...		4,000	
Cost in Dept. C:			
Materials (400 × $1.75)...................................	$700		
Labor (400 × 75% × $1.20)..............................	360		
Factory overhead (400 × 75% × $.60)	180	1,240	10,540
Total production costs accounted for..			$55,060

overhead would be recorded in the journals and ledgers. After all entries have been made, the work in process accounts in the general ledger should have balances that equal the cost assigned to work in process on the cost of production summaries. If desired, a departmental cost work sheet can be prepared as illustrated in Chapter 6.

UNITS LOST IN PRODUCTION

In many industries that have a process manufacturing operation, the process is of such a nature that there will always be some loss of units during the process due to evaporation, shrinkage, spillage, or other factors. The effect of such losses is that the number of units completed during a given period of time plus the number of units still in process at the end of the period will be less than the number of units in process at the beginning of the period plus the number of units placed in process during the period.

Normal losses are inherent to the manufacturing process and cannot be avoided; they represent a necessary cost of producing the good units. The usual procedure is to treat normal losses as **product costs**, that is, to include the cost of the lost units in the cost of all units finished or still in process. The effect is that the unit cost of the remaining good units is greater than if there had been no losses, since there are a smaller number of units over which to spread the production costs for the period. The following examples illustrate the procedures involved.

Illustrative Problem No. 1 – Units lost in the first department.

Assume that materials, labor, and factory overhead are applied evenly throughout the process and that the monthly production report for Department A reports the following data:

Units started in process..		10,000
Units finished and transferred to the next department.............	9,000	
Units still in process, one-half completed	800	9,800
Units lost in production...		200

This report is significant to the factory management, who review these figures to determine whether they represent normal unavoidable losses or abnormal losses which require action. With the production figures above and the costs of production for the month, the cost accountant can prepare the cost of production summary shown on the next page.

Notice that on the cost of production summary, the lost units have not been considered; they have been completely ignored in the calculation of equivalent production and in the determination of in-

CHEMICAL REFINING CORPORATION
Cost of Production Summary — Department A
For the Month Ended July 31, 19--

Cost of production for month:

Materials	$18,800
Labor	9,400
Factory overhead	4,700
Total costs to be accounted for	$32,900

Unit output for month:

Finished and transferred to Dept. B during month	9,000
Equivalent units of work in process, end of month (800 units, one-half completed)	400
Total equivalent production	9,400

Unit cost for month:

Materials ($18,800 ÷ 9,400)	$2.00
Labor ($9,400 ÷ 9,400)	1.00
Factory overhead ($4,700 ÷ 9,400)	.50
Total	$3.50

Inventory costs:

Cost of goods finished and transferred to Dept. B during month (9,000 × $3.50)		$31,500
Cost of work in process, end of month:		
Materials (800 × ½ × $2)	$800	
Labor (800 × ½ × $1)	400	
Factory overhead (800 × ½ × $.50)	200	1,400
Total production costs accounted for		$32,900

ventory costs. If the units had not been lost but had been finished, equivalent production would have been 9,600 units, and the unit costs for materials, labor, and factory overhead would have been lower. The cost of the lost units is absorbed by the production for the month.

Illustrative Problem No. 2 – Units lost in subsequent department.

The July production report for Department B reflects the following data:

Units received from Department A		9,000
Units finished and transferred to finished goods	8,000	
Units still in process, two-thirds completed	750	8,750
Units lost in production		250

On the cost of production summary, the procedures are identical to those for Department A through the calculation of unit costs for the month. The 250 units lost in the department during the period are ignored in the computations, so that the higher unit costs for the month reflect the absorption of the costs relating to the lost units.

Before determining the cost of the goods finished and in process at the end of the month, however, a new computation must be made. The 250 units that were lost in Department B were ignored in determining unit costs for Department B, but these units carried from Department A a cost of $3.50 each, which must now be taken into consideration.

CHEMICAL REFINING CORPORATION
Cost of Production Summary — Department B
For the Month Ended July 31, 19—

Cost of production for month:		
Materials	$15,300	
Labor	10,200	
Factory overhead	6,375	
Total		$31,875
Cost of goods received from Dept. A during month.........		31,500
Total costs to be accounted for		$63,375
Unit output for month:		
Finished and transferred to finished goods during month		8,000
Equivalent units of work in process, end of month (750 units, two-thirds completed)		500
Total equivalent production		8,500
Unit cost for month:		
Materials ($15,300 ÷ 8,500)		$1.80
Labor ($10,200 ÷ 8,500)		1.20
Factory overhead ($6,375 ÷ 8,500)...........................		.75
Total		$3.75

Inventory costs:

Cost of goods finished and transferred to finished goods:			
Cost in Dept. A (8,000 × $3.60, adjusted unit cost).		$28,800	
Cost in Dept. B (8,000 × $3.75)		30,000	$58,800
Cost of work in process, end of month:			
Cost in Dept. A (750 × $3.60, adjusted unit cost)....		$ 2,700	
Cost in Dept. B:			
Materials (750 × ⅔ × $1.80)	$900		
Labor (750 × ⅔ × $1.20)	600		
Factory overhead (750 × ⅔ × $.75)..........	375	1,875	4,575
Total production costs accounted for			$63,375

During the month, 250 of the 9,000 units transferred from Department A were lost in Department B. Therefore, the cost transferred of $31,500 must now be spread over the remaining 8,750 units, producing a unit cost of $3.60. This new cost is called the **adjusted unit cost** in the cost of production summary. The adjustment of unit cost does not affect Department A's cost of production summary, since the units were lost in Department B.

Another way of making this calculation is as follows:

Units from Dept. A lost in Dept. B..	250
Multiplied by the unit cost from Dept. A	$3.50
Cost applicable to the units lost..	$875.00
Number of units transferred from Dept. A..	9,000
Number of units lost..	250
Number of units remaining...	8,750

The cost applicable to lost units must be spread over the remaining units:

$$\frac{\$875}{8,750} = \$.10 \text{ adjustment in unit cost.}$$

Original unit cost..	$3.50
Add adjustment in unit cost..	.10
Adjusted unit cost	$3.60

Illustrative Problem No. 3 – Units lost at the end of the process.

In the previous illustrations, the units lost were treated as though they had never been put into production. Both finished goods and units still in process absorbed the cost of the lost units. However, if units are lost at the end of the process or are rejected at the point of final inspection, the cost of the lost units may be absorbed by the completed units only. In this case, no part of the loss is charged to the units remaining in process. The units lost are included in the number of units used to determine equivalent production and unit costs are then calculated in the usual way, thus producing a lower unit cost than if the lost units had been ignored. This unit cost is applied to goods finished and transferred, to those still in process, and to those units that were lost. The cost assigned to lost units is then added to the cost of the goods completed, and this total cost is transferred to the next department or to Finished Goods. The unit cost of the goods transferred will, of course, be higher than the monthly unit cost of production. These calculations are shown on the following cost of production summary, using the same data as that used on page 278.

The preceding discussion has considered only normal losses, with the cost of lost units being treated as a product cost, that is, charged to the remaining units. But **abnormal losses** may also occur. Such losses are not inherent to the manufacturing process and are

CHEMICAL REFINING CORPORATION
Cost of Production Summary — Department A
For the Month Ended July 31, 19––

Cost of production for month:	
Materials	$18,800
Labor	9,400
Factory overhead	4,700
Total costs to be accounted for	**$32,900**
Unit output for month:	
Finished and transferred to Dept. B during month	9,000
Equivalent units of work in process, end of month	
(800 units, one-half completed)............................	400
Lost in process	200
Total equivalent production	9,600
Unit cost for month:	
Materials ($18,800 ÷ 9,600)	$1.958
Labor ($9,400 ÷ 9,600)..	.979
Factory overhead ($4,700 ÷ 9,600)..........................	.490
Total	$3.427

Inventory costs:

Cost of goods finished and transferred to Dept. B during month (9,000 × $3.427).....................................	$30,843	
Add cost of units lost (200 × $3.427).......................	686	
Total cost of good units finished and transferred to Department B during month (9,000 × $3.503*) ...		$31,529
Cost of work in process, end of month:		
Materials (800 × ½ × $1.958)..............................	$ 783	
Labor (800 × ½ × $.979)	392	
Factory overhead (800 × ½ × $.49)......................	196	1,371
Total production costs accounted for		**$32,900**

*200 units lost × $3.427 = $686 cost of lost units.
$686 ÷ 9,000 units completed = $.076 unit cost adjustment for lost units.
$3.427 + $.076 = $3.503 adjusted unit cost of units completed.

not expected under normal, efficient operating conditions. Units lost under these circumstances would be included in the calculation of equivalent production and unit costs as shown in the preceding example of units lost at the end of the process. However, abnormal losses are not included as part of the cost of transferred or finished goods, but are treated as a **period cost**, that is, charged to a separate expense account and shown as a separate item of expense on the current income statement. If the loss of units in the previous example were considered to be abnormal, the cost transferred to the next department would be $30,843, $686 would be charged to Abnormal

Loss of Units, and the cost of work in process would be unchanged at $1,371.

Illustrative Problem No. 4 – Abnormal loss of units at the beginning of the process.

If an abnormal loss occurs at the beginning of processing in a department, only materials and/or transferred-in costs are affected. Since these units are lost early in the process, no labor or overhead should be added for these lost units. Using the Department A data, the abnormal loss is calculated and accounted for as follows:

CHEMICAL REFINING CORPORATION
Cost of Production Summary — Department A
For the Month Ended July 31, 19—

Cost of production for month:		
Materials		$18,800
Labor		9,400
Factory overhead		4,700
Total costs to be accounted for		$32,900
Unit output for month:		
Materials:		
Finished and transferred to Dept. B during month		9,000
Equivalent units of work in process, end of month (800 units, one-half completed)		400
Lost in process		200
Total equivalent production		9,600
Labor and factory overhead:		
Finished and transferred to Dept. B during month		9,000
Equivalent units of work in process, end of month (800 units, one-half completed)		400
Total equivalent production		9,400
Unit cost for month:		
Materials ($18,800 ÷ 9,600)		$1.9583
Labor ($9,400 ÷ 9,400)		1.0000
Factory overhead ($4,700 ÷ 9,400)		.5000
Total		$3.4583
Inventory costs and abnormal loss:		
Cost of goods finished and transferred to Dept. B (9,000 × $3.4583)		$31,125
Cost of work in process, end of month:		
Materials (800 × ½ × $1.9583)	$783	
Labor (800 × ½ × $1.00)	400	
Factory overhead (800 × ½ × $.50)	200	1,383
Cost of abnormal loss (200 × $1.9583)		392
Total production costs accounted for		$32,900

The journal entry to transfer costs would be as follows:

Work in Process — Department B..................	31,125	
Abnormal Loss of Units	392	
Work in Process — Department A................		31,517

UNITS GAINED IN PRODUCTION

With some manufactured products, the addition of materials in a department after the first increases the number of units being processed. For example, if a liquid product is produced, and 1,000 gallons of materials were put into production in the first department and transferred to the next department, the addition of 500 gallons of another material in the second department increases the number of units being manufactured to 1,500. This increase in units has the opposite effect of lost units and requires an adjustment to the unit cost in the second or subsequent departments. The calculation of this adjusted unit cost is similar to that made when units are lost, except that the total cost for the original units must be spread over a greater number of units in the subsequent department, thereby reducing the unit cost.

To illustrate, assume that a concentrated detergent, Super-Glo, is manufactured. During the month 10,000 gallons of the partially processed product have been transferred to Department B at a cost of $15,000, or a unit cost of $1.50. In Department B, 5,000 gallons of additional materials are added to these units in process. As these materials are added, the mixing and refining of the liquid involves the equal application of materials, labor, and overhead. A production report shows that 13,000 gallons were completed and transferred to finished goods, leaving 2,000 gallons in process, one-half completed. The cost of production summary is on page 285. The cost transferred from Department A for 10,000 gallons was $15,000, or a unit cost of $1.50. The addition of 5,000 gallons in Department B increases the liquid in process to 15,000 units. The cost from Department A of $15,000 must now be spread over these 15,000 units, resulting in an adjusted unit cost of $1.00.

It is possible in a manufacturing process as illustrated that, in addition to gaining a number of units, some units will also be lost during processing in Department B. This factor presents no additional problem, since the equivalent production and unit costs are calculated as though the lost units had not existed, and the type of computation shown in the preceding example would be the same. As mentioned previously in this chapter, if management wishes to have a dollar accounting for lost units, then the number lost would be

SUPER-GLO MANUFACTURING COMPANY
Cost of Production Summary — Department B
For the Month Ended May 31, 19——

Cost of goods received from Dept. A during month (10,000 gallons × $1.50)		$15,000
Cost of production for month:		
Materials	$ 7,700	
Labor	3,500	
Factory overhead	2,800	14,000
Total costs to be accounted for		$29,000
Unit output for month:		
Finished and transferred to finished goods		13,000
Equivalent units of work in process, end of month (2,000 gallons, one-half completed)		1,000
Total equivalent production		14,000
Unit cost for month:		
Materials ($7,700 ÷ 14,000)		$ .55
Labor ($3,500 ÷ 14,000)		.25
Factory overhead ($2,800 ÷ 14,000)		.20
Total		$1.00
Inventory costs:		
Cost of goods finished and transferred to finished goods:		
Cost in Dept. A (13,000 × $1.00, adjusted unit cost)	$13,000	
Cost in Dept. B (13,000 × $1.00)	13,000	$26,000
Cost of work in process, end of month:		
Cost in Dept. A (2,000 × $1.00, adjusted unit cost)	$ 2,000	
Cost in Dept. B:		

Materials (2,000 × ½ × $.55)	$550		
Labor (2,000 × ½ × $.25)	250		
Factory overhead (2,000 × ½ × $.20)	200	1,000	3,000
Total production costs accounted for			$29,000

included in equivalent production as though no loss had occurred. The unit cost would be computed and a dollar cost assigned to lost units by multiplying the unit cost by the number of units lost.

EQUIVALENT PRODUCTION — FIRST-IN, FIRST-OUT (FIFO) METHOD

The previous discussion and illustrations have used the average method of costing. As mentioned in Chapter 6, another method of costing commonly used is the **first-in, first-out (fifo)** method. This approach assumes that costs of the current period are first applied to complete the beginning units in process; secondly, to start and finish a number of units; and finally, to start other units in process.

The two problems which follow illustrate this method of costing compared with average costing. When studying these examples, note that fifo costing differs from average costing only if there are units in process at the start of the period; if there is no beginning work in process, both methods will produce the same results.

Also note that under the fifo method, if units are lost, there must be a decision made as to whether these units are from the beginning inventory in process or from the units started during the period. Assuming that unit costs differ from one period to the next, this decision is necessary in order to determine which unit cost should be adjusted.

Whether the fifo or the average cost method is used, the first step in preparing the cost of production summary is to list the costs that must be accounted for, that is, the beginning balance of work in process, the current period's costs of production, and the cost of units transferred from a prior department, if any. With the fifo method, there is no necessity to break down the cost of the beginning work in process into its cost elements as is required with the average cost method.

The second step under the fifo method, as with the average cost procedure, is to determine the unit output for the month. If there were units in process at the start of the period, the total equivalent production figures for the fifo method will differ from those for the average cost method because the unit output required to complete the beginning work in process must also be calculated.

Illustrative Problem No. 1 – Fifo cost method compared with average cost method — materials added at start of process.

Assume that in Department 1, materials are added at the start of processing, and labor and factory overhead are applied evenly throughout the process. The production report for March reflects the following data:

Units in process, beginning of month, two-thirds completed	3,000
Units started in process	9,000
Units finished and transferred to Department 2	8,000
Units in process, end of month, one-half completed	4,000

Cost data are as follows:

Beginning work in process, prior month's cost:	
Materials	$ 9,600
Labor	3,600
Factory overhead	2,800
Total	$16,000

Current month's production costs:

Materials	$27,000
Labor	16,000
Factory overhead	8,000
Total	$51,000

Using the fifo method, a cost of production summary is prepared as shown on the following page. For comparative purposes, a cost of production summary under the average cost method is shown on page 289.

There were 3,000 units in process at the beginning of the month; these units were complete as to materials and two-thirds complete as to labor and factory overhead.

In the current month, no materials had to be added to these units; however, the equivalent of 1,000 units (3,000 × ⅓) of labor and overhead had to be applied to these units to finish them in Department 1.

Of the 8,000 units finished and transferred to Department 2 during the month, 3,000 were from the beginning units in process; therefore, 5,000 units must have been fully manufactured during the month. Under the fifo cost method, the beginning units in process are not merged with the units started and finished during the month.

The calculation of equivalent production for the ending work in process is the same under fifo as under the average cost method. There are 4,000 units in process with all materials and with one half of the labor and overhead. Thus, the equivalent production for materials is 4,000 units, and for labor and overhead, 2,000 units.

The calculation of unit costs with the fifo method takes into consideration only the current period data. The total cost of each element — materials, labor, and factory overhead — is divided by the equivalent production for the month to determine the unit cost for each element. The cost of the beginning work in process is not merged with current costs under the fifo method as it is under the average cost method.

When assigning costs to the units finished and transferred, the average cost approach simply charges the 8,000 units transferred with the total unit cost of $6.09. Under the fifo method, however, two calculations are necessary to determine the cost assigned to units transferred. First, the 3,000 units in process at the beginning of the month were complete as to materials, so no cost for materials is added. However, the units had been two-thirds completed during the previous month as to labor and overhead and therefore must have been completed as to the other one third during the current month. Thus, one third of the current period's unit cost for labor

Fifo Method

GAGE MANUFACTURING COMPANY
Cost of Production Summary — Department 1
For the Month Ended March 31, 19--

Cost of work in process, beginning of month		$16,000
Cost of production for month:		
Materials	$27,000	
Labor	16,000	
Factory overhead	8,000	51,000
Total costs to be accounted for		**$67,000**

Unit output for month:

	Materials	Labor and Factory Overhead
To complete beginning units in process........................	—0—	1,000
Units started and finished during month.......................	5,000	5,000
Ending units in process	4,000	2,000
Total equivalent production	9,000	8,000

Unit cost for month:	
Materials ($27,000 ÷ 9,000).....................................	$3.00
Labor ($16,000 ÷ 8,000)...	2.00
Factory overhead ($8,000 ÷ 8,000)............................	1.00
Total	$6.00

Inventory costs:		
Cost of goods finished and transferred to Department 2 during month:		
Beginning units in process:		
Prior month's cost..	$16,000	
Current cost to complete:		
Materials	—0—	
Labor (3,000 × ⅓ × $2)	2,000	
Factory overhead (3,000 × ⅓ × $1).................	1,000	$19,000
Units started and finished during month (5,000 × $6.00)		30,000
Total cost transferred (8,000 × $6.125)		$49,000
Cost of work in process, end of month:		
Materials (4,000 × $3)	$12,000	
Labor (4,000 × ½ × $2)	4,000	
Factory overhead (4,000 × ½ × $1).........................	2,000	18,000
Total production costs accounted for		**$67,000**

and overhead is assigned to each of the 3,000 units and then added to the $16,000 cost carried over from the prior period.

Second, the 5,000 units fully manufactured during the month are priced at the unit cost of $6 for the period. The total accumulated

Average Cost Method

GAGE MANUFACTURING COMPANY
Cost of Production Summary — Department 1
For the Month Ended March 31, 19—

Cost of work in process, beginning of month:		
Materials	$ 9,600	
Labor	3,600	
Factory overhead	2,800	$16,000
Cost of production for month:		
Materials	$27,000	
Labor	16,000	
Factory overhead	8,000	51,000
Total costs to be accounted for		$67,000
Unit output for month:		
Materials:		
Finished and transferred to Dept. 2 during month		8,000
Work in process, end of month		4,000
Total equivalent production		12,000
Labor and factory overhead:		
Finished and transferred to Dept. 2 during month		8,000
Work in process, end of month		2,000
Total equivalent production		10,000
Unit cost for month:		
Materials ($36,600 ÷ 12,000)		$3.05
Labor ($19,600 ÷ 10,000)		1.96
Factory overhead ($10,800 ÷ 10,000)		1.08
Total		$6.09
Inventory costs:		
Cost of goods finished and transferred to Dept. 2 during month (8,000 × $6.09)		$48,720
Cost of work in process, end of month:		
Materials (4,000 × $3.05)	$12,200	
Labor (4,000 × ½ × $1.96)	3,920	
Factory overhead (4,000 × ½ × $1.08)	2,160	18,280
Total production costs accounted for		$67,000

cost of the 3,000 units in process at the beginning of the month and the cost of the 5,000 units started and finished during the month is then transferred to Department 2. Note that when making this transfer of cost, the costs related to the starting units in process lose their identity and are merged with the costs of those units started and finished during the current period.

The costs assigned to the ending work in process inventory are determined in the same manner under the fifo method as under the average cost approach. The 4,000 units are complete as to materials and are charged with the full unit cost; they are one-half complete as to labor and overhead and are allocated one half of the unit cost. Although the method of calculation is the same, the total costs charged to the ending units in process differ between the fifo and average cost methods because of the difference in unit costs which result under each procedure.

Illustrative Problem No. 2 – Fifo cost method compared with average cost method — materials added at end of process and units lost during process.

Assume that in Department 2 materials are added at the end of the process and labor and factory overhead are applied evenly throughout the process. The production for March reflects the following information:

Units in process, beginning of month, three-fourths completed............	2,000
Units received from Department 1	8,000
Units finished...	8,000
Units in process, end of month, one-half completed...........................	1,000
Units lost...	1,000

Cost data are as follows:
Beginning work in process, prior month's cost:

Prior department cost...	$12,000
Materials..	—0—
Labor...	4,160
Factory overhead	3,000
Total..	$19,160
Cost of units received from Department 1	$49,000

Current month's production costs:

Materials..	$16,000
Labor...	21,000
Factory overhead	14,000
Total..	$51,000

The cost of production summary for Department 2 is shown on the following page, using the fifo method, and on page 292, using the average cost method. In the cost of production summary using the fifo method, the costs to be accounted for are listed and then the unit output for the period is determined. In this department, materials are added at the end of the process; therefore, in order to finish the 2,000 units in process at the beginning of the period, all of the materials had to be added — a total of 2,000. Three fourths of the labor and factory overhead had been applied to these units in process during the prior period, so one fourth of these cost elements would be applied in the current month to finish the 2,000 units — an equivalent of 500 units.

Fifo Method

GAGE MANUFACTURING COMPANY
Cost of Production Summary — Department 2
For the Month Ended March 31, 19--

Cost of work in process, beginning of month			$ 19,160
Cost of goods received from Dept. 1 during month.......			49,000
Cost of production for month:			
Materials		$16,000	
Labor		21,000	
Factory overhead		14,000	51,000
Total costs to be accounted for			$119,160

Unit output for month:

	Materials	Labor and Factory Overhead
To complete beginning units in process..................	2,000	500
Units started and finished during month.................	6,000	6,000
Ending units in process	—0—	500
Total equivalent production	8,000	7,000

Unit cost for month:		
Materials ($16,000 ÷ 8,000)		$2.00
Labor ($21,000 ÷ 7,000)..		3.00
Factory overhead ($14,000 ÷ 7,000).......................		2.00
Total		$7.00

Inventory costs:			
Cost of goods finished:			
Beginning units in process:			
Prior month's cost..		$19,160	
Current cost to complete:			
Materials (2,000 × $2)		4,000	
Labor (2,000 × ¼ × $3)		1,500	
Factory overhead (2,000 × ¼ × $2)...............		1,000	$ 25,660
Units started and finished during month:			
Cost in Dept. 1 (6,000 × $7*).........................		$42,000	
Cost in Dept. 2 (6,000 × $7)		42,000	84,000
Total (8,000 × $13.7075)			$109,660
Cost of work in process, end of month:			
Cost in Dept. 1 (1,000 × $7*).............................		$ 7,000	
Cost in Dept. 2:			
Materials		—0—	
Labor (1,000 × ½ × $3)		1,500	
Factory overhead (1,000 × ½ × $2)................		1,000	9,500
Total production costs accounted for			$119,160

*The adjusted unit cost is calculated as follows:

Units received from Dept. 1 during the current month	8,000
Units lost in Dept. 2...	1,000
Units remaining...	7,000

Cost transferred from Dept. 1 — $49,000 ÷ 7,000 units = $7 adjusted unit cost.

Of the eight thousand units completed during the period, 2,000 were in process at the start of the month; therefore, 6,000 have been fully manufactured during the current month. The 1,000 units in pro-

Average Cost Method

GAGE MANUFACTURING COMPANY
Cost of Production Summary — Department 2
For the Month Ended March 31, 19--

Cost of work in process, beginning of month:			
Cost in Dept. 1		$12,000	
Cost in Dept. 2:			
Materials	—0—		
Labor	$4,160		
Factory overhead..................................	3,000	7,160	$ 19,160
Cost of goods received from Dept. 1 during month.......			48,720
Cost of production for month:			
Materials	$16,000		
Labor	21,000		
Factory overhead	14,000	51,000	
Total costs to be accounted for			$118,880
Unit output for month:			
Materials finished during month			8,000
Labor and overhead:			
Finished during month		8,000	
Work in process, end of month		500	8,500
Unit cost for month:			
Materials ($16,000 ÷ 8,000)			$2.00
Labor ($25,160 ÷ 8,500)			2.96
Factory overhead ($17,000 ÷ 8,500)......................			2.00
Total			$6.96
Inventory costs:			
Cost of goods finished:			
Cost in Dept. 1 (8,000 × $6.74667*)....................		$53,973	
Cost in Dept. 2 (8,000 × $6.96)...........................		55,680	$109,653
Cost of work in process, end of month:			
Cost in Dept. 1 (1,000 × $6.74667*)....................		$ 6,747	
Cost in Dept. 2:			
Materials		—0—	
Labor (1,000 × ½ × $2.96).............................		1,480	
Factory overhead (1,000 × ½ × $2.00)		1,000	9,227
Total production costs accounted for			$118,880

*The adjusted unit cost is calculated as follows:

Total units processed during the month that had been received from Dept. 1............................	10,000
Units lost...	1,000
Units remaining..	9,000

Total cost from Dept. 1 — $60,720 ÷ 9,000 = $6.74667 adjusted unit cost.

cess at the end of the month have had no materials added but are one-half complete as to labor and overhead — an equivalent of 500 units.

Notice that with both the fifo and average cost methods, the units lost in processing are ignored for purposes of calculating the unit output. This procedure is based on the assumption that the losses are normal and occur during the process. If the losses were incurred at the end of the process, or were abnormal, the lost units would be included in the determination of equivalent production under either method, and a separate dollar accounting would be made for these units.

As in Department 1, unit cost under the fifo method is determined by dividing the current period's cost of each element by the unit output for the period. Under the average cost method, unit cost is calculated by dividing the merged costs of the current period and those carried over as work in process by the unit output, which is determined by merging current production and the units in process at the beginning of the period.

In determining the total costs to be charged to the beginning work in process, the balance from the prior month is added to the costs incurred to complete these units in the current period. The 2,000 units are charged for the full unit cost of materials and with one fourth of the current unit costs for labor and overhead. This computation is not made under the average cost method.

Under the fifo method, when calculating the cost to be allocated to those units fully manufactured during the month, the lost units must be taken into consideration, and the unit cost from the prior department must be adjusted. As mentioned previously, a determination must be made as to whether the lost units are from those in process at the beginning of the period or from those received during the period. In this case, the assumption is made that the units lost are from those received from Department 1 during the month.

Eight thousand units had been received but 1,000 units were lost in processing, leaving 7,000 units in Department 2 that had been received during the month from Department 1. The cost transferred from Department 1 during the period, $49,000, is divided by the 7,000 units remaining, to result in an adjusted unit cost from Department 1 of $7. The 6,000 units started and finished during the month are charged with the $7 adjusted unit cost from the prior department as well as the $7 current unit cost in Department 2.

Under the average cost method, all of the units that had come from Department 1, whether this month or last month, must be considered in determining the adjusted unit cost. The 2,000 units in process at the beginning of the period, as well as the 8,000 units received during the month, are included in the calculation, and the prior department cost of $12,000, carried over from the prior month, is added to the current month's cost transferred from Department 1. The total prior department cost of $60,720 is divided by the 9,000 remaining units to produce an adjusted unit cost of $6.74667. The 8,000 units completed during the period are charged with this unit cost as well as with the current unit cost in Department 2 of $6.96.

The calculation of the costs to be charged to the units in process at the end of the month is similar under either the fifo or the average cost method. The resulting figures differ as a result of the differences between prior department and current month unit costs under the two methods.

In comparing the fifo and the average cost methods, the argument for fifo is that units started within the current period are valued at the current period's costs and are not distorted by the merging of these costs with costs from the preceding period. The units and costs in the beginning inventory maintain their separate identity while they are in the department. Use of the fifo method, however, means that the units in the beginning inventory are valued, when completed, at a cost that represents neither the prior cost nor the current period's cost, but a combination of the two. Also, the identity of the beginning units in process is typically not maintained when these units are transferred to the next department, so the cost of these units is usually combined with the cost of units fully manufactured during the month.

The average cost method has the advantage that all units completed during the period have the same unit cost assigned to them; therefore, this method is easier to use than the fifo cost method. In the final analysis, however, a manufacturing concern should choose the method which most accurately depicts to management the unit cost of producing in that firm's particular industrial and economic environment.

JOINT PRODUCTS AND BY-PRODUCTS

In many industries, the manufacturing process is such that from one or more materials started in process, two or more distinct products are derived. Examples of these industries are petroleum refineries, lumber mills, and meat packing plants. Petroleum yields gasoline, heating oils, and lubricants. Lumber mills produce various grades of lumber and salable sawdust. Meat packing processes result in a variety of different cuts of meat and other products. The several items obtained from a common process are divided into two categories: those that are the primary objectives of the process are called **joint products**, while secondary products with relatively little value are designated as **by-products**.

Accounting for Joint Products

The costs of materials, labor, and overhead incurred during the process are called **joint costs**. When the separate products become identifiable, that is, at the **split-off point**, the manufacturing costs up to that point cannot usually be specifically identified with any one of the individual products. Therefore, some method must be adopted to equitably allocate the joint costs to each of the products. If further processing of any of the products is required, these additional costs are applied directly to the specific products as discussed in this and previous chapters.

Typical bases for the apportionment of joint costs to joint products are as follows:

(1) A physical unit of measure such as volume, weight, size, or grade.
(2) Relative sales value of each product (or adjusted sales value).
(3) Chemical, engineering, or other types of analyses.

The allocation of joint costs according to **physical unit of measure** is a simple method of apportionment in which each product is assumed to have received similar benefits from the process and therefore is charged with a proportionate share of the total processing costs.

To illustrate, assume that the Chemi-Pro Co. produces two liquid products from one process. In the manufacturing process, various materials are mixed in a huge vat and allowed to settle, so that a light liquid rises to the top and a heavier liquid settles to the bottom of the vat. The products, A and B, are drawn off separately and piped directly into tank cars for shipment. The costs of materials, labor, and overhead total $120,000 to produce 20,000 gallons of A and 10,000 gallons of B. The allocation of costs would be:

Product	Units (Gals.)	Percent of Total Quantity	Assignment of Joint Costs
A	20,000	66⅔%	$ 80,000
B	10,000	33⅓	40,000
Total	30,000	100 %	$120,000

This method is satisfactory if all of the units manufactured are quite similar in their revenue-producing ability. It would not be satisfactory if it created large variances in gross margins of the products. It could also conceivably allocate to a product costs that would be greater than the sales value of that product.

Because the allocation of costs based on physical measure can be misleading, the assignment of costs in proportion to the **relative sales value** of each product is more commonly used. This method assumes a direct relationship between selling price and joint costs and follows the logic that the greatest share of joint cost should be assigned to the product that has the highest value.

Assume the same facts as given for Chemi-Pro Co. and assume that Product A sells for $5.00 a gallon and Product B for $8.50 a gallon. Using the relative sales value method, costs of $120,000 would be allocated as follows:

Product	Units Produced (Gals.)		Unit Selling Price (per Gal.)		Total Sales Value	Percent of Sales Value (Rounded)	Assignment of Joint Costs
A	20,000	×	$5.00	=	$100,000	54%	$ 64,800
B	10,000	×	8.50	=	85,000	46	55,200
Total	30,000				$185,000	100%	$120,000

Some companies make a further refinement of this method by subtracting the estimated selling expenses for each product from its sales value to determine the net realizable value of the product. If a product is to be processed further after the point of separation, costs should not be assigned on the basis of ultimate sales value because the additional processing adds value to the product. In this case, an **adjusted sales value** is used which takes into consideration the cost of the processing after split-off.

Assume that Chemi-Pro Co. market researchers determine that Product B would have a better market if the product is sold in powder form in individual packages. After studying this proposition, the company decides to pipe Product B into ovens to dehydrate it. The resulting powder is packaged in one-pound packages that will sell for $21 each.

During the month of October, when the new process began, the costs of materials, labor, and factory overhead in the Mixing and Settling Department were $99,000, $6,000, and $15,000 respectively, and 20,000 gallons of Product A were transferred to tank cars. In the Baking Department, costs totaled $5,000 for baking and packaging the 10,000 gallons of Product B received from Mixing and Settling and 5,000 one-pound packages were produced.

The assignment of costs of $120,000 in the Mixing and Settling Department, using the adjusted sales value method, is as follows:

Product	Units Produced		Unit Selling Price		Ultimate Sales Value	Less Cost After Split-Off	Sales Value at Split-Off	Percent of Sales Value	Assignment of Joint Costs
A	20,000 gals.	×	$ 5.00	=	$100,000	—0—	$100,000	50%	$ 60,000
B	5,000 lbs.*	×	21.00	=	105,000	$5,000	100,000	50	60,000
Total					$205,000	$5,000	$200,000	100%	$120,000

*10,000 gallons of liquid is further processed into 5,000 lbs. of powder.

The allocated cost of Product A is transferred to a finished goods inventory account. The assigned cost of Product B is transferred to a work in process account to which the additional costs of processing are also charged. The total cost of Product B is then transferred to a finished goods inventory account.

Occasionally, the makeup of the joint products is such that chemical or engineering analyses, or some other type of examination of component parts, can be employed to determine the amount of raw materials present in each completed product. This procedure is complex and must be carried out by highly qualified experts, but the accountant's allocation of costs, based on these analyses, follows the procedures previously discussed.

If the Chemi-Pro Co. found, upon analysis, that 40% of the raw materials introduced into the process were present in the finished Product A and 60% in Product B and that labor and overhead were added evenly, the following allocation of costs could be made.

		Allocated to Products	
October Processing Costs (A/B)		A	B
Materials.....................	$ 99,000 (40/60)	$39,600	$59,400
Labor.........................	6,000 (50/50)	3,000	3,000
Factory overhead..........	15,000 (50/50)	7,500	7,500
Total......................	$120,000	$50,100	$69,900

Accounting for By-Products

In accounting for by-products, the common practice is to make no allocation of the processing costs up to the split-off point. Costs incurred up to that point are chargeable to the main products. If no further processing is required to make the by-products marketable, they may be accounted for by debiting an inventory account, By-Products, and crediting Work in Process for the estimated sales value of the by-products recovered. Under this procedure, the estimated sales value of the by-products is treated as a reduction in cost of the main products and is so reflected in the inventory costs section of the cost of production summary. If the by-products are sold for more or less than the estimated sales value, the difference may be credited or debited to Gain and Loss on Sales of By-Products.

Assume that the production management of the Chemi-Pro Co. finds that nonusable residue at the bottom of the vat can be sold for $2,000 without further processing. Also assume that other data for the month of November are the same as for October. A cost of production summary, as shown below, reflects the assignment of joint costs under the adjusted sales value method, and uses the by-product value as a reduction in the cost of the joint products and as the cost assigned to the by-product.

CHEMI-PRO CO.
Cost of Production Summary — Mixing and Settling Department
For the Month Ended November 30, 19--

Cost of production for month:

Materials	$ 99,000
Labor	6,000
Factory overhead	15,000
Total costs to be accounted for	**$120,000**

Unit output for month:

Finished and transferred to finished goods (Product A)	20,000
Finished and transferred to Baking Department (Product B)	10,000
Total	30,000

Unit cost for month:

Materials ($99,000 ÷ 30,000)	$3.30
Labor ($6,000 ÷ 30,000)	.20
Factory overhead ($15,000 ÷ 30,000)	.50
Total	$4.00

Total costs to split-off point	$120,000
Less market value of by-product	2,000
Total cost to be assigned to joint products finished and transferred	$118,000

Inventory costs:

Cost of goods finished (Product A) and transferred to finished goods*	$ 59,000
Cost of goods finished (Product B) and transferred to Baking Department*	59,000
Cost of by-product finished and transferred to by-product inventory	2,000
Total production costs accounted for	**$120,000**

*50% × $118,000

In many instances, the sales value of the by-product will be so insignificant or so uncertain, due to an unstable market, that the cost of the main products will not be reduced. In this case, no entry for the by-product is made at the point of separation. When the by-product is sold, the transaction is recorded by debiting Cash or Accounts Receivable and crediting By-Product Sales or Miscellaneous Income. The revenue account will usually be treated as "other income" on the income statement, although some companies, if the amount is significant, will show this revenue as sales income, as a deduction from the cost of the main products sold, or as a reduction in the total cost of the main products manufactured.

If further processing is required to make the by-product salable, an account entitled By-Products in Process may be opened, and all subsequent processing costs incurred are charged to that account. As with other products, when the processing is completed, an entry is made to transfer the costs from the in-process account to an inventory account.

SELL OR PROCESS FURTHER

There are some instances in which a manufacturing organization may produce goods ready for sale that could be sold for a higher price if given additional processing. In this case, management must make a decision whether to sell these units or process them further. In considering the alternative courses of action, the increase in gross margin generated by further processing must be determined.

Assume that Product A of the Chemi-Pro Co. could be sold for $6 a gallon if it is packaged in 5-gallon cans rather than being transported in bulk. Assume further that the by-product could be sold for $4,000 with further processing. Using the data given, the following analysis could be made:

Product	Allocated Cost of Product	Cost of Additional Processing	After Additional Processing			Gross Margin Without Further Processing	Increase (Decrease) in Gross Margin
			Cost of Product	Sales Value	Gross Margin		
A	$59,000	$5,000(1)	$64,000	$120,000	$56,000	$41,000(3)	$15,000
By-product	2,000	2,100(2)	4,100	4,000	(100)	—0—	(100)

(1) Cost of additional materials
   20,000 gals. ÷ 5 = 4,000 cans × 50¢ cost per can = $2,000
   Cost of additional labor and overhead......................   3,000
                                                            $5,000

(2) Cost of additional labor and overhead...................... $2,100

(3) $100,000 − $59,000 = $41,000

Based on this analysis, Chemi-Pro would benefit by further processing Product A but would incur no advantage through additional processing of the by-product. Before coming to a final conclusion however, the company must consider other factors, such as the effect on the market, the volume that can be sold, the amount of promotional effort required, the ramifications of setting up an additional process, and the long-run advantages and disadvantages of such a venture.

QUESTIONS

1. Under what conditions may the unit costs of materials, labor, and overhead be computed by using only one equivalent production figure?

2. When is it necessary to use separate equivalent production figures in computing the unit costs of materials, labor, and overhead?

3. If materials are not put into process uniformly, what must be considered when determining the cost of the ending work in process?

4. In what way does the cost of production summary on page 272 differ from the cost of production summaries presented in Chapter 6? What is the reason for this difference in treatment?

5. Explain why the total number of units completed during a month plus the number of units in process at the end of a month, may be less than the total number of units in process at the beginning of the month plus the number of units placed in process during the month.

6. What is the usual method of handling the cost of normal processing losses?

7. If some units are normally lost during the manufacturing process and all units absorb the cost, what effect does this have on the unit cost of goods finished during the period and work in process at the end of the period?

8. In what way is the cost of units normally lost in manufacturing absorbed by the unit cost for the period?

9. What computations must be made if units are lost in a department other than the originating one?

10. What is the method for handling the cost of units lost or rejected at the end of a process?

11. Describe the method of treatment for the cost of abnormal processing losses.

12. What computations must be made if materials added in a department increase the number of units being processed?

13. If materials added in a department increase the number of units being processed and units are also lost through evaporation in that same department, what calculations must be made, assuming the company follows the practice of letting all units absorb the cost of lost units?

14. Differentiate between the average cost method and the first-in, first-out cost method.

15. Define:

    (a) Joint products   **(c)** Joint costs
    (b) By-products   **(d)** Split-off point

16. (a) Name three methods of allocating joint costs. **(b)** Under what conditions might each of the three methods be used?

17. Describe two ways of accounting for by-products for which no further processing is required.

18. What basic decision is involved in determining whether to sell certain products or to process them further?

EXERCISES

Note: The average cost method is to be used with Exercises 1 through 6.

1. Using the data given for Cases 1–3, compute the separate equivalent units of production, one for materials and one for labor and overhead, under each of the following assumptions (labor and factory overhead are applied evenly during the process in each assumption):

    (a) All materials go into production at the beginning of the process.
    (b) All materials go into production at the end of the process.
    (c) 75% of the materials go into production at the beginning of the process and 25% when the process is one-half completed.

Case 1 — Started in process 10,000 units; finished 8,000 units; work in process, end of period 2,000 units, three-fourths completed.

Case 2 — Opening inventory 5,000 units, three-fifths completed; started in process 20,000 units; finished 22,000 units; work in process, end of period 3,000 units, one-fourth completed.

Case 3 — Opening inventory 2,000 units, one-half completed, and 6,000 units, one-fourth completed; started in process 27,000 units; finished 29,000 units; closing inventory goods in process 3,000 units, one-third completed, and 3,000 units, one-half completed.

2. The following data appeared in the accounting records of The Beal Manufacturing Company:

Started in process...	12,000 units
Finished and transferred	10,500 units
Work in process, end of month	1,500 units ($^2/_5$ completed)
Materials	$3,600
Labor	$4,440
Factory overhead	$2,220

Case 1 — All materials are added at the beginning of the process and labor and factory overhead are added evenly throughout the process.

Case 2 — One half of the materials are added at the start of the manufacturing process and the balance of the materials are added when the units are one-half completed. Labor and factory overhead are applied evenly during the process.

Using the above information, calculate for each case **(a)** the unit cost of materials, labor, and factory overhead for the month, **(b)** the cost of the units finished during the month, and **(c)** the cost of the units in process at the end of the month.

3. Assuming that all materials are added at the beginning of the process and the labor and factory overhead are applied evenly during the process, compute the figures to be inserted in the blank spaces of the following data.

	Case 1	Case 2	Case 3
Units in process, beginning of period	300	None	———
Materials cost in process, beginning of period..	$ 915	None	$ 568
Labor cost in process, beginning of period...	$ 351	None	$ 200
Overhead cost in process, beginning of period..	$ 300	None	$ 188
Units started in process.............................	———	———	19,200
Units transferred	1,300	8,000	———
Units in process, end of period	200	———	1,400
Stage of completion	1/4	———	1/5
Equivalent units — materials......................	———	———	
Equivalent units — labor and factory overhead...	———	———	18,440
Materials cost current month	$ 3,660	$13,120	$———
Labor and factory overhead current month ..	$ 5,100	$16,200	$———
Materials unit cost for period	$———	$ 1.60	$ .30
Labor and factory overhead unit cost for period...	$———	$ 2.00	$ .20

4. The Jorcano Manufacturing Company uses a process cost system to account for the costs of its only product, Product D. Production begins in the Fabrication Department where units of raw materials are molded into various connecting parts. After fabrication is complete, the units are transferred to the Assembly Department. There are no materials added in the Assembly Department. After assembly is complete, the units are transferred to the Packaging Department where packing materials are placed around the units. After the units are ready for shipping, they are sent to a shipping area.

At year end, June 30, the following inventory of Product D is on hand:

(1) No unused raw materials or packing materials.
(2) Fabrication Departments — 300 units, ⅓ complete as to raw material and ½ complete as to direct labor.
(3) Assembly Department — 1,000 units, ⅖ complete as to direct labor.
(4) Packaging Department — 100 units, ¾ complete as to packing materials and ¼ complete as to direct labor.
(5) Shipping area — 400 units.

Determine: **(a)** the number of equivalent units of raw materials in all inventories at June 30; **(b)** the number of equivalent units of fabrication department direct labor in all inventories at June 30; **(c)** the number of equivalent units of packing materials in all inventories at June 30.

(AICPA adapted)

5. The Greentree Products Company manufactures a liquid product. Due to the nature of the product and the process, units are regularly lost during production. Goods finished in the Mixing Department are transferred to the Refining Department. The following summaries were prepared for the month of January.

	Units	
Production Summary	**Mixing Dept.**	**Refining Dept.**
Started in process or received from prior department......	10,000	8,000
Finished and transferred to the next department or the stockroom...	8,000	7,000
In process, end of the month..	1,000	500
Stage of completion..	1/4	1/2
Lost in process..	1,000	500
Cost Summary		
Materials..	$33,000	$7,250
Labor..	4,950	3,625
Factory overhead..	3,300	7,250

Calculate the unit cost for materials, labor, and factory overhead for January and show the costs of units transferred and in process for **(a)** the Mixing Department and **(b)** the Refining Department.

6. A company manufactures a liquid fertilizer Super-Gro. The basic ingredients are put into process in Department 1. In Department 2, other materials are added that increase the number of units being processed by 50%. There are only two departments in the factory.

	Units	
Production Summary	**Dept. 1**	**Dept. 2**
Started in process...	18,000	
Received from prior department....................................		14,000
Added to units in process		7,000
Finished and transferred	14,000	15,000
In process, end of month...	4,000	6,000
Stage of completion...	1/4	1/2
Cost Summary		
Materials..	$45,000	$18,000
Labor..	30,000	13,500
Factory overhead..	15,000	4,500

On the basis of the information given above, calculate the following for each department: **(a)** unit cost for the month for materials, labor, and factory overhead; **(b)** the cost of the units transferred; and **(c)** the cost of the work in process.

7. Using the data given below for Cases 1–3 and the fifo cost method, compute the separate equivalent units of production, one for materials and one for labor and overhead, under each of the following assumptions (labor and factory overhead are applied evenly during the process in each assumption):

  (a) All materials go into production at the beginning of the process.
  (b) All materials go into production at the end of the process.
  (c) 75% of the materials go into production at the beginning of the process and 25% when the process is one-half completed.

Case 1 — Started in process 10,000 units; finished 8,000 units; work in process, end of period 2,000 units, three-fourths completed.

Case 2 — Opening inventory 5,000 units, three-fifths completed; started in process 20,000 units; finished 22,000 units; work in process, end of period 3,000 units, one-fourth completed.

Case 3 — Opening inventory 2,000 units, one-half completed, and 6,000 units, one-fourth completed; started in process 27,000 units; finished 29,000 units; closing inventory work in process 3,000 units, one-third completed, and 3,000 units, one-half completed.

Compare your answers with those of Exercise 1 on the average cost basis.

8. Assume each of the following conditions concerning the data given below:

(1) All materials are added at the beginning of the process.
(2) All materials are added at the end of the process.
(3) One half of the materials are added at the beginning of the process and the balance of the materials are added when the units are three-fourths completed.

In all cases, labor and factory overhead are added evenly throughout the process.

Production Summary

	Units		
	Dept. 1	**Dept. 2**	**Dept. 3**
Work in process, beginning of month	3,000	1,500	1,200
Stage of completion	1/2	3/5	4/5
Started in process	18,000	16,000	21,000
Finished and transferred	19,000	15,500	21,000
Work in process, end of month	2,000	2,000	1,200
Stage of completion	1/4	4/5	1/5

Compute separate equivalent units of production, one for materials and one for labor and factory overhead for each of the conditions listed, using **(a)** the average cost method and **(b)** the fifo cost method.

9. The Grand Valley Lumber Co. processes rough timber to obtain three grades of finished lumber, Nos. 1, 2, and 3. The company allocates costs to the joint products on the basis of market value. During the month of May, total production costs of $26,000 were incurred in producing the following:

Grade	Thousand Board Feet	Selling Price per 1,000 Board Feet
No. 1	100	$200
No. 2	300	100
No. 3	500	160

Draft the general journal entry to transfer the finished lumber to separate inventory accounts.

10. The LaBreck Company's joint cost of producing 1,000 units of Product A, 500 units of Product B, and 500 units of Product C is $100,000. The unit sales values of the three products at the split-off point are Product A — $20; Product B — $200; Product C — $160. Ending inventories include 100 units of Product A, 300 units of Product B, and 200 units of Product C.

Compute the amount of joint cost that would be included in the ending inventory valuation of the three products **(a)** on the basis of their relative sales value and **(b)** on the basis of physical units.

(AICPA adapted)

11. The Kingston Chemical Co. manufactures product X. During the process, a by-product, AX, is obtained and placed in stock. The estimated sales value of AX produced during the month of April is $1,020. Assume that the value of the by-product is treated as a reduction of production cost.

Prepare the general journal entry for April to record **(a)** the placing of AX in stock and, **(b)** the sale of three fourths of the AX for $800.

12. The Broadbeck Manufacturing Co. makes one main product, X, and a by-product, Z, which splits off from the main product when the work is three-fourths completed. Product Z is sold without further processing and without being placed in stock. During June, $800 is realized from the sale of the by-product.

Journalize the entries to record the recovery and sale of the by-product on the assumption that the recovery is treated as: **(a)** a reduction in the cost of the main product; **(b)** other income.

PROBLEMS

Note: The average cost method is to be used with Problems 1 through 7.

7-1. Cost of production summaries, one department, two months; journal entries. Manufacturing data for the months of January and February in Department A of the Ace Manufacturing Co. are shown below.

	January	February
Materials used	$8,000	$7,140
Labor	$5,700	$4,896
Factory overhead	$3,800	$3,264
Finished and transferred to Dept. B	3,600	3,200
Work in process, end of month	400	600
Stage of completion	1/2	1/3

All materials are added at the start of the process. Labor and factory overhead are added evenly throughout the process. There were no units in process at the beginning of January. Goods finished in Department A are transferred to Department B for further processing.

Required: **(1)** From an analysis of this information, prepare a cost of production summary for each month. **(2)** Journalize the entries necessary to record each month's transactions.

7-2. Cost of production summaries, three departments; departmental cost work sheet; journal entries; statement of cost of goods manufactured. The Dugan Manufacturing Company is engaged in the manufacture of a cement sealing compound called Patchtite. The process requires that the product pass through three departments:

Dept. 1 — Sorting and Cleaning
Dept. 2 — Mixing
Dept. 3 — Clarifying and Packaging

In Department 1, all materials are put into production at the beginning of the process; in Department 2, materials are put into production evenly throughout the process; and in Department 3, all materials are put into production at the end of the process. In each department it is assumed that the labor and factory overhead are applied evenly throughout the process.

At the end of January, the production reports for the month show the following:

	Dept. 1	Dept. 2	Dept. 3
Started in process.................................	50,000	....	....
Received from prior department.............	....	40,000	30,000
Finished and transferred........................	40,000	30,000	28,000
Finished and on hand	....	5,000	....
Work in process, end of month...............	10,000	5,000	2,000
Stage of completion..............................	1/2	1/4	3/4

The cost summary for January shows the following:

	Dept. 1	Dept. 2	Dept. 3
Materials..	$22,500	$23,200	$ 9,800
Labor..	7,200	14,500	4,720
Factory overhead.................................	10,800	14,500	7,965
	$40,500	$52,200	$22,485

Required: **(1)** Prepare a cost of production summary for each department for January. **(2)** Prepare a departmental cost work sheet for January. **(3)** Prepare the required general journal entries to record the January operations. **(4)** Prepare a statement of cost of goods manufactured for the month ended January 31.

7-3. Equivalent production; unit costs; cost of work in process. The Walsch Company manufactures a single product, a mechanical device known as "Klebo." The company maintains a process cost type of accounting system.

The manufacturing operation is as follows:

Material K, a metal, is stamped to form a part which is assembled with one of the purchased parts "X." The unit is then machined and cleaned, after which it is assembled with two units of part "Y" to form the finished device known as a "Klebo." Spray priming and enameling is the final operation.

Time and motion studies indicate that of the total time required for the manufacture of a unit, the first operation required 25% of the labor cost, the first assembly an additional 25%, machining and cleaning 12.5%, the second assembly 25%, and painting 12.5%. Factory overhead is considered to follow the same pattern by operations as does labor.

The following data are presented to you as of October 31, the end of the first month of operation:

Material K purchased — 100,000 lbs.	$25,000
Part X purchased — 80,000 units	16,000
Part Y purchased — 150,000 units	15,000
Primer and enamel used	1,072
Direct labor — cost	45,415
Factory overhead	24,905

	Units
Units finished and sent to finished goods warehouse	67,000
Units assembled but not painted	5,000
Units ready for the second assembly	3,000
Inventories at the end of the month:	
Finished units	7,500
Material K (lbs.)	5,800
Part X (Units of part X)	5,000
Part Y (units of part Y)	6,000
Klebos in process (units)	8,000

Required: (1) A schedule of equivalent units of production for labor. (2) A schedule of total and unit costs incurred in production for:

(a) Each kind of material   (c) Factory overhead
(b) Labor cost   (d) Total cost of production

(3) A schedule of detailed materials, labor, and factory overhead costs assigned to the units left in process.   (AICPA adapted)

7-4. Lost units; cost of production summaries. The Parker Products Co. uses the process cost system. Following is a record of the factory operations for the month of October:

Production Summary

	Units
Started in process	12,500
Finished and transferred to stockroom	9,500
In process, end of the month, one-half completed	1,000

Cost Summary

Materials	$12,000
Labor	6,000
Factory overhead	9,000

Required: Prepare a cost of production summary for each of the following conditions. **(1)** The cost of lost units is absorbed by all units. **(2)** The cost of lost units is charged only to units completed. **(3)** The cost of lost units is charged to an expense account.

7-5. Lost units; cost of production summaries. The Mantis Manufacturing Company manufactures a single product that passes through two departments: Extruding and Finishing-Packing. The product is shipped at the end of the day in which it is packed. The production in the Extruding and Finishing-Packing Departments does not increase the number of units started.

The cost and production data for January are as follows:

Cost Data	Extruding Department	Finishing-Packing Department
Work in process, January 1:		
Cost from preceding department	—	$60,200
Materials..	$ 5,900	—
Labor..	1,900	1,500
Factory overhead	1,400	2,000
Costs added during January:		
Materials..	20,100	4,400
Labor..	10,700	7,720
Factory overhead	8,680	11,830
Percentage of completion of work in process:		
January 1:		
Materials..	70%	0%
Labor..	50	30
Factory overhead	50	30
January 31:		
Materials..	50	0
Labor..	40	35
Factory overhead	40	35
Production Data		
Units in process, January 1	10,000	29,000
Units in process, January 31	8,000	6,000
Units started or received from preceding department........	20,000	22,000
Units completed and transferred or shipped	22,000	44,000

In the Extruding Department, materials are added at various phases of the process. All lost units occur at the end of the process when the inspection operation takes place.

In the Finishing-Packing department, the materials added consist only of packing supplies. These materials are added at the midpoint of the process when the packing operation begins. Cost studies have disclosed that one half of the labor and overhead costs apply to the finishing operation and one half to the packing operation. All lost units occur during the finishing operation. All of the work in process in this department at January 1 and January 31 was in the finishing operation phase of the manufacturing process.

Required: (1) Compute the units lost, if any, for each department during January. (2) Prepare a cost of production summary for each department for January. The report should disclose the equivalent units of production for the calculation of unit costs for each department for January, the departmental total cost, and cost per unit (for materials, labor, and overhead) of the units transferred to the finishing-packing department and for units shipped. Assume that January production and costs were normal. (Submit all supporting computations in good form.)

(AICPA adapted)

7-6. *Units gained and lost; cost of production summaries.* The Sandy Manufacturing Co. uses the process cost system. There are three departments, A, B, and C. In Department A, all of the materials are put into production at the beginning of the process; in Department B, no materials are added to the process; in Department C, all of the materials are put into production at the beginning of the process. The materials added in Department C increase the number of units being processed by 25%. Labor and factory overhead are incurred uniformly throughout the process in all departments. Losses of units in any department are considered unavoidable due to the nature of the manufacturing process and can occur at any time during the process.

Following is a record of the factory operations for May:

Cost Summary

	Dept. A	Dept. B	Dept. C
Materials	$25,000		$15,000
Labor	10,800	$ 6,910	10,150
Factory overhead	8,100	6,910	7,250

Production Summary

	Units		
	Dept. A	Dept. B	Dept. C
Started in process	11,000		
Received from prior department		8,500	6,000
Added to units in process			1,500
Finished and transferred	8,500	6,000	7,000
Units in process, end of month	1,500	1,820	500
Stage of completion	1/3	1/2	1/2

Required: Prepare a cost of production summary for each department for the month of May.

7-7. *Fifo cost method; cost of production summary.* The Small-Line Products Co. uses the fifo cost method. Following is a record of the factory operations for the month of October:

Production Summary	Units
Work in process, beginning of month, one-fourth completed	5,000
Started in process	13,000
Finished and transferred to stockroom	11,000
Work in process, end of month, three-fourths completed	7,000

Cost Summary

Work in process, beginning of month	$ 3,750
Materials	18,000
Labor	24,000
Factory overhead	12,000

Required: Prepare a cost of production summary for the month.

7-8. Fifo cost method; lost units; cost of production summary. The Biltimar Company manufactures gewgaws in three steps or departments. The Finishing Department is the third and last step before the product is transferred to finished goods inventory.

All materials needed to complete the gewgaws are added at the beginning of the process in the Finishing Department, and lost units, if any, occur only at this point. The company uses the fifo cost method in its accounting system and has accumulated the following data for July for the Finishing Department:

Production of gewgaws:	Units
In process, July 1 (labor and factory overhead three-fourths complete)	10,000
Transferred from preceding department during July	40,000
Finished and transferred to finished goods inventory during July	35,000
In process, July 31 (labor and factory overhead one-half complete)	10,000

Cost of work in process inventory, July 1:	
Cost from preceding departments	$ 38,000
Cost added in Finishing Department prior to July 1:	
Materials	21,500
Labor	39,000
Factory overhead	42,000
Total	$140,500

Gewgaws transferred to the Finishing Department during July had costs of $140,000 assigned from preceding departments.

During July, the Finishing Department incurred the following production costs:

Materials	$ 70,000
Labor	162,500
Factory overhead	130,000
Total	$362,500

Required: (1) Calculate the number of gewgaws lost in production during July. (2) Prepare a cost of production summary for July.

(AICPA adapted)

7-9. Fifo cost method; equivalent production; units gained and lost. Poole, Inc., produces a chemical compound by a unique chemical process which Poole has divided into two departments, A and B, for accounting purposes. The process functions as follows:

(a) The formula for the chemical compound requires one pound of Chemical X and one pound of Chemical Y. In the simplest sense, one pound of Chemical X is processed in Department A and transferred to Department B for further processing where one pound of Chemical Y is added when the process is 50% complete. When the processing is complete in Department B, the finished chemical compound is transferred to finished goods. The process is continuous, operating twenty-four hours a day.

(b) Normal processing losses occur in Department A. Five percent of Chemical X is lost in the first few seconds of processing.

(c) No processing losses occur in Department B.

(d) In Department A, conversion costs are incurred uniformly throughout the process and are allocated to good pounds produced because processing losses are normal.

(e) In Department B, conversion costs are allocated equally to each equivalent pound of output.

(f) Poole's unit of measure for work in process and finished goods inventories is pounds.

(g) The following data are available for the month of October:

	Department A	Department B
Work in process, October 1......................	8,000 pounds	10,000 pounds
Stage of completion of beginning inventory (one batch per department)............	3/4	3/10
Started or transferred in.........................	50,000 pounds	?
Transferred out..................................	46,500 good pounds	?
Work in process, October 31....................	?	?
Stage of completion of ending inventory (one batch per department)..................	1/3	1/5
Total equivalent pounds of material added in Department B.................................	—	44,500 pounds

Required: (1) Determine the amounts indicated by the question marks. **(2)** Prepare schedules computing equivalent "good" pounds of production (materials and conversion costs) for Department A and for Department B for the month of October, using the first-in, first-out method for inventory cost.

(AICPA adapted)

7-10. *Allocation of joint costs*. Miller Manufacturing Company buys zeon for $.80 a gallon. At the end of processing in Department 1, zeon splits off into Products A, B, and C. Product A is sold at the split-off point with no further processing. Products B and C require further processing before they can be sold; Product B is processed in Department 2 and Product C is processed in Department 3. Following is a summary of costs and other related data for the year ended December 31.

	Dept. 1	Dept. 2	Dept. 3
Cost of zeon...	$ 96,000	—	—
Direct labor...	14,000	$45,000	$ 65,000
Factory overhead.....................................	10,000	21,000	49,000
Total...	$120,000	$66,000	$114,000

	Product A	Product B	Product C
Gallons sold...	20,000	30,000	45,000
Gallons on hand at December 31................	10,000	—	15,000
Sales in dollars......................................	$30,000	$96,000	$141,750

There were no inventories on hand at the beginning of the year, and there was no zeon on hand at the end of the year. All gallons on hand at the end of the year were complete as to processing. Miller uses the relative-sales-value method of allocating joint costs.

Required: (1) Calculate the allocation of joint costs. (2) Calculate the cost of Product B sold.   *(AICPA adapted)*

7-11. *Allocation of joint costs.* The Harrison Corporation produces three products — Alpha, Beta, and Gamma. Alpha and Gamma are joint products, while Beta is a by-product of Alpha. No joint cost is to be allocated to the by-product. The production processes for a given year are as follows:

(a) In Department One, 110,000 pounds of raw material, Rho, are processed at a total cost of $120,000. After processing in Department One, 60% of the units are transferred to Department Two and 40% of the units (now Gamma) are transferred to Department Three.

(b) In Department Two, the material is further processed at a total additional cost of $38,000. Seventy percent of the units (now Alpha) are transferred to Department Four and 30% emerge as Beta, the by-product, to be sold at $1.20 per pound. Selling expenses related to disposing of Beta are $8,100.

(c) In Department Four, Alpha is processed at a total additional cost of $23,660. After this processing, Alpha is ready for sales at $5 per pound.

(d) In Department Three, Gamma is processed at a total additional cost of $165,000. In this department, a normal loss of units of Gamma occurs which equals 10% of the good output of Gamma. The remaining good output of Gamma is then sold for $12 per pound.

Required: (1) Prepare a schedule showing the allocation of the $120,000 joint cost between Alpha and Gamma using the relative sales value approach. The net realizable value of Beta should be treated as an addition to the sales value of Alpha. (2) What is the cost of Alpha transferred to finished goods, assuming that the net realizable value of Beta available for sale is to be deducted from the cost of producing Alpha?   *(AICPA adapted)*

7-12. *Allocation of joint costs; sell or process further.* From a particular joint process, Watkins Company produces three products, X, Y, and Z. Each product may be sold at the point of split-off or processed further. Additional processing requires no special facilities, and production costs of further processing are entirely variable and traceable to the products involved. During one year, all three products were processed beyond split-off. Joint production costs for the year were $60,000. Sales values and costs needed to evaluate Watkins' production policy follow:

| | | | Additional Costs and Sales Values If Processed Further | |
Product	Units Produced	Sales Values at Split-Off	Sales Values	Added Costs
X	6,000	$25,000	$42,000	$9,000
Y	4,000	41,000	45,000	7,000
Z	2,000	24,000	32,000	8,000

Joint costs are allocated to the products in proportion to the relative physical volume of output.

Required: Prepare an analysis to show which products Watkins should subject to additional processing in order to maximize profits.

(AICPA adapted)

8

Standard Cost Accounting— Materials and Labor

In previous chapters cost control has been emphasized. The primary means of control discussed was the comparison of current costs with historical costs — costs of yesterday, last week, last month, or last year. When a current cost differed from an earlier cost in an unfavorable manner, it was shown that management should immediately investigate the cause of this variation and try to eliminate it before the results became too costly. It was also indicated that management has the responsibility not only to watch for these fluctuations and attempt to correct them but also to consider all possible ways of controlling costs.

While this method of cost control is useful, there is the danger that management will tend to become complacent if the costs of manufacturing do not differ significantly from period to period. There may be a feeling that the manufacturing operation is efficient because unit and overall costs are stabilized at a certain level. But stability of costs does not necessarily indicate efficiency when the earlier costs with which current costs are compared may reflect inefficiency. There is always the possibility that costs can be utilized more effectively.

The purpose of **standard cost accounting** is to monitor costs and measure efficiency. This system is not a third cost accounting method, but is used with either job order or process manufacturing operations. It is based on a predetermination of what it should cost to manufacture a product and the subsequent comparison of the actual costs with the established standard. Any deviation from the standard can be quickly detected and responsibility pinpointed so that appropriate action can be taken to eliminate inefficiencies or to take advantage of efficiencies.

Standard costs are usually determined for a period of one year and are revised annually. However, if cost analyses during the year indicate that a standard is incorrect, or if a significant change has occurred in costs or other related factors, management should not hesitate to adjust the standard accordingly.

TYPES OF STANDARDS

A **standard** is a norm against which performance can be measured. The objective of setting standards is to promote efficiency and to control costs by assigning responsibility for deviations from the standards. Also, a standard can motivate employees by providing a goal for achievement. But a question that often arises is "What is the proper standard to use?" A company can estimate materials, labor, and factory overhead usage and costs, but what about the unforeseen costs, such as spoilage, lost time, and equipment breakdowns? Should these items be considered in determining the standard cost to manufacture a product?

Some companies set their standards at the maximum degree of efficiency. Costs are determined by considering estimated materials, labor, and overhead costs, the condition of the factory and machinery, and time for rest periods, holidays, and vacations; but no allowances are made for inefficient conditions such as lost time, waste, or spoilage. This **ideal standard** can be achieved only under the most efficient operating conditions, and therefore it is practically unattainable, giving rise to unfavorable variances. Companies using this type of utopian standard feel that it provides a maximum objective for which to strive in the attempt to improve efficiency. There is, however, a psychological disadvantage — the factory personnel may become discouraged and lose their incentive to meet standards which are almost impossible to attain except under perfect operating conditions.

Recognizing this potential problem, most companies set attainable or reasonable standards that include such factors as lost time, spoilage, or waste. These companies realize that some inefficiencies cannot be completely eliminated, and so they design a standard that can be met or even bettered in efficient production situations. The primary concern of the manufacturer should be to set a standard that is high enough to provide motivation and promote efficiency, yet not so high that it is unreasonable and thus unattainable.

STANDARD COST PROCEDURES

Standard cost accounting is based on the following procedures:

(1) Standard costs are determined for the three elements of cost — direct materials, direct labor, and factory overhead.

(2) The standard costs, the actual costs, and the variances, or differences between the two, are recorded in appropriate accounts.

(3) All variances are analyzed and investigated and appropriate action taken.

Determination of Standard Costs for Materials and Labor

The first step, the determination of standard costs for manufacturing a product, is a complex task that requires considerable experience and familiarity with manufacturing operations as well as cooperation between employees in various departments of the factory. The cost accountant may be consulted to help determine historical costs, to point out prevalent trends, and to otherwise assist in accomplishing the job. In setting a **materials cost standard**, the production engineering department may be consulted to determine the amounts and types of materials that are needed, and the purchasing agent must apply knowledge of suppliers' markets to calculate the costs of these materials.

In determining what the **labor cost standard** for a unit of product should be, the heads of various departments might be asked to contribute their knowledge of the operations that are necessary to process a product. The services of work-study engineers may be utilized to establish the time necessary to perform each operation, and the personnel manager may be consulted regarding prevailing wage rates for the various types of labor needed.

Historical costs and processes should be studied to gain familiarity with these items, but the persons who set the standards should also consider the trends that may change the gathered data in the future. In setting standards for materials and labor, factors to be considered might include:

(1) The trend of prices for raw materials.

(2) The uses of different types of materials due to new processing or market developments.

(3) The effect on labor rates of negotiations with labor unions.

(4) The possible saving of labor time due to the use of more modern machinery and equipment.

The following illustrates a simple standard cost summary:

HALL PLASTICS, INC.
Standard Cost Summary
Product X

Materials — 1 lb. @ $2 per lb.	$2.00
Labor — ½ hr. @ $5 per hr.	2.50
Factory overhead	1.00
Standard cost per unit..	$5.50

The development of factory overhead standards will be discussed in the following chapter.

Recording Standard Costs for Materials and Labor

Once the standard cost for manufacturing a product has been determined, the second phase of the system can be put into effect: the standard costs, the actual costs, and the variances are recorded in the various journals and transferred to the general ledger. Usually this process takes place at the end of the month.

Determination of Variances. A **variance** represents the difference, during an accounting period, between the actual and the standard costs of materials, labor, and overhead. The variances measure efficiencies or inefficiencies in usage (quantity of materials used or number of labor hours worked) and cost (price of materials and hourly wage rates).

Assume that the production report of Hall Plastics, Inc., whose standard cost summary is shown above, indicates that equivalent production for the month, calculated as discussed in previous chapters, was 10,000 units. The standard cost of this production is determined as follows:

Materials cost — 10,000 units × $2.00...	$20,000
Labor cost — 10,000 units × $2.50...	25,000
Factory overhead cost — 10,000 units × $1.00..............................	10,000
Total standard cost of manufacturing 10,000 units	$55,000

Assume that the materials requisitions, the time tickets or payroll records, and the factory overhead records indicate the following actual costs of manufacturing these units:

Cost of direct materials used (11,000 lbs. @ $1.90)	$20,900
Cost of direct labor (4,500 hrs. @ $5.50).....................................	24,750
Factory overhead applied	10,000
Total actual cost of manufacturing 10,000 units	$55,650

The cost accountant can now compare the standard with the actual costs to determine whether any variances exist. This analysis is done as follows:

	Standard Cost	Actual Cost	Net Variances — Favorable or (Unfavorable)
Materials....................................	$20,000	$20,900	$(900)
Labor...	25,000	24,750	250
Factory Overhead	10,000	10,000	———
Total...	$55,000	$55,650	$(650)

The information presented by these comparative figures is significant to the extent that it shows that the total actual manufacturing costs have exceeded the standards previously established. The variances indicate that the cost of materials was $900 higher than it should have been, and that the cost of labor was $250 less than the established standards, resulting in an overall unfavorable variance of $650. For these figures to be of value, however, a further breakdown of the variances must be made.

The accounts used to indicate the materials and labor variances are as follows:

Materials Quantity (Usage) Variance — indicates the actual quantity of direct materials used above or below the standard quantity for the actual level of production at standard price.

Materials Price Variance — reflects the actual unit cost of materials above or below the standard unit cost, multiplied by the actual quantity of materials used.

Labor Efficiency (Usage) Variance — indicates the number of actual direct labor hours worked above or below the standard for the actual level of production at standard price.

Labor Rate (Price) Variance — represents the average of the actual hourly rates paid above or below the standard hourly rate, multiplied by the actual number of hours worked.

A debit balance in any of these accounts indicates an unfavorable variance; that is, actual costs have exceeded the established standard cost. A credit balance reflects a favorable variance, meaning that actual costs were less than the standard cost.

Formulas which are commonly used to calculate the materials and labor variances are on page 319, using the figures previously presented for materials and labor.

This type of analysis points out the effects of the deviations from the standard. The manufacturing effort exceeded the established materials standard for 10,000 units which, at a standard price of $2.00

Formula for Calculating Materials Variances

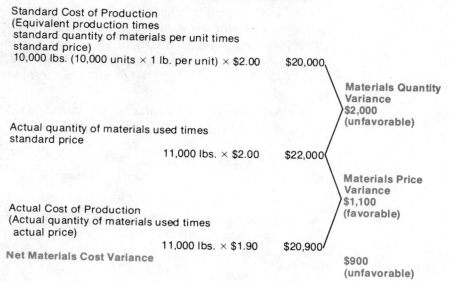

Standard Cost of Production
(Equivalent production times
standard quantity of materials per unit times
standard price)
10,000 lbs. (10,000 units × 1 lb. per unit) × $2.00 $20,000

Materials Quantity Variance $2,000 (unfavorable)

Actual quantity of materials used times
standard price
                          11,000 lbs. × $2.00 $22,000

Materials Price Variance $1,100 (favorable)

Actual Cost of Production
(Actual quantity of materials used times
  actual price)
                          11,000 lbs. × $1.90 $20,900

Net Materials Cost Variance $900 (unfavorable)

Formula for Calculating Labor Variances

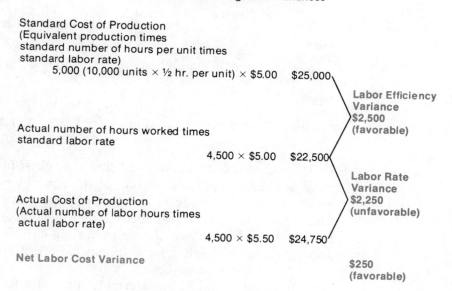

Standard Cost of Production
(Equivalent production times
standard number of hours per unit times
standard labor rate)
    5,000 (10,000 units × ½ hr. per unit) × $5.00 $25,000

Labor Efficiency Variance $2,500 (favorable)

Actual number of hours worked times
standard labor rate
                          4,500 × $5.00 $22,500

Labor Rate Variance $2,250 (unfavorable)

Actual Cost of Production
(Actual number of labor hours times
  actual labor rate)
                          4,500 × $5.50 $24,750

Net Labor Cost Variance $250 (favorable)

per pound, created an unfavorable quantity variance of $2,000 (1,000 pounds used in excess of standard × $2.00). This variance was partially offset by the fact that the 11,000 pounds of materials used were obtained at a cost below standard, thereby creating a favorable price variance of $1,100 (11,000 pounds used at a saving of $.10 per pound).

The calculation of labor variances indicates a favorable labor efficiency variance of $2,500, because the number of hours worked was 500 hours below the standard for the production of 10,000 units (500 hours times the standard rate of $5.00). However, during the period, a labor rate higher than standard was paid, creating an unfavorable rate variance of $2,250 (4,500 hours paid at a rate $.50 over standard).

Another method of calculating the variances, which displays the specific deviations from standard, is as follows:

	Standard Quantity or Hours	Actual Quantity or Hours	Difference	Standard Cost	Variance
Materials Quantity Variance	10,000 lbs.	11,000 lbs.	1,000 lbs. (unf.)	$2.00 lb.	$2,000 (unf.)
Labor Efficiency Variance	5,000 hrs.	4,500 hrs.	500 hrs. (fav.)	$5.00 hr.	$2,500 (fav.)

	Standard Cost	Actual Cost	Difference	Actual Quantity or Hours	Variance
Materials Price Variance	$2.00 lb.	$1.90 lb.	$.10 (fav.)	11,000 lbs.	$1,100 (fav.)
Labor Rate Variance	$5.00 hr.	$5.50 hr.	$.50 (unf.)	4,500 hrs.	$2,250 (unf.)

It is important to understand that the terms **favorable** and **unfavorable** indicate only a deviation of the actual cost below or above standard. Further analysis and investigation may indicate that the unfavorable variance is not necessarily reflecting an inefficiency, nor is the favorable variance always indicating a desirable situation. An apparently unfavorable condition may be offset completely by a favorable situation. In any event, all variances, favorable or unfavorable, must be analyzed to determine the cause for and the effect of the deviations. Appropriate action should then be taken to improve the problem areas.

Accounting Procedure. The work in process account is always debited with the standard cost of equivalent production for the period. The materials inventory account is credited for the actual cost of materials issued to the factory as indicated by materials requisitions and inventory ledger cards. The payroll account is credited with the actual cost of labor incurred for the period. The differences between the debits (at standard costs) and the credits (at actual costs) are debited or credited to the variance accounts. The standard cost of units finished is transferred from Work in Process to Finished Goods.

To illustrate, use the figures previously presented for materials and labor costs.

1. To record the entry for direct materials cost:

Work in Process.....................................	20,000	
Materials Quantity Variance......................	2,000	
Materials Price Variance.........................		1,100
Materials		20,900

2. To record the entry for direct labor cost:

Work in Process.....................................	25,000	
Labor Rate Variance................................	2,250	
Labor Efficiency Variance		2,500
Payroll		24,750

3. To record the entry applying factory overhead to work in process (assuming no variances):

Work in Process.....................................	10,000	
Factory Overhead		10,000

4. To record the entry for finished goods (assuming no beginning or ending inventory of work in process, 10,000 units @ $5.50):

Finished Goods......................................	55,000	
Work in Process......................................		55,000

Under a standard cost system, the balance sheet of Hall Plastics, Inc., would reflect inventories for work in process and finished goods at standard cost, while the materials inventory account would be shown at actual cost. This procedure will be followed in this text. The materials inventory account, however, may also be shown at standard cost, as explained below.

Alternative Method of Recording Materials Cost. Some companies recognize the materials price variance at the time the materials are purchased. The logic used is that the deviation of cost above or below standard is known at this time, so there is no reason for delaying the recognition of this variance until the materials are used. In this case a **purchase price variance** is recorded.

Using the above price figures and assuming that 12,000 pounds are purchased, the purchase entry under this method is as follows:

Materials (12,000 lbs. @ $2.00 standard price)	24,000	
Materials Purchase Price Variance............		1,200
Accounts Payable (12,000 lbs. @ $1.90 actual price)		22,800

Under these conditions, the materials inventory account on the balance sheet would reflect standard cost. At the time of materials usage, there would be no price variance to record, and the quantity variance would be recorded as follows:

Work in Process (10,000 lbs. @ $2.00 standard price).....................................	20,000	
Materials Quantity Variance.......................	2,000	
Materials (11,000 lbs. @ $2.00)................		22,000

Another benefit of using this method is that the individual materials inventory accounts are maintained at standard cost. This saves record-keeping expense because it is necessary to keep track only of the quantities purchased, issued, and on hand. It is not necessary to post individual materials costs nor to continuously calculate dollar amounts on the inventory ledger cards. Because the materials inventory account is kept at standard cost, the balance, in dollars, can be determined at any time by multiplying the standard price times the quantity on hand.

If the materials purchase price variance account has a balance at the end of the accounting period, the amount is used to adjust the materials inventory account from standard to actual cost.

Disposition of Standard Cost Variances. At the end of the accounting period, the variances of actual cost from standard must be reflected in some appropriate manner on the financial statements. There are different approaches for handling these items:

1. Some companies prorate these variances to cost of goods sold, work in process, and finished goods. The net effect of this method is the adjustment of these expense and inventory accounts to actual or historical cost. The logic is that standard costs are important for management's evaluation of operations but are not proper for external financial reports; therefore, the variances, being a part of actual manufacturing cost, should be included in inventory costs. When this method is followed, the allocation of materials, labor, and overhead variances will be in proportion to the standard materials, labor, and overhead costs included in cost of goods sold, work in process, and finished goods.

2. A more common approach, however, is to show the unfavorable net variance as an addition to the cost of goods sold for the period and the favorable net variance as a deduction. This would be reflected in the income statement shown at the top of the next page.

The basis for this approach is that these variances are the result of favorable or unfavorable conditions or inefficiencies during the

Sales..		$100,000
Cost of goods sold at standard.........................	$80,000	
Add unfavorable variance:		
Materials quantity variance..........................	800	
	$80,800	
Less favorable variances:		
Materials price variance.............................. $410		
Labor efficiency variance............................ 100		
Labor rate variance.................................... 105	615	
Cost of goods sold (actual).............................		80,185
Gross margin on sales (actual cost).................		$ 19,815

period, and so they should be charged or credited to the period. These items should not be charged to future periods by including them in inventory costs.

3. If the variances are significant or have been caused by the use of an incorrect standard, then the variances should be allocated to inventory and to cost of goods sold, and the standard cost adjusted accordingly.

4. If production is seasonal, with extreme peaks and valleys during the year, variances should be shown as deferred charges or credits on interim balance sheets, using the logic that they would be mostly offset in future periods. At the end of the year, however, some disposition of these variances, as described above, must be made, and the variance accounts closed.

5. If the variances are due to abnormal or unusual circumstances, such as strikes, fires, storms, or floods, there is justification for charging off these items as extraordinary losses on the income statement.

The material in this text will, unless otherwise indicated, use the more common approach of reflecting the materials and labor variances as adjustments to the standard cost of goods sold, as illustrated in Item 2. Variances of factory overhead costs, to be discussed in the next chapter, would also be reflected in the statements in a similar manner. Illustration 8-1 will aid the student in understanding the cost flow through a standard cost system.

Analyses of Variances

In analyzing materials and labor variances, two factors are considered — **usage** and **price**. The cost accountant considers the quantity of materials used, the cost per unit of each type of material, the number of direct labor hours worked, and the cost of each labor

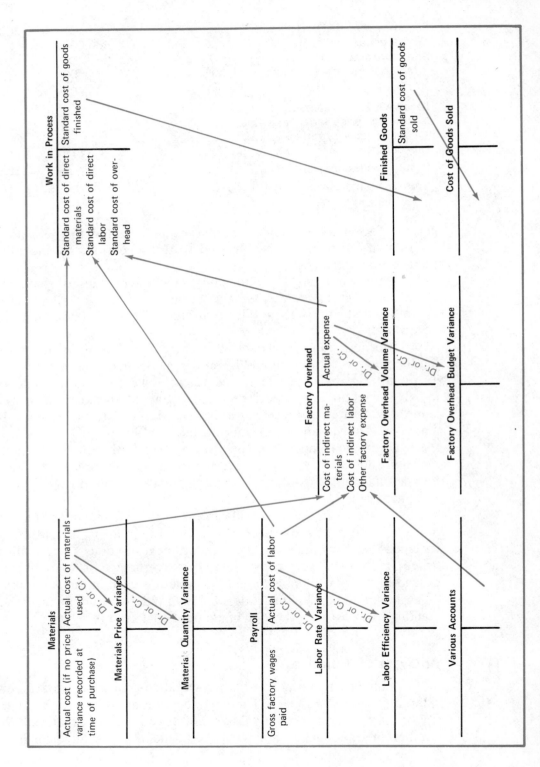

ILLUSTRATION 8-1   Cost Flow Through a Standard Cost System

hour. If management can discover in what respect the usage and/or price differ from standard, the reason for this variance can be determined, and action can be taken to correct any deficiency before the loss becomes significant.

In analyzing the materials cost variance, the usage of materials might be above, below, or at standard, or the cost per unit of the materials used might be above, below, or at standard. This relevant information is required by management in order to make intelligent decisions. Consider the following three possibilities in the manufacture of 10,000 units:

Example 1:

Standard cost, 10,000 lbs. of materials @ $2.00	$20,000
Actual cost, 10,000 lbs. of materials @ $2.09	20,900
Unfavorable price variance	$ (900)

This analysis shows that the factory usage of materials is at standard, but the price of the materials is not. The variance is caused by the fact that the company used materials costing $.09 more than the standard price. With 10,000 pounds used, this $.09 per unit variance causes a total variance of $900.

Management now has the data with which to investigate why the materials cost per unit is higher than the standard of $2.00 per pound. There are several possibilities, some of which are:

(1) Inefficient purchasing methods.
(2) Use of a slightly different material as an experiment.
(3) Increase in market price.

Inefficient purchasing can be corrected by better planning and by careful selection of suppliers. If the different material (2) is adopted by the company for use in its manufacturing operations, the standard cost per unit of materials will have to be increased. The standard cost would also have to be increased if the situation mentioned in (3) is found to be the cause of the variance and is considered to be a permanent condition.

This example illustrates the principle that any variance, favorable or unfavorable, must be carefully investigated so that corrective action can be taken. This action may involve elimination of inefficiencies or a change in the standard cost of the product.

Example 2:

Standard cost, 10,000 lbs. of materials @ $2.00	$20,000
Actual cost, 10,450 lbs. of materials @ $2.00	20,900
Unfavorable quantity variance	$ (900)

In this case, the cost of the materials is at standard but the materials usage is not. The manufacturing operation used 450 pounds of materials more than it should have, as indicated by the standard. This additional 450 pounds at a cost of $2.00 created the variance of $900 over standard cost.

As with the previous example, management must now determine why the extra materials were used. Again, there are various circumstances that might have created this situation. Some are:

(1) Materials were spoiled or wasted. This loss could have been due to the fact that a different type of material was used, that workers were careless, or that supervisory personnel were lax. If possible, this condition must be eliminated.

(2) More materials were deliberately used per manufactured unit as an experiment to determine if the quality of the product could be increased. If management decides to continue this usage, the standard cost per unit must be changed.

An analysis of the cause of this variance might also result in the elimination of inefficiencies or in a change in the standard cost.

Example 3:
Standard cost, 10,000 lbs. of materials @ $2.00 .... $20,000
Actual cost, 11,000 lbs. of materials @ $1.90 20,900
Unfavorable variance.. $ (900)

In this example, a combination of usage and price variances causes the overall unfavorable variance. The factory has used 1,000 pounds of materials over standard but has purchased these materials at a cost which is $.10 below standard. Once again management should investigate the reason for the usage of additional materials and take appropriate action. It is important to recognize that the price variance of $.10 will also be investigated. The fact that this variance is favorable, below standard cost, is no reason for production personnel to be complacent and to ignore it. This "better" price may have been created by more efficient buying techniques, a bargain purchase, or a general price reduction. On the other hand, materials of a lesser quality may have been purchased, thereby reducing the quality of the product and possibly causing an unfavorable effect on the marketing of the product.

It is also possible that the greater usage of materials may be related to the lower price. Waste and spoilage might be created by (1) use of cheaper materials, or by (2) unfamiliarity in the use of a different material by the production workers. Of course, an investigation may reveal that the standard was not properly determined and should be revised.

The important points that have been illustrated by the three examples with identical net variances are these:

(1) The total variance between standard and actual cost must be broken down by usage and price.

(2) The variances in usage and price, whether unfavorable or favorable, must be analyzed as to cause and effect. Variances may be stated in dollar amounts, or in terms of units such as pounds or hours. The method chosen should be that which is of greatest benefit in aiding analysis.

(3) Appropriate action must be taken. This action might include a change in methods of manufacturing, supervision, or purchasing, or a change in the standard cost of the product. It might involve taking advantage of efficient operations or functions. If the standard cost is changed, the units in inventory are often revalued at the new figure.

The same principles of analysis apply to the labor cost variances. Three similar examples are presented below.

Example 1:

Standard cost, 5,000 hrs. @ $5.00 per hr.	$25,000
Actual cost, 5,000 hrs. @ $4.95 per hr.	24,750
Favorable rate variance	$ 250

Example 2:

Standard cost, 5,000 hrs. @ $5.00 per hr.	$25,000
Actual cost, 4,950 hrs. @ $5.00 per hr.	24,750
Favorable efficiency variance	$ 250

Example 3:

Standard cost, 5,000 hrs. @ $5.00 per hr.	$25,000
Actual cost, 4,500 hrs. @ $5.50 per hr.	24,750
Favorable variance	$ 250

In the first instance, it is apparent that the number of actual labor hours was at standard, but the cost per hour was lower than the standard of $5. Although this situation appears to be favorable, the reason and the possible effect must still be determined. It may be that the personnel department is doing a more efficient job in hiring qualified employees and should be commended; or it may be that less-than-qualified workers are being hired at a lower rate, possibly reducing the quality of the work on the product. This second condition would not be acceptable.

The second example indicates that the labor rate is at standard, but the time required was 50 hours below standard. Again, the question is, "why?" It is possible that the speed of production has been increased and the employees are working too fast to do top quality work. This possibility could have an adverse effect on sales. Again, of course, there is the possibility that the manufacturing and/or supervisory functions have become more efficient so that more work is done in less time.

In the third example, a saving of 500 hours is indicated, but there has been a payment per hour of $.50 in excess of standard. These two factors could be related. The hiring of more highly skilled and higher paid personnel quite often results in a reduction in the number of hours worked. But, as with the other examples, management must investigate carefully and determine the cause and the effect of the variances in usage and price. If the labor efficiency variance is unfavorable, it may have been caused by the use of unskilled workers or it may be due to time lost because of machine breakdowns, improper scheduling of production, or an inefficient flow of materials to the production line.

The analyses of materials and labor variances do not stand alone; it is very possible that a difference above or below standard of one is directly tied to a variance of the other. For example, the hiring of more highly skilled personnel at a higher labor rate does not always reduce the number of hours worked, but it may reduce the amount of materials lost through spoilage. Conversely, the use of less skilled workers at a lower rate may cause greater materials loss. In examining any variance, management should look closely at the relationship of that variance to other variances.

Features of Standard Cost Accounting

Some features of standard cost accounting must be emphasized. First, the actual unit cost of manufacturing a product is not determined; only the total actual costs and the total standard costs are gathered.

Second, the fact that standards are based on estimates does not make them unreliable. A close examination and analysis of variances will quickly indicate whether the manufacturing operation is inefficient or whether the standards are reasonable.

Third, standards will change as conditions change. Permanent changes in prices, processes, or methods of operating may indicate the need for adjustment of the standards.

Fourth, the purpose of using a standard cost accounting system is to provide continual incentive for factory personnel to keep costs and performance in line with predetermined management objectives. As mentioned earlier in the chapter, comparisons between actual costs and the predetermined standards are much more effective than comparisons between current actual costs and actual costs of prior periods.

Fifth, a standard cost accounting system, through the recording and analysis of manufacturing cost variances, helps focus management's attention on these questions:

(1) Were materials purchased at prices above or below standard?
(2) Were materials used in quantities above or below standard?
(3) Is labor being paid at rates above or below standard?
(4) Is labor being used in amounts above or below standard?

Finally, although the discussion in this text indicates that variances are determined at the end of the month, most manufacturing companies calculate variances on a weekly, or even daily, basis to allow for more timely action in correcting inefficiencies or taking advantage of efficiencies. The variances for the month, however, are still recorded in the accounts at the end of the month.

Illustration of Standard Cost in a Departmentalized Factory

The following example demonstrates standard cost accounting procedures in a factory having two departments.

Standard Cost Summary

	Dept. A	Dept. B	Total
Materials:			
5 lbs. @ $1.00 lb.	$ 5		
1 lb. @ $2.00 lb.		$ 2	$ 7
Labor:			
1 hour @ $4.00	4		
2 hours @ $5.00		10	14
Factory overhead:			
Per unit	1	2	3
Total	$10	$14	$24

Production Report for the Month

	Dept. A	Dept. B
Beginning units in process	None	None
Units finished and transferred	2,200	1,800
Ending units in process	None	400
Stage of completion		½

Units pass through Department A to Department B. In both departments, materials, labor, and overhead are added evenly throughout the process. Actual costs for the month, as determined from materials requisitions, payroll records, and factory overhead records are as follows:

	Dept. A		Dept. B		Total
Direct materials:					
12,000 lbs. @ $ .95.............	$11,400				
1,900 lbs. @ $2.10............				$ 3,990	$15,390
Direct labor:					
2,000 hrs. @ $4.05...........	8,100				
4,100 hrs. @ $4.95...........				20,295	28,395
Factory overhead:					
Indirect materials..............	$ 400		$1,000		
Indirect labor..............	600		1,000		
Other items..............	1,200	2,200	2,000	4,000	6,200
		$21,700		$28,285	$49,985

From the data given on the standard cost summary, the cost accountant can determine the standard costs of production. To facilitate the comparison of these figures with actual costs and the determination of variances, the accountant may use a form similar to that shown in Illustration 8-2.

Using the data given, the specific variances for materials and labor can be determined as follows:

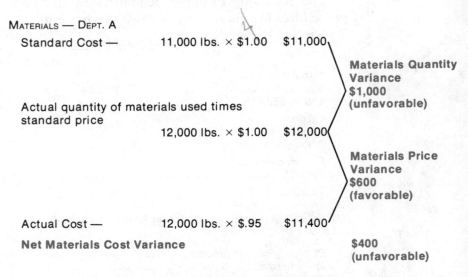

MATERIALS — DEPT. A

Standard Cost —   11,000 lbs. × $1.00 $11,000

                                                          Materials Quantity
                                                          Variance
                                                          $1,000
                                                          (unfavorable)

Actual quantity of materials used times
standard price

                          12,000 lbs. × $1.00 $12,000

                                                          Materials Price
                                                          Variance
                                                          $600
                                                          (favorable)

Actual Cost —   12,000 lbs. × $.95 $11,400

Net Materials Cost Variance $400
                                                          (unfavorable)

One thousand pounds of materials in excess of standard were used in Department A, which, at the standard cost of $1.00, caused an unfavorable variance of $1,000. If prices had not changed, there would have been no other variances. But prices did change — 12,000 pounds of materials at a cost of $.05 below standard resulted in a favorable price variance of $600. The two variances combined resulted in a net unfavorable materials cost variance of $400 in Department A.

	Dept. A Equivalent Production of 2,200 Units			Dept. B Equivalent Production of 2,000 Units			Total		
	Standard Cost	Actual Cost	Variance Favorable (Unfavorable)	Standard Cost	Actual Cost	Variance Favorable (Unfavorable)	Standard Cost	Actual Cost	Variance Favorable (Unfavorable)
Materials:									
11,000 lbs. @ $1.00	$11,000	$11,400	$(400)						
12,000 lbs. @ $.95									
2,000 lbs. @ $2.00				$4,000	$3,990	$10	$15,000	$15,390	$(390)
1,900 lbs. @ $2.10									
Labor:									
2,000 hours @ $4.00	8,800	8,100	700						
2,000 hours @ $4.05									
4,000 hours @ $5.00				20,000	20,295	(295)	28,800	28,395	405
4,100 hours @ $4.95									
Factory overhead:									
Standard cost per unit $1.00	2,200	2,200	—						
Actual cost									
Standard cost per unit $2.00				4,000	4,000	—	6,200	6,200	—
Actual cost									
Total	$22,000	$21,700	$300	$28,000	$28,285	$(285)	$50,000	$49,985	$15

ILLUSTRATION 8-2 Calculation of Variances

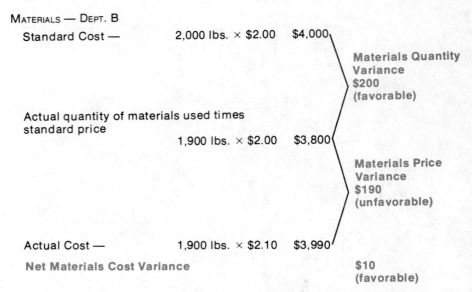

Materials — Dept. B

Standard Cost — 2,000 lbs. × $2.00 $4,000

Materials Quantity Variance $200 (favorable)

Actual quantity of materials used times standard price

1,900 lbs. × $2.00 $3,800

Materials Price Variance $190 (unfavorable)

Actual Cost — 1,900 lbs. × $2.10 $3,990

Net Materials Cost Variance $10 (favorable)

In this case, Department B used 100 pounds of materials less than standard. At a standard cost of $2.00 per pound, the favorable quantity variance was $200. But this variance was partially offset by the unfavorable price variance created by the increase in the cost per unit of the materials of $.10. With 1,900 pounds being used, the price variance was $190 above standard. The two variances resulted in a net favorable materials cost variance of $10 in Department B.

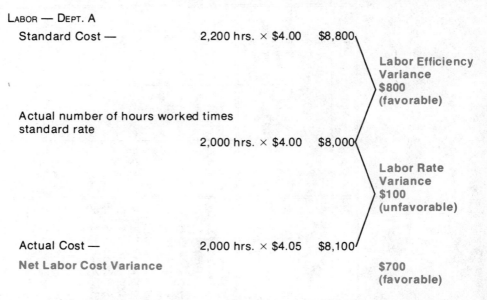

Labor — Dept. A

Standard Cost — 2,200 hrs. × $4.00 $8,800

Labor Efficiency Variance $800 (favorable)

Actual number of hours worked times standard rate

2,000 hrs. × $4.00 $8,000

Labor Rate Variance $100 (unfavorable)

Actual Cost — 2,000 hrs. × $4.05 $8,100

Net Labor Cost Variance $700 (favorable)

During the month, this department saved 200 hours by working fewer hours than the number established as a standard for the number of units produced. At a standard cost of $4.00 per hour, a favorable efficiency variance of $800 was realized. The average hourly rate of pay, however, was $.05 above standard so there was also an unfavorable rate variance. The company paid $.05 more per hour than the standard rate for 2,000 hours of work or a total of $100.

LABOR — DEPT. B

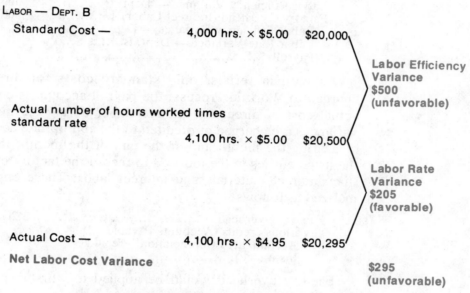

Standard Cost —	4,000 hrs. × $5.00	$20,000

Labor Efficiency
Variance
$500
(unfavorable)

Actual number of hours worked times standard rate

4,100 hrs. × $5.00 $20,500

Labor Rate
Variance
$205
(favorable)

Actual Cost —   4,100 hrs. × $4.95 $20,295

Net Labor Cost Variance

$295
(unfavorable)

Department B used 100 hours more than the standard and therefore, at the standard rate of $5.00, had an unfavorable efficiency variance of $500. Because the actual rate paid was $.05 below standard, there was a favorable rate variance of $205, determined by multiplying the 4,100 hours actually worked by this $.05 rate difference. (For the purposes of discussion in this chapter, no variances have been reflected for factory overhead. This type of variance will be discussed in detail in the next chapter.)

The following journal entries can now be made:

Work in Process — Dept. A	11,000	
Work in Process — Dept. B	4,000	
Materials Quantity Variance — Dept. A	1,000	
Materials Price Variance — Dept. B	190	
Factory Overhead (Indirect Materials)	1,400	
Materials Price Variance — Dept. A		600
Materials Quantity Variance — Dept. B		200
Materials		16,790

Note that the accounts for work in process are charged for the standard cost of direct materials, the materials account is credited at actual cost for all direct and indirect materials used, and the variance accounts are debited if unfavorable and credited if favorable. (If this company followed the practice of recording the materials price variance at time of purchase, no price variances would be recorded at this time.)

Work in Process — Dept. A	8,800	
Work in Process — Dept. B.......................	20,000	
Labor Rate Variance — Dept. A	100	
Labor Efficiency Variance — Dept. B	500	
Factory Overhead (Indirect Labor)	1,600	
Labor Efficiency Variance — Dept. A		800
Labor Rate Variance — Dept. B...............		205
Payroll		29,995

As with materials, only standard costs for direct labor are charged to Work in Process; the payroll account is credited for the actual cost of direct and indirect labor during the month; and the variances are charged or credited to the appropriate accounts.

During the month and at the end of the month, there would be the usual entries in the journals to record the factory overhead other than indirect materials and indirect labor. These entries are summarized as follows:

Factory Overhead	3,200	
Various credits (Accounts Payable, Accumulated Depreciation, Prepaid Insurance)..		3,200

Factory overhead would be applied to work in process by the following entry:

Work in Process — Dept. A (2,200 units × $1)...	2,200	
Work in Process — Dept. B (2,000 units × $2)...	4,000	
Factory Overhead		6,200

The entries are then made to transfer the standard cost of units finished in Department A to Department B and from Department B to finished goods.

Work in Process — Dept. B.......................	22,000	
Work in Process — Dept. A		22,000
(2,200 units @ $10)		
Finished Goods......................................	43,200	
Work in Process — Dept. B.....................		43,200
(1,800 units @ $24)		

After these entries have been posted, the general ledger accounts would reflect the data as shown below in "T" account form.

MATERIALS		WORK IN PROCESS — DEPT. A		WORK IN PROCESS — DEPT. B	
	16,790	11,000	22,000	4,000	43,200
		8,800		20,000	
		2,200		4,000	
		22,000		22,000	
				6,800 50,000	

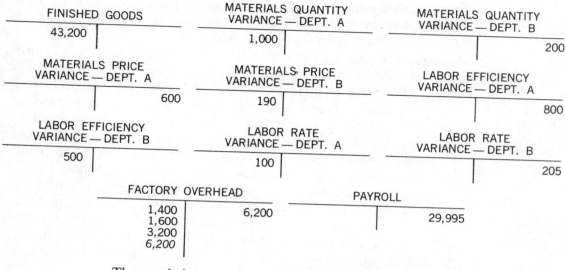

FINISHED GOODS		MATERIALS QUANTITY VARIANCE — DEPT. A		MATERIALS QUANTITY VARIANCE — DEPT. B	
43,200		1,000			200

MATERIALS PRICE VARIANCE — DEPT. A		MATERIALS PRICE VARIANCE — DEPT. B		LABOR EFFICIENCY VARIANCE — DEPT. A	
	600	190			800

LABOR EFFICIENCY VARIANCE — DEPT. B		LABOR RATE VARIANCE — DEPT. A		LABOR RATE VARIANCE — DEPT. B	
500		100			205

FACTORY OVERHEAD		PAYROLL	
1,400	6,200		29,995
1,600			
3,200			
6,200			

The work in process account for Department A has no balance because all work has been completed in this department and transferred to Department B. The work in process account for Department B has a balance of $6,800 accounted for as follows:

Cost in Department A — 400 units @ $10	$4,000
Cost in Department B — 400 units @ $7 (one-half completed)	2,800
	$6,800

Additional entries, not shown above, would have been made during the month for purchases of materials, vouchering and payment of payrolls, and recording of cost of goods sold.

Mix and Yield Variances

It is quite common for more than one material to be required in a production process. The proportion or ratio of each material to the others is called the **mix**. Quite often, in industries such as petroleum manufacturing, textiles, chemicals, foundries, rubber goods, and food processing, the mix of materials is deliberately changed from the standard formula. This may be for various reasons, such as (1) achieving economy, (2) an experimental change in the quality of the product, or (3) because a given material is in short supply or is not available. Sometimes a change in mix will affect the **yield**, which is the number of units produced from a standard amount of materials introduced into the process. For example: If the standard calls for 2 gallons of Material X and 1 gallon of Material Y to produce 3 gallons of Product Z, the mix ratio is ⅔ of X to ⅓ of Y. The yield is three units of Z. If the ratio of ⅔ Material X to ⅓ Material Y is altered in the production process, there has been a change in mix. If the ratio of 3 gallons of input materials to 3 gallons of output product is different, there has been a change in yield.

As discussed earlier, the materials quantity variance measures the cost of the actual quantity of direct materials used above or below the standard quantity for the actual level of production. If there has been a change in the mix, further analysis must be made to determine the effect of this change. This involves breaking down the materials quantity variance into a mix variance and a yield variance.

A **mix variance** shows the change in cost that results from changing the proportions of materials added to the production mix. It measures the effect of using a different combination of materials. In the previous example, if Materials X and Y were used in equal proportions, the standard mix has changed, and a mix variance would be calculated. This variance is determined by measuring the difference in cost, at standard prices, between the actual mix of quantities used and the standard mix of the total quantity used.

A **yield variance** measures whether a change in mix affected the yield, and shows the difference in cost that results if the actual yield (output) varies from the standard quantity of yield determined for a given input of materials. In the previous example, if the mix was changed and 3 gallons of direct materials did not produce 3 gallons of product, the yield has also changed and a yield variance should be determined. This variance is calculated by measuring the difference between the actual quantity of materials used, at standard mix and prices, and the standard quantity of materials allowed for the actual amount of production, at standard prices.

To illustrate, assume that the standards for materials are as follows:

Material	Quantity	Mix Ratio	Price per Pound	Total Cost
A	60 lbs.	60%	$1	$ 60
B	40	40	$3	120
	100 lbs.	100%		$180

Yield = 100 lbs. of finished product.

Also assume that the production records for the month show that 100 pounds of finished product were manufactured at the following cost:

Material	Quantity	Price per Pound	Total Cost
A	90 lbs. ×	$1	$ 90
B	20 ×	$3	60
	110 lbs.		$150

The materials quantity variance would be calculated as follows:

Material	100 Finished Units				
	Actual Quantity	Standard Quantity	Quantity Difference	Standard Price	Quantity Variance
A...	90 lbs.	60 lbs.	(30 lbs.) (U) ×	$1	$(30) (U)
B...	20	40	20 (F) ×	$3	60 (F)
	110 lbs.	100 lbs.	(10 lbs.) (U)		$ 30 (F)

The mix variance is then calculated:

Material	Actual Quantity	Actual Quantity Converted to Standard Mix	Quantity Difference	Standard Price	Mix Variance
A....................	90 lbs.	66 lbs. (60% × 110 lbs.)	(24) lbs. (U) ×	$1	$(24) (U)
B....................	20	44 (40% × 110 lbs.)	24 (F) ×	$3	72 (F)
	110 lbs.	110 lbs.	–0–		$ 48 (F)

The mix variance is favorable because the actual mix of materials cost less than the standard mix. This was because more of the lower cost Material A was used and less of the higher priced Material B.

The yield variance is determined as follows:

Material	Actual Quantity Converted to Standard Mix	Standard Quantity (100 units)	Quantity Difference	Standard Price	Yield Variance
A...............................	66 lbs.	60 lbs.	(6) lbs. (U)	$1	$ (6) (U)
B...............................	44	40	(4) (U)	$3	(12) (U)
	110 lbs.	100 lbs.	(10) lbs. (U)		$(18) (U)

This analysis indicates that it took 110 pounds of input materials, rather than the standard 100 pounds, to produce 100 finished units. This creates an unfavorable yield variance which may have been caused by **(1)** the use of an inferior grade of materials, **(2)** loss of units due to the different mix, or **(3)** rejection of units of poorer quality.

Note that the total of the mix and yield variances equals the quantity variance.

Mix variance..	$48 (F)
Yield variance..	(18) (U)
Quantity variance...	$30 (F)

These variances may be developed for internal use only, in which case only the materials quantity variance would be recorded in a journal entry, as discussed earlier in the chapter. However, if the mix and yield variances are to be recorded in the accounts in lieu of a materials quantity variance, the journal entry is as follows (assuming no price variance):

Work in Process..	180	
Materials Yield Variance	18	
Materials Mix Variance		48
Materials		150

This same type of analysis can be applied to labor mix and yield. A change in labor mix would be created if the relative proportions of skilled (higher paid) and unskilled (lower paid) workers were changed due to (1) economy measures, (2) absentee workers, (3) a shortage of one type of labor, or (4) problems in scheduling. In this case, a mix variance would be determined. Because this type of variation from the standard labor mix usually would affect hours worked and unit yield, a yield variance would also be calculated.

Assume that the direct labor standard for manufacturing a unit of product is as follows:

Class 1 labor — 1 hour @ $10................................	$10
Class 2 labor — 1 hour @ $5.................................	5
Total direct labor cost per unit............................	$15

Due to a shortage of skilled laborers, it was necessary to hire additional unskilled workers to complete the production process. The production data are as follows:

Number of units manufactured................................	1,000
Direct labor cost:	
Class 1 labor — 900 hours @ $10.........................	$9,000
Class 2 labor — 1,300 hours @ $5........................	$6,500

The labor variances would first be calculated in the usual way:

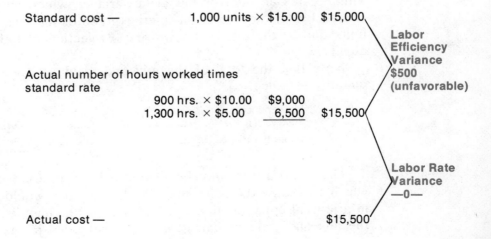

Standard cost —   1,000 units × $15.00 $15,000

Labor Efficiency Variance $500 (unfavorable)

Actual number of hours worked times standard rate

     900 hrs. × $10.00 $9,000
   1,300 hrs. × $5.00 6,500 $15,500

Labor Rate Variance —0—

Actual cost — $15,500

There is no labor rate variance because the two classes of workers were paid standard hourly rates for their classification. The labor efficiency variance is $500 and is unfavorable. This variance seemingly results because the number of hours worked (2,200) exceeded the standard number of hours (2,000) allowed for the production of 1,000 units. However, the breakdown of the efficiency variance into labor mix and yield variances will provide a more definitive analysis. The calculation is as follows:

Labor Class	Actual Hours	Actual Hours Converted to Standard Mix		Quantity Difference	Standard Price	Mix Variance	
1	900	1,100	(50%)	200 hrs. (F)	$10	$2,000	(F)
2	1,300	1,100	(50%)	(200) hrs. (U)	5	(1,000)	(U)
	2,200	2,200		–0–		$1,000	(F)

The mix variance is favorable because more lower paid workers were used in place of higher paid workers, but when this type of variance arises, management must be concerned as to whether the quality of the product and the yield were affected.

The yield variance is determined next:

Labor Class	Actual Hours Converted to Standard Mix		Standard Hours (1,000 units)	Quantity Difference		Standard Price	Yield Variance	
1	1,100	(50%)	1,000	(100) hrs.	(U)	$10	$(1,000)	(U)
2	1,100	(50%)	1,000	(100)	(U)	5	(500)	(U)
	2,200		2,000	(200) hrs.	(U)		$(1,500)	(U)

The yield variance is unfavorable because 2,200 hours of labor produced only 1,000 units, rather than 1,100 units as prescribed by the standards. The total of the mix variance ($1,000 favorable) and the yield variance ($1,500 unfavorable) equals the amount of the efficiency variance ($500 unfavorable). Because a change in materials and/or labor mix can affect yields, costs, and quality of the product, management will carefully study these variances to determine the potential effect of nonstandard mix.

QUESTIONS

1. Give a simple explanation of the function and objective of standard cost accounting.
2. Distinguish between standard cost and actual cost of production.
3. What is a "standard"?

4. What are the specific procedures upon which a standard cost accounting system is based?
5. State briefly how standards are determined for materials and labor costs.
6. What is a variance?

7. When are variances usually recorded in the journals?

8. Explain price and quantity variances in relation to materials costs.

9. Explain rate and efficiency variances in relation to labor costs.

10. Is a favorable variance "good" and an unfavorable variance "bad"? Explain.

11. Are actual costs or standard costs charged to Work in Process?

12. Are the inventory accounts — Finished Goods, Work in Process, and Materials — valued at actual cost or standard cost?

13. What two things must the cost accountant consider when breaking down a variance into its components? Explain.

14. What might cause the following variances?

   (a) An unfavorable materials price variance.

   (b) A favorable materials price variance.

   (c) An unfavorable materials quantity variance.

   (d) A favorable materials quantity variance.

   (e) An unfavorable labor rate variance.

   (f) A favorable labor rate variance.

   (g) An unfavorable labor efficiency variance.

   (h) A favorable labor efficiency variance.

15. Is it possible that a variance of one type might be partially or fully offset by another variance? Explain.

16. If, in a given period, the total actual cost of all materials used is exactly the same as the standard cost so that there is no net variance, is there any reason for further analyzing the data? Explain.

17. Explain a mix variance.

18. Explain a yield variance.

EXERCISES

The following data are to be used for Exercises 1 through 5:

The standard operating capacity of The Maximum Manufacturing Co. is 1,000 units. A detailed study of the manufacturing data relating to the production of one product revealed the following:

1. Two pounds of materials are needed to produce one unit.
2. The standard unit cost of materials is $3 per pound.
3. It takes one hour of labor to produce one unit.
4. The standard labor rate is $5 per hour.
5. Standard overhead for this volume is $3,000.

The following is required for each Case in each Exercise 1 through 5:

(a) Set up a standard cost summary showing the standard unit cost. **(b)** Analyze the variances and prepare entries in general journal form to record the transfer of **(1)** materials costs, **(2)** labor costs, and **(3)** overhead costs to the work in process account. When making these entries, indicate the types of variances, and state whether each variance is favorable or unfavorable. **(c)** Prepare the entry in general journal form to record the transfer of costs to the finished goods account.

1. 1,000 units were started and finished.

Case 1. All prices and quantities for the cost elements are standard, except for materials cost which is $2.95 per pound.

Case 2. All prices and quantities for the cost elements are standard, except that 2,100 pounds of materials were used.

2. 1,000 units were started and finished.

Case 1. All prices and quantities are standard, except for the labor rate which is $5.10 per hour.

Case 2. All prices and quantities are standard with the exception of labor hours which totaled 900.

3. All of the deviations listed in Excercises 1 and 2 took place, and 1,000 units were started and finished.

4. All of the deviations listed in Exercises 1 and 2 took place, and 950 units were started and finished.

5. All of the deviations listed in Exercises 1 and 2 took place, and 1,050 units were started and finished.

6. A manufacturing plant produces an average of 10,000 units each month. The factory standards are 20,000 hours of direct labor and 10,000 pounds of materials for this volume. The standard cost of direct labor is $4.50 per hour, and of materials, $2.00 per pound. The standard factory overhead at this level of production is $5,000.

During the current month the production and cost reports reflected the following information:

Beginning units in process...	None
Units finished...	9,500
Units in process, end of month...	None
Direct labor hours worked	20,000
Pounds of materials used...	9,400
Cost of direct labor	$89,000
Cost of materials used..	$19,740

On the basis of the above information: **(a)** prepare a standard cost summary; **(b)** calculate the materials and labor cost variances and indicate whether they are favorable or unfavorable using formulas as shown on page 319; and **(c)** calculate the materials and labor cost variances, using a schedule similar to that shown on page 320.

7. The normal capacity of a manufacturing plant is 30,000 direct labor hours and 20,000 units per month. A finished unit requires 5 pounds of materials at an estimated cost of $1 per pound. The estimated cost of labor is $5.50 per hour. It is estimated that overhead for a month will be $18,000.

During the month of March, 27,200 direct labor hours were worked at an average rate of $5.45 an hour. The number of units produced was 18,000, using 88,000 pounds of materials at a cost of $1.02 per pound.

Prepare **(a)** a standard cost summary showing the standard unit cost, and **(b)** entries in general journal form to charge materials and labor to Work in Process. Indicate whether the variances are favorable or unfavorable.

8. Assume that during the month of April the production report of the company in Exercise 7 revealed the following information:

Units produced during the month	21,000
Direct labor hours for the month	31,000
Materials used (in pounds)	106,000
Labor rate per hour	$5.52
Materials cost per pound	$ .99

Prepare entries in general journal form to charge materials and labor to Work in Process. Indicate whether variances are favorable or unfavorable.

9. From an analysis of the data presented below, determine the actual quantity of materials used and the actual price per pound as well as the actual direct labor hours incurred and the actual cost per hour.

	Standard Quantity or Hours	Standard Price or Rate	Variances Materials Quantity	Variances Materials Price
Materials	(pounds)			
(a)	2,200	$ 2.05	$ 205 Unf.	$115 Fav.
(b)	800	11.00	110 Fav.	79 Fav.
(c)	10,000	3.00	1,200 Unf.	520 Unf.
			Labor Efficiency	Labor Rate
Labor	(hours)			
(d)	5,600	5.00	$ 500 Unf.	$285 Fav.
(e)	8,800	4.50	900 Fav.	430 Unf.
(f)	11,500	5.25	1,575 Fav.	560 Unf.

10. Last year Crowley Corporation adopted a standard cost system. Labor standards were set on the basis of time studies and prevailing wage rates. Materials standards were determined from materials specifications and the prices then in effect.

At June 30, the end of the current fiscal year, a partial trial balance revealed the following:

	Debit	Credit
Materials Price Variance		25,000
Materials Quantity Variance	9,000	
Labor Rate Variance	30,000	
Labor Efficiency Variance	7,500	

Standards were set at the beginning of the year and have remained unchanged. All inventories are priced at standard cost. What conclusions can be drawn from each of the four variances shown in Crowley's trial balance?

(AICPA adapted)

PROBLEMS

8-1. Materials and labor variance analyses. The standard cost summary of the Arrow Mfg. Co. is shown below, together with production and cost data for the period.

Standard Cost Summary

Materials:		
2 gallons A @ $.50	$1.00	
2 gallons B @ $1.00	2.00	$3.00
Labor:		
1 hour @ $5.00		5.00
Factory overhead:		
$.50 per direct labor hour		.50
Total standard unit cost		$8.50

Production and Cost Summary

Units completed during the month	9,000
Ending units in process (one-fourth completed)	2,000
Gallons of Material A used	21,000
Gallons of Material B used	20,000
Direct labor hours worked	10,000
Cost of Material A used	$10,080
Cost of Material B used	$20,000
Cost of direct labor	$48,500

One gallon each of Materials A and B are added at the start of processing. The balance of the materials are added when the process is two-thirds complete. Labor and overhead are added evenly throughout the process.

Required: On the basis of this information: **(1)** Calculate equivalent production. **(2)** Calculate materials and labor variances and indicate whether they are favorable or unfavorable, using formulas shown on page 319. **(3)** Explain all variances by preparing a schedule similar to the one on page 320. **(4)** Determine the cost of materials and labor in the work in process account at the end of the month. **(5)** Prove that all materials and labor costs have been accounted for.

8-2. *Variance analysis, journal entries, other analyses.* Cost and production data for the Metal Products Company are presented below.

Standard Cost Summary

	Dept. I	Dept. II	Total
Materials:			
4 units @ $ .50...	$2		
1 unit @ $1.00...		$1	$ 3
Labor:			
1 hour @ $4.00..	4		
1 hour @ $5.00..		5	9
Factory overhead:			
Per unit	1	2	3
	$7	$8	$15

Production Report

	Dept. I	Dept. II
Beginning units in process	None	None
Units finished and transferred	6,000	5,000
Ending units in process...	2,000	1,000
Stage of completion...	½	½

Cost Data

	Dept. I		Dept. II
Direct materials:			
30,000 units @ $.52...........................	$15,600		
5,500 units @ $.95..............................			$ 5,225
Direct labor:			
6,800 hours @ $4.00..........................	27,200		
5,600 hours @ $5.10..........................			28,560
Factory overhead:			
Indirect materials..............................	$ 500		$1,000
Indirect labor...................................	2,000		5,000
Other...	4,500	7,000	5,000 11,000

Required: (1) Calculate net variances for materials, labor, and factory overhead.

(2) Calculate specific materials and labor variances by department.

(3) Prepare all journal entries to record production costs in Work in Process and Finished Goods.

(4) Prove balances of Work in Process for both departments.

(5) Prove that all costs have been accounted for.

Note: Assume that materials, labor, and overhead are added evenly throughout the process.

(6) If 4,000 units were sold @ $25 each, **(a)** what is the gross margin based on standard cost? **(b)** what is the gross margin based on actual cost?

8-3. *Analysis of materials and labor variances.* The Organet Stamping Company manufactures a variety of products made of plastic and aluminum components. During the winter months, substantially all of the production capacity is devoted to the production of lawn sprinklers for the following spring and summer seasons. Other products are manufactured during the remainder of the year.

The company has developed standard costs for its several products. Standard costs for each year are set in the preceding October. The standard cost of a sprinkler for the current year is $2.50, computed as follows:

Direct materials:		
Aluminum	— 0.2 lbs. @ $.40 per lb.	$ .08
Plastic	— 1.0 lbs. @ $.38 per lb.	.38
Production labor	— 0.3 hrs. @ $4.00 per hr.	1.20
Factory overhead	....	.84
Total	....	$2.50

During February, 8,500 good sprinklers were manufactured. The following costs were incurred and charged to production:

Materials requisitioned for production:		
Aluminum	— 1,900 lbs. @ $.40 per lb.	$ 760
Plastic — Regular grade	— 6,000 lbs. @ $.38 per lb.	2,280
Low Grade*	— 3,500 lbs. @ $.38 per lb.	1,330
Production labor — 2,700 hrs.	....	11,600
Factory overhead	....	7,140
Costs charged to production	....	$23,110

Materials price variations are not determined by usage, but are charged to a materials price variation account at the time the invoice is entered. All materials are carried in inventory at standard prices. Materials purchases for February were:

Aluminum	— 1,800 lbs. @ $.48 per lb.	$ 864
Plastic — Regular grade	— 3,000 lbs. @ $.50 per lb.	1,500
Low grade*	— 6,000 lbs. @ $.29 per lb.	1,740

*Due to plastic shortages, the company was forced to purchase lower grade plastic than called for in the standards. This increased the number of sprinklers rejected on inspection.

Required: Calculate price and usage variances for each type of material and for labor.

(CMA adapted)

8-4. *Materials and labor variances analyses.* The Bronson Company manufactures a fuel additive which has a stable selling price of $40 per drum. The company has been producing and selling 80,000 drums per month.

In connection with your examination of the financial statements of Bronson Company for the year ended September 30, you have been asked to review some computations made by Bronson's cost accountant. Your working papers disclose the following about the company's operations:

Standard costs per drum of product manufactured:

> Materials:
> 8 gallons of Miracle Mix @ $2 .... $16
> 1 empty drum 1 $17
> Direct labor — 1 hour... $ 5
> Factory overhead... $ 6

Costs and expenses during September:

> Miracle Mix: 500,000 gallons purchased at a cost of $950,000; 650,000 gallons used
> Empty drums: 94,000 purchased at a cost of $94,000; 80,000 used
> Direct labor: 82,000 hours worked at a cost of $414,100
> Factory overhead: $768,000

Required: Prepare a schedule computing the following variances for September:

(1) Materials quantity variance
(2) Materials price variance (determined at time of purchase)
(3) Labor efficiency variance
(4) Labor rate variance   *(AICPA adapted)*

8-5. Calculation of materials and labor variances. The Carberg Corporation manufactures and sells a single product. The cost system used by the company is a standard cost system. The standard cost per unit of product is shown below:

> Materials — one pound plastic @ $2.00..................................... $ 2.00
> Direct labor — 1.6 hours @ $4.00...   6.40
> Factory overhead...   4.45
> Total... $12.85

The charges to the manufacturing department for November, when 5,000 units were produced, are given below:

> Materials — 5,300 pounds @ $2.00.. $10,600
> Direct labor — 8,200 hours @ $4.10...   33,620
> Factory overhead...   23,815
> Total... $68,035

The purchasing department normally buys about the same quantity as is used in production during a month. In November, 5,200 pounds were purchased at a price of $2.10 per pound.

Required: Calculate the following variances from standard costs for the data given:

(1) Materials quantity
(2) Materials price (at time of purchase)
(3) Labor efficiency
(4) Labor rate   *(CMA adapted)*

8-6. *Allocation of variances.* The Butrico Manufacturing Corporation uses a standard cost system which records raw materials at actual cost, records materials price variances at the time that raw materials are issued to work in process, and prorates all variances at year end. Variances associated with direct materials are prorated based on the direct materials balances in the appropriate accounts, and variances associated with direct labor are prorated based on the direct labor balances in the appropriate accounts. The following information is available for Butrico for the year ended December 31.

Raw materials inventory at December 31	$ 65,000
Finished goods inventory at December 31:	
Direct materials	87,000
Direct labor	130,500
Applied factory overhead	104,400
Cost of goods sold for the year ended December 31:	
Direct materials	348,000
Direct labor	739,500
Applied factory overhead	591,600
Materials quantity variance (favorable)	15,000
Materials price variance (unfavorable	10,000
Labor efficiency variance (favorable)	5,000
Labor rate variance (unfavorable)	20,000
Factory overhead applied	696,000

There were no beginning inventories and no ending work in process inventory.

Required: Determine the following:

(1) The amount of materials price variance to be prorated to finished goods inventory at December 31.

(2) The total amount of direct materials cost in the finished goods inventory at December 31, after all variances have been prorated.

(3) The total amount of direct labor cost in the finished goods inventory at December 31, after all variances have been prorated.

(4) The total cost of goods sold for the year ended December 31, after all variances have been prorated. *(AICPA adapted)*

8-7. *Analysis of materials and labor variances.* Tolbert Manufacturing Company uses a standard cost system in accounting for the cost of production of its only product, Product A. The standards for the production of one unit of Product A are as follows:

Direct materials: 10 feet of Item 1 at $.75 per foot and 3 feet of Item 2 at $1.00 per foot.
Direct labor: 4 hours at $6.00 per hour.
Factory overhead: applied at 150% of standard direct labor costs.

There was no inventory on hand at July 1. Following is a summary of costs and related data for the production of Product A during the following year ended June 30.

100,000 feet of Item 1 were purchased at $.78 per foot.
30,000 feet of Item 2 were purchased at $.90 per foot.

8,000 units of Product A were produced which required 78,000 feet of Item 1, 26,000 feet of Item 2, and 31,000 hours of direct labor at $6.10 per hour.

6,000 units of Product A were sold.

At June 30, there are 22,000 feet of Item 1, 4,000 feet of Item 2, and 2,000 completed units of Product A on hand. All purchases and transfers are "charged in" at standard.

Required: Calculate the following:
(1) Materials quantity variance for Item 1.
(2) Materials quantity variance for Item 2.
(3) Materials price variance for Item 1 (recorded at purchase).
(4) Materials price variance for Item 2 (recorded at purchase).
(5) Labor efficiency variance.
(6) Labor rate variance.   *(AICPA adapted)*

8-8. Materials mix and yield variances. Using the data presented in Problem 8-3, calculate materials mix and yield variances.

8-9. Materials mix and yield variances. Using the data given in Problem 8-7, calculate materials mix and yield variances.

8-10. Labor efficiency, rate, mix and yield variances. The direct labor standard for the Brit Company is as follows:

Class A labor — 2 hours @ $12	$24
Class B labor — 3 hours @ $6	18
Standard direct labor cost per unit	$42

During the month 2,000 units were manufactured. Actual labor costs were as follows:

Class A labor — 4,200 hours @ $12.00	$50,400
Class B labor — 6,000 hours @ $5.75	34,500

Required: (1) Calculate the following:
(a) Labor efficiency variance.
(b) Labor rate variance.
(c) Labor mix variance.
(d) Labor yield variance.

(2) Explain what might have caused the mix and yield variances.

9

Standard Cost Accounting—
Factory Overhead

The determination of the factory overhead cost standard per unit involves the estimation of factory overhead cost at the standard, or normal, level of production, considering historical data (adjusted for distorting items in the past such as strikes and fire losses) and future changes and trends. This estimated factory overhead cost is divided by the standard number of units to be produced to determine the standard unit cost. For example, assume that the standard amount of production is 1,000 units. At this level of activity, the standard factory overhead is determined to be as follows:

Depreciation on building and machinery	$ 4,000
Taxes and insurance on building and machinery	1,000
Supervisory salaries	4,000
Maintenance costs	2,000
Supplies	1,000
Total standard factory overhead	**$12,000**

Dividing the standard factory overhead of $12,000 by 1,000 units to be produced results in a standard unit cost for overhead of $12. If equivalent production during the period is exactly 1,000 units, Work in Process will be charged with $12,000 of factory overhead (1,000 units × $12 per unit). As illustrated in the following journal entry and "T" accounts, if the actual factory overhead was $12,000, all of this cost would be applied to the work in process account, and there would be no over- or underapplied overhead.

Work in Process	12,000	
Factory Overhead		12,000
To apply factory overhead to work in process.		

WORK IN PROCESS		FACTORY OVERHEAD	
12,000		12,000 (actual costs recorded from various journals)	12,000 (standard cost applied to work in process)

If the actual overhead was higher than $12,000, as illustrated in the following account, Factory Overhead would have a debit balance of $400 after $12,000 of standard cost has been applied to Work in Process. This balance reflects the amount of factory overhead cost that was not charged to or absorbed by the goods produced. This unabsorbed cost represents the amount of overhead incurred over and above the standard for this level of production. The balance in the account would be considered an unfavorable variance.

FACTORY OVERHEAD	
12,400 (actual costs recorded from various journals) *400*	12,000 (standard cost applied to work in process)

TWO-VARIANCE METHOD OF ANALYSIS

Two methods are commonly used for analyzing overhead variances: the **two-variance method** and the **three-variance method**. Additional variances can be calculated, but most companies limit their analyses to one of these two methods. The most commonly used approach, the two-variance analysis, is discussed on the following pages; the three-variance method is discussed at the end of the chapter.

Budget Variance

In the previous example, the factory incurred actual overhead cost that exceeded the standard for this level of production; the resulting variance is called an unfavorable **budget**, or **controllable**, variance. As with any variance, the cause must be immediately determined and action taken to eliminate inefficient conditions.

Conversely, as shown below, if the actual factory overhead had been $11,800, or less than the standard indicated, the factory overhead account would have a credit balance of $200 after $12,000 had

FACTORY OVERHEAD	
11,800 (actual costs recorded from various journals)	12,000 (standard cost applied to work in process) *200*

been applied to the work in process account. This credit balance indicates a favorable budget variance: the factory did not incur as much overhead as was allowed by the standard at this level of production. However, the variance must still be analyzed and investigated even though it appears to be favorable, because underspending can affect the quality of the product.

The underlying principle of budget variance analysis is that a comparison must be made between the actual factory overhead for a given period and the standard amount of overhead allowed by the budget at a given level of production. Differences are classified as favorable or unfavorable budget or controllable variances.

If the actual level of production differs from the standard level, it is reasonable to assume that the standard budgeted amount of factory overhead for the actual level of production would differ from the standard budgeted amount for the standard level of production. This difference is the result of the behavior of the fixed and variable cost items included in the overhead estimate. As discussed in previous chapters, fixed cost items tend to remain the same in total dollars despite normal fluctuations in production, while total variable costs tend to vary more or less proportionately to the changes in production.

In the example given previously, the items of depreciation, taxes, insurance, and supervisory salaries are common items of fixed expense, while maintenance costs and supplies are usually in the category of variable cost.

Assuming that the actual level of production in the previous example on page 349 was 900 units, or 90% of the planned production of 1,000 units, the standard amount of factory overhead allowed in the budget for this level of production might be as follows:

Depreciation on building and machinery (fixed)............................	$ 4,000
Taxes and insurance on the above (fixed)	1,000
Supervisory salaries (fixed)...	4,000
Maintenance costs, 90% × $2,000 (variable)	1,800
Supplies, 90% × $1,000 (variable)...	900
Total standard factory overhead	$11,700

The fixed costs remain the same as budgeted at 1,000 units of production, but the variable costs are lower. Production of 900 units is equal to 90 percent of normal production, so the cost of maintenance is budgeted at $1,800 (90 percent of $2,000). The cost of supplies is shown to be $900 (90 percent of $1,000).

Assume that with production of 900 units, the actual factory overhead recorded is $11,700, which is the amount budgeted for this level of production. There will be no budget variance because the actual costs are equal to the costs budgeted for the actual number of units produced. However, another variance, the volume variance, must now be given consideration.

Volume Variance

At the beginning of the period, the standard cost per unit for overhead was determined to be $12; therefore, Work in Process will be charged the standard overhead cost of $12 for each unit produced. In the previous example, the amount of factory overhead applied to production would be $10,800 (900 units × $12). Thus, an unfavorable variance of $900 appears which is caused by the difference between the actual overhead of $11,700 and the standard overhead applied to work in process, $10,800.

FACTORY OVERHEAD

11,700 (actual costs recorded from various journals) 900	10,800 (standard cost applied to work in process)

This variance is called a **volume** variance because it is the result of operating at a level of production different from the standard, or normal, level. If the normal level of production had originally been set at 900 units and the budgeted overhead at $11,700, the standard cost would have been $13 per unit. If 900 units had been produced, the amount charged to Work in Process would have been $11,700 (900 units × $13), and there would have been no variance.

Another way of determining this variance is as follows:

Standard Level of Production — 1,000 units

Fixed cost:
Depreciation	$ 4,000	
Taxes and insurance	1,000	
Supervisory salaries	4,000	
Total	$ 9,000	
Application rate per unit		$ 9

Variable cost:
Maintenance	$ 2,000	
Supplies	1,000	
Total	$ 3,000	
Application rate per unit		3
Total standard factory overhead	$12,000	
Total application rate per unit		$12

Actual Level of Production — 900 units

	Budget	Applied	Variance
Fixed cost (applied at $9 per unit)	$ 9,000	$ 8,100	$900
Variable cost (applied at $3 per unit)	2,700	2,700	–0–
Total factory overhead	$11,700	$10,800	$900

The volume variance can be very significant because it indicates that production was below the established standard. If management feels that 1,000 units should have been produced during the period, it will be concerned that only 900 units were produced and will investigate to determine the cause. This reduced production may be the result of inefficiencies in labor or supervision, machine breakdowns due to faulty maintenance or any number of unfavorable conditions. On the other hand, this level of production might indicate a normal seasonal fluctuation which would be offset by higher than normal production in other periods. It is possible also, if the drop in production is not seasonal, that the factory is not at fault. Production may have been deliberately reduced because sales were not as high as predicted, in which case the marketing department could be held accountable for the situation.

Whatever the circumstances, if the factory is producing below its normal capacity, it has idle, and possibly wasted, excess capacity. If it is producing above its normal capacity, it may be subject to inefficient operating conditions and excess costs. These types of situations must be constantly scrutinized by management, which has the ultimate responsibility of planning and implementing the most efficient production methods and schedules.

Determination of Variances

Assume the following facts for the accounting period:

Standard overhead cost per unit	$12
Number of units manufactured	900
Actual factory overhead	$11,000
*Standard factory overhead budgeted for the actual level of production	$11,700

*See page 351.

The actual overhead costs incurred during the month are recorded in the various journals by methods previously discussed and posted to the factory overhead account in the general ledger.

At the end of the accounting period, the following journal entry would be made and reflected in the accounts as shown:

Work in Process	10,800	
Factory Overhead		10,800

        To apply factory overhead to production —
        900 units equivalent production at standard
        cost of $12 per unit.

WORK IN PROCESS		FACTORY OVERHEAD	
10,800		11,000 (actual costs recorded from various journals) *200*	10,800 (standard cost applied to work in process)

As was indicated, the factory overhead account has a debit balance of $200, which represents unabsorbed or underapplied factory overhead. The $200 is the net variance, and the debit balance shows that it is unfavorable. This net unfavorable variance can be analyzed in more detail. Illustrated below is the formula for calculating factory overhead variances using the the two-variance method.

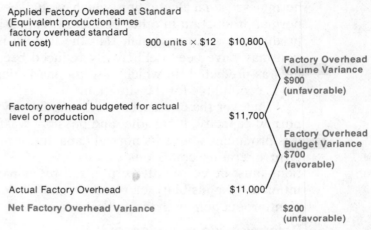

Formula for Calculating Factory Overhead Variances Using Two-Variance Method

Applied Factory Overhead at Standard
(Equivalent production times
factory overhead standard
unit cost)　　　　　　　900 units × $12　　$10,800

　　　　　　　　　　　　　　　　　Factory Overhead
　　　　　　　　　　　　　　　　　Volume Variance
　　　　　　　　　　　　　　　　　$900
　　　　　　　　　　　　　　　　　(unfavorable)

Factory overhead budgeted for actual
level of production　　　　　　　　　$11,700

　　　　　　　　　　　　　　　　　Factory Overhead
　　　　　　　　　　　　　　　　　Budget Variance
　　　　　　　　　　　　　　　　　$700
　　　　　　　　　　　　　　　　　(favorable)

Actual Factory Overhead　　　　　　　$11,000

Net Factory Overhead Variance　　　　　　　　$200
　　　　　　　　　　　　　　　　　(unfavorable)

The amount of overhead applied to production is $900 less than the amount of overhead budgeted for the actual level of production. This variance is unfavorable because fixed overhead was underabsorbed by production. It is a volume variance because it was created when the actual production of 900 units was less than the planned or standard production of 1,000 units. The amount of actual factory overhead was $700 less than the amount budgeted at the actual level of production, creating a seemingly favorable condition and resulting in a favorable budget variance.

After the analysis of the variances, the following journal entry can be made:

Factory Overhead Volume Variance................　900
　　Factory Overhead Budget Variance..............　　　　700
　　Factory Overhead ....　　　　200

This entry closes out the account for factory overhead and records the variances in individual accounts.

The entries to apply overhead and to record the variances may be combined in the following manner:

Work in Process ....　10,800
Factory Overhead Volume Variance................　900
　　Factory Overhead Budget Variance..............　　　　700
　　Factory Overhead ....　　　　11,000

Production below the standard number of units will always produce an unfavorable volume variance for the reasons previously explained. Conversely, production greater than the standard number of units will always cause a favorable volume variance. Assume the following facts for the period:

Standard overhead cost per unit	$ 12
Number of units manufactured (120% of normal production)	1,200
Actual factory overhead	$15,000
Standard factory overhead budgeted for the actual level of production:	
Depreciation	$ 4,000
Taxes and insurance	1,000
Supervisory salaries	4,000
Maintenance costs (120% × $2,000)	2,400
Supplies (120% × $1,000)	1,200
Total standard factory overhead	$12,600

Under these circumstances, the work in process account would be charged with $14,400 applied factory overhead (standard cost of $12 per unit × 1,200 units of equivalent production). The factory overhead account, as reflected below, would have a debit balance of $600 which represents a net unfavorable variance. Analysis of this variance is as shown below.

FACTORY OVERHEAD

15,000 (actual costs recorded from various journals)	14,400 (standard cost applied to work in process)
600	

The breakdown of the net variance shows that there is a favorable volume variance, because factory overhead was overabsorbed in production when the actual volume of production was higher than

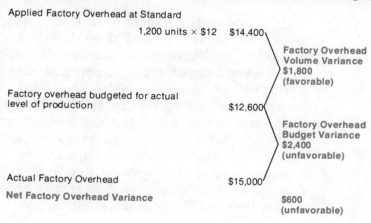

Applied Factory Overhead at Standard

1,200 units × $12 $14,400

Factory Overhead Volume Variance $1,800 (favorable)

Factory overhead budgeted for actual level of production $12,600

Factory Overhead Budget Variance $2,400 (unfavorable)

Actual Factory Overhead $15,000

Net Factory Overhead Variance $600 (unfavorable)

the established standard. The unfavorable budget variance indicates that the actual overhead exceeded the amount budgeted, or allowed, at the standards for the actual level of production.

Both variances should be investigated to determine their cause and effect. The favorable volume variance may be due to a normal seasonal fluctuation that was anticipated, and it may offset all or part of the previous unfavorable volume variances that arose during periods of low production. However, this level of production may have occurred because the company received more orders for goods than it had anticipated. From the standpoint of increased profits, this factor is favorable; however, if the factory worked beyond an established efficient capacity of production, the quality of the product may have suffered.

The unfavorable budget variance should be scrutinized carefully to determine why the costs were higher than they should have been, where the responsibility for this condition lies, and what steps should be taken to keep these costs under control in the future. This variance could be the result of several factors, such as laxity in purchasing, inefficiency in supervision, or weak control of expenditures. However, some portion of the budget variance may result from additional machine maintenance and repair costs, which are attributable to the increased use of facilities at the higher level of production.

On the financial statements, the overhead variances will usually be treated as additions to or deductions from the standard cost of goods sold. If the variances are material, seasonal, or due to unusual circumstances, they will be treated as discussed in Chapter 8.

BUDGETED FACTORY OVERHEAD

In previous pages, there were several references to the standard amount of factory overhead allowed, or budgeted, at different levels of production. These dollar amounts are predetermined; that is, the expense is estimated at the beginning of the year, before production is started, for varying levels of production. Using these predetermined figures, the cost accountant can determine the factory overhead variances by converting the production report data into standard costs and then comparing these costs with the actual costs that have been posted to the overhead accounts. The purpose of the following section is to discuss the procedures by which the accountant determines in advance what these standard amounts of factory overhead will be at different levels of production.

Budgets

Most successful companies today make use of operating budgets to help them in their constant effort to analyze and control operations, keep costs in line, and reduce expenses. A **budget** is a planning device that helps a company set goals, and it is a gauge against which the results can be measured. Many heads of households are familiar with the basic aspects of budgeting whereby they estimate their income for the following year, determine what their living expenses will be, and then, depending on the figures, reduce unnecessary spending, set up a savings plan, or possibly determine additional ways to supplement their income. During the year, they compare their budget with their actual income and expenditures to be sure that expenses do not exceed income, thereby causing financial embarrassment.

Budgeting in business and industry is a formal method of providing for detailed financial planning. It encompasses the coordination and control of every item of significance in the balance sheet and income statement. Its purpose is to help the company reach its objectives, both long-term and short-term. If the principles of budgeting are carried out in a proper manner, the company can be assured that it will efficiently use all of its resources and achieve the most favorable results possible in the long run.

Basically, the primary objective of any company is to maximize its net income, or attain the highest volume of sales at the lowest possible cost. Planning and control are absolutely essential in achieving this goal, and the process of budgeting produces the framework within which the organization can reach this objective. The budget then becomes a roadmap which guides management along the way and lets them know when the company is straying from its planned route. It is a chart of the course of operations and, in addition to forecasting costs and profits as a means of controlling costs, it requires those in authority in all areas of the business to analyze carefully all aspects of their responsibility for costs, and also to analyze company strengths and weaknesses.

Principles of Budgeting. The general principles of budgeting are these:

(1) Management must clearly define its objectives.
(2) Goals must be realistic and possible to attain.
(3) Because the budgeting process involves looking to the future, the development of the budget must carefully consider economic developments, the general business climate, and the condition of the industry, as well as changes and trends that may influence sales and costs. Historical data should be used only as a stepping-off point for projections into the future.

(4) There must be a plan, which is consistently followed, to constantly analyze the actual results as compared with the budget.

(5) The budget must be flexible enough so that it can be modified in the light of changing conditions; it must not be so restrictive that changes cannot be made where more favorable results are foreseeable.

(6) Responsibility for forecasting costs must be clearly defined, and accountability for actual results must be enforced. This principle encourages careful analysis and precise evaluation.

Preparing the Budget. This section is not intended to be an exhaustive survey of budgeting, but is principally concerned with the preparation of the production plan and the manufacturing expense budget. However, a brief discussion of other budgets is appropriate, so that the cost accountant can see how all budgets are interrelated and how the budget for the factory is influenced by the other budgets.

Forecast of Sales. In preparing a budget, all the items of income and expense should be considered. The best starting point is a forecast of sales, followed by a determination of inventory policy, a production plan, a budget of manufacturing costs, and a budget for all administrative and selling expenses. The resulting amount is the budgeted net income for the year. A balance sheet forecast should also be prepared, concerned primarily with cash, receivables, and capital additions.

Although all of the aforementioned budgets are important, the **forecast of sales** is especially significant, because management must use this information as a basis for preparing all other budgets. This forecast is concerned with projecting the volume of sales both in units and dollars. In estimating the sales for the forthcoming year, the sales department must take into consideration present and future economic situations; it must research and carefully analyze market prospects for its products; it must consider the development of new products and the discontinuance of old products. It must make these analyses by territory, by type of product, and possibly by type of customer. Marketing researchers should also carefully survey and evaluate consumer demand. After this detailed examination, the mix of the products to be sold can be determined, as well as the volume and the sales price.

Inventory and Production Planning. After the sales mix and volume plans have been made, the factory can proceed with the determination of production requirements. In a simple situation, assuming one product, stable production throughout the year, and an ending inventory 2,000 units greater than the beginning inventory, the number of units to be produced can be calculated as follows:

Units to be sold...	100,000
Ending inventory required	4,500
Total..	104,500
Beginning inventory..	2,500
Units to be manufactured	102,000
Units per month (102,000 ÷ 12)...	8,500

In actual practice, this computation is more complex. Management must try to achieve a satisfactory balance between production, inventory, and the timely availability of goods to be sold. For example, if the company's sales are seasonal rather than evenly distributed throughout the year, stable production might produce the following situation:

NUMBER OF UNITS

	Produced	Sold	On Hand
Beginning balance			2,500
January	8,500	1,000	10,000
February..	8,500	2,000	16,500
March	8,500	3,000	22,000
April...	8,500	10,000	20,500
May	8,500	15,000	14,000
June	8,500	15,000	7,500
July..	8,500	12,000	4,000
August	8,500	9,000	3,500
September...	8,500	9,000	3,000
October..	8,500	8,000	3,500
November..	8,500	8,000	4,000
December..	8,500	8,000	4,500
Total	102,000	100,000	

The problem created here is that the company must have enough storage facility to handle as many as 22,000 units. However, most of this space would be unused during several months of the year, resulting in a waste of invested capital for inventory and storage facilities and expenditures for upkeep, insurance, and taxes that provide no direct benefit. In this situation, a manufacturing concern might lease some storage facilities during the peak months, thereby requiring a much smaller company-owned facility. However, leasing may present problems of inconvenience, expense, and unavailability of the facilities at the right time and in the right place. In addition, during some months the company would have a considerable amount of capital tied up in finished goods which are threatened by obsolescence.

Another solution is for management to schedule different levels of production each month in order to maintain a stable inventory and to minimize the number of units stored. The following table shows this approach:

NUMBER OF UNITS

	Produced	Sold	On Hand
Beginning balance			2,500
January	1,500	1,000	3,000
February	2,500	2,000	3,500
March	3,000	3,000	3,500
April	10,000	10,000	3,500
May	15,000	15,000	3,500
June	15,000	15,000	3,500
July	12,000	12,000	3,500
August	9,500	9,000	4,000
September	9,500	9,000	4,500
October	8,000	8,000	4,500
November	8,000	8,000	4,500
December	8,000	8,000	4,500
Total	102,000	100,000	

This alternative requires minimum storage space and related expenses, but it creates a new problem: the factory must have enough facilities to handle the peak production of 15,000 units, but these facilities would be from 50 percent to 90 percent idle during some months. A possible solution is to have a smaller facility and to engage two or three shifts of employees during the busier months. Although the facility investment problem is reduced, a bigger problem is created because the working force can vary by 1,000 percent from the slowest period to the most active. This condition would require hiring new employees in the earlier months as production is climbing, with the problem of the high cost of recruiting and training as well as the problem of quality production with new, possibly inexperienced employees. In the later months, as production drops, many workers would be laid off, creating considerable additional expense for unemployment compensation as well as hardship for the employees and a feeling of ill will toward the company.

Management is often faced with the problem of determining which course to follow — whether to maintain stable production, with the necessity of providing for storage capacity, the tie-up of capital funds in inventory, and the possibility of obsolescence; or to maintain a stable inventory, with all of the ensuing expenses of personnel and facilities. Most companies will carefully analyze the alternatives and arrive at a plan that represents a reasonable compromise between the two alternatives.

Budgets for Manufacturing Costs and Administrative and Selling Expenses. Once the production schedule has been determined, the **budget for manufacturing costs** can be prepared which involves determining the costs of materials, labor, and factory overhead for each month (or week, or even day) of the coming year. After standard costs have been determined, this calculation, whether for one or for several products, is relatively simple for direct materials and direct labor, involving the extension of the number of units to be produced times the standard cost per unit. However, the forecast of the factory overhead is more involved and will be considered in detail later in this section. When the level of activity has been determined for sales and production, the **budgets for administrative, selling**, and **other expenses** can be prepared. As with other forecasts, the planners must take into consideration not only the planned volume for the company but also economic conditions, trends for local and national wages and salaries, and other expenses.

Other Budgets. Completion of these budgets permits the determination of the **budgeted income statement** for the year. It should be recognized that, although the discussion to this point has centered around units and dollars, the forecasts would also be used for planning the hiring (or laying off) of personnel, scheduling the purchases of materials, arranging for necessary facilities, developing sales promotion, and other appropriate functions.

The balance sheet budgets can now be prepared. The **cash budget** shows the anticipated flow of cash and the timing of receipts and disbursements based upon projected revenues, the production schedule, and expenses. Using this budget, management can plan for necessary financing or for temporary investment of surplus funds. The **budget for receivables**, based on anticipated sales, credit terms, the economy, and other relevant factors, will influence the cash budget by showing when cash can be expected from the turnover of inventory and receivables. A **liabilities budget** is also necessary, reflecting how the cash position will be affected by payment of these items.

The company may prepare a **capital additions budget**, which is a plan for the timing of acquisitions of buildings, equipment, or other significant assets during the year. This plan ties in with the sales and production plans and may influence the cash budget for expenditures to the extent that additional financing may be necessary.

Teamwork and cooperation in preparing the budgets are absolutely necessary. The sales, engineering, manufacturing, and accounting divisions of the company must work together to produce meaningful forecasts, because many of the estimates depend on the plans of other departments. Also, a considerable amount of coordination is required. For example, the sales goal must be compatible with the production that can be attained with the facilities available; at the same time, the amount and scheduling of production relies heavily on the needs of the marketing department. As mentioned before, some budgets can be prepared only after certain others have been completed, and they will be influenced by these other plans.

Another point to be made is that the budgets are not necessarily prepared sequentially. After the sales forecast in units is made, the manufacturing division can begin working on the production schedule and the manufacturing expense budget; the sales department can start preparing its budget for selling expenses; and the administrative expense forecast can begin. The receivables turnover schedule can also be made at this point, and possibly the capital expenditures budget can be prepared. The cash budget and the schedule of liabilities and payments cannot be considered until all of the aforementioned items are completed.

Evaluating Budget Performance. If a budget is to be used successfully as a mangement tool for control, the actual results must be periodically compared with the budgeted figures, and the differences must be thoroughly analyzed. Without this constant follow-up and analysis, the budget is a useless item. This principle has been discussed previously in connection with standard costs, and the same application may be made to the other planned amounts, both by unit and by dollar volume. If variances are found to exist in the number of units sold or manufactured, or in the dollar amounts of sales or expenses, or in other budgeted items, a careful evaluation of the variances must be made and responsibility determined.

Typically, performance reports are prepared for and distributed to the people who are accountable for the actual results. For example, all supervisors and department heads receive reports for their respective departments. The vice president in charge of production receives information on all elements of manufacturing involving the production and service departments. The president of the company receives reports on all divisions of the business — manufacturing, sales, and administrative. These reports should clearly reflect the variances from budget in all areas so that appropriate action can be taken.

Flexible Budgeting. The comparison of actual results with the budget to see if the planned objectives are being met leads to the use of **flexible budgeting**. This concept, which was introduced in Chapter 4, will be discussed from the standpoint of the factory overhead budget, but the principles are applicable to any item of expense that involves fixed and variable elements.

Implementation of a flexible budget involves planning what will happen to a company under varying sets of conditions: for example, the sale of 10,000 units per month rather than 9,000; the production of 15,000 units per month rather than 17,000; the effect of the addition or replacement of a machine in a department; or the development of new products or the discontinuance of the old. In other words, the company plans in advance what the effect will be on revenue, expense, and profit if sales or production differ from the budget. To illustrate, if budgeted sales for a month are $100,000 and the budgeted selling expense is $25,000, it is reasonable to assume that if actual sales are $80,000, the actual selling expense would be less than $25,000. If production volume was 10,000 units rather than a budgeted 9,000, the cost of production would logically be greater than the amount budgeted for 9,000 units.

The flexible budget is influenced by the presence of fixed and variable costs as discussed in Chapter 4. **Fixed costs** have been previously defined as those costs that do not change as production changes over a given range. They are a function of time and generally will be incurred regardless of the level of production. These expenses, such as straight-line depreciation, insurance, taxes, supervisory salaries, and others, will remain the same in dollar total, except in the extreme case of a major change in production which will require more or fewer machines, facilities, and supervisory personnel.

Many costs do vary in total dollar amount in proportion to any change in production. These **variable costs**, which are a function of activity, include direct labor, direct materials, indirect labor, and maintenance costs. It is because of these variable elements that the total cost differs from amounts originally budgeted when the level of production is different. If the manufacturer has budgeted production of 5,000 units for the month at a cost of $50,000 and the actual production is more or less than 5,000 units, there would be little value in comparing the actual cost of production with the items making up the $50,000 budget. Under such operating conditions, a flexible budget is useful because it shows the planned expenses at various levels of production. Thus, management can quickly determine variances by comparing the actual costs with what the costs of production should have been at the actual level of production.

Preparing the Flexible Budget for Factory Overhead. Determining the standard overhead cost per unit and preparing the flexible budget for factory overhead follow the basic principles which were suggested for determining standards for materials and labor costs. All costs that might be incurred must be carefully considered. Prior costs, as adjusted, must be studied as well as the effect of new costs, future economic conditions, changes in processes, and trends. As with other standards, the individuals responsible must have considerable experience in and familiarity with manufacturing operations.

Because costs are affected by the level of production, the first step is to determine what should be the standard volume of production. **Standard production** is the volume on which the initial calculation of costs is based. There are several approaches used to determine this figure and several related definitions of manufacturing capacity. Some of these types of capacity are as follows:

(1) **Theoretical capacity** represents the maximum number of units that can be produced with the completely efficient use of all available facilities and personnel. Generally, this production level is almost impossible to attain. It represents a rigid standard for the factory because it requires maximum production with no allowance for inefficiencies of any kind.

(2) **Practical capacity** is the level of production that provides complete utilization of all facilities and personnel, but allows for some idle capacity due to operating interruptions such as machinery breakdowns, idle time, and other inescapable inefficiencies.

(3) **Normal capacity** is the level of production that will meet the normal requirements of ordinary sales demand over a period of years. Although it conceivably can be equal to or greater than practical capacity, normal capacity usually does not involve a plan for maximum usage of manufacturing facilities but allows for some unavoidable idle capacity and some inefficiencies in operations. Most manufacturing firms use this level of capacity for budget development because it represents a logical balance between maximum production capacity and that capacity which is demanded by actual sales volume. Furthermore, over a period of years, all factory overhead expense will normally be absorbed by production. The following discussion will assume the use of normal capacity for planning purposes.

To illustrate the flexible budget, the following figures were determined to be the factory overhead costs at the normal or standard volume of 1,000 units. (To simplify the illustration, only a few overhead classifications are used. In actual practice there would be many types of expenses broken down into fixed and variable categories.)

Standard production — 1,000 units
Standard direct labor hours — 2,000

Fixed cost:

Depreciation of building and equipment.....................	$ 4,000	
Property tax and insurance	1,000	
Supervisory salaries	4,000	
Total fixed cost..		$ 9,000

Variable cost:

Maintenance...	$ 2,000	
Supplies	1,000	
Total variable cost..		3,000
Total factory overhead cost...		$12,000

Standard factory overhead application rate per direct labor hour:
Fixed cost ($9,000 ÷ 2,000 hours) $4.50
Variable cost ($3,000 ÷ 2,000 hours)..   1.50
Total factory overhead rate ($12,000 ÷ 2,000 hours)...................... $ 6.00
Standard overhead cost per unit ($12,000 ÷ 1,000 units).............. $12.00

As discussed in Chapter 4, factory overhead can be applied to work in process using different bases, such as direct labor hours, direct labor cost, or machine hours. One of the most commonly used bases is the direct labor hours method, in which overhead is applied in relation to the standard number of direct labor hours allowed for the current actual production.

In the preceding schedule, both standard units and standard hours are given, because production may be expressed in terms of units or the standard number of direct labor hours allowed for the actual production. Whichever base for measuring production is chosen, the results are not affected. Based on the budget above, if 900 units are manufactured, Work in Process would be charged with $10,800 (900 × $12) for factory overhead. If production is expressed in terms of standard direct labor hours, in this case 1,800 (900 units × 2 hours), Work in Process would still be charged with $10,800 (1,800 × $6).

The flexible budget for this illustration is shown below. The individuals responsible for the work have determined what the fixed and variable costs will be at various levels of production. Notice that the

FACTORY OVERHEAD COST BUDGET

Percent of Normal Capacity	80%	90%	(Normal) 100%	110%	120%
Number of units	800	900	1,000	1,100	1,200
Number of standard direct labor hours.	1,600	1,800	2,000	2,200	2,400
Budgeted factory overhead:					
Fixed cost:					
Depreciation of building and equipment	$ 4,000	$ 4,000	$ 4,000	$ 4,000	$ 4,000
Property taxes and insurance	1,000	1,000	1,000	1,000	1,000
Supervisory salaries	4,000	4,000	4,000	4,000	4,000
Total fixed cost........................	$ 9,000	$ 9,000	$ 9,000	$ 9,000	$ 9,000
Variable cost:					
Maintenance................................	$ 1,600	$ 1,800	$ 2,000	$ 2,200	$ 2,400
Supplies	800	900	1,000	1,100	1,200
Total variable cost....................	$ 2,400	$ 2,700	$ 3,000	$ 3,300	$ 3,600
Total factory overhead cost...............	$11,400	$11,700	$12,000	$12,300	$12,600

standard volume of production is expressed as being 100 percent of capacity. This production level is not necessarily the maximum capacity of the manufacturing facility; but it does represent, considering sales demand, the most efficient use of the present facilities under normal operating conditions, with some allowance for operating interruptions. A factory can always produce more than the normal volume by working overtime, adding a shift, or by squeezing in more machinery and workers; but these conditions are not normal. Since it is not uncommon to operate above or below normal, the flexible budget shows expense amounts for production above and below normal capacity of 100 percent.

Using the Flexible Budget. If actual production for a given period is exactly 1,000 units, the accountant can compare total or individual factory overhead costs incurred with these budgeted figures and determine variances as shown below.

FACTORY OVERHEAD COST VARIANCES

Normal production.......................... 1,000 units (or 2,000 direct labor hours)
Actual production.......................... 1,000 units (or 2,000 direct labor hours)

	Budget	Actual	Variances Favorable (Unfavorable)
Fixed cost:			
Depreciation of building and equipment.............................	$ 4,000	$ 4,000	
Property taxes and insurance.......	1,000	1,000	
Supervisory salaries....................	4,000	4,000	
Total fixed cost........................	$ 9,000	$ 9,000	
Variable cost:			
Maintenance..............................	$ 2,000	$ 2,500	$(500)
Supplies.....................................	1,000	900	100
Total variable cost	$ 3,000	$ 3,400	$(400)
Total factory overhead cost.............	$12,000	$12,400	$(400)

The net unfavorable variance is considered a budget, or controllable, variance because production was at normal capacity, eliminating the possibility of a volume variance.

Usually, however, factory activity will not be exactly at the normal level. The volume of production invariably fluctuates to a certain extent from the standard level because it is affected by such things as vacations, holidays, absentee employees, work interruptions, and equipment breakdowns. If a seasonal factor is involved, the fluctuation from one month to the next could be significant. Under these circumstances, the flexible budget provides the budgeted figures for the actual levels of production rather than the established normal level.

Upon receiving the report on actual volume for the period, the accountant can determine what the factory overhead costs should have been at that volume and compare these with the actual costs to determine variances. If the volume of production falls between two of the amounts shown in the budget, an approximation of budgeted cost can be interpolated as shown below:

Actual production 850 units (85%)	
Budgeted cost at 90%	$11,700
Budgeted cost at 80%	11,400
Difference...	$ 300
Range between volume levels	10%

Dividing the difference of $300 by 10 determines an additional cost of $30 for each percentage point increase.

Next lower budgeted volume..	80%
Costs at 80% volume..	$11,400
Plus (5 × $30)...	150
Budgeted costs at 85% volume...	$11,550

Semifixed and Semivariable Costs. The preceding method of determining the budgeted amount of factory overhead at a level of production different from that given in the budget is satisfactory if the overhead increases evenly throughout each range of activity, as would be the case if all costs were either fixed or variable. However, if there are significant semifixed or semivariable costs, then this method would not always be accurate enough for the most efficient evaluation.

Semifixed, or **step, costs** are those that tend to remain the same in dollar amount through a certain range of activity but increase when production exceeds certain limits. For example, the salary of a department head is generally considered a fixed cost, because no other department head will be employed through a given range of activity, and the salary cost will not change as the volume fluctuates. But if the production level exceeds a given number of units, an assistant department head might have to be employed to aid in supervising the greater number of workers that would be necessary. In this case, the fixed expense for supervisory personnel would increase, as illustrated below.

Percent of Normal Capacity	80%	90%	100%	110%	120%	130%
Fixed cost.....................	$20,000	$20,000	$20,000	$20,000	$28,000	$28,000
Variable cost.................	24,000	27,000	30,000	33,000	36,000	39,000
Total factory overhead....	$44,000	$47,000	$50,000	$53,000	$64,000	$67,000

In this case, if the actual volume of production falls into the range between 110% and 120%, the use of interpolation to determine budgeted expense would probably not be satisfactory. A careful analysis of the expenses would need to be made, without the use of interpolation, to determine whether more supervisory personnel would be needed at 119% of capacity or 111% of capacity, for example.

Semivariable costs are those that may change with production but not necessarily in direct proportion. For example, if a company incurs expense to train new employees before they go into the factory, this expense will increase as production increases and new employees are hired. But if the volume of production decreases and no new employees are hired, there will be no training expense.

The existence of semifixed or semivariable costs indicates an even greater need for careful analysis and evaluation of the costs at each level of production. A statistical analysis of semivariable expenses was discussed in Chapter 4. The approach in this chapter, however, assumes that fixed costs remain constant and variable costs vary evenly throughout the ranges of activity given unless stated otherwise.

Service Department Budgets and Variances

The preparation of a budget for a service department follows the same procedure as that for production departments. Expenses at different levels of production are estimated, and a standard rate for application of service department expenses to production departments is determined based on the type of service provided and the estimated usage by the production departments. The production departments will take these expenses into consideration in setting up their budgets.

During the period, the production departments are charged with service department expenses at the standard rate using their actual activity base, such as kilowatt hours or hours of maintenance labor. At the end of the period, the service department's actual expenses are compared with the amount charged to the production departments to determine the variances.

Summary

A summarization of the budgeting process for the factory, the determination of standard costs, and the segregation of the variances is illustrated on the following page.

1 **A Sales Forecast** in units, considering the

2 **Inventory Policy**, minimum-maximum and stable or fluctuating, helps in developing the

3 **Production Plan** in units and by periods.
This information aids in developing the

4 (a)	4 (b)	4 (c)
Requirements for Direct Materials (quantities and prices)	**Requirements for Direct Labor** (hours and rates)	**Requirements for Indirect Costs, Facilities, and Supplies** (fixed and variable costs)

From this information is developed the

5 (a)	5 (b)	5 (c)
Direct Materials Budget	**Direct Labor Budget**	**Factory Overhead Budget**

From these budgets are developed the

6 (a)	6 (b)	6 (c)
Standard Unit Cost for Direct Materials	**Standard Unit Cost for Direct Labor**	**Standard Unit Cost for Factory Overhead**

(These figures combined determine the **Standard Unit Cost for the Product.**)

7 These unit costs, when multiplied by the equivalent production for the period, determine the amount to be charged to Work in Process for each element of production cost. The costs in 6 (a) and (b) above are

8 (a)	8 (b)	
multiplied by the actual quantity of direct materials used.	multiplied by the actual direct labor hours worked.	

8 (c)

From the flexible budget is determined the budgeted factory overhead cost, using the standard hours allowed at the actual level of production.

The comparison of 7 and 8 determines the

9 (a)	9 (b)	9 (c)
Materials Quantity Variance	**Labor Efficiency Variance**	**Factory Overhead Volume Variance**

The comparison of 8 above with the actual cost for the period determines the

10 (a)	10 (b)	10 (c)
Materials Price Variance*	**Labor Rate Variance**	**Factory Overhead Budget Variance**

Unless the materials price variance is recognized at the time of purchase.

THREE-VARIANCE METHOD OF ANALYSIS

The **three-variance method** of factory overhead cost analysis, although not as common as the two-variance method, is used by many manufacturers. This method breaks down the difference between actual and applied overhead into three variances: **(1) efficiency, (2) capacity,** and **(3) budget (spending).**

The **efficiency variance** measures the difference between the overhead applied (standard hours at the standard rate) and the actual hours worked multiplied by the standard rate. It indicates the effect on fixed and variable overhead costs when the actual hours worked are more or less than standard hours allowed for the production volume. Unfavorable variances may be caused by inefficiencies in the use of labor or by other conditions; favorable efficiency variances might indicate an opposite situation.

The **capacity variance** indicates that the volume of production was more or less than normal. It reflects an under- or overabsorption of fixed costs and is measured by the difference between the actual hours worked, multiplied by the standard overhead rate, and the budget allowance based on actual hours worked. It indicates that the actual hours of work were more or less than the normal hours used in determining the overhead rate. This variance is considered the responsibility of management and can be due to expected seasonal variations, or it can be caused by changes in the volume of production due to poor scheduling of production, improper use of labor, strikes, or other causes.

The **budget**, or **spending**, **variance** reflects the difference between the amount allowed by the budget for the actual hours worked and the actual costs incurred. The saving or overspending is chargeable to a manager or a departmental supervisor who is responsible for the costs.

The budget variances here must not be confused with those used for the two-variance method; the calculations of these variances are slightly different and result in a sharper distinction in variances. The primary difference between the two methods of variance analysis is that the three-variance method determines the budget allowance based on actual hours worked rather than on the standard number of hours for the units produced.

Many accountants feel that the budgeted allowance for overhead is more appropriately based on actual labor hours than on standard labor hours. They believe there is a more definite relationship between actual hours worked and the factory expense involved and feel that the three-variance method provides a more precise analysis of overhead costs.

The following example illustrates the three-variance method, using the flexible budget presented on page 365. Assume that production was 900 units, direct labor hours worked were 1,900, and actual factory overhead totaled $12,000.

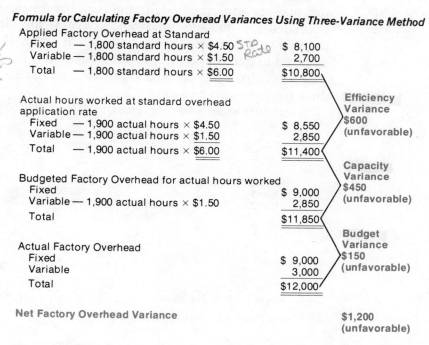

Formula for Calculating Factory Overhead Variances Using Three-Variance Method

Applied Factory Overhead at Standard

Fixed	— 1,800 standard hours × $4.50 *STD Rate*	$ 8,100
Variable	— 1,800 standard hours × $1.50 *Rate*	2,700
Total	— 1,800 standard hours × $6.00	$10,800

Rates from page 364.5

Actual hours worked at standard overhead application rate

Fixed	— 1,900 actual hours × $4.50	$ 8,550
Variable	— 1,900 actual hours × $1.50	2,850
Total	— 1,900 actual hours × $6.00	$11,400

Efficiency Variance $600 (unfavorable)

Budgeted Factory Overhead for actual hours worked

Fixed	$ 9,000
Variable — 1,900 actual hours × $1.50	2,850
Total	$11,850

Capacity Variance $450 (unfavorable)

Actual Factory Overhead

Fixed	$ 9,000
Variable	3,000
Total	$12,000

Budget Variance $150 (unfavorable)

Net Factory Overhead Variance $1,200 (unfavorable)

Whichever method is used, two- or three-variance, the overhead applied to production is the same because this figure is based on the standard number of labor hours allowed for the actual production. Similarly, the actual overhead would be the same. Therefore, the net variance in overhead would be the same in either approach.

The efficiency variance illustrated is unfavorable because the number of labor hours worked was more than standard. In this case, the excess of 100 hours times the standard overhead application rate of $6 equals the variance of $600 and reflects the underabsorption of fixed and variable costs.

The budgeted overhead, based on the actual hours worked, is calculated in this manner: the flexible budget is used to determine the amount of fixed overhead allowed, $9,000. Variable cost in the flexible budget is $1.50 per direct labor hour, and is multiplied by the actual number of hours worked to equal $2,850. The capacity variance theoretically reflects the cost of unused plant facilities and involves only fixed costs. At 1,900 actual labor hours worked, $8,550 (1,900 × $4.50) should have been absorbed in Work in Process, leaving $450 of fixed cost unabsorbed. This variance is similar to the volume variance under the two-variance method but is based on actual hours worked rather than the standard hours allowed for 900 units.

The budget variance, which is similar to the budget variance in the two-variance method, is unfavorable because actual overhead exceeded the budgeted allowance. Again, the amount differs from the two-variance method because actual rather than standard hours are used to determine the budgeted amount.

For comparison purposes, the two-variance method would produce the following results:

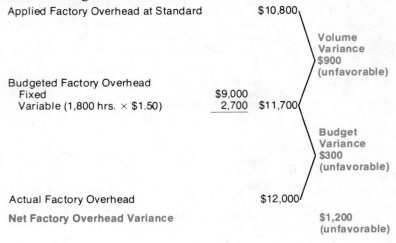

Applied Factory Overhead at Standard		$10,800	
			Volume Variance $900 (unfavorable)
Budgeted Factory Overhead			
Fixed	$9,000		
Variable (1,800 hrs. × $1.50)	2,700	$11,700	
			Budget Variance $300 (unfavorable)
Actual Factory Overhead		$12,000	
Net Factory Overhead Variance			**$1,200 (unfavorable)**

The following is presented as an aid to understanding the three-variance method:

	Fixed Cost	Variable Cost	Total	
Applied overhead...	$8,100	$2,700	$10,800	
Actual hours at standard rate............................	8,550	2,850	11,400	
Overhead underabsorbed (efficiency variance)....	$ 450	$ 150	$ 600	(1)
Actual hours at standard rate............................	$8,550	$2,850	$11,400	
Budgeted allowance...	9,000	2,850	11,850	
Overhead underabsorbed (capacity variance)......	$ 450	—0—	$ 450	(2)
Budgeted allowance...	$9,000	$2,850	$11,850	
Actual overhead cost	9,000	3,000	12,000	
Overhead underabsorbed (budget variance)........	$—0—	$ 150	$ 150	
Total overhead underabsorbed...........................	$ 900	$ 300	$ 1,200	

    (1) If the labor hours had been efficiently used, 950 units (1,900 ÷ 2 hours per unit) would have been produced. Factory overhead applied would have been $11,400 (950 units × $12), and there would have been no efficiency variance.

(2) Normal capacity is 2,000 direct labor hours. Since only 1,900 hours were worked, the planned capacity was not fully utilized; therefore, all of the fixed overhead was not absorbed by production. Variable cost is not affected. Another way of calculating this variance is: Normal hours (2,000) − actual hours (1,900) = 100 idle hours × the fixed overhead application rate ($4.50) = $450 unfavorable capacity variance.

QUESTIONS

1. How is the standard cost per unit for factory overhead determined?

2. How is factory overhead cost applied to work in process in a standard cost accounting system?

3. What is a budget variance?

4. Why is it important to determine budget variances?

5. Distinguish between fixed and variable costs and give examples of each.

6. What is a volume variance?

7. What is the significance of a volume variance?

8. If production is more or less than the standard volume, is it possible that there would be no budget or volume variances? Explain.

9. What is a budget?

10. What is the advantage of using budgets for business and industry?

11. What are the six principles of good budgeting?

12. Which budget must be prepared before the others? Why?

13. If the sales forecast estimates that 50,000 units of product will be sold during the following year, should the factory plan on manufacturing 50,000 units in the coming year? Explain.

14. Discuss the advantages and disadvantages of **(a)** a stable production policy and **(b)** a stable inventory policy for a company that has greatly fluctuating sales during the year.

15. After budgets have been prepared in units and dollars, what other activities can be planned?

16. What is a flexible budget?

17. Define **(a)** theoretical capacity, **(b)** practical capacity, and **(c)** normal capacity.

18. Is it possible for a factory to operate at more than 100 percent of capacity?

19. If a factory operates at 100 percent of capacity one month, 90 percent of capacity the next month, and at 105 percent of capacity the next, will a different cost per unit be charged to Work in Process each month for factory overhead?

20. At the end of the current fiscal year, the trial balance of Crowley Corporation revealed the following debit balances:

Budget Variance — $2,000
Volume Variance — $75,000

What conclusions can be drawn from these two variances?

(AICPA adapted)

EXERCISES

1. The normal capacity of a manufacturing plant is 5,000 units per month. Fixed overhead at this volume is $2,500 and variable overhead is $7,500. Additional data are as follows:

	Month 1	Month 2
Actual production (units)...	5,200	4,800
Actual factory overhead	$9,900	$9,500

(a) Determine the amount of factory overhead allowed for the actual levels of production. (b) Calculate variances for each month for factory overhead. Indicate whether these variances are favorable or unfavorable.

2. The standard capacity of a factory is 10,000 units per month. Cost and production data are as follows:

Standard application rate for fixed overhead	$.50 per unit
Standard application rate for variable overhead......................	$1.50 per unit
Production — Month I	9,000 units
Production — Month II	10,500 units
Actual factory overhead — Month I	$18,200
Actual factory overhead — Month II	$22,000

(a) Determine the amount of factory overhead allowed for the actual volume of production each month. (b) Calculate the variances for factory overhead, indicating whether these variances are favorable or unfavorable. (c) Explain the significance of the variances.

The following data and instructions are to be used for Exercises 3 through 5:

The normal operating capacity of the Ludlow Mfg. Co. is 1,000 units. At this level of production, the standard factory overhead is $3,000 (fixed costs, $1,000; variable costs, $2,000).

For each exercise below, prepare the general journal entry to record the application of factory overhead to work in process and to record the variances and state whether each variance is favorable or unfavorable.

3. Equivalent production — 1,000 units; actual factory overhead — $3,200.

4. Equivalent production — 950 units; actual factory overhead — $3,200.

5. Equivalent production — 1,050 units; actual factory overhead — $3,200.

6. The normal capacity of a manufacturing plant is 30,000 direct labor hours or 20,000 units per month. Standard fixed costs are $6,000 and variable costs are $12,000.

Data for two months are as follows:	March	April
Units produced	18,000	21,000
Factory overhead incurred..	$16,600	$19,100

For each month, prepare general journal entries to charge overhead to Work in Process and to record variances. Indicate the types of variances and state whether each variance is favorable or unfavorable.

7. The overhead application rate for a company is $2.50 per unit, made up of $1.00 for fixed overhead and $1.50 for variable overhead. Normal capacity is 10,000 units. In one month there was an unfavorable budget variance of $500. Actual overhead for the month was $27,000. What was the amount of factory overhead applied to work in process?

8. The sales department of your company has forecast sales in March to be 10,000 units. Additional information is as follows:

Finished goods inventory, March 1 .... 2,000 units
Finished goods inventory required, March 31............................. 3,000 units

Materials used in production:

	Inventory March 1	Required Inventory March 31	Standard Cost
A (one gallon per unit)....................	500 gal.	1,000 gal.	$2 per gal.
B (one pound per unit)	1,000 lbs.	1,000 lbs.	$1 per lb.

Prepare **(a)** a production budget for March (in units), and **(b)** a materials budget for the month (in units and dollars).

PROBLEMS

9-1. Overhead application rate; calculation of all variances. Milner Manufacturing Company uses a job order costing system and standard costs. It manufactures one product whose standard cost is as follows:

Materials, 20 yards @ $.90 per yard $18
Direct labor, 4 hours @ $6.00 per hour... 24
Total factory overhead, applied at five-sixths of direct labor (the ratio of
   variable costs to fixed costs is 3 to 1)... 20
Total unit cost... $62

The standards are set based on normal activity of 2,400 direct labor hours.

Actual activity for the month of October was as follows:

Materials purchased, 18,000 yards @ $.92 .... $16,560
Materials used, 9,500 yards
Direct labor, 2,100 hours @ $6.10 12,810
Total factory overhead, 500 units actually produced.................... 11,100

Required: (1) Compute the variable factory overhead rate per direct labor hour and the total fixed factory overhead based on normal activity. **(2)** Prepare a schedule computing the following variances for the month of October:

    (a) Materials quantity variance.
    (b) Materials price variance (at time of purchase).
    (c) Labor efficiency variance.
    (d) Labor rate variance.
    (e) Overhead budget (controllable) variance.
    (f) Overhead volume variance.

Indicate whether each variance is favorable or unfavorable.

(AICPA adapted)

9-2. Journal entries; variance analysis; other analyses. Cost and production data for the Office Products Co. are as follows:

Standard Cost Sheet
(Normal capacity — 1,000 units)

	Dept. A	Dept. B	Total
Materials:			
I — 2 lbs. @ $2	$ 4		
II — 2 lbs. @ $1		$ 2	$ 6
Labor:			
2 hours @ $5	10		
1 hour @ $6		6	16
Factory overhead: (per standard labor hour)			

Fixed	Variable			
$2	$1	6		
1	3		4	10
Total		$20	$12	$32

Production Report

	Dept. A	Dept. B
Beginning units in process	None	None
Units finished and transferred	1,000	900
Ending units in process	200	100
Stage of completion	½	½

Cost Data

	Dept. A		Dept. B	
Direct materials used:				
I — 2,300 lbs.		$ 4,715		
II — 1,850 lbs.				$ 1,813
Direct labor:				
2,150 hours		10,965		
1,000 hours				5,900
Factory overhead:				
Indirect materials	$1,000		$ 500	
Indirect labor	1,300		1,000	
Other	4,400	6,700	2,250	3,750
Total		$22,380		$11,463

During the month 850 units were sold at $50 each.
Note: Materials, labor, and overhead are added evenly throughout the process.

Required: (1) Prepare all entries, in general journal form, to record all transactions and variances. (Use the two-variance method for overhead variance analysis.) (2) Prove balances of Work in Process in both departments. (3) Prove that all costs have been accounted for. (4) Determine the gross margin:

      (a) at standard cost   **(b)** at actual cost

9-3. Flexible budget; overhead variance analysis. Presented below are the monthly factory overhead cost budget at normal capacity of 5,000 units or 20,000 direct labor hours and the production and cost data for a month.

Factory Overhead Cost Budget

Fixed cost:		
Depreciation on building and machinery.....................	$1,200	
Taxes on building and machinery............................	500	
Insurance on building and machinery........................	500	
Superintendent's salary....................................	1,500	
Supervisors' salaries	2,300	
Maintenance wages...	1,000	$7,000
Variable cost:		
Repairs..	$ 400	
Maintenance supplies	300	
Other supplies..	200	
Payroll taxes...	800	
Small tools...	300	2,000
Total standard factory overhead		$9,000

Production and Cost Data

Number of units produced..	4,000
Factory overhead:	
Depreciation on building and machinery.....................	$1,200
Supervisors' salaries	2,300
Insurance on building and machinery........................	480
Maintenance supplies	200
Maintenance wages	1,050
Other supplies..	150
Payroll taxes	650
Repairs	275
Small tools...	170
Superintendent's salary	1,500
Taxes on building and machinery...........................	525

Required: Use the factory overhead cost budget for instructions (1) through (4):

(1) Assuming that variable costs will vary in direct proportion to the change in volume, prepare a flexible budget for production levels of 80 percent, 90 percent, and 110 percent. Also determine the rate for application of factory overhead to work in process at each level of volume.

(2) Prepare a flexible budget for production levels of 80 percent, 90 percent, and 110 percent, assuming that variable costs will vary in direct proportion to the change in volume but with the following exceptions:

- **(a)** At 110 percent of capacity, an assistant department head will be needed at a salary of $10,500 annually.
- **(b)** At 80 percent of capacity, the repairs expense will drop to one half of the amount at 100 percent capacity.
- **(c)** Maintenance supplies expense will remain constant at all levels of production.
- **(d)** At 80 percent of capacity, one part-time maintenance worker, earning $6,000 a year, will be laid off.
- **(e)** At 110 percent of capacity, a machine not normally in use and on which no depreciation is normally recorded will be used in production. Its cost was $12,000 and it has a ten-year life.

(3) Using the flexible budget prepared in (1), determine the budgeted cost at 92 percent of capacity using interpolation.

(4) Using the flexible budget prepared in (1), determine the budgeted cost at 104 percent of capacity using a method other than interpolation.

(5) Using the production and cost data for a month and the flexible budget prepared in (1):

- **(a)** Determine the variances.
- **(b)** Explain the meaning of the variances.
- **(c)** Prepare a schedule comparing the actual and budgeted items and showing the variance for each item of factory overhead. Indicate unfavorable variances by putting them in parentheses.

9-4. *Variance analysis*. Ross Shirts, Inc., manufactures short- and long-sleeve men's shirts for large stores. Ross produces a single quality shirt in lots to each customer's order and attaches the store's label to each. The standard costs for a dozen long-sleeve shirts are:

Direct materials...	24 yards @ $ .55	$13.20
Direct labor..	3 hours @ $4.90	14.70
Factory overhead	3 hours @ $2.00	6.00
Standard cost per dozen..........................		$33.90

During October, Ross worked on three orders for long-sleeve shirts. Job cost records for the month disclose the following:

Lot	Units in Lot	Materials Used	Hours Worked
30	1,000 dozen	24,100 yards	2,980
31	1,700 dozen	40,440 yards	5,130
32	1,200 dozen	28,825 yards	2,890

The following information is also available:

- **(a)** Ross purchased 95,000 yards of materials during the month at a cost of $53,200. The materials price variance is recorded when goods are purchased and all inventories are carried at standard cost.
- **(b)** Direct labor incurred amounted to $54,450 during October. According to payroll records, production employees were paid $4.95 per hour.
- **(c)** Overhead is applied on the basis of direct labor hours. Factory over-

head totaling $22,800 was incurred during October.

(d) A total of $288,000 was budgeted for overhead for the year based on estimated production at the plant's normal capacity of 48,000 dozen shirts per year. Overhead is 40 percent fixed and 60 percent variable at this level of production.

(e) There was no work in process at October 1. During October, Lots 30 and 31 were completed, and all materials were issued for Lot 32, which was 80 percent completed as to labor.

Required: (1) Prepare a schedule computing the standard cost for October of Lots 30, 31, and 32. **(2)** Prepare a schedule computing the materials price variance for October and indicate whether the variance is favorable or unfavorable. **(3)** For each lot produced during October, prepare schedules computing the following (and indicate whether the variances are favorable or unfavorable):

(a) Materials quantity variance in yards.
(b) Labor efficiency variance in hours.
(c) Labor rate variance in dollars.

(4) Prepare a schedule computing the total budget and volume overhead variances for October and indicate whether the variances are favorable or unfavorable.

(AICPA adapted)

9-5. Schedule of production and standard cost; variance analysis; mix and yield variances. Conti Pharmaceutical Company processes a single compound-product known as NULAX and uses a standard cost accounting system. The process requires preparation and blending of three materials in large batches with a variation from the standard mixture sometimes necessary to maintain quality. Conti's cost accountant became ill at the end of October and you were engaged to determine standard costs of October production and explain any differences between actual and standard costs for the month. The following information is available for the Blending Department:

(a) The standard cost card for a 500-pound batch shows the following standard costs:

	Quantity	Price	Total Cost	
Materials:				
Mucilloid	250 lbs.	$ .14	$35	
Dextrose..................................	200 lbs.	.09	18	
Ingredients	50 lbs.	.08	4	
Total per batch	500 lbs.			$ 57
Labor:				
Preparation and blending	10 hours	$6.00		60
Factory Overhead:				
Variable.....................................	10 hours	$1.00	$10	
Fixed	10 hours	.30	3	13
Total standard cost per 500-pound batch				$130

(b) During October, 410 batches of 500 pounds each of the finished compound were completed and transferred to the Packaging Department.

(c) Blending Department inventories totaled 6,000 pounds at the beginning of the month and 9,000 pounds at the end of the month (assume both inventories were completely processed but not transferred, and consisted of materials in their standard proportions). Inventories are carried in the accounts at standard cost prices.

(d) During the month of October, the following materials were purchased and put into production:

	Pounds	Price	Total Cost
Mucilloid	114,400	$.17	$19,448
Dextrose..	85,800	.11	9,438
Ingredients	19,800	.07	1,386
Total	220,000		$30,272

(e) Wages paid for 4,212 hours of direct labor at $6.25 per hour amounted to $26,325.

(f) Actual overhead costs for the month totaled $5,519.

(g) The standards were established for a normal production volume of 200,000 pounds (400 batches) of NULAX per month. At this level of production, variable factory overhead was budgeted at $4,000 and fixed factory overhead was budgeted at $1,200.

Required: (1) Prepare a schedule for the Blending Department presenting the computations of the following:

(a) October production in both pounds and batches.

(b) The standard cost of October production itemized by components of materials, labor, and overhead.

(2) Prepare schedules computing the differences between actual and standard costs and analyzing the differences as:

(a) Materials variances (for each material) caused by:
   (1) Quantity difference.
   (2) Price difference.

(b) Labor variances caused by:
   (1) Efficiency difference.
   (2) Rate difference.

(c) Overhead variances caused by:
   (1) Budget factors.
   (2) Volume factors.

(3) Calculate materials mix and yield variances.

(AICPA adapted)

9-6. Analyses. On May 1, Bovar Company began the manufacture of a new mechanical device known as "Dandy." The company installed a standard cost system in accounting for manufacturing costs. The standard costs for a unit of Dandy are as follows:

Raw materials (6 lbs. @ $1 per lb.)..	$ 6
Direct labor (1 hour @ $6 per hour)...	6
Overhead (50% of direct labor costs)...	3
	$15

The following data were obtained from Bovar's records for the month of May:

	Units
Actual production of Dandy	4,000
Units sold of Dandy	2,500

	Debit	Credit
Sales		$50,000
Purchases (26,000 pounds)	$27,300	
Materials price variance	1,300	
Materials quantity variance	1,000	
Direct labor rate variance	760	
Direct labor efficiency variance		1,200
Manufacturing overhead total variance	500	

The amount shown above for materials price variance is applicable to raw materials purchased during May.

Required: Compute each of the following items for Bovar for the month of May. Show computations in good form.
(1) Standard quantity of raw materials allowed (in pounds).
(2) Actual quantity of raw materials used (in pounds).
(3) Standard hours allowed.
(4) Actual hours worked.
(5) Actual direct labor rate.
(6) Actual total overhead.

(AICPA adapted)

9-7. Three-variance overhead analysis. Using the data provided in Problem 9-2, calculate the overhead cost variances under the three-variance method.

9-8. Variance analysis using the three-variance method for overhead costs. The Jones Furniture Company uses a standard cost system in accounting for its production costs.

The standard cost of a unit of furniture follows:

Lumber, 100 feet @ $150 per 1,000 feet		$15.00
Direct labor, 4 hours @ $5 per hour		20.00
Factory overhead: Fixed (15% of direct labor)	$3.00	
Variable (30% of direct labor)	6.00	9.00
Total unit cost		$44.00

The following flexible monthly overhead budget is in effect:

Direct Labor Hours	Estimated Overhead
5,200	$10,800
4,800	10,200
4,400	9,600
4,000 (normal capacity)	9,000
3,600	8,400

The actual unit costs for the month of December were as follows:

Lumber used (110 feet @ $120 per 1,000 feet).............................	$13.20
Direct labor (4¼ hours @ $5.12 per hour)	21.76
Factory overhead ($10,560 ÷ 1,200 units)	8.80
Total actual unit cost	$43.76

Required: Prepare a schedule which shows an analysis of each element of the total variance from standard cost for the month of December. (Use the three-variance method for overhead costs).

(AICPA adapted)

9-9. Journal entries; three-variance analysis; income statement. The Smith Company uses a standard cost system. The standards are based on a budget for operations at the rate of production anticipated for the current period. The company records in its general ledger variations in materials prices and usage, wage rates, and labor efficiency. The accounts for manufacturing costs reflect variations in activity from the projected rate of operations, variations of actual expense from amounts budgeted, and variations in the efficiency of production.

Current standards are as follows:

Direct materials:

Material A..	$1.20 per unit
Material B..	2.60 per unit
Direct labor..	6.05 per hour

	Special Widgets	Deluxe Widgets
Finished products (content of each unit):		
Material A..	12 units	12 units
Material B	6 units	8 units
Direct labor	14 hours	20 hours

The general ledger does not include a finished goods inventory account; costs are transferred directly from Work in Process to Cost of Goods Sold at the time finished products are sold.

The budget and operating data for the month of August are summarized as follows:

Budget:	
Projected direct labor hours	9,000
Fixed factory overhead...	$ 4,500
Variable factory overhead...	13,500
Selling expense	4,000
Administrative expense...	7,500
Operating data:	
Sales:	
500 special widgets..	$85,000
100 deluxe widgets..	25,000
Purchases:	
Material A — 8,500 units...	$ 9,725
Material B — 1,800 units	5,635

Materials requisitions:	**Material A**	**Material B**
Issued from stores:		
Standard quantity..	8,400 units	3,200 units
Over standard..	400 units	150 units
Returned to stores......................................	75 units	none

Direct labor hours:	
Standard	9,600 hours
Actual	10,000 hours

Wages paid:	Expenses:	
500 hours @ $6.10	Manufacturing............	$20,125
8,000 hours @ 6.00	Selling.......................	3,250
1,500 hours @ 5.90	Administrative............	6,460

Required: **(1)** Prepare journal entries to record operations for the month of August. Show computations of the amounts used in each journal entry. Materials purchases are recorded at standard. **(2)** Prepare an income statement for the month supported by an analysis of variations.

(AICPA adapted)

10

Cost Analysis for Management Decision Making

The features which distinguish cost accounting from managerial accounting are not well defined. To a great degree the differences between the two areas are subjective. Most cost accounting textbooks (including this textbook) give considerable attention to the managerial uses of cost data by interweaving the data uses and management needs as part of the discussions involving the cost systems. Most managerial accounting textbooks include at least some discussion of cost systems and the accumulation and processing of cost data. However, the more comprehensive the coverage of cost accounting systems (job order, process, and standard cost), the more analytical and methodical can be the approach to resolving the special problems which are encountered internally by manufacturing firms.

Most special studies which generate investigatory reports for management make use of the regularly accumulated cost data and at times also create required additional data. These reports are prepared for internal use and are not distributed to external parties. This additional, not-regularly-accumulated data require an understanding of new financial data terminology which is not regularly used in operational cost accounting systems. These terms are more appropriately identified with the special purpose reports and studies which are prepared exclusively for internal management decision making. In the sections that follow, these new terms will be described or defined in order to make them part of a working vocabulary.

DIRECT COSTING

The **direct costing method** charges the product with only the costs that vary directly with volume — direct materials, direct labor, and variable factory overhead. The term "direct costing" is generally accepted to identify the method; however, an equally descriptive term such as "variable costing" could be used.

Direct Costing v. Absorption Costing

The alternative to direct costing is the **absorption costing method** (the method used in the preceding nine chapters), whereby both fixed and variable expenses are charged to the product. The absorption, or "full cost," method charges the product with period costs, which are a function of time and are not affected by volume changes. **Period costs** are the costs that would be incurred whether or not products are manufactured. An example of a period cost is depreciation expense which has been calculated on a straight-line basis. The total amount of depreciation expense will be unchanged no matter what volume of production is attained.

Period costs include not only costs associated with the plant and its equipment but also the costs incurred to maintain the company organization. These costs, therefore, are both manufacturing and nonmanufacturing types which are incurred when the organization begins its operations and are continued throughout the firm's existence. The period costs represent the firm's fixed costs for a given period, and under direct costing they are charged against the income generated during the period.

To illustrate the differences between direct costing and absorption costing, assume the following conditions for a 3-month period:

Selling price per unit	$11
Variable cost per unit:	
Direct cost — materials	$ 2
— labor	2
Indirect cost — variable factory overhead	1
Variable cost per unit	$ 5
Fixed cost per unit:	
Fixed factory overhead for the year	$108,000
Normal production for the year in units	36,000
Fixed cost per unit — ($108,000 ÷ 36,000)	$ 3

	Units Produced	Units Sold
January	3,000	1,500
February	500	2,000
March	4,000	2,000

There are no beginning inventories for January.

The comparative production report in Illustration 10-1 shows that standard costs are being charged to the products. Note that under the traditional absorption costing method, the goods manufactured in January have absorbed the standard costs of the direct materials, direct labor, and both fixed and variable factory overhead, totaling $8 per unit. Under the direct costing method, the fixed factory overhead is not charged to the manufacturing process, resulting in a unit cost of $5.

COMPARATIVE PRODUCTION REPORT						
	January (3,000 units)		February (500 units)		March (4,000 units)	
	Absorption Costing	Direct Costing	Absorption Costing	Direct Costing	Absorption Costing	Direct Costing
Direct materials	$ 6,000	$ 6,000	$ 1,000	$ 1,000	$ 8,000	$ 8,000
Direct labor	6,000	6,000	1,000	1,000	8,000	8,000
Variable factory overhead...........	3,000	3,000	500	500	4,000	4,000
Fixed factory overhead	9,000	——	1,500	——	12,000	——
Total cost................................	$24,000	$15,000	$ 4,000	$ 2,500	$32,000	$20,000
Unit cost.................................	$8	$5	$8	$5	$8	$5

FIXED OVERHEAD ABSORPTION						
Average fixed factory overhead ...	$ 9,000	$ 9,000	$ 9,000	$ 9,000	$ 9,000	$ 9,000
Fixed factory overhead absorbed	9,000	——	1,500	——	12,000	——
Under- (over-) absorbed factory overhead.................................	—0—	$ 9,000	$ 7,500	$ 9,000	$(3,000)	$ 9,000

ILLUSTRATION 10-1   Comparison of Manufacturing Costs for Absorption and Direct Costing Methods

The illustration also presents a comparison of the average fixed factory overhead of $9,000 ($108,000 ÷ 12) per month with the amount that is applied to production, using each of the two methods. In January, 3,000 units are manufactured, and the manufacturing costs under absorption costing include $9,000 ($3 × 3,000) in fixed factory overhead. February manufacturing costs covering the 500 units produced include fixed factory overhead of $1,500, and the manufacturing costs for March include $12,000. The result of the overhead charges is that in February $7,500 of fixed expense is not absorbed in manufacturing costs; but in March, the fixed overhead is overabsorbed by $3,000. These variances of underabsorbed and overabsorbed factory overhead are reflected in the income statements for February and March as an addition to and a deduction from cost of goods sold, respectively. Under the direct costing method, no fixed factory overhead expenses are charged to production in any month. These fixed costs appear as an expense on each month's income statement.

An examination of the comparative income statements in Illustration 10-2 reveals the effect that fluctuating production has on reported income under the absorption costing method. Although sales in February are higher than in January, the net income decreased from $2,500 in January to a net loss of $3,500 in February under the absorption method. This decrease is caused in part by adding $7,500 of underabsorbed overhead at the end of February to the cost of goods sold.

COMPARATIVE INCOME STATEMENTS
For Three Months Ended March 31, 19--

	January		February		March	
	Absorption Costing	Direct Costing	Absorption Costing	Direct Costing	Absorption Costing	Direct Costing
	(1,500 units)		(2,000 units)		(2,000 units)	
Sales	$16,500	$16,500	$22,000	$22,000	$22,000	$22,000
Cost of goods sold	12,000	7,500	16,000	10,000	16,000	10,000
Under- (over-) absorbed factory overhead	——	——	7,500	——	(3,000)	——
Gross margin (loss)	$ 4,500		$(1,500)		$ 9,000	
Contribution margin*		$ 9,000		$12,000		$12,000
Fixed factory overhead..........................		9,000		9,000		9,000
Selling and administrative expenses	2,000	2,000	2,000	2,000	2,000	2,000
Net income (loss)	$ 2,500	$(2,000)	$(3,500)	$ 1,000	$ 7,000	$ 1,000

COMPARATIVE SCHEDULE OF COST OF GOODS SOLD
For Three Months Ended March 31, 19--

Finished goods inventory, January 1	——	——	$12,000	$ 7,500	——	——
Cost of goods manufactured..................	$24,000	$15,000	4,000	2,500	$32,000	$20,000
Goods available for sale.........................	$24,000	$15,000	$16,000	$10,000	$32,000	$20,000
Less finished goods inventory, March 31.	12,000	7,500	——	——	16,000	10,000
Cost of goods sold	$12,000	$ 7,500	$16,000	$10,000	$16,000	$10,000

*Contribution margin is a term commonly used in direct costing to denote the excess of revenue over variable costs.

ILLUSTRATION 10-2   Comparison of Net Income for Absorption and Direct Costing Methods

In March the sales are the same as in February, but reported net income increased from a $3,500 net loss in February to a $7,000 net income in March. This increase is due to the increased production which caused considerably more of the fixed factory overhead to be absorbed in product cost in March than in February. In fact, overhead is overabsorbed in March, and this overabsorption is shown as a decrease in cost of goods sold on the March statement.

A study of the income statement under the direct costing method shows that as sales increase in February, income also increases. When sales remain the same in March as they were in February, income does not change.

With the absorption costing method, inventories are normally reported at a higher figure than under the direct costing method, because fixed costs are deferred by being included in the cost of inventory. This element of fixed cost will not be reported as a deduction from revenue until the goods are sold and the unit cost becomes an expense in the cost of goods sold section of the income statement. Under the direct costing method, no fixed costs are deferred; they are charged against revenue in the period in which they are incurred.

Merits and Limitations of Direct Costing

The merits of direct costing may be viewed in terms of the usefulness of the data obtained from it as well as its conformity with accepted accounting theory.

Some members of company management believe that the direct costing method furnishes more understandable data regarding costs, volumes, revenues, and profits to a management not expert in accounting techniques and procedures. It presents the cost data as they are related to revenue in a simplified form without distorting profits during periods of fluctuating production and sales, since variable production costs will tend to move in the same direction as sales. Furthermore, management planning is aided, because direct costing presents a much clearer picture of the effect of additional production on costs and income. From the production report on page 386, management can ascertain that any units produced and sold over and above normal production will cost $5 each and will therefore produce a gross profit of $6 each. Management may find that it can get additional orders for goods by selling the units at a special price of $9. In periods of low production, when plant capacity is not being fully utilized, production and sale of these additional items can produce an additional income of $4 per unit.

Although direct costing has attracted an increasing amount of attention, it is still a controversial subject, because it does not conform to accepted accounting theory. The measurement of income, in traditional accounting theory, is based on the matching of revenue with associated costs. Under absorption costing, product costs include all variable and nonvariable costs. These costs are matched with the sales revenue in the period in which the goods are sold. The direct cost method, however, matches only the variable manufacturing costs with revenue.

There are other limitations and criticisms of direct costing. Even when sophisticated statistical techniques are used to separate costs into variable and fixed groups, these techniques may lead to erroneous conclusions. The procedures often use historical data adjusted for future expectations in order to establish the groups; but unforeseen occurrences may have a significant effect on such established cost categories. To avoid overlooking significant changes in cost behavior patterns, therefore, a systematic review of the costs and the statistical techniques should be provided in the system. Any unexpected change can then be analyzed for its effect on the categories of costs so that faulty data will not be used in the formulation of company directives.

Direct costing is also criticized because no fixed factory overhead cost is included in work in process or finished goods inventories. In the opinion of the direct costing opponents, both fixed and variable costs are incurred in manufacturing products. Since the inventory figures do not reflect the total cost of production, they do not present a realistic cost valuation.

Adjustments can be made to the inventory figures to reflect actual cost on published financial reports while retaining the benefits of direct costing internally for income analysis purposes. In the example given, the unit cost was $5 under the direct costing method and $8 under the absorption method. The latter method reflects 60% more cost than the first method; therefore, inventories could be adjusted as follows:

	Ending Inventory Under the Direct Costing Method	Direct-Absorption Cost Ratio ($8 ÷ $5)	Ending Inventory Under the Absorption Costing Method
January	$ 7,500	×160%	$12,000
February	None		None
March	$10,000	×160%	$16,000

Direct costing for external reports has not received wide recognition because it is not accepted by many authorities. For example, it has not been discussed directly in any of the American Institute of Certified Public Accountants' research bulletins. In Accounting Research Bulletin No. 43, which deals with acceptable inventory costs, it is implied that fixed cost should be included as a part of the factory overhead in inventory cost. The American Accounting Association, in its 1957 Revision of Accounting and Reporting Standards for Corporate Financial Statements, states that the omission of any element of manufacturing cost is not acceptable. The regulations of the Internal Revenue Code specifically bar the use of direct costing. The National Association of Accountants, which is primarily interested in reporting the practices of firms and does not issue judgments on accounting practices, seems to be the only major accounting group which favors direct costing.

SEGMENT REPORTING FOR PROFITABILITY ANALYSIS

Segment reporting provides data which can be used by management to evaluate the operations and profitability of individual segments within a company. A **segment** may be a division, a product line, a sales territory, or other identifiable organizational unit.

The results of a segment profitability analysis may be questioned as to validity if it is based on absorption costing data. This is due to the fact that the measure of each company segment's profitability may be distorted by arbitrarily assigning indirect costs to the segments being examined. The contribution margin approach (as used in direct costing), which separates the fixed and variable elements that comprise cost, is often used to overcome these objections.

Segment profitability analysis requires that all costs be classified into one of two categories: direct or indirect. A **direct (traceable) cost** is a cost that can be traced to the segment being analyzed. Direct costs include both variable and fixed costs that are directly identifiable with a specific segment. An **indirect cost** is a nontraceable cost, which is referred to in segment analysis as a **common cost**. Under the contribution margin approach, only those costs which are directly traceable to a segment are assigned to the segment. The excess of segment revenue over direct costs assigned to the segment is the **segment margin**. Common costs are excluded from the computation of the segment margin.

Although common costs cannot be directly identified with a specific segment, they are identifiable as common to all segments at a particular level of an organization. Often the differences between direct and common costs are not markedly distinctive; however, the costs which will disappear when the segment is eliminated by the company should be classified as direct costs. Costs which are difficult to classify should not be assigned without a careful evaluation.

The more refinement and sophistication attempted in segment reporting, the larger the amount of costs that will become common costs. For instance, if a company consists of two divisions, each division manager's salary would be a direct cost to each division. However, if each division manufactured two products, each division's product segment report would classify the manager's salary as a common cost. An arbitrary allocation of the manager's salary to a product would distort the profitability shown for each product.

The following is an illustration of two segment reports: (1) by divisions and (2) by products for one of the divisions. The assumed company is divided into two divisions, and each division manufactures two products.

SEGMENT REPORT BY DIVISIONS

SEGMENT REPORT BY PRODUCTS — DIVISION ONE

	Total Company	Division One	Division Two	Total Division One	Product A	Product B
Sales..................................	$1,000,000	$750,000	$250,000	$750,000	$500,000	$250,000
Less variable costs	700,000	600,000	100,000	600,000	400,000	200,000
Contribution margin.............	$ 300,000	$150,000	$150,000	$150,000	$100,000	$ 50,000
Less direct fixed costs:						
Production........................	$ 50,000	$ 25,000	$ 25,000	$ 20,000	$ 15,000	$ 5,000
Administration	75,000	40,000	35,000	15,000	10,000	5,000
Total direct fixed costs.......	$ 125,000	$ 65,000	$ 60,000	$ 35,000	$ 25,000	$ 10,000
Segment margin...................	$ 175,000	$ 85,000	$ 90,000	$115,000	$ 75,000	$ 40,000
Less common fixed costs:						
Selling..............................	$ 30,000					
Production........................				$ 5,000		
Administration	20,000			25,000		
Total common fixed costs...	$ 50,000			$ 30,000		
Segment margin..................				$ 85,000		
Net income........................	$ 125,000					

An analysis of the segment report by divisions reveals that the division segment margin was $175,000 for the total company. Division One contributed $85,000 to the margin and Division Two, $90,000. The direct fixed costs chargeable to the divisions totaled $125,000, and the nonallocated common fixed costs totaled $50,000.

When Division One is isolated and analyzed to determine how each product contributed to the segment margin of $85,000, the direct fixed costs chargeable to the individual products amount to $35,000. Product A is charged $25,000 and Product B, $10,000. Division One has nonallocated common fixed costs of $30,000, not directly chargeable to either product.

These reports reveal how costs shift from one category to another depending on the segment under scrutiny. Each segment report prepared for a company isolates those costs, variable and fixed, that can be charged directly to the segment elements. As different segments are analyzed, these costs may be direct costs in one segment and indirect (common) costs in another segment.

The divisions' contribution margins are determined by subtracting the variable costs from the sales. The contribution margin can be used as a guide in making management decisions in regard to short-run problems such as pricing of special orders.

The direct fixed costs which are chargeable to each segment are subtracted from the contribution margin to determine the segment margin. The segment margin can be used as a guide relating to the segment's long-run profitability. In other words, it measures the ability of the division or product to recover not only the assigned variable costs but also the direct fixed costs which must be recovered in order to keep the company solvent in the long-run.

The remaining revenue, after direct variable and fixed costs have been deducted, is the amount left to be applied toward the unallocated common costs and the net income of the company as a whole. The segment margin analysis is particularly beneficial as an aid to making decisions which relate to a company's long-run requirements and performance, such as changing production capacities, product pricing policies, and selecting a segment's expected return on investment.

COST-VOLUME-PROFIT ANALYSIS

The net income earned by a business is a measure of management's success in attaining its goals. In planning, management must anticipate how selling prices, costs, expenses, and profits will react to changes in activity with the activity measured in terms of capacity or volume. When the degree of variability in costs is known, the effect of volume changes can be predicted.

Cost-volume-profit analysis is an analytical technique which uses the degrees of cost variability for measuring the effect of changes in volume on resulting profits. Such analysis assumes that the plant assets of the firm will remain the same in the short-run; therefore, the established level of fixed cost will also remain unchanged during the period being studied.

Break-Even Analysis

The usual starting point in C-V-P analysis is the determination of a firm's break-even point. The **break-even point** can be defined as the point at which sales revenue is adequate to cover all costs to manufacture and sell the product but no profit is earned. The equation can be stated as follows:

Sales revenue (to break even) = Cost to manufacture + Cost to sell

Break-even analysis relies on segregating costs according to their degree of variability. The established groupings are usually classed as variable and fixed costs and expenses, and the break-even equation is rewritten as follows:

$$\text{Sales revenue (to break even)} = \text{Fixed costs} + \text{Variable costs}$$

The annual income statement for the Comco Manufacturing Company in condensed form is shown below.

COMCO MANUFACTURING COMPANY
Income Statement
For the Year Ended December 31, 19--

Net sales (10,000 units at $10)		$100,000
Cost of goods sold:		
Materials	$20,000	
Labor	25,000	
Factory overhead	15,000	60,000
Gross margin on sales..		$ 40,000
Operating expenses:		
Selling expense	$15,000	
Administrative expense	10,000	25,000
Net income		$ 15,000

The costs and expenses of the Comco Manufacturing Company were analyzed and classified as follows:

Items	Total	Variable Costs	Fixed Costs
Materials...	$20,000	$20,000	
Labor...	25,000	25,000	
Factory overhead.................................	15,000	10,000	$ 5,000
Selling expense....................................	15,000	10,000	5,000
Administrative expense.........................	10,000	5,000	5,000
	$85,000	$70,000	$15,000

The analysis shows that variable costs are 70% of net sales ($70,000 ÷ $100,000).

The break-even equation in mathematical terms is as follows:

$$\text{Break-even sales volume} = \frac{\text{Total fixed costs}}{1 - (\text{Total variable costs} \div \text{Total sales volume})}$$

Using this equation, the break-even point for the Comco Manufacturing Company would be:

$$\text{Break-even sales volume} = \frac{\$15,000}{1 - (\$70,000 \div \$100,000)}$$

$$= \frac{\$15,000}{1 - .70}$$

$$= \frac{\$15,000}{.30}$$

$$= \$50,000$$

The break-even point can also be calculated in terms of units by using the following equation:

$$\text{Break-even sales volume} = \frac{\text{Total fixed cost}}{\text{Sales price per unit} - \text{Variable cost per unit}}$$

Using this equation, the break-even point for the Comco Manufacturing Company would be:

$$\text{Break-even sales volume} = \frac{\$15,000}{\$10 - \$7}$$

$$= \frac{\$15,000}{\$3}$$

$$= 5,000 \text{ units}$$

The break-even point can be rechecked, if desired, as follows:

Sales at break-even point	$50,000
Less variable costs at break-even point (70% × $50,000)	35,000
Margin available for fixed costs	$15,000
Less fixed costs	15,000
Net income (loss)	—0—

Break-Even Chart. The break-even point can also be graphically depicted by a break-even chart as in Illustration 10-3. A fixed cost line, a total cost line, and a sales revenue line are plotted on the chart, and the point at which the cost and sales lines intersect is the break-even point.

Break-Even Analysis for Management Decisions. Break-even analysis can be used to help management when a decision must be made and several alternatives exist. This analysis is based on the conditions that variable costs will vary in constant proportion to the sales volume and the fixed costs will be fixed over a prescribed range of activity. If management, therefore, wishes to test new proposals that will change the percentage of variable costs to sales volume, or

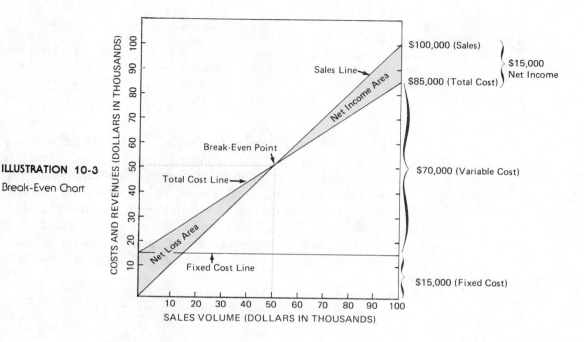

ILLUSTRATION 10-3
Break-Even Chart

the total amount of fixed costs, or even a combination of these changes, the basic break-even equation can be used to calculate the results.

For example, assume that the Comco Manufacturing Company, now that it has established its break-even point in sales volume at $50,000, wishes to determine the point at which an $18,000 net income can be expected. The $18,000 net income is viewed as a nonvariable factor, and the sales volume would be calculated as follows, using a modified equation:

$$\text{Sales volume} = \frac{\text{Total fixed costs} + \text{Net income}}{1 - (\text{Total variable costs} \div \text{Total sales volume})}$$

$$= \frac{\$15,000 + \$18,000}{1 - (\$70,000 \div \$100,000)}$$

$$= \frac{\$33,000}{1 - .70}$$

$$= \frac{\$33,000}{.30}$$

$$= \$110,000$$

The new conditions can be checked, in income statement form, as follows:

Sales	$110,000
Less variable costs (70% × $110,000)	77,000
Margin available for nonvariable factors...................................	$ 33,000
Less fixed costs	15,000
Net income	$ 18,000

Further assume that the management of Comco Manufacturing Company, fearing that changing economic conditions may make it difficult for the company to attain the present sales volume, wants to analyze the effect on the break-even point of increasing the percentage of variable costs to sales and lowering the fixed costs. The management believes that fixed costs can be reduced to $5,000, with a corresponding increase in the percentage of variable costs to 80%.

The break-even sales volume calculated with these conditions is as follows:

$$\text{Break-even sales volume} = \frac{\$5,000}{1 - .80}$$

$$= \frac{\$5,000}{.20}$$

$$= \$25,000$$

If the proposed shift from fixed costs to variable costs is accomplished, the break-even point is reduced from $50,000 to $25,000. The higher the variable costs, the smaller the risk of not attaining the expected break-even point. On the other hand, if the sales volume exceeds expectations, a large portion of the sales revenue will be used to cover the variable costs, and therefore a smaller net income must be anticipated.

To illustrate, assume the Comco Manufacturing Company achieves a sales volume of $200,000; with a variable cost percentage of 70%, the net income would amount to $45,000. If the fixed costs were reduced to $5,000 and the variable cost percentage increased to 80%, the profit would be only $35,000, a reduction of $10,000 at the same sales volume.

	Variable Cost Rate	
	70%	**80%**
Sales...	$200,000	$200,000
Variable costs	140,000	160,000
Margin available for nonvariable factors	$ 60,000	$ 40,000
Fixed costs	15,000	5,000
Net income...	$ 45,000	$ 35,000

Contribution Margin Ratio and Margin of Safety

Two terms frequently used in cost-volume-profit relationships are *contribution margin* and *margin of safety*. The **contribution margin** is the difference between the sales revenue and the total variable costs and expenses. When an income statement depicts the contribution margin, it can be used by management as a tool for studying the effects of changes in sales volume. The **contribution margin ratio**, which is also referred to as the **profit-volume ratio**, is the relationship of contribution margin to sales. The profit-volume ratio, however, is a misleading term, since the ratio is not determined by dividing profits by sales, nor can it be applied to sales revenue to estimate profits and losses.

The **margin of safety** indicates the amount that sales can decrease before the company will suffer a loss. The **margin of safety ratio** is a relationship computed by dividing the difference between the total sales and the break-even point sales by the total sales.

The following data are used to illustrate the two terms:

Sales (10,000 units @ $100)	$1,000,000	100%
Variable costs	600,000	60
Contribution margin	$ 400,000	40%
Fixed costs	300,000	30
Net income	$ 100,000	10%

The contribution margin is $400,000. The contribution margin ratio is calculated as follows:

$$\text{Contribution margin ratio} = \frac{\text{Total sales} - \text{Variable costs}}{\text{Total sales}}$$

$$= \frac{\$1,000,000 - \$600,000}{\$1,000,000}$$

$$= \frac{\$400,000}{\$1,000,000}$$

$$= 40\%$$

Using the contribution margin ratio of 40%, the break-even point can be calculated as follows:

$$\text{Break-even sales volume} = \frac{\text{Fixed costs}}{\text{Contribution margin ratio}}$$

$$= \frac{\$300,000}{.40}$$

$$= \$750,000$$

The margin of safety ratio (M/S) is calculated as follows:

$$\text{Margin of safety ratio} = \frac{\text{Total sales} - \text{Break-even sales volume}}{\text{Total sales}}$$

$$= \frac{\$1,000,000 - \$750,000}{\$1,000,000}$$

$$= \frac{\$250,000}{\$1,000,000}$$

$$= 25\%$$

Using the previous data, the margin of safety is 25% of the total sales, or $250,000. If the break-even sales equal $750,000 but the total expected sales are $1,000,000, the M/S ratio shows that the $1,000,000 in sales can decline by 25% before it reaches the firm's break-even level.

Since the margin of safety is directly related to net income, the M/S ratio can be used to calculate the net income as follows:

$$\text{Net income} = \text{Contribution margin ratio} \times \text{Margin of safety ratio}$$
$$= 40\% \times 25\%$$
$$= 10\%$$

If the contribution margin ratio and the net income percentage have been calculated, the margin of safety ratio can then be determined as follows:

$$\text{Margin of safety ratio} = \frac{\text{Net income percentage}}{\text{Contribution margin ratio}}$$

$$= \frac{.10}{.40}$$

$$= 25\%$$

Cost-Volume-Profit Limitations

Cost-volume-profit analysis assumes that all factors used in the analysis except volume will remain constant for a given period of time. This assumption may be questioned, for it is unrealistic to assume that the established relationship between sales and production will remain as forecast, or even that the sales mix, as established, will remain constant. Some costs and expenses are relatively unpredictable except over very limited ranges of activity. Even price changes that have not been predicted can occur, and the outcome will be substantially affected.

The results from a cost-volume-profit analysis must be interpreted by giving recognition to the basic assumption that the analysis is based on static relationships. Anticipated results depend on the stability of the relationships as they have been established. If a fairly stable set of relationships cannot be established, a series of analyses should be prepared which recognizes the changing sets of circumstances.

COSTS FOR DECISION MAKING

In the previous discussion, it was stated that management, in forecasting, must give recognition to how selling prices, costs and expenses, and profits will react to activity (volume) changes in a firm. However, there are many kinds of problems that are not exclusively associated with activity. In such problems, the analyst is responsible for supplying the quantitative information that will reflect the effect of the alternative choices available in a given situation. These problems may be associated with the expansion or contraction of operations (deleting or adding products), increasing or decreasing the volume of a product or a product line, changing the channel of distribution (selling to wholesalers or selling directly to retailers), selecting between alternative raw materials, selling or further processing a product, and so on. Some of the cost concepts which are related to these problems are discussed in the following section.

Relevant Costs

When comparing alternatives, **relevant costs** are those costs which are expected to differ from one alternative to another. Other terms are often used for relevant costs, such as **marginal costs**, **differential costs**, and **incremental costs**, but whatever the term used, these costs will change according to the choice of alternatives.

Costs which are not affected by the choice to be made are termed **irrelevant costs**. For example, assume that the use of a higher quality material is being considered in order to reduce losses from spoiled and defective materials. Such costs as insurance, depreciation, and property tax on the plant would probably not be changed by the decision; therefore, these costs would be disregarded for purposes of comparing alternatives. The relevant and irrelevant costs must be carefully isolated so that management can make the most satisfactory decision.

Escapable and Inescapable Costs

Many costs which are directly chargeable to an operating department would be eliminated if that department's operations were discontinued. These costs are called **escapable costs**. The costs that would be merely shifted or apportioned to the remaining operational departments are called **inescapable costs**. Escapable and inescapable classifications of departmental costs are important when management is considering whether or not to discontinue a product, a departmental operation, or a company division or plant.

For example, if a production department in a manufacturing plant is discontinued, the direct materials, direct labor, and factory overhead created by the department's operations would be eliminated. These costs are escapable. However, the apportioned costs, such as depreciation on the building and the department's share of the heat, light, and power, would be assigned to other departments and would thus be classified as inescapable.

Sunk Costs

A **sunk cost** is the investment that has been made in a tangible productive asset or an intangible right. This investment can be recovered only by using the asset over its service life. Sunk costs are historical costs that have been created by an irrevocable past decision which cannot be changed by any future decision.

For example, assume a replacement is being considered for a machine which originally cost $20,000 and has accumulated depreciation of $10,000. If the machine is scrapped, a loss of $10,000 would result. However, except for the effect on the income tax liability, such a loss should not be included in the consideration for replacement. The undepreciated book value of the existing asset is a sunk cost and is entirely irrelevant to the decision. In this case, the only pertinent information is a comparison of the effect of the two machines on income and the return on the additional investment. Recovery of the book value of the old asset is not possible; therefore, the asset may be considered to be used "free" in manufacturing operations. Although there would be a recorded loss if the asset is scrapped, this loss should be attached to a "wrong" decision of the past, not to the future use of the asset.

Out-of-Pocket Costs

Costs which will require additional cash expenditures immediately or in the future are called **out-of-pocket costs**. This condition is in contrast to sunk costs, in which the expenditure has already been made and will not be affected by the decision under consideration. Out-of-pocket costs are usually relevant costs because they vary with different alternatives.

Suppose a steel manufacturer maintains its own fleet of trucks to bring coke and coal to its mill. The company is considering selling the trucks and contracting with a private trucking firm for delivery of the required fuel. Irrelevant to this decision is the sunk cost of the investment in trucks. The relevant costs are the out-of-pocket costs that will be incurred by the contract and the future costs for maintenance, repairs, insurance, gasoline, tires, and oil that will be eliminated if the company decides to sell the trucks.

Imputed Costs and Opportunity Costs

In decision making, costs do not always involve cash expenditures. In some cases, additional costs must be assigned or imputed before a fair comparison between alternatives can be made. **Imputed costs** are hypothetical costs which are not recognized by the traditional accounting system. For example, interest expense is considered a cost only if it is paid or is part of a legal obligation, whereas the interest on capital invested in the firm is not usually recognized as a business cost. However, in the evaluation of a project, failure to give effect to the interest on capital investment may result in an erroneous decision.

Assume that a company is deciding which of two projects it will undertake — Project A, which requires an investment of $100,000, or Project B, requiring $120,000. Both projects are expected to return $30,000 of income, and the risk factors are equal. Using the value of money established by the company, the interest on capital could be directly included as part of the project cost.

Opportunity cost, another type of imputed cost, is the cost associated with a course of action that deprives the company of the opportunity to pursue some other course of action. For example, a company owns a vacant warehouse which is being considered for use as an additional manufacturing facility. The warehouse can be rented to another company for $50,000 per year. In evaluating the expansion proposal, a charge of $50,000 should be included as an opportunity cost.

Replacement Cost

The amount that was actually paid for an asset is its **historical cost**. The **replacement cost** is the cost of the same asset at current market prices or current construction costs. In periods of inflation, the use of historical costs results in an overstatement of profits, because part of the reported net income is being plowed back into the business as inventories and fixed assets are replaced at higher costs. For making some decisions, converting to replacement costs may be considered necessary in order to provide a more realistic measurement of profit.

Suppose inventories are purchased for $100,000 and later sold for $125,000. If no other expenses are incurred, a profit of $25,000 would be realized from the transaction. If, however, $110,000 is required to replace the inventory, there may be some argument whether the profit on the previous transaction was $25,000 or only $15,000. To further emphasize the importance of this inflationary factor, assume that the company has paid out the $25,000 profit as a dividend to its stockholders. It would then have to borrow $10,000 to replace the inventory.

Using only historical cost data, $25,000 is the amount subject to income taxes. Since an inflationary trend has been the economic tendency over the past few years, businesses would like to make replacement cost adjustments to historically-computed profits in order to lessen their income tax liabilities. Pressure is increasing to accept financial statements reported on a replacement cost basis because management believes that such statements more fairly represent the current financial position of their firms.

DIFFERENTIAL COST ANALYSIS

All management requirements cannot be satisfied by one concept or combination of cost data. The designated purpose for which a cost measurement is to be made needs to be studied carefully to determine what items should be included in a specific cost analysis. These studies should then provide a series of alternative solutions which compare different sets of relevant cost data. Studies which highlight the significant cost data of alternatives are referred to as **differential cost analyses**.

Assume a company, now operating at 80% capacity, has been asked by a one-time purchaser to sell additional units at less than its established sales price. A study would be made to determine the difference in costs at the two volume levels.

The company produces 30,000 units at 80% of its total capacity. Its fixed factory overhead costs are $20,000, and it sells each unit for $10. A new customer wishes to purchase 7,500 units for $4 per unit. Should the company agree to the terms or reject the offer?

The variable production costs per unit are:

Direct materials	$2.00
Direct labor	1.00
Variable overhead	.75
Total variable cost per unit	$3.75

At the present level of operations, the total production cost per unit is $4.42 ([(30,000 units × $3.75) + $20,000] ÷ 30,000 units). If the additional units are produced and fixed factory overhead cost is included, the unit cost would be $4.28 ([(37,500 units × $3.75) + 20,000] ÷ 37,500 units). Since the new customer is offering only $4 per unit, the company apparently should not accept such an offer.

However, if the fixed factory overhead cost is not considered and only the differential costs per unit are used, the offer of $4 would result in additional revenue of $.25 per unit. If the order is accepted, the overall gross margin would be increased by $1,875, as shown below.

	Accept Order	Reject Order
Sales:		
30,000 units @ $10	$300,000	$300,000
7,500 units @ $4	30,000	—0—
Total	$330,000	$300,000
Cost of goods sold	160,625*	132,500**
Gross margin on sales	$169,375	$167,500
*37,500 units × $3.75 (variable cost)		$140,625
Fixed cost		20,000
Total		$160,625
**30,000 units × $3.75 (variable cost)		$112,500
Fixed cost		20,000
Total		$132,500

The differential cost concept is applicable only when there is excess capacity that can be utilized at little or no increase in fixed cost. Also, in accepting additional orders at selling prices below the usual price levels, care should be exercised so that regular customers will not expect the same price treatment for their purchases.

Operation Versus Shutdown

Differential cost analysis can also be used to determine whether it is better to shut down a division or to operate at a loss.

Suppose a division is operating at 40% of capacity and producing 80,000 units. The March income statement shows the following:

Sales — 80,000 units @ $10		$800,000
Less:		
Variable costs — 80,000 units @ $8	$640,000	
Fixed costs	160,000	800,000
Net income		$ —0—

A new competitor has entered the market, so division management anticipates a decline from the March sales volume for the next few months. However, due to a strong advertising and sales effort now being undertaken, management feels that eventually the sales volume will increase, although there is little hope of increasing revenue in the immediate future. If the division is temporarily shut down, not all fixed costs can be eliminated. Estimates indicate that $60,000 of the $160,000 in fixed costs will be retained. Management states that it would like to continue production as long as the operating loss would be less than the shutdown cost.

Pro forma statements at various capacities show the following:

Capacity	0%	20%	25%	30%	35%	40%
Number of units	Shutdown	40,000	50,000	60,000	70,000	80,000
Sales ($10 per unit)	—0—	$400,000	$500,000	$600,000	$700,000	$800,000
Variable cost ($8 per unit)	—0—	320,000	400,000	480,000	560,000	640,000
Marginal contribution	—0—	$ 80,000	$100,000	$120,000	$140,000	$160,000
Fixed costs	$ 60,000	160,000	160,000	160,000	160,000	160,000
(Loss)	$(60,000)	$(80,000)	$(60,000)	$(40,000)	$(20,000)	$ —0—

Not until sales fall below the 50,000 unit level (25% of capacity) will the loss from continuing operations be greater than the cost of shutting down completely. The division should therefore continue operations as long as capacity is above 25%. Since an advertising campaign is being undertaken to improve the prestige of the product, an intangible factor worthy of consideration is keeping the product on the buyers' shelves, although it is presently unprofitable for the division.

Make or Buy Decisions

A company may buy a finished part that could perhaps be more economically manufactured in its own plant. For example, assume that 40,000 parts are purchased each month at a unit price of $1 per part. All the tools and necessary skills required for manufacturing this part are available in Department A.

Department A has a total potential capacity of 30,000 direct labor hours per month. The present capacity is 24,000 direct labor hours, or 80%. Analyses of its factory overhead costs are:

	Budgeted (80%) 24,000 Hours		Normal (100%) 30,000 Hours	
	Total Costs	Per Hour Costs	Total Costs	Per Hour Costs
Fixed costs	$ 72,000	$3.00	$ 72,000	$2.40
Variable costs	48,000	2.00	60,000	2.00
Total	$120,000	$5.00	$132,000	$4.40
Differential cost			$ 12,000	$ .60

The costs to manufacture 40,000 parts are:

Materials	$ 2,000
Labor, 6,000 Hours @ $4	24,000
Total	$26,000
Add differential cost	12,000
Total cost to manufacture parts	$38,000
Cost per unit, $38,000 ÷ 40,000	$ .95

Since Department A is presently operating at 80% of its total capacity, the company can save $2,000 ($40,000 − $38,000) by making the 40,000 parts rather than buying them. If the 80% capacity level in Department A is temporary, this factor must be considered before the final decision is made. The estimated savings may not be realized if the excess capacity of the department will soon be needed for the company's regularly manufactured products.

Equipment Replacement Decisions

An older machine may still have a substantial operating life remaining, but replacement may be considered when a newer, more efficient machine is being marketed. The company already owns the old machine; the decision to purchase it has already been made. The replacement decision, therefore, focuses on retaining the old or buying the new machine.

To illustrate, assume a machine was acquired 4 years ago for $70,000 and has an estimated remaining useful life of 10 years. The machine is depreciated on a straight-line basis and has no salvage value. The present book value of the machine is $50,000 ($70,000 − $20,000). A new machine is now being marketed that can produce the same number of units as the old machine, but at a substantially lower variable cost per unit. The new machine will cost $60,000 and is expected to last for 10 years and have no salvage value. A trade-in allowance of $12,000 will be received for the old machine.

The annual variable and fixed costs expected to be incurred in producing 100,000 units of product on the old and new machines are as follows:

	Old	New
Variable out-of-pocket costs	$70,000	$50,000
Fixed out-of-pocket costs	10,000	10,000
Depreciation	5,000	6,000
Total	$85,000	$66,000
Expected savings		$19,000
Cost per unit	$.85	$.66

The analysis does *not* give consideration to:

(1) The trade-in allowance.
(2) The fact that the new equipment is not required to maintain present production.
(3) The taxes to which part of the additional savings is subject.

Following is a revision of the analysis to include these considerations:

	Old	New
Variable out-of-pocket costs	$70,000	$50,000
Fixed out-of-pocket costs	10,000	10,000
Depreciation:		
1/10 of $12,000 (trade-in)*	1,200	
1/10 of $60,000		6,000
Additional costs for new machine:		
Interest on average investment**		4,800
Additional income taxes***		9,500
Total costs	$81,200	$80,300
Cost per unit	$.812	$.803

*Book value of old equipment, $50,000, is a sunk cost recoverable only through continued use. Cost of old equipment for decision purposes is trade-in value of $12,000, depreciated over remaining 10 years.

**Additional investment of $48,000 required for the new machine is removed from working capital. Assuming a rate of 10% can be earned on $48,000, the opportunity to earn $4,800 per year is being sacrificed.

***Assuming a 50% income tax rate — 50% of the expected annual savings ($19,000) would be paid out in taxes — $9,500.

It still appears that the company would save by acquiring the new machine, but the saving is not so large when the sunk cost and the opportunity cost are taken into consideration. If there are any other factors that will change if the new machine is purchased, they should also be included in the cost of the new machine as relevant costs. Such factors may include special electrical wiring, additional power costs, installation costs, and additional space costs.

Operate-the-Department or Lease-the-Space Decisions

A company may consider leasing space in which it has been operating a department. For example, assume that a large manufacturer maintains a hardware and supply department somewhat similar to a retail hardware store. The effort involved to maintain the department causes management to investigate the possibility of leasing this operation to an outside company that specializes in hardware sales. This hardware specialty firm has offered $20,000 annually for the lease. If the offer is accepted, the equipment presently in the department would be sold for a nominal amount.

The following figures reflect the revenue and expense for the hardware department; in addition to the operating expenses, an average inventory of $50,000 must be maintained.

	Hardware	Other Departments	Total
Gross margin on sales	$50,000	$1,000,000	$1,050,000
Operating expenses	40,000	850,000	890,000
Income before income taxes	$10,000	$ 150,000	$ 160,000

The decision whether or not to lease requires consideration of:

(1) The escapable and the inescapable expenses involved in eliminating the department.

(2) The sunk costs in equipment in the department.

(3) An imputed interest cost on the inventory investment that would be released to earn revenue if operations in the Hardware Department were eliminated.

The following are escapable and inescapable costs:

	Hardware	Other Departments	Total
Gross margin on sales	$50,000	$1,000,000	$1,050,000
Escapable costs:			
Salaries, supplies, bad debts, etc.	$22,000	$ 600,000	$ 622,000
Depreciation	1,000	30,000	31,000
Total escapable costs	$23,000	$ 630,000	$ 653,000
Inescapable costs:			
Building maintenance, utilities, office expenses, etc.	17,000	220,000	237,000
Total costs	$40,000	$ 850,000	$ 890,000
Income before income taxes	$10,000	$ 150,000	$ 160,000

When the Hardware Department is eliminated, the gross margin and the escapable costs of the department will vanish. The inescapable costs will become an added cost to the remaining departments, as shown below:

Gross margin on sales		$1,000,000
Less escapable costs		630,000
Total		$ 370,000
Less: Other departments — inescapable costs	$220,000	
Hardware Department — inescapable costs	17,000	237,000
Operating income		$ 133,000
Add other revenue:		
Lease rent	$ 20,000	
Interest on investment*	4,000	24,000
Income before income taxes		$ 157,000

*$50,000 (investment in inventory) × 8% (assumed annual interest rate) = $4,000

The depreciation expense charged to the Hardware Department reflects a sunk cost that is irrelevant to the decision; therefore, the $1,000 depreciation expense should be added to the income of the Hardware Department.

Income — including Hardware Department	$160,000
Add Hardware Department depreciation expense	1,000
Total income — including Hardware Department	$161,000
Income — leasing Hardware Department's space	157,000
Income — decrease	$ 4,000

The Hardware Department's contribution to the company's profitability may also be viewed as follows:

	Hardware
Gross margin on sales	$50,000
Less escapable costs — excluding depreciation	22,000
Remainder of gross margin	$28,000
Less: Lease rent $20,000	
Interest on investment 4,000	24,000
Hardware Department's contribution	$ 4,000

It appears that an offer of $20,000 for a department earning only $10,000 should be accepted, according to the financial data gathered by the traditional accounting system. However, when costs of the department are classified as escapable and inescapable, the attractiveness of the lease offer is diminished. Even considering the potential revenue from the lease rental and the interest on investment, the net productivity of the space, as measured by the net income, is not enhanced by leasing. In fact, the company would lose $4,000 from its overall earnings if the department were eliminated.

DISTRIBUTION COSTS

Cost accounting is frequently thought of as a method of accounting only for the costs of manufacturing. However, "cost," as a general term, covers more than merely manufacturing costs; it should include all of the costs of doing business. In other words, efficient control of all costs should cover both the production costs and the **distribution costs** — costs incurred to sell and deliver the product.

In recent years, state and federal laws prohibiting discriminatory sale prices and the problems of increasing competition, have forced accountants to devote more time to the study of distribution costs. An attempt is being made to determine, by means of close and careful analysis, the answers to such questions as:

1. How much of the selling and administrative expense is allocable to each type of product sold?
2. How much of the selling and administrative expense is allocable to each particular sales office?
3. How much of the selling and administrative expense is allocable to each salesperson?
4. How much of the selling and administrative expense is allocable to each order sold?

Allocating Distribution Costs

To illustrate some of the difficulties to be encountered, assume a company that sells bakery products also operates a fleet of delivery trucks to distribute the finished items. Each driver is a salesperson; therefore each truck is a combination sales and delivery truck. At each stop, the driver takes an order from the store manager for bread, cakes, cookies, and other bakery products carried on the truck and then stocks the shelves. In one store, fifteen minutes may be spent selling four dozen loaves of bread, two dozen breakfast rolls, and a dozen boxes of doughnuts; while in another store it may require forty-five minutes to sell only a dozen loaves of bread. Suppose the daily costs of the operation are: $50 for the salesperson-driver's salary; $30 for truck depreciation; $15 for gasoline and oil; and $5 for miscellaneous operating expenses.

How much of the total truck expense is chargeable to each sale? Should it be allocated on the basis of the number of sales made? Should it be allocated on the basis of the time spent at each stop by the driver? What is the cost of selling a loaf of bread, a dozen doughnuts, or a package of breakfast rolls?

These questions are not academic, and businesses devote a considerable amount of time attempting to arrive at meaningful answers to such questions. The following example will show the usefulness of distribution cost studies.

Assume that a company is making three products, A, B, and C. The manufacturing cost per unit is as follows:

A $10
B 15
C 5

During one month, 1,000 units of each product are sold at $15, $18, and $6 each, respectively. The gross margin for the month would be $9,000 ($39,000 − $30,000). If the selling and administrative expense for the month is $4,000, the net income for the month would be $5,000, a result which the management would probably regard as satisfactory.

Now assume that study indicates that the distribution cost per product is as follows:

Expense	A	B	C	Total
Selling expenses:				
Salaries	$ 300	$ 200	$ 300	$ 800
Commissions			500	500
Advertising	600	200	200	1,000
Telephone and telegraph	40		60	100
Sales manager's salary	133	133	134	400
Miscellaneous selling expense	127	17	56	200
Total selling expense	$1,200	$ 550	$1,250	$3,000
Administrative expense	300	350	350	1,000
Total	$1,500	$ 900	$1,600	$4,000
Cost per unit	$1.50	$.90	$1.60	

In order to arrive at these figures, it was necessary to make a study of the prevailing conditions and to allocate the various expenses to the products on some reasonable basis. For example, sales salaries might be allocated to the products on the basis of time reports showing the amount of time devoted to selling each product. Advertising might be allocated on the basis of the number of square inches of advertising space purchased for advertising each product. The sales manager's salary might be allocated evenly among the products. Miscellaneous selling expense might be allocated on the basis of the number of orders received for each product or the value of each product sold. There is no standard basis for allocating such expenses, but every effort should be made to use a reasonable basis for allocating each type of expense to the various products.

Using the cost and sales data on page 409, it becomes apparent that a profit is actually being made only on Products A and B. Product C is being sold at a loss. The following table, based on the sales for the month, shows the extent of the gain and loss:

Product	Cost to Make	Cost to Sell	Total Cost	Selling Price	Profit (Loss)
A	$10,000	$1,500	$11,500	$15,000	$3,500
B	15,000	900	15,900	18,000	2,100
C	5,000	1,600	6,600	6,000	(600)
Total	$30,000	$4,000	$34,000	$39,000	$5,000

As a result of the analysis of distribution costs, management determines that the company might make more money by selling less. If the sale of Product C were discontinued, the profit would be greater by the amount of the loss being sustained on C. However, if a more intensive study were undertaken, it may show that Products A and B could not sustain their profit margins if the costs charged to Product C had to be charged to A and B. Also, the intangible benefits derived from continuing to carry Product C must be given consideration.

Determining the Optimum Size of the Sales Force

Another distribution cost problem may be the determination of the optimum size of sales force a company should maintain. This problem requires a study of the marginal income that could result from hiring additional salespeople. The sales saturation point is reached when the marginal revenue from sales generated by one additional salesperson is less than the marginal costs that apply to that person.

Suppose three salespeople are used in a regional area where the following sales have been made during the past three years:

Salesperson	19X1	19X2	19X3
1	$128,000	$132,000	$135,000
2	94,000	98,000	100,000
3	90,000	95,000	95,000
	$312,000	$325,000	$330,000

The sales record of the three salespeople indicates that a dramatic increase in sales should not be expected, although sales have improved a small amount in total each year.

The total costs of the company are analyzed and classified into fixed and variable categories. The costs directly related to selling activities are then summarized to determine whether an increase or decrease in the number of salespeople would be justified. The analysis, which uses only variable factors, is as follows:

Number of Salespeople	Estimated Potential Sales	Variable Factory Costs	Sales Commissions	Other Variable Costs	Total Variable Costs	Marginal Sales	Marginal Costs	Marginal Profit or (Loss)
1	$135*	$ 65	$20.25	$ 25.90	$111.15	$135	$111.15	$23.85
2	235	120	35.25	45.20	200.45	100	89.30	10.70
3	330	170	47.25	73.40	290.65	95	90.20	4.80
4	410	225	57.00	97.60	379.60	80	88.95	(8.95)
5	480	270	66.00	127.30	463.30	70	83.70	(13.70)

*All figures are in thousands of dollars.

Each of the three salespeople employed by the company produces a marginal profit that ranges from $23,850 to $4,800. An additional salesperson should not be added, because that person's marginal contribution would be a loss of $8,950. Although the marginal costs will decline by increasing the volume, the sales dollars generated at the higher production levels are not adequate to improve the company's profitability. The fifth salesperson, for example, would add $70,000 to sales; but the additional costs of using the fifth person would be $83,700.

The preceding illustration shows how the size of a sales force can be determined. Often, however, this problem is resolved through intuition rather than by analysis of quantitative data, even though the problem is very significant for most businesses.

QUESTIONS

1. Distinguish between absorption costing and direct costing.
2. What effect will application of the direct costing method have on the income statement and the balance sheet?

3. What are the advantages and disadvantages derived from use of the direct costing method?
4. Why are there objections to using absorption costing when segment reports of profitability are being prepared?

5. What are common costs?

6. How is a contribution margin determined and of what importance is it to management?

7. What are considered direct costs in segment analysis?

8. What is generally the measure of success in a business?

9. What is cost-volume-profit analysis?

10. What is the break-even point?

11. Distinguish between contribution margin and the margin of safety ratio.

12. Distinguish between relevant and irrelevant costs.

13. Distinguish between escapable and inescapable costs?

14. Define sunk costs.

15. What are out-of-pocket costs?

16. Do all decision-making costs involve cash expenditures?

17. Distinguish between historical and replacement costs. Why are replacement costs becoming more important to many businesses today?

18. What is differential cost analysis?

19. What is the purpose of an operation versus shutdown study?

20. What is the importance of make or buy studies for a company?

21. What are the alternatives that should be considered in equipment replacement problems?

22. What are some of the important factors to be considered in operate or lease decisions?

23. What are distribution costs?

24. What is the purpose of the analysis of distribution costs?

25. In cost analysis, what governs which costs are to be included in the study?

EXERCISES

1. The Packaging Products Co. uses a process cost system and applies actual factory overhead to work in process at the end of the month. The following data are taken from the records for the month of January:

Direct materials	$200,000
Direct labor	$100,000
Variable factory overhead	$ 80,000
Fixed factory overhead	$120,000
Selling and administrative expenses	$ 40,000
Units produced	50,000
Units sold	40,000
Selling price per unit	$ 15

There were no beginning inventories and no work in process at the end of the month.

From the information presented above, determine the cost of the ending inventory; **(a)** Under the absorption costing method, and **(b)** under the direct costing method.

2. Using the information presented in Exercise 1, prepare comparative income statements for January **(a)** under absorption costing, and **(b)** under direct costing.

3. A company had income of $50,000 using direct costing for a given period. Beginning and ending inventories for the period were 13,000 units and 18,000 units, respectively. If the fixed overhead application rate was $2 per unit, what was the income using absorption costing?

4. The Shop Company is planning to produce two products, A and B. Shop is planning to sell 100,000 units of A at $4 a unit and 200,000 units of B at $3 a unit. Variable costs are 70% of sales for A and 80% of sales for B. In order to realize a total profit of $160,000, what must the total fixed costs be?

5. A company has prepared the following statistics regarding its production and sales at different capacity levels.

Capacity level............................	60%	80%	100%	120%
Units.....................................	60,000	80,000	100,000	120,000
Sales.....................................	$300,000	$400,000	$500,000	$600,000
Total costs:				
Variable.............................	$120,000	$160,000	$200,000	$240,000
Fixed.................................	200,000	200,000	200,000	200,000
Total costs..........................	$320,000	$360,000	$400,000	$440,000
Net profit (loss).......................	$(20,000)	$ 40,000	$100,000	$160,000

(a) At what point is break-even reached in sales? In capacity? (b) If the company is operating at 60% capacity, should it accept an offer from a customer to buy 10,000 units at $2 per unit?

6. The Zi-Toes Company manufactures a novelty product that sells for $1.95 per unit. A competitor is now producing a similar product; the demand for the Zi-Toes product has declined and the selling price has dropped to $1.25. Management is considering shutting down operations rather than continuing at a loss. A new product is being developed and will be marketed in the near future.

The 100% capacity level of the plant produces 200,000 units. The production costs are:

Variable costs (materials, labor, and factory overhead)............. $.90 per unit
Fixed costs... $70,000

If the plant is completely shut down, it is estimated that $20,000 of the fixed costs will still be incurred. At the new selling price of $1.25, it is estimated that 150,000 units can be sold.

(a) Should the plant continue to operate at a loss or shut down? Show computations. (b) When should shutdown occur?

7. Boyer Company manufactures basketballs. The forecasted income statement for the year before any special orders is as follows:

	Amount	Per Unit
Sales...	$4,000,000	$10.00
Manufacturing cost of goods sold...............................	3,200,000	8.00
Gross profit...	$ 800,000	$ 2.00
Selling expenses..	300,000	.75
Operating income...	$ 500,000	$ 1.25

Fixed costs included in the forecasted income statement are $1,200,000 in manufacturing cost of goods sold and $100,000 in selling expenses.

A special order offering to buy 50,000 basketballs for $7.50 each was made to Boyer. There will be no additional selling expenses if the special order is accepted. Assuming Boyer has sufficient capacity to manufacture 50,000 more basketballs, by what amount would operating income be increased or decreased as a result of accepting the special order?   (AICPA adapted)

8. Cardinal Company needs 20,000 units of a certain part to use in its production cycle. The following information is available:

Cost to Cardinal to make the part:	
Direct materials	$ 4
Direct labor	16
Variable factory overhead...	8
Fixed factory overhead applied	10
Total...	$38
Cost to buy the part from the Oriole Company........................	$36

If Cardinal buys the part from Oriole instead of making it, Cardinal could not use the released facilities in another manufacturing activity. Sixty percent of the fixed factory overhead applied will continue regardless of what decision is made.

In deciding whether to make or buy the part, what are the total relevant costs to make the part?   (AICPA adapted)

9. A company purchases a finished part that it could manufacture. This part is bought in quantities of 100,000 per month at a cost of $5 each. The department in which the part can be manufactured is now at 60% of its total capacity and its monthly factory overhead budget shows:

Capacity...................	60%	80%	100%	120%
Direct labor hours......	60,000	80,000	100,000	120,000
Variable costs	$120,000	$160,000	$200,000	$240,000
Fixed costs	240,000	240,000	240,000	240,000
Total....................	$360,000	$400,000	$440,000	$480,000

Estimates indicate that the additional costs for producing the finished part would include $1.00 per unit for materials and 40,000 hours of labor at $3.75 per hour.

This department has been operating at a level far below its total capacity for some time, and it is anticipated that the present level of operations will continue unless a new product is developed by the company which will require the use of this department.

Does it appear advisable to make or buy the finished part? Show computations.

10. Equipment that a company is considering replacing was purchased 3 years ago for $39,000. Its remaining useful life is estimated
to be 10 years with no salvage value. The new equipment will operate
more efficiently at a higher rate of speed, thereby reducing the variable operating costs. The new equipment will cost $50,000, have a
useful life of 10 years and no salvage value. A trade-in allowance of
$7,000 will be given for the old equipment. No additional costs for
removal of the old equipment and installation of the new equipment
are anticipated. The company pays income tax at the 50% rate and
estimates that it should earn 10% interest on its investments. The
following are estimated costs of the old and new equipment at the
normal 100,000 unit level:

	Old	New
Variable costs — out-of-pocket	$50,000	$40,000
Fixed costs — out-of-pocket	8,000	10,000
Depreciation	3,000	5,000
	$61,000	$55,000
Expected savings		$ 6,000
Cost per unit	$.61	$.55

Should the company replace the old equipment? Show computations.

11. A manufacturer has been offered a lease of $25,000 for space
now being used by a small division of the company. The leasing company will supply its own equipment and furnishings. The manufacturer
estimates interest on investment at the rate of 10%. An analysis
shows the following escapable and inescapable costs (the division to
be leased carries an average inventory of $80,000):

	Division to be Leased	Other Divisions	Total
Gross margin on sales	$50,000	$700,000	$750,000
Escapable costs:			
Other than depreciation	$30,000	$400,000	$430,000
Depreciation	3,000	40,000	43,000
	$33,000	$440,000	$473,000
Inescapable costs	10,000	140,000	150,000
Total costs	$43,000	$580,000	$623,000
Income before income tax	$ 7,000	$120,000	$127,000

Should the division be leased? Show computations.

12. The Dexter Manufacturing Co. wishes to determine the profitability of its products and asks the cost accountant to make a comparative
analysis of sales, cost of sales, and distribution costs of each product
for the year. The accountant gathers the following information which
will be useful in preparing the analysis:

	Product		
	X	Y	Z
Number of units sold	30,000	20,000	20,000
Number of orders received	5,000	2,500	1,000
Selling price per unit	$50	$75	$100
Cost per unit	$30	$50	$ 70

Advertising expenses total $600,000 for the year, an equal amount being expended to advertise each product. The sales representative's commission is based on the selling price of each unit and is 10% for Product X, 15% for Product Y, and 20% for Product Z. The sales manager's salary of $75,000 per year is allocated evenly to each product. Other miscellaneous selling and administrative expenses are estimated to be $10 per order received.

Prepare an analysis for the Dexter Manufacturing Co. that will show in comparative form the net income derived from the sale of each product for the year.

PROBLEMS

10-1. *Absorption and direct cost income statements.* The Rod Manufacturing Co. has determined the cost of manufacturing a unit of product to be as follows, based on normal production of 100,000 units per year:

Direct materials	$5	
Direct labor	4	
Variable factory overhead	3	$12
Fixed factory overhead		6
		$18

Operating statistics for the month of August and September are:

	August	September
Units produced	12,000	6,000
Units sold	6,000	10,000
Selling and administrative expense	$12,000	$12,000

The selling price is $20 per unit. There were no inventories on August 1, and there is no work in process at September 30.

Required: Prepare comparative income statements for each month under **(1)** the absorption costing method and **(2)** the direct costing method.

10-2. *Segmented income statement.* The Davcoe Manufacturing Company manufactures two products. Boeld and Knotboeld, which are sold in two territories designated by the company as East Territory and West Territory. The income statement prepared for the company shows the product line segments.

DAVCOE MANUFACTURING COMPANY
Income Statement

	Total Sales	Product Lines			
		Boeld		Knotboeld	
Sales............................	$1,000,000	$600,000	100%	$400,000	100.0%
Less variable expenses....	600,000	450,000	75	150,000	37.5
Contribution margin........	$ 400,000	$150,000	25%	$250,000	62.5%
Less direct fixed costs.....	200,000	50,000		150,000	
Segment margin	$ 200,000	$100,000		$100,000	
Less common fixed costs .	100,000				
Net income	$ 100,000				

The territorial product sales are:

	East	West
Boeld...	$400,000	$200,000
Knotboeld	200,000	200,000
Total....................................	$600,000	$400,000

The common fixed costs are partially identifiable with the East Territory, the West Territory, and the general administration as follows:

East Territory..	$ 40,000
West Territory	30,000
General administration....................................	30,000
Total common fixed costs	$100,000

Required: (1) Prepare a segmented income statement by territories. The direct fixed costs of the product lines should be treated as common fixed costs on the segmented statement being prepared. (2) What is the significance of this analysis?

10-3. Break-even analysis. The production of a new product required the Snowblo Manufacturing Company to lease additional plant facilities. Based on studies, the following data have been made available:

Estimated annual sales — 24,000 units

Estimated costs:	Amount	Per Unit
Materials	$ 96,000	$4.00
Direct labor	14,400	.60
Factory overhead	24,000	1.00
Administrative expense	28,800	1.20
Total	$163,200	$6.80

Selling expenses are expected to be 15% of sales and net income is to amount to $1.02 per unit.

Required: (1) The selling price per unit. (2) An income statement for the year. (3) A break-even point expressed in dollars and in units assuming that overhead and administrative expense are fixed but other costs are fully variable. *(AICPA adapted)*

10-4. Break-even point: absorption and direct cost analysis. The Jutson Company has a maximum productive capacity of 210,000 units per year. Normal capacity is 180,000 units per year. Standard variable manufacturing costs are $11 per unit. Fixed factory overhead is $360,000 per year. Variable selling expense is $3 per unit and fixed selling expense is $252,000 per year. The unit sales price is $20.

The operating results for the year are: sales, 150,000 units; production, 160,000 units; beginning inventory, 10,000 units; and the net unfavorable variance for standard variable manufacturing costs, $40,000. All variances are written off as additions to (or deductions from) the standard cost of sales.

Required: (1) What is the break-even point expressed in dollar sales? **(2)** How many units must be sold to earn a net income of $60,000 per year? **(3)** How many units must be sold to earn a net income of 10% on sales? **(4)** Prepare a formal income statement for the year under:

  (a) Absorption costing.   **(b)** Direct costing.

(5) Explain briefly the difference in net income between the two income statements.   *(AICPA adapted)*

10-5. Contribution margin and break-even analysis. Axa Company operates its production department only when orders are received for one or both of its products, two sizes of metal discs. The manufacturing process begins with the cutting of doughnut-shaped rings from rectangular strips of sheet metal; these rings are then pressed into discs. The sheets of metal, each 4 feet long and weighing 32 ounces, are purchased at $1.36 per running foot. The department has been operating at a loss for the past year as shown below:

Sales for the year..	$172,000
Expenses	177,200
Net loss for the department	$ (5,200)

The following information is available:

(a) Ten thousand 4-foot pieces of metal yielded 40,000 large discs, each weighing 4 ounces and selling for $2.90 and 40,000 small discs, each weighing 2.4 ounces and selling for $1.40.

(b) The company has been producing at less than normal capacity and has had no spoilage in the cutting step of the process. The skeletons remaining after the rings have been cut are sold for scrap at $.80 per pound.

(c) The variable conversion cost of each large disc is 80% of the disc's direct materials cost, and the variable conversion cost of each small disc is 75% of the disc's direct materials cost. Variable conversion costs are the sum of direct labor and variable overhead.

(d) Fixed costs were $86,000.

Required: (1) For each of the parts manufactured, prepare a schedule computing:

 (a) Unit materials cost after deducting the value of salvage

(b) Unit variable conversion cost
(c) Unit contribution margin
(d) Total contribution margin for all units sold

(2) Assuming you computed the materials cost for large discs at $.85 each and for small discs at $.51 each, compute the number of units the company must sell to break even based on a normal production capacity of 50,000 units. Assume no spoiled units and a product mix of one large disc to each small disc.

(AICPA adapted)

10-6. *Analysis of an unprofitable product.* The Creek Company manufactures and sells three different products — A, B, and C. Projected income statements by product line for the year ended December 31, are presented below:

	A	B	C	Total
Units sold	10,000	500,000	125,000	635,000
Sales	$925,000	$1,000,000	$575,000	$2,500,000
Variable cost of units sold	$285,000	$ 350,000	$150,000	$ 785,000
Fixed cost of units sold	304,200	289,000	166,800	760,000
Gross margin	$335,800	$ 361,000	$258,200	$ 955,000
Variable general and administrative expenses	$270,000	$ 200,000	$ 80,000	$ 550,000
Fixed general and administrative expenses	125,800	136,000	78,200	340,000
Income (loss) before income tax	$(60,000)	$ 25,000	$100,000	$ 65,000

Production costs are similar for all three products. The fixed general and administrative expenses are allocated to products in proportion to revenues. The fixed cost of units sold is allocated to products by various bases, such as square feet for factory rent and machine hours for repairs, etc.

The management is concerned about the loss for Product A and is considering two alternative courses of corrective action.

Alternative A — The company would purchase some new machinery for the production of Product A. This new machinery would involve an immediate cash outlay of $650,000. Management expects that the new machinery would reduce variable production costs so that total variable costs (cost of units sold and general and administrative expenses) for Product A would be 52% of Product A revenues. The new machinery would increase total fixed costs allocated to Product A to $480,000 per year. No additional fixed costs would be allocated to Products B or C.

Alternative B — The company would discontinue the manufacture of Product A. Selling prices of Products B and C would remain constant. Management expects that Product C production and revenues would increase by 50% . Some of the present machinery devoted to Product A could be sold at scrap value which equals its removal costs.

The removal of this machinery would reduce fixed costs allocated to Product A by $30,000 per year. The remaining fixed costs allocated to Product A include $155,000 of rent expense per year. The space previously used for Product A can be rented to an outside organization for $157,500 per year.

Required: Prepare a schedule analyzing the effect of Alternative A and Alternative B on projected total company income before income taxes.

(AICPA adapted)

10-7. Analysis of discontinuing an operation. The L & L Publishing Company is in the business of publishing and printing guide books and directories. The board of directors has engaged you to make a cost study to determine whether the company is economically justified in continuing to print, as well as publish, its books and directories. You obtain the following information from the company's cost accounting records for the preceding fiscal year:

| | **DEPARTMENTS** | | | |
	Publishing	Printing	Shipping	Total
Salaries and wages....................	$375,000	$200,000	$20,000	$ 595,000
Telephone and telegraph	22,000	6,000	1,000	29,000
Materials and supplies...............	100,000	400,000	20,000	520,000
Occupancy costs.......................	100,000	110,000	12,000	222,000
General and administrative expenses.................................	80,000	70,000	8,000	158,000
Depreciation...........................	10,000	80,000	10,000	100,000
	$687,000	$866,000	$71,000	$1,624,000

Additional data:

(a) A review of personnel requirements indicates that if printing is discontinued, the publishing department will need one additional clerk at $8,000 per year to handle correspondence with the printer. Two layout planners and a proofreader will be required at an aggregate annual cost of $27,000; other personnel in the printing department can be released. One mailing clerk, at $7,000, will be retained; others in the shipping department can be released. Employees whose employment was being terminated would immediately receive, on the average, three months' termination pay. The termination pay would be amortized over a five-year period.

(b) Long distance telephone and telegraph charges are identified and distributed to the responsible department. The remainder of the telephone bill, representing basic service at a cost of $4,000, was allocated in the ratio of 10 to publishing, 5 to printing, and 1 to shipping. The discontinuance of printing is not expected to have a material effect on the basic service cost.

(c) Shipping supplies consist of cartons, envelopes, and stamps. It is estimated that the cost of envelopes and stamps for mailing material to an outside printer would be $5,000 per year.

(d) If printing is discontinued, the company would retain its present building, but would sublet the space previously occupied by printing at an

annual rental of $50,000. Taxes, insurance, heat, light, and other oc-
cupancy costs would not be significantly affected.

(e) One cost clerk would not be required ($8,000) if printing is discontin-
ued. Other general and administrative personnel would be retained.

(f) Included in administrative expenses is interest expense on a 5% mort-
gage loan of $500,000.

(g) Printing and shipping room machinery and equipment having a net
book value of $300,000 can be sold without gain or loss. These funds
in excess of termination pay would be invested in marketable securities
earning 8%.

(h) The company has received a proposal for a five-year contract from an
outside printer, under which the volume of work done last year would
be printed at a cost of $800,000 per year.

(i) Assume continued volume and prices at last year's level.

Required: Prepare a statement in comparative form showing the costs
of operation of the printing and shipping departments under the present arrangement and under an arrangement in which inside printing is
discontinued. Summarize the net saving or extra cost in case printing
is discontinued.   *(AICPA adapted)*

10-8. *Optimum size of sales force.* A new company has completed a
study showing that if 5 salespeople are hired, the sales to be made by
each salesperson would be as follows:

Salesperson	Sales
1	$100,000
2	90,000
3	80,000
4	70,000
5	60,000
	$400,000

An analysis of the total costs of the company shows that variable
costs associated with the different levels of sales are:

Sales	Variable Costs
$100,000	$ 70,000
190,000	145,000
270,000	225,000
340,000	310,000
400,000	395,000

Each salesperson will be paid a commission of 5% on total sales.

Required: Determine the number of salespeople the company should
hire. Show computations.

10-9. *Expanding a market with a special order.* Nubo Manufacturing,
Inc., is presently operating at 50% of practical capacity, producing
annually about 50,000 units of a patented electronic component.
Nubo recently received an offer from a company in Yokohama, Japan,
to purchase 30,000 components at $6 per unit, FOB Nubo's plant.

Nubo has not previously sold components in Japan. Budgeted production costs for 50,000 and 80,000 units of output follow:

Units	50,000	80,000
Costs:		
Direct materials	$ 75,000	$120,000
Direct labor	75,000	120,000
Factory overhead	200,000	260,000
Total cost	$350,000	$500,000
Cost per unit	$7.00	$6.25

The sales manager thinks the order should be accepted, even if it results in a loss of $1 per unit, because the sales may build up future markets. The production manager does not wish to have the order accepted primarily because the order would show a loss of $.25 per unit when computed on the new average unit cost. The treasurer has made a quick computation indicating that accepting the order will actually increase gross margin.

Required: (1) Explain what apparently caused the drop in cost from $7 per unit to $6.25 per unit when budgeted production increased from 50,000 to 80,000 units. Show supporting computations. (2) Explain:

(a) Whether (either or both) the production manager or the treasurer is correct.

(b) Why the conclusions of the production manager and treasurer differ.

(3) Explain why each of the following may affect the decision to accept or reject the special order:

(a) The likelihood of repeat special sales and/or all sales to be made at $6 per unit.

(b) Whether the sales are made to customers operating in two separate, isolated markets or whether the sales are made to customers competing in the same market.

10-10. Distribution cost analysis. Boots Corporation's actual and standard distribution cost data for the month of January follow.

	Budget at Standard Cost	Actual Operations
Sales	$750,000	$750,000
Direct distribution costs:		
Selling	$ 12,000	$ 15,000
Shipping salaries	7,000	9,450
Indirect distribution costs:		
Order-filling	17,250	21,500
Other	2,100	2,500
Total costs	$ 38,350	$ 48,450

Additional data:

(a) Boots Corporation sells a single product for $10 per unit.

(b) Shipping salaries and indirect distribution costs-other are allocated on the basis of shipping hours.

(c) January shipping hours data follow:

	Shipping Hours
Budgeted	3,500
Standard operating level	4,400
Actual..	4,500

(d) Order-filling costs are allocated on the basis of sales and are comprised of freight, packing, and warehousing costs. An analysis of the amount of these standard costs by unit order-size follows:

	Order-Filling Standard Costs Classified by Unit Order-Size			
Unit-Volume Classifications	1–15	16–50	Over 50	Total
Freight......................................	$1,200	$1,440	$2,250	$ 4,890
Packing	2,400	3,240	4,500	10,140
Warehousing	600	720	900	2,220
Total.....................................	$4,200	$5,400	$7,650	$17,250
Units sold	12,000	18,000	45,000	75,000

Required: (1) Compute rate and efficiency variances from standard cost for:

(a) Shipping salaries.

(b) Indirect distribution costs-other. The analysis should compare actual costs and standard costs at the standard operating level.

(2) Management realizes that the distribution cost per unit decreases with an increase in the size of the order and, hence, wants to revise its unit sales prices upward or downward on the basis of the quantity ordered to reflect the allocated freight, packing, and warehousing standard costs. Management assumes that the revised unit prices will require no changes in standards for sales volume, the number of units sold in each order-size classification and the profit per unit sold.

(a) For each unit-volume classification, prepare a schedule computing the standard cost per unit for each order-filling cost: freight, packing, and warehousing. Use the format shown in Item (d) above.

(b) Prepare a schedule computing the revised unit sales prices for each unit-volume classification.

(AICPA adapted)

INDEX